PREFACE

Work with young offenders is essentially a multi-disciplinary activity. It also takes place within a labyrinthine legal framework. Our aim has been to pull together legal material of practical and policy relevance to both students and the whole range of professionals and lay people involved in working with, or making decisions about, young people in the youth justice system. It is a task which has not to the best of our knowledge been previously undertaken, and for which, we feel a collaborative multi-disciplinary approach is peculiarly appropriate.

We started work in 1992, when the Criminal Justice Act 1991 was newly implemented and still intact. All those who work within the criminal justice system — whether as judges, magistrates, justices' clerks, advocates, probation staff, local authority social workers or police officers — will, we feel confident, have some sympathy with our predicament since that time. The shifting sands of the legislative and policy initiatives of the last three years have left no part of the subject matter of the book untouched. The Criminal Justice Act 1993 and the Criminal Justice and Public Order Act 1994 have been accompanied by a seemingly remorseless bombardment of guidance in the form of revisions of Codes of Practice and National Standards as well as Departmental Circulars — some related to the content of the Acts and others reversing previously well established policies set out in earlier guidance.

We are all too aware that the end product may seem somewhat bloodless, a dry legal text which is light on "policy and practice" and fails to do justice to the realities of life for a depressingly large proportion of young people in Britain today. For many teenagers experiencing poverty, fear of violence or harassment and with little prospect of employment, crime may be a routine means of survival. While the prevailing view casts adolescents as the predominant crime problem, it is easy to forget the extent to which young people experience victimisation and the denial of legitimate opportunity. We could not hope to do justice to the expanding literature detailing the lives and crime patterns of young offenders. We fully admit these shortcomings which are a reflection not of ignorance but of the impossibility of including an adequate criminological and social policy perspective within the limits of this volume.

Whilst we have commented on and revised each other's drafts, and share responsibility for the whole, the actual writing was divided: Ball wrote the Introduction, Part I and Chapters 3 and 8; McCormac wrote Chapters 4–7, and Stone, Chapters 9–25. The major part of the typescript was delivered to the long-suffering and supportive publishers in January

1995, and we hope that we have been able to incorporate all subsequent changes up to the end of July 1995.

With three authors acknowledgements could proliferate, and it is not therefore possible to refer individually to all those whose help and support has gone towards the production of this book. However, those most closely and practically involved deserve a particular mention: Nigel Stone would like to acknowledge the unstinting efforts of Erica Barr in decoding his handwriting and processing the manuscript so skilfully, Kevin McCormac pays tribute to Carmella Beech, who speedily and accurately transcribed his material with patience and good humour, and Caroline Ball is endlessly grateful to her colleagues in the School of Social Work at the University of East Anglia for stimulation and encouragement.

Caroline Ball, Kevin McCormac and Nigel Stone

August 1995

T181
3861
SNP
(Bal)

YOUNG OFFENDERS
Law, Policy and Practice

4 Week

This book is due for return c

Australia

The Law Book Company
Brisbane ● Sydney ● Melbourne ● Perth

Canada

Carswell
Ottawa ● Toronto ● Calgary ● Montreal ● Vancouver

Agents
Steimatzky's Agency Ltd, Tel Aviv;
N.M. Tripathi (Private) Ltd, Bombay;
Eastern Law House (Private) Ltd, Calcutta;
M.P.P. House, Bangalore;
Universal Book Traders, Delhi;
Aditya Books, Delhi;
Macmillan Shuppan K.K., Tokyo;
Pakistan Law House, Karachi, Lahore

YOUNG OFFENDERS
Law, Policy and Practice

Caroline Ball,

Kevin McCormac

and

Nigel Stone

LONDON
SWEET & MAXWELL
1995

Published in 1995 by Sweet & Maxwell Limited of South Quay Plaza,
183 Marsh Wall, London E14 9FT
Computerset by Tradespools
Printed and bound in Great Britain by Butler and Tanner Ltd,
Frome and London

No natural forests were destroyed to make this product, only farmed
timber was used and replanted

A CIP catalogue record for this book is available from the
British Library

ISBN 0421 489405

*The cover photograph is reproduced by kind permission of Hulton
Deutsch Collection Limited*

CONTENTS

TABLE OF CASES

All references are to paragraph numbers

TABLE OF STATUTES

All references are to paragraph numbers

xxxi

TABLE OF STATUTORY INSTRUMENTS

All references are to paragraph numbers

PART I

Chapter 1

Young Offenders and the Police

THE POLICE AND CRIMINAL EVIDENCE ACT AND THE CODES OF PRACTICE

Juveniles suspected by the police of involvement in the commission of offences are subject to the same provisions regarding police investigations and interrogation as adults, with additional safeguards. The Police and Criminal Evidence Act 1984 (PACE), with its accompanying Codes of practice (revised in 1995), provided the first comprehensive statutory framework regulating police powers of arrest and interrogation, replacing the administrative 'Judges' Rules'. The Act was the product of years of debate about and proposals for reform of the existing rules of the criminal process. The tension between the police, seeking extension of their powers to investigate offences and apprehend and interrogate offenders, and those concerned to protect suspects from the perceived excesses of police powers is a continuing one. Amendments to PACE recently introduced by the Criminal Justice and Public Order Act 1994, together with substantial changes to the Codes of Guidance under the Act (see below), appear to amount to a significant tilt of the balance towards the police at the cost of the protection of more vulnerable defendants including those vulnerable through youth (Fenwick, 1995).

In addition to statutory amendment, since 1986 the provisions of the **1–002** Act have been defined and refined by a substantial body of case law augmented by publication of the findings of research undertaken by the Home Office, and other studies funded by the Economic and Social Science Research Council. The Act and interpretation of its accompanying Codes of Practice continue to be the subject of commentary, most recently in the Report of the Royal Commission on Criminal Justice (1993a), many of whose recommendations, including that in regard to the right to silence, were subsequently rejected by the Home Secretary (Fenwick, 1995).

The Act is supplemented by five Codes of Practice issued by the Secretary of State and substantially revised in 1995. These cover:

A. the exercise by police officers of statutory powers of stop and search

B.   the searching of premises by police officers and the seizure of property found by police officers on persons and premises

C.   the detention, treatment and questioning of persons by police officers

D.   the identification of persons by police officers

E.   The tape recording of interviews by police officers at police stations with suspected persons

Codes A to D in their original form came into effect when the Act was implemented in 1986 and Code E in 1988. Codes A-D were revised 1991, and the current revision came into effect in 1995.

1-003   The status of the Codes of Practice is somewhat unusual, in that they are not, as was intended by the Royal Commission on Criminal Procedure (1981), contained in subordinate legislation. On the other hand their status is clearly greater than that of ministerial guidance. This is because the Police and Criminal Evidence Act 1984 requires the Secretary of State to prepare and publish drafts of any codes and consider any representations made on them, before laying the Code before both Houses of Parliament, after which they may be brought "into operation by order made by statutory instrument" (PACE, s.67(4)). As Zander (1995) suggests, this involves a lengthy process of "open government" with the codes going through several drafts as a result of wide ranging consultation before presentation to Parliament. The fact that the codes are not in the form of statutory instruments may lessen their legal status, but it also allows the language in which they are drafted to be more "user friendly", and the inclusion of 'Notes for Guidance.' These notes are not part of the code. They are intended, as their title suggests, to provide guidance "to police officers and others about (its) application and interpretation" (Code C,1.3). In practice it has been suggested that it is doubtful whether the technical difference between the Codes and the notes of guidance is a clear one despite the presumption that whilst breach of the Codes is automatically a breach of the police disciplinary code, breach of the notes of guidance would not be (Zander, 1995).

1-004   The Codes of Practice are admissible in evidence; "and if any provision of such code appears to the court or tribunal conducting the proceedings to be relevant to any question arising in the proceedings it shall be taken into account in determining that question." (s.67(11)). The extent to which a breach of the codes results in evidence being excluded is a matter for the judge. Case law reviewed by Zander (1995) suggests that judges interpret the provisions of sections 76 and 78 to exclude evidence or quash convictions on the basis of breaches of the codes, to an extent that might not have been anticipated (Part V). In regard to young offenders the decisions in *Fogah* [1989] Crim.L.R. 141 and *Absolam* [1988] 88 Cr.App.R.332 support Zander's thesis (See below, para. 1–011). The document containing the codes has to be available at all police stations for consultation by police officers, detained persons and members of the public.

The investigation of crime **1–005**

To the police officer investigating a crime, the age of the offender, unless it becomes apparent that he or she is under the age of ten and therefore below the age of criminal responsibility, only becomes an issue when the officer wishes to search or question the suspect. If the suspected offender is under ten the investigation will be concluded without the possibility of charge (C&YPA 1963, s.16). If any persons suspected of involvement in the offence are between 10 and 16 years, the police will have to observe the extra safeguards provided for young offenders whenever the police are carrying out investigations or interviewing suspects. Any provisions under PACE and its accompanying Codes of Practice or other legislation which give children and other vulnerable persons special protection, apply in addition to that provided by the Act and Codes for all persons.

Prior to the 1990 revision of the codes there were no special provisions relating to young offenders in regard to the investigation of crime. Juveniles were treated as adults at the earlier stage of the process, despite the fact that young people, and especially black young people, are likely in many areas to be subject to rather more intensive attention from the police than adults (Home Office 1994). The first Home Office Circular on PACE (88/1985) issued to the police and the courts gave the following guidance:

> "In any situation where a constable exercises a power of search under this Act, the co-operation of the citizen should not be taken as implying consent, and the exercise of the power should be noted in the appropriate record. Whilst it is legitimate to invite co-operation from the public in circumstances where there is no power to require it, the subject of a voluntary search must properly understand the position and not be left with the impression that a power is being exercised."

However, as Zander comments "there are too many situations where **1–006** the concept of consensual search has been used as a way of avoiding the main thrust of the safeguards." (1995 at p. 8) As a result of early concerns that police officers were able to avoid the restrictions in Code A regarding searches by classifying too many as 'voluntary', the 1991 revision provided additional guidance as regards all suspects. The most recent version states that in circumstances in which he is searching a person on a voluntary basis, "an officer should always make it clear that he is seeking the consent of the person concerned to the search being carried out by telling the person that he need not consent and that without his consent he will not be searched" (Code A 1D). Improper action in this respect will invalidate a voluntary search. The Code goes on to make it clear that juveniles should not be invited to submit to a voluntary search:

"Juveniles, persons suffering from a mental handicap and others who appear not to be capable of giving an informed consent should not be subject to a voluntary search." (Code A, Notes of Guidance, 1E)

1-007 Interviews

The provisions of sections 76 to 78 of the Police and Criminal Evidence Act 1984 reflect the extent to which the questioning of suspects and the making of admissions are of such importance in the detection of crime and the conviction of offenders that detailed rules are needed to ensure that questioning is fairly conducted and recorded. Where a police officer conducts an interview with a person suspected of an offence he must administer the caution, the wording of which has been substantially amended to reflect the end to the right to silence:

> "You do not have to say anything. But it may harm your defence if you do not mention when questioned something which you later rely on in court. Anything you do say may be given in evidence." (Code C, 10.4)

If a juvenile is cautioned in the absence of the appropriate adult, the caution must be repeated in the adult's presence (*ibid.* 10.6). As Bevan and Lidstone (1991) suggest in many circumstances the recognised stages of police investigation—suspicion, caution, questioning and arrest—do not necessarily follow that sequence. More importantly the borderline between questioning that follows suspicion and that which does not require a caution, in that is directed at preliminary matters such as discovering identity or whereabouts, is frequently blurred. As Evans and Ferguson observed, information obtained from informal questioning of juveniles, for instance in the car travelling to the police station, may subsequently be used as the basis for formal interrogations (1991).

1-008 Interviews at school

Juveniles may only be interviewed at school "in exceptional circumstances" and then only where the principal or his nominee agrees (Code C, 11.15), and in the presence of an appropriate adult (see para. 1-028 below). Every effort should be made to notify the juvenile's parents and the appropriate adult if that is someone different. Failing that the head teacher or a nominee may act as appropriate adult provided the juvenile is not suspected of an offence against the educational establishment.

1-009 Arrest

Police powers of arrest are set out in Part III of PACE. Young people are only treated differently from adults to the extent that Code C provides that they should preferably not be arrested at school unless this is unavoidable, in which case the head teacher or the head teacher's nominee must be informed.(Code C, Notes for Guidance 11C).

Children under ten years
A child under the age of 10 years is below the age of criminal responsibility and should not be arrested (Children and Young Persons Act 1963, s.16). Where an arrest of a child who later turns out to be below that age takes place the child should be released as soon as it becomes apparent that they are under ten years (PACE, s.34(2) and see para. 1–014, below).

JUVENILES AT THE POLICE STATION   1–010

General
The provisions of Part IV of PACE, which is concerned with detention at a police station following arrest, and of Part V on the questioning and treatment of persons by the police, apply to juveniles in the same way as to adults, with additional safeguards. The need for a range of additional safeguards for juveniles and other vulnerable groups is set out with great clarity in the Code of Practice for the Detention, Treatment and Questioning of Persons by Police Officers issued under PACE:

> "It is important to bear in mind that, although juveniles or persons who are mentally ill or handicapped are often capable of providing reliable evidence, they may, without knowing or wishing to do so, be particularly prone in certain circumstances to provide information which is unreliable, misleading or incriminating. Special care should therefore always be exercised in questioning such a person and the appropriate adult should be involved if there is any doubt about a person's age, mental state or capacity. Because of the risk of unreliable evidence it is also important to obtain corroboration of any facts admitted whenever possible." (Notes of Guidance, 11B)

The consequences of failure to exercise such care in an interview which **1–011** under the Code of Practice is not limited to questioning in a police station, were confirmed in the case of *Delroy Fogah* [1989] Crim.L.R. 141 in which a 16 year old boy suspected of robbery was asked a series of questions in the street by police officers during which he confessed to involvement in the robbery. At the Crown Court the judge, following the decision in *Absolam* (1988) 88 Cr.App.R.332, held that the questions amounted to an interview and, as the interview took place in the absence of an appropriate adult, the confession could not be admitted.

Arrested juveniles   1–012
For the purposes of Part IV of PACE which provides the statutory framework for detention by the police, both as regards condition and duration, an "arrested juvenile" means "a person arrested with or without a warrant who appears to be under the age of 17" (s.37(15)). In this chapter all references to juveniles will be to 10 to 16 year olds except

5

where reference is made to the separation of 17 year olds from adult defendants.

A person is in police detention for the purposes of the Police and Criminal Evidence Act (s.118(2)) if—

> "(a)   he has been taken to a police station after being arrested for an offence. ... or
>
> (b)   he is arrested at a police station after attending voluntarily at the station or accompanying a constable to it. ..."

1–013   The custody officer

The Act requires that detention of arrested persons must be at a police station designated by a chief officer to be used for the purpose of detaining arrested persons (s.35) and that each designated station must have a custody officer, preferably of the rank of sergeant or above whose role is clearly separated from that of the investigating officer (s.36(5)). The duties of the custody officer are to ensure that all persons in detention at police stations are treated in accordance with the Act and the Codes of Practice issued under the Act, and that all matters required to be recorded are recorded in the custody record which must be opened when the arrested person appears before the custody officer. It is the custody officer therefore who has responsibility for ensuring that juveniles detained at police stations are treated in accordance with the provisions of the Act and the Codes of Practice, which apply to all detained persons and that the additional safeguards in that and other legislation which apply only to juveniles are met.

1–014   Police protection under the Children Act 1989

When the person arrested is a child the custody officer has to determine whether the child is aged ten years and therefore capable of criminal responsibility (C&YPA 1963, s.16). If a child under ten is mistakenly arrested and brought to a police station the custody officer must normally arrange for the child's immediate release (PACE, s.34(2)). If, however, the circumstances are such that " a constable has reasonable cause to believe that the child would otherwise be likely to suffer significant harm" the child (who for the purposes of the Children Act 1989 is a person under the age of 18 (s.105)) may be taken into police protection under the Children Act 1989, s.46(1).

The child may only be kept in police protection for a maximum of 72 hours, and as soon as is possible the constable concerned must ensure that the case is inquired into by the officer designated by the chief officer of the police area. Once that officer has completed his or her inquiry the child must be released from police protection unless there is still reasonable cause to believe that he or she would be likely to suffer significant harm if released (s. 46(3)(e) and (5)).

1–015   As well as arranging for the designated officer to make inquiries the constable who has taken a child into police protection must inform the parents and other people specified in section 46(4), the local authority in whose area the child was found, and that in which the child normally resides, and the child, of the steps that have been and are proposed to be taken. In the case of the child an explanation must also be given of the reasons for the police actions and such efforts as are reasonably practicable must be taken to discover the child's wishes and feelings. The constable must also ensure that, if not released, the child is moved to accommodation provided by the local authority (s.43(3)(f)).

The designated officer, as well as inquiring into the case, has a number of other responsibilities. In appropriate cases, where protection is needed for longer than the 72 hours of police protection, this could include applying, on behalf of the local authority for the area in which the child is normally resident, for an emergency protection order under section 44, although this will more usually be done by the local authority.

Guidance under the Children Act emphasises the need for inter-agency liaison between the police and local authorities in order to ensure "that no child taken into police protection need be accommodated in a police station, and that his reception into local authority accommodation is achieved with the minimum of trauma" (Department of Health 1990, para. 4.77).

Release or detention   1–016

Apart from the need to discharge a child who is below the age of criminal responsibility or possibly to take him or her into police protection under the Children Act, the custody officer has to decide whether any person detained at a designated police station should be charged or released, or detained, with or without charge. If the person is charged he must be released with or without bail, unless:

s.38(1)

(a)(i) "his name or address cannot be ascertained or the custody officer has reasonable grounds for doubting whether a name or address furnished by him as his name or address is his real name and address;

(ii) the custody officer has reasonable grounds for believing that the detention of the person arrested is necessary for his own protection or to prevent him from causing physical injury to any other person or from causing loss of or damage to property; or

(iii) the custody officer has reasonable grounds for believing that the person arrested will fail to appear in court to answer to bail or that his detention is necessary to prevent him from interfering with the administration of justice or with the investigation of offences or of a particular offence;"

or, in addition, in the case of a juvenile only:
"the custody officer has reasonable grounds for believing that he ought to be detained in his own interests." s.38(1)(b)(ii).

1–017 The most often quoted illustration of the sort of circumstances in which it was envisaged that a juvenile might need to be detained in his own interests is that given in the Committee stage debate on PACE (Hansard, Committee E, February 14, 1984, col. 1127). It was suggested that where a runaway juvenile boarding a train in the North of England without paying his fare was arrested and charged in London, and his parents could not collect him until the next day, it would not be in his interests to release him on to the streets overnight.

The general principle in section 34(1) is followed by a general duty imposed on the custody officer that a person in police detention must be immediately released if at any time:

s.34(2)

"(a) he becomes aware that the grounds for detention of that person have ceased to apply; and

(b)   he is not aware of any other grounds on which the continued detention of that person could be justified under the provisions of this Part of the Act."

If the custody officer decides that he has sufficient evidence to charge a person with the offence for which he was arrested, the person must be charged, either on bail or without bail (s.37(7)). If at the time of release no decision has been taken as to whether the person is to be prosecuted or not, the custody officer must inform him (s.37(8)). This will be the case with most juveniles, since the decision as to whether the offender will be charged or cautioned may not be made immediately (see Chapter 2).

1–018 Juveniles arrested on a warrant
Juveniles arrested on a warrant must not be released

"... unless the juvenile or a parent or guardian (with or without sureties) enters into a recognisance for such amount as the custody officer at the police station where he is detained considers will secure his attendance at the hearing of the charge; and the recognisance entered into in pursuance of this section may, if the custody officer thinks fit, be conditioned for the attendance of the parent or guardian at the hearing in addition to the child or young person." (C&YPA 1969, s.29, substituted by PACE 1984, Sched. 6, para. 19(b)).

1–019 Detention in Custody before charge
Under section 37 the custody officer who does not have sufficient evidence to charge the person before him may only authorise the detention of the arrested person if he has reasonable grounds to believe that detention without charge is necessary "to secure or preserve evidence relating to an offence for which he is under arrest or to obtain such evidence by questioning him" (s.37(2)). Where a custody officer authorises such detention he must make a written record of the grounds for the detention, and, unless one of the exceptions set out in section

37(6) apply, inform the arrested person of the grounds for his detention and of his rights, as set out in Code of Practice C, paras 3.1–3.4. These rights are:

(1) to have someone informed of his detention;

(2) to consult a solicitor; and

(3) to consult the Code of Practice governing detention or any other Code of Practice.

In addition to oral information the detained person, whether adult or 1–020 juvenile, must be given a written statement of these three rights and sign an acknowledgement on the custody record. Research undertaken by the Home Office Research and Planning Unit and by a team at the University of Hull suggests that police practices in giving information to juveniles about these rights and the take-up of them, exhibit various differences from adult suspects which may place juveniles at a disadvantage, both generally as regards information about their rights and specifically in regard to legal advice (Brown, *et al.*, 1992; Dixon, 1990).

1. The right of an arrested person to have someone informed 1–021
It is the right of anyone to have a friend or relative or other person who is known to him or who is likely to take an interest in his welfare told that he has been arrested and is being detained at a police station (PACE, s.56(1)). Children and young people up to the age of 16 who have been arrested or detained under the prevention of terrorism provisions have additional rights under section 57 of PACE (which amended section 34(2) of the Children and Young Persons Act 1933). The 1933 Act provided that where a child or young person has been arrested reasonable steps must be taken to inform his parent or guardian. Section 57, and the accompanying Codes and notes of Guidance, re-affirm and extend the provision in relation to detention and interrogation of children and young people by requiring that:

"(2) Where a child or young person is in police detention, such steps as are practicable shall be taken to ascertain the identity of a person responsible for his welfare.

(3) If it is practicable to ascertain the identity of a person responsible for the welfare of the child or young person, that person shall be informed, unless it is not practicable to do so—

(a) that the child or young person has been arrested;

(b) why he has been arrested; and

(c) where he is being detained."

Subsection (4) requires such information to be given "as soon as it is practicable to do so."

The person to be informed is widely defined to include the child's 1–022 parent or guardian or "any other person who has for the time being assumed responsibility for his welfare". This definition is further elaborated in Code C, 3.7:

> "If the person is a juvenile, the custody officer must, if it is practicable, ascertain the identity of a person responsible for his welfare. That person may be his parent or guardian (or if he is in care, the care authority or voluntary organisation) or any other person who has for the time being, assumed responsibility for his welfare. That person must be informed as soon as practicable that the juvenile has been arrested, why he has been arrested and where he is detained. This right is in addition to the juvenile's right in section 5 of the code not to be held incommunicado"

The person informed of the juvenile's arrest will generally also act as an 'appropriate adult' for the purposes of Code C (see para. 1–028 below) although this will not always be the case.

1–023   Children in care or under supervision

Note 3C of the Code further provides:

> "If the juvenile is in the care of a local authority or voluntary organisation but is living with his parents or other adults responsible for his welfare then, although there is no legal obligation on the police to inform them, they as well as the local authority or organisation should normally be contacted unless suspected of involvement in the offence concerned. Even if a juvenile in care is not living with his parents, consideration should be given to informing them as well."

Compliance with these requirements, apart from representing good practice, might be seen as more important now than at the time the note of guidance was drafted since, following implementation of the Children Act 1989, a care order gives parental responsibility to a local authority together with, rather than, instead of, the parents. (s.33)

Where a juvenile is known to be the subject of a supervision order reasonable steps must be taken to notify the person supervising him (Code C, 3.8).

1–024   **2. The right to legal advice**

As Cape (1993) suggests, although the traditional view has been that the trial "is the crowning glory of the adversarial criminal justice system", most cases are in fact won or lost at the police station, and it is here, where "Confessions, sometimes false confessions, are obtained from suspects, evidence is gathered, deals are done, which will inevitably influence the course of subsequent events" (p. 1), that the advice of a skilled lawyer is essential. Under section 58 of the Act a person who is in police detention is entitled, if he so requests, to consult a solicitor privately at any time, and as soon as is practicable unless any of the exceptions set out in section 58(8) apply, and in any event within 36 hours of being detained. The duty solicitor scheme originally established under section 59 of the Police and Criminal Evidence Act 1984 which now comes under the Legal Aid Act 1988 is intended to provide free legal advice round the clock on request to anyone held at a police station. These provisions have resulted in a significant increase in the proportion of suspects who request legal advice (Brown, *et al.*, 1992; Dixon, 1990), although a study undertaken for the Lord Chancellor's Department by researchers from the University of Birmingham Law School suggests that there is some evidence that custody officers use a variety of devices to discourage suspects from seeking legal advice (Sanders, *et al.*, 1989). The Code requires that the additional information — that the advice is free and may be given in private — is provided, although researchers express concern that even where they are told of the right to legal advice the additional information about its being free and private may not be given in a substantial proportion of cases. They also expressed concern that the duty to remind detained people that they have a right to legal advice at crucial stages of the interview process was often ignored (Brown, *et al.* 1992).

Where the appropriate adult is not present when the custody officer **1–025** informs a juvenile of the reasons for his detention and of his right to legal advice, that information should be repeated in the presence of the detained person when the person acting as appropriate adult arrives (Code C, para. 3.11). However it is clearly intended that the right of the appropriate adult to request a solicitor is an additional one that exists to protect the rights of juveniles or others at risk, who may not understand details of their right to legal advice when it is initially given to them by the custody officer, rather than the adult being the arbiter of whether or not the juvenile gets legal advice. Not only did researchers find that the request rate for legal advice for juveniles was below that for adults, but also that it fluctuated greatly between police stations. In one study a third of juveniles were informed of their rights in a cursory way or they were not given the opportunity to exercise those rights, in that for instance "Brief expositions of rights were sometimes but a prelude to telling juveniles that the next step would be to get in touch with his or her parents, and they would decide whether a solicitor was necessary" (*ibid.* at 75). The researchers suggest that this practice continues despite the terms of the revised Code which makes it clear that if a juvenile wishes to have a solicitor that request should be dealt with at once and not delayed until the arrival of the appropriate adult (C3.13 and 3G).

Both Dixon (1990) and Brown, *et al.* (1992) found that there were delays in implementing juveniles' rights which were compounded if the decision to request legal advice was delayed until the arrival of the appropriate adult.

3.The right to consult the Codes

Research evidence suggests that very few detainees ask to see the Codes, and that those who do are put off by their length and complexity (Brown, *et al.*, 1992).

1-026 THE "APPROPRIATE ADULT"

The Royal Commission on Criminal Procedure which reported in 1981 felt it essential that a juvenile being interviewed should have an adult, other than the police present, and that:

> "the adult should be someone in whom the juvenile has confidence, his parents or guardian, or someone else he knows, a social worker or school teacher. Juveniles may not as readily understand the significance of questions or of what they themselves say and are likely to be more suggestible than adults. They may need the support of an adult presence; of someone to befriend, advise and assist them to make their decisions." (para.4.103)

1-027   The requirements

The requirement that when the police wish to interview an arrested juvenile, whether at a police station or not, they may only do so in the presence of an appropriate adult, unless the circumstances are such as to pose an immediate danger to persons or serious harm to property (Code C, 11.14 and Annex C), was introduced as a result of this recommendation. The courts have interpreted the requirement strictly and have excluded admissions made in the absence of an appropriate adult as being unreliable under section 76 of the Act (*Delroy Fogah* [1989] Crim.L.R. 141). Research evidence also suggests that urgent interviews without an appropriate adult are rarely undertaken with juveniles; Brown and his colleagues (1992) only reporting two cases in a sample of 1000.

1-028   Definition of 'appropriate adult'

The 'Appropriate adult' is defined in the first part of Code C:

> "1.7 In this Code "the appropriate adult" means:
>
> (a)   in the case of a juvenile:
>
> > (i)   his parent or guardian (or if he is in care, the care authority or voluntary organisation). The term "in care" is used in this code to cover all cases in which a juvenile is "looked after" by a local authority under the terms of the Children Act 1989;
> >
> > (ii)   a social worker; or
> >
> > (iii) failing either of the above, another responsible adult aged 18 or over who is not a police officer or employed by the police."

Although the child's parent or guardian should normally be the 'appropriate adult' the Notes for Guidance to section 1 of Code C detail circumstances in which someone else should take on the role:

> "A person, including a parent or guardian, should not be an appropriate adult if he is suspected of involvement in the offence in question, is the victim, is a witness, is involved in the investigation or has received admissions prior to attending to act as the appropriate adult. If the parent of a juvenile is estranged from the juvenile, he should not be asked to act as the appropriate adult if the juvenile expressly and specifically objects to his presence." (Note 1C)

Similarly if a child in care admits an offence to a social worker, it is **1–029** suggested that:

> "If a juvenile admits an offence to or in the presence of a social worker other than during the time that the social worker is acting as the appropriate adult for that juvenile, another social worker should be the appropriate adult in the interests of fairness." (Note 1D)

Problems arise for police custody officers when parents refuse to attend or juveniles express extreme reluctance to have their parents or guardians notified. In such circumstances a local authority social worker, if one is available, or another adult nominated by the juvenile should be sought. The Code specifically provides that a solicitor or lay visitor who is present in a professional capacity may not act as appropriate adult (Note 1F), though there is some doubt as to whether the prohibition extends to unqualified employees of law firms.

The role 1–030

The appropriate adult has an important role to play:

> "He should be informed that he is not expected to act simply as an observer; and also that the purposes of his presence are, first, to advise the person being questioned and to observe whether or not the interview is being conducted properly and fairly, and, secondly, to facilitate communication with the person being interviewed." (Code C, 11.16)

The custody officer must explain the role of the appropriate adult to the juvenile and inform him that he has the right to consult privately with the adult at any time (Code C, 3.12).

The role of appropriate adult is, therefore, the potentially difficult one **1–031** of providing support whilst not interfering with the proper conduct of the interrogation. It is very much in the juvenile's interests that the adult should be both sympathetic to, and understanding of, the young persons's predicament and fulfil their role positively. In practice both these conditions, that of suitability to act as, and competence in performing the role of appropriate adult, can prove problematic.

1-032 Competence to act

There is a presumption that a parent will be competent to act, but this presumption does not extend to parents who are estranged from their children (see Note 1C above) nor to those without the mental ability to recognise the hazardous nature of their child's situation. Prior to amendment of Note 1C, in *D.P.P. v. Blake* [1989] 1 W.L.R. 432, the Divisional Court held that an estranged parent whom an arrested juvenile did not wish to attend could not be regarded as an 'appropriate adult'. The facts of the case, which raise questions of principle which it is suggested go beyond the issue addressed in the revision to Note 1C, were that a 16 year old girl, who was not in care, but lived in a hostel on a voluntary basis, was detained on suspicion of starting a fire at the hostel. She initially refused to give her father's name and address and had asked instead for her social worker to be contacted. The local authority indicated that their policy was not to send a social worker unless it was impossible to contact any other suitable person willing to attend the interview. The police eventually persuaded the girl that her refusal to divulge information regarding her father would prolong her detention. When the interview began he asked her if she was all right and she ignored him, no conversation took place regarding the alleged offence or the reason for her arrest and detention. The girl made a full confession which the justices excluded from being given in evidence at her trial under section 76(2) of PACE. The Divisional Court upheld the justices' decision. The court also urged local authorities to reconsider, if the result of following their existing policy would be to fail to provide an 'appropriate adult' to assist an arrested juvenile when requested to do so.

> "The justices, in my view, were entitled to find that the estranged parent of a child, whom the child did not wish to attend her interview at the police station, did not come within the spirit of the code of practice.....It is clear from the way in which they have expressed themselves that they were far from satisfied that such an estranged parent would fulfil the objectives of ensuring a fair interview of a juvenile when that juvenile had expressly and with some steadfastness, made it plain that she did not wish the parent to attend.......There is no point in a police officer seeking to protect a juvenile by persisting with taking steps to facilitate the attendance of an adult, parent or otherwise, whom the juvenile has made plain he or she does not want present." (*Per* Auld J. at 439)

> "The appropriate adult cannot, in my judgement, be a person with whom the juvenile has not empathy. Plainly, there was no empathy here. In that circumstance, the definition in Note C13C to the code cannot be met." (*Per* Mann L.J. at 440)

1-033 Nor can a parent who has not the mental capacity to appreciate the gravity of the situation or the role he or she is expected to fulfil be properly regarded as an 'appropriate adult' regardless of whether the police were aware of this at the time. In *Morse* [1991] Crim. L.R. 195, it was held that empathy with the interviewee was not enough. Medical evidence, given on appeal subsequent to conviction based on evidence of several admissions made by a 16 year old at an interview at which the defendant's father acted as 'appropriate adult', showed that the father had an IQ of between 60 and 70, was virtually illiterate and probably incapable of understanding the gravity of his son's situation. There was no question of any impropriety on the part of the police.

The test, it is suggested in commentary on the case, "... being whether **1–034** the evidence would have such an adverse effect on the fairness of the proceedings that it ought not to be admitted". This test was applied in *W. and Another* [1994] Crim.L.R. 130 when the Court of Appeal held that a mentally ill mother who would, had she been suspected of an offence, have herself been entitled to the assistance of an appropriate person, could nonetheless act as appropriate adult for her 13 year old daughter. The trial judge formed the view that, since he was satisfied that the interview had been conducted fairly and was not overly long, the mother was capable of giving her daughter appropriate support despite her illness.

Effectiveness in the role of 'appropriate adult'   1–035
Even if they are competent to act, experience would suggest that in the role of appropriate adult, both parents and social workers very often, for a variety of reasons, fail to provide effective support. Evans (1993b) in research into police interviews with juveniles, funded by the Royal Commission on Criminal Justice, found that approximately three quarters of all parents and other appropriate adults who attended interviews made "no contribution whatsoever" and that when they did contribute parents "were as likely to be unsupportive. ... as supportive of their children" (p. 39). As Dixon (1989) suggests:

> "Like suspects some parents can be disorientated, scared and compliant to police requests. It should not be forgotten that, in the Confait investigation, the inaccurate confessions were countersigned by some of the suspects' parents (although they were not present at the original interrogations)". (p. 119)

A Policy Studies Institute report based on research undertaken before **1–036** the PACE provisions were implemented suggested:

> "the adult usually has little or no knowledge of what kinds of approach or questioning are allowed and consequently says nothing or does not interfere with any questioning or behaviour by the officers that he [sic] disapproves of. Thus it is common for the adult to acquiesce in hectoring questioning, thinking it is 'normal'. ..."
> (Smith and Gray, 1985 at 476)

The tape recording of interviews should now militate against overtly 'hectoring' questioning, but there is reason to believe that many parents will not act in a supportive way, either because they are overwhelmed by the experience, or because the see their role as being " to assist the police in extracting 'the truth' from their children, often by means which police officers could not use in their presence". (Dixon, 1990 at 118; Evans, 1993b) If parents go too far in putting pressure on their children the evidence could be excluded as having been obtained 'by oppression' under PACE 1984, s.76(2), or as being 'unfair' under section 78. However it was recently decided that admonitions by parents to their children to "tell the truth", even forcefully expressed, do not provide grounds for excluding admissions providing that the police questioning was fair (*Jefferson, Skeritt and Keogh, The Times*, June 22, 1993).

1-037　　Juveniles may not get a much better deal from having a social worker to act as their appropriate adult (Thomas, 1994). Social workers get little training for the role, nor do they receive particularly useful advice from their professional organisation, the British Association of Social Workers, which in 1987 was advising its members to inform suspects of their right to silence, but not offering them any advice as to when refusal to answer questions might be appropriate. (Kay and Quao, 1987) Many social workers feel threatened by the police culture which they perceive as hostile, and were observed by researchers to be often as unfamiliar as parents with the boundaries of what is acceptable in regard to the police questioning of suspects (Sanders, *et al.* 1989). As Evans (1993b) suggests the fact that professionals acting as appropriate adults "are either not aware of, ignore or are unable or unwilling to assert themselves in order to ensure that the PACE code of practice which emphasise the potential vulnerability of juveniles is implemented", may allow the police to "exploit the interrogative susceptibility of suspects".

1-038 ACCOMMODATION OF DETAINED JUVENILES

The Code provides that juveniles should not be detained in police cells

"unless no other secure accommodation is available and the custody officer considers that it is not practicable to supervise him if he is not placed in a cell or the custody officer considers that a cell provides more comfortable accommodation than other secure accommodation in the police station",

and that a juvenile may not be placed in a cell with a detained adult (Code C, 8.8). If he is placed in a cell the reasons must be recorded (8.12). Guidance provides that whenever possible a juvenile held in a cell should be visited more regularly than the hourly intervals specified for adults (Code C, 8.10).

1-039 Time limits on detention without charge
The rules regarding time limits on detention without charge and reviews of detention under Part IV of PACE 1984 apply to juveniles in the same way as to adult detainees, except that when an arrested juvenile is transferred to local authority accommodation the custody officer ceases to be subject to the duty to ensure that all the provisions of

the Act and the codes set out in section 39(1) are complied in regard to him (s.39(4)).

The maximum period for which an arrested person can ordinarily be detained at a police station without charge is 24 hours; detention beyond 24 hours is only permissible in respect of 'serious arrestable offences' (PACE, s.41). A superintendent or more senior police officer may authorise continued detention for up to 12 hours beyond the 24 hours if there are reasonable grounds for believing that such detention is necessary to secure or preserve evidence, or obtain it by questioning, and if certain other conditions are satisfied. A magistrates' court may issue a warrant for up to a further 36 hours on the same criteria, and that may be extended for a further 36 hours up to an absolute maximum of 96 hours. A detainee must appear before the magistrates on the applications for warrants for further detention and may be legally represented (s.43).

IDENTIFICATION

The provisions of PACE 1984, Part V apply to juveniles in the same way as to adults with additional protection in the form of consents by parents or guardians.

Fingerprints
The taking of fingerprints requires consent to be given by the appropriate person, that is to say the person themselves if they are aged 17 years or over, the young person and parent or guardian for 14–16 year olds and only the parent and guardian for a child aged 10–13 (Code D, 1.11). Where a juvenile is in the care of the local authority or a voluntary agency a representative of the authority or agency may consent as parent or guardian (Note of Guidance, 1E). The police must give reasons for taking the prints and inform the suspect that they will be destroyed in certain circumstances (see below). Where fingerprints are taken at a police station, consent must be given in writing (3.1) and the reason for taking the fingerprints must be entered on the custody record.

Fingerprints may be taken without the appropriate person's consent either after charge for a recordable offence, or if a police officer of at least the rank of superintendent authorises the taking of fingerprints on the grounds there are reasonable grounds for suspecting the involvement of the person whose fingerprints are to be taken in a criminal offence, and for believing that his fingerprints will tend to confirm or disprove the persons involvement (para. 3.2). Where fingerprints are taken without consent, the person must be told the reason why they are being taken and this must be recorded in the custody book. Fingerprints may also be taken without consent from convicted persons where they were not taken during the course of investigations, and there is a power of arrest for this purpose.

1–041　Body samples

The Act, amended by Part IV of the CJ&POA 1994, distinguishes between two kinds of body samples. Intimate samples, which are dealt with in section 62, include blood, semen or other tissue fluid, urine, saliva, pubic hair, a swab taken from a person's body orifice other than the mouth, and, following the recommendation of the Royal Commission on Criminal Justice (1993), dental impressions. Non-intimate samples include samples, other than intimate samples, or a foot print or print of any other part of the body except a hand, and "a swab taken from any part of a person's body including the mouth but not any other body orifice" (s.65(3)c).

1–042　Intimate samples

The taking of intimate samples, which apart from urine and saliva can only be performed by a doctor or dentist, requires the permission of an officer of or above the rank of superintendent. That authority can only be given if the offence in question is a recordable offence, and there are reasonable grounds for believing that the sample will tend to confirm or disprove the suspect's involvement in the offence (s. 62).

The taking of an intimate sample requires the written consent of the suspect. The same consent rules as for the taking of fingerprints apply to the taking of intimate samples from juveniles; consent must be given by a parent or guardian for a child aged 10 to 13 years and by both the young person and a parent or guardian for those aged 14 to 16. When consent is being invited an officer must tell the suspect that the required authorisation has been given, and the nature of the offence in which it is suspected that he or she is involved.

1–043　　Although the taking of an intimate sample requires consent and a reminder to the person to be searched of his entitlement to legal advice, there is no requirement to advise the suspect that he may refuse consent, nor that the sample cannot be taken without consent. Refusing consent is not neutral, in that under the Police and Criminal Evidence Act, s.62(10) the court may "draw such inferences from refusal as appear proper; and the refusal may, on the basis of such inferences, be treated as, or as capable of amounting to, corroboration of any evidence against the person in relation to which the refusal is material".

The provisions of the subsection clearly diminish the protection of the requirement for consent, however Code D, para. 5.2 provides some protection with the requirement that before consent to the taking of an intimate sample is sought the person must be warned that a refusal may be treated as corroborating relevant prosecution evidence.

The PACE provisions on intimate samples do not apply to samples taken under sections 5 to 12 of the Road Traffic Act 1972 (drink/driving provisions).

1–044　Non-intimate samples

These normally require consent, with the same provisos for juveniles as with intimate samples. However, an officer of the rank of superintendent or above can authorise the compulsory taking of non intimate samples where the offence is a recordable one and there are reasonable grounds for believing that the sample will tend to confirm or disprove the suspect's involvement. The suspect must be informed of the authorisation, and the grounds on which it has been given before the sample is taken, and the reason has to be recorded as soon as possible after the sample is taken (PACE, s.63(8A)).

Identification by witnesses   1–045
The Code of Practice on Identification (Code D) provides four alternative methods that can be used in disputed identification cases: an identification parade, a group identification, a video film, and a confrontation. The participation of a juvenile in any of these requires the presence of an appropriate adult (Code D, 1.14) and requirements regarding the suspects consent are as set out above. A full account of the procedures police have to follow in regard to disputed identification are described and discussed elsewhere (Bevan and Lidstone, 1990, pp. 379–390).

CHARGING OF DETAINED JUVENILES   1–046

Under paragraph 16 of Code C when it is decided that there is sufficient evidence to charge a juvenile, and that there is sufficient evidence for a prosecution to succeed, and that person has said all that he wishes to say about the offence, he should be brought without delay before the custody officer in the presence of the appropriate adult. The custody officer must administer the caution before either charging the juvenile or informing him that he may be prosecuted. The mandatory notice with the particulars of any offence with which the juvenile is charged must be given to the appropriate adult as well as to the juvenile.

After a person has been charged or informed that he or she may be prosecuted for an offence, no further questions may be put unless they are necessary

> "for the purpose of preventing or minimising harm or loss to some other person or to the public or for clearing up any ambiguity in a previous answer or statement, or where it is in the interests of justice that the person should have put to him and have an opportunity to comment on information concerning the offence which has come to light since he was charged or informed that he might be prosecuted. Before any such questions are put to him, he shall be warned that he does not have to say anything but anything he does say may be given in evidence and reminded of his right to legal advice ..." (Code C, 16.5).

Detention of juveniles after charge   1–047
When a juvenile is charged he must be released unless the conditions for refusing to release an adult with or without bail are met (PACE, s.38(1)(a)). If a juvenile is detained he must be brought before a

magistrates court in accordance with the provisions of section 46(1), as soon as is practicable and in any event, in almost all circumstances, not later than the day following charge.

Section 38 presumes that all detained juveniles will be accommodated by the local authority:

> "(6) Where a custody officer authorises an arrested juvenile to be kept in police detention under subsection (1) above, the custody officer shall, unless he certifies—
>
> > (a) that, by reason of such circumstances as are specified in the certificate, it is impracticable for him to do so, or
> >
> > (b) in the case of an arrested juvenile who has attained the age of 12 years, that no secure accommodation is available and that keeping him in other local authority accommodation would not be adequate to protect the public from serious harm from him,
>
> secure that the arrested juvenile is moved to local authority accommodation".

1–048　Section 38(6) as amended by the C.J.A 1991, s.59 and the C.J.P.O.A 1994, s.24, provides the only circumstances in which the police can keep a 12–16 year old in police custody. The revised Code provides:

> "Where a juvenile is charged with an offence and the custody officer authorises his continued detention he must try to make arrangements for the juvenile to be taken into care of a local authority to be detained pending appearance in court unless he certifies that it is impracticable to do so, or, in the case of a juvenile of at least 12 years of age, no secure accommodation is available and there is a risk to the public of serious harm from that juvenile ..." (16.6)

To reinforce this the Notes for Guidance (16B) state:

> "Except as provided in 16.6 above, neither a juvenile's behaviour nor the nature of the offence with which he is charged provides grounds for the custody officer to decide that it is impracticable to seek to arrange for his transfer to the care of the local authority. Similarly, the lack of secure local authority accommodation shall not make it impracticable for the custody officer to transfer him. The availability of secure accommodation is only a factor in relation to a juvenile aged 12 or over when the local authority accommodation would not be adequate to protect the public from serious harm from the juvenile. The obligation to transfer a juvenile to local authority accommodation applies as much to a juvenile charged during the daytime as it does to a juvenile to be held

overnight, subject to a requirement to bring the juvenile before a court under s.46 of the Police and Criminal Evidence Act 1984."

The guidance suggests that the effect of the revised subsection is to require that all juveniles who are not released on bail should be transferred to local authority accommodation with two exceptions.

i) Any juvenile aged 10–16 years   1–049

Any juvenile may be held by the police themselves if the custody officer certifies that it is impracticable to make the transfer to local authority accommodation.

ii) 12–16 year olds

Under the Police and Criminal Evidence Act, s.38 (6)

(6) "(b) in the case of an arrested juvenile who has attained the age of 12 years, that no secure accommodation is available and that keeping him in any other local authority accommodation would not be adequate to protect the public from serious harm from him, secure that the arrested juvenile is moved to local authority accommodation.

(6A) In this section—   1–050
'local authority accommodation' means accommodation provided by or on behalf of a local authority (within the meaning of the Children Act 1989);
'secure accommodation' means accommodation provided for the purposes of restricting liberty;
'sexual offence' and 'violent offence' have the same meaning as in Part I of the Criminal Justice Act 1991;
and any reference, in relation to an arrested juvenile charged with a violent or sexual offence, to protecting the public from serious harm from him shall be construed as reference to protecting members of the public from death or serious personal injury, whether physical or psychological, occasioned by such further offences committed by him.

(6B) Where an arrested juvenile is moved to local authority accommodation under subsection (6) above it shall be lawful for any person acting on behalf of the authority to detain him."

Detention of seventeen year olds   1–051
Under the Criminal Justice Act 1991 17 year olds come within the provisions of section 31 of the Children and Young Persons Act 1933 under which children and young persons detained in a police station, being conveyed to or from, or waiting to attend or return from a criminal court must be separated from adults who have been charged with criminal offences. The only exceptions being if the adults are relatives or adults with whom the juvenile is jointly charged.

For all other pre-trial purposes seventeen year olds are regarded as adults.

Chapter 2

Diversion from the Criminal Process

2–001 The diversion of offenders of all ages from the criminal process, through informal or formal cautions, has its roots in the discretion, in the hands of the police since the first forces were formed, to decide to take no action or to administer a caution instead of proceeding to prosecution. Official policy on the use of cautions has been set out in a series of Home office circulars, the most recent of which is HOC 18/1994. The circulars from the early 1970s up to 59/1990 reflect a policy aimed at encouraging, at first for juveniles but more recently also for adults, the diversion of offenders from the criminal process. Despite official guidance favouring the use of cautioning, the fact that cautioning has never been put on a statutory footing has made the practice particularly vulnerable to discrepant interpretation both as between one police force and another, and even within a single force (Ditchfield, 1976; Tutt and Giller, 1983; Giller and Tutt, 1987; Evans and Wilkinson, 1990).

In order to set these shifting policies in context this chapter considers the origins and growth in the use of cautioning for juveniles. It also examines the issues raised by the exercise of police discretion unfettered by legislation, and recurrent pressures on the government to reduce idiosyncratic interpretation of guidance by placing cautioning on a statutory footing.

2–002 Historical development

Prior to 1954 when the Home Office first collected and published overall numbers of offenders who had received police cautions, broken down by age, offence type, and sex, there was no means of determining the prevalence of the use of cautioning, nor of comparing rates between different forces. Certainly in commentaries and departmental reports prior to the mid 1960s the practice attracted as many or possibly more disparaging comments than those in favour, in regard to its use for juveniles in circumstances where there was no accompanying supportive intervention. This attitude has to be seen in the light of the prevailing 'welfare' orientation, based on a medical model of diagnosis and cure which underpinned policy, practice and legislation relating to young offenders from the mid 1920s onwards (Pratt, 1986). For instance Elkin commenting in 1938 on the fact that the Chief Constable of

Stockport's report for 1936 revealed that almost as many juveniles were cautioned (82) as were dealt with by the juvenile courts (95) for indictable offences:

"... it is a dangerous theory that delinquency amongst the very young can be regarded more lightly than the offences of older children or young persons. It is important to prevent the formation of delinquent habits at an early stage, and a failure to apply any constructive treatment to a small child may enormously increase the difficulties of those who have to handle him later." (Elkin, 1938 at 139)

During the late 1940s and early 1950s rapidly rising crime rates amongst **2–003** juveniles led a number of police forces to introduce inter-agency liaison schemes which undertook preventative work with offenders who had received cautions and also with substantial numbers of children perceived to be 'at risk', but who had no offences recorded against them. As Pratt points out these schemes had the effect of bringing many more juveniles into contact with the police:

"Policing such a terrain where calls for action were to be based on perceived departures from the norm rather than crime *per se*, opened up an infinite variety of behaviour for scrutiny and circumstances requiring investigation". (Pratt, 1986 at 220)

In the late 1950s the Departmental Committee on Children and Young Persons, chaired by Viscount Ingleby, heard several witnesses strongly supporting the police liaison schemes, as well as representatives of magistrates and probation officers who, perceiving diversion from court as a threat to their territory, did not. The Committee expressed reservations about the extension of cautioning in general, coming down firmly against any expansion of police liaison schemes, mainly on the grounds that

"... the process of following up the child and his family involves the juvenile liaison officer in work that nowadays is recognised as a skill to be acquired by special training in case-work which the juvenile liaison officer has no opportunity to receive. It is work that should be done by other social agencies." (Home Office, 1960, para. 138)

The change of attitude to cautioning from the belief in the therapeutic **2–004** value of a court appearance expressed by Elkin (1938) and the Ingleby Committee, towards concern to avoid where possible a child being stigmatised by a court appearance is apparent from the mid 1960s onwards.

"Since a conviction may have serious consequences for a young person's career, there is a natural reluctance to prosecute..... A caution spares offenders the stigma of a court appearance, and may preserve whatever deterrent effect is presented by the threat of prosecution. A caution may be given in the hope that if a juvenile is not immediately treated as a delinquent then there is less chance of his behaving like one in the future." (Home Office, 1960, para. 147)

2–005 The White Paper *The Child the Family, and the Young Offender,* proposed avoiding the stigma of criminality with a shift away from criminal proceedings towards a wholly treatment based model of family councils (Home Office, 1965), and its somewhat less radical successor *Children in Trouble* (Home Office, 1968) which preceded the Children and Young Persons Act 1969, set out proposals to reduce drastically the numbers of juveniles appearing in court. As a consequence of these policies the use of cautioning rose during the late 1960s. The 1969 Act, which had it been fully implemented would have effectively decriminalised the juvenile court (Bottoms, 1974), did not, owing to a change of government, come into force even in part until 1971. Despite this delay the principle of avoiding criminal proceedings for juveniles wherever possible was on the statute book, and cautioning for the first and only time gained statutory recognition in section 5(2) of the 1969 Act:

> "A qualified informant shall not lay an information in respect of an offence if the offender is a young person unless it would not be adequate for the case to be dealt with by a parent, teacher or other person or by means of a caution from a constable ..."

2–006 Anticipating full implementation, many police forces reviewed their policies and set up new Juvenile Bureaux or Juvenile Liaison Schemes (not to be confused with the earlier ones of the same name) to provide an inter-agency forum for decision making regarding whether juveniles reported for committing offences should be cautioned, prosecuted, or the police should take no further action (Ditchfield, 1976). Many researchers and commentators have questioned whether the apparent dramatic rise in the use of police cautions during this period shown in table 1) and subsequently (table 2) accurately reflects numbers of children diverted from court appearances (Ditchfield, 1976; Giller and Tutt, 1983; Pratt, 1986). The evidence suggests that it is more likely to be a manifestation of police net widening through proceeding to the stage of recording cautions against many young offenders who would previously have not featured in criminal statistics, having been dealt with by means of an informal admonition (Giller and Tutt, 1987).

2–007 *Table 1Juveniles cautioned as a percentage of known offenders (indictable and non-indictable offences) 1960–1974*

Age group	1960	1968	1970	1972	1974
10–13	33.0	39.1	51.7	65.7	66.2
14–16	21.2	18.6	25.5	34.1	36.1

(Criminal Statistics 1991, Home Office)

The expansion in the use of cautioning from the mid 1960s was by no means universal. Home Office statistics and research studies have consistently shown wide discrepancies as between cautioning policies and practices in different police authorities (Evans, 1993). In 1981 the variation for males under 17 cautioned for indictable offences covered 32 percentage points from a high of 64 per cent in Lincolnshire to a low of 32 per cent in South Wales with a national average of 47 per cent. By 1985 the use of cautioning for the same group had further increased to a national average of 60 per cent, but so had the range—from a high of 84 per cent in Northamptonshire to 48 per cent in Humberside. As the researchers (Giller and Tutt, 1987) suggest criminal statistics demonstrate that 'Justice by geography continues despite attempts to reduce diversity by exhortation in the form of central government circular' (at 374).

Home Office circular 14/1985 encouraged police forces both to **2–008** increase their use of cautioning and to follow consistent policies based on general principles spelt out in the guidelines attached to the circular. The policy thrust in regard to juveniles was unambiguously set out in the introduction to the guidelines:

> "It is recognised both in theory and in practice that delay in the entry of a young person into the formal criminal justice system may help to prevent his entry into that system altogether. The Secretary of State commends to chief officers the policy that the prosecution of a juvenile is not a step to be taken without the fullest consideration of whether the public interest (and the interest of the juvenile concerned) may be better served by a course of action which falls short of prosecution. Thus chief officers will wish to ensure that their arrangements for dealing with juveniles are such that prosecution will not occur unless it is absolutely necessary ..."

A particular warning was issued in paragraph 7 of the Circular regarding the dangers of 'net widening'. The following years saw a further dramatic increase in the use of cautioning; by 1990, 75 per cent of males under 17 were being cautioned for indictable offences nationally, and the variation between police forces with the highest and lowest rates had dropped to 24 percentage points.(Home Office Statistics 1991). Following further guidance to chief officers contained in circular 59/1990 which replaced 14/1985 and for the first time included National Standards for the cautioning of offenders, in 1991 the national rate rose to 76 per cent but the range of variation had increased to 30 per cent (60 per cent–90 per cent) (Table 2). This may have reflected differing rates in assimilating the new guidance into police force standing orders, or organisational differences between police forces as well as the individual policies of a few chief or even divisional officers (Evans, 1991).

2–009 *Table 2 Male Offenders aged 10–13 and 14–16 cautioned, as a percentage of all offenders found guilty or cautioned for indictable offences 1981–1994*

Year	10–13 years	14–16 years
1981	68	35
1982	70	38
1983	74	42
1984	75	45
1985	79	51
1986	81	55
1987	86	59
1988	86	60
1989	88	64
1990	90	69
1991	90	70
		14–17 years
1992	91	63
1993	90	62
1994	87	59

(Criminal Statistics, Home Office 1995).

2–010 Inter-agency diversionary programmes

Following partial implementation of the C&YPA 1969 variously named inter-agency liaison groups were set up to encourage diversion from court and the provision of intermediate treatment for offenders. Their description, constitution and working practices were, as with all other parts of the youth justice system, immensely varied. A local survey, for instance, revealed that in neighbouring counties 'juvenile bureaux' which dealt with what are ultimately police decisions regarding 'no further action', caution, of referral for process, in one authority involved senior staff from the police, social services, probation and the education welfare service in weekly meetings, whereas in the other similar decisions were made by individual Chief Superintendents on the basis of a paper information gathering exercise (Ball, 1985). In many authorities throughout the 1980s these inter-agency fora, whatever their name—and encouraged by Home Office guidance—achieved increasing success in both diverting most minor offenders from the courts and persuading the courts to use community based rather than custodial sentences (Bowden and Stevens, 1986; Gibson, *et al.* 1994). Other police forces continued, however, to ignore the guidance and routinely process disproportionately large numbers of young offenders through the juvenile courts (Giller and Tutt, 1987).

2–011 Current policy and practice

Home Office Circular 59/1990 was based on research undertaken by the University of Birmingham which not only showed the continuing disparity amongst cautioning rates between and within police areas referred to above, but also a sharp fall-off in cautioning rates between 16 and 17 year olds, with a 16 year old being four times as likely to receive a caution as a 17 year old. The 1990 circular for the first time established National Standards for cautioning based on a uniform set of principles. Contrary to the guidance to chief officers contained in its predecessor, the 1994 circular (18/1994) does not appear to be based on research into the effects of the previous circular, nor on any clearly stated policy aims. Whatever the intention there is little doubt that it represents a significant shift away from the policies set out in circulars 14/1985 and 59/1990, which positively encouraged the diversion from formal legal process of as many juveniles and adults as possible, towards one which discourages the use of more than one caution, and removes juveniles from the category of vulnerable people in the National Standards for cautioning (Ball, 1994; Stone, 1994b; Evans, 1994). This change of policy, which may well be in contravention of treaty obligations under the United Nations Convention on the Rights of the Child, is likely to result in a very substantial increase in the numbers of young offenders appearing before youth courts (Cavadino, 1995) (Table 2).

Previous guidance recognised the importance of cautioning as a **2–012** means of keeping offenders of all ages out of the courts, whilst accepting that cautioning rates for "the young, the elderly and infirm and other vulnerable groups will tend to be higher than for others" (59/1990, para. 5). In 18/1994, para. 5 the emphasis is different:

"Nor does the presumption in favour of diverting juveniles from the courts mean that they should automatically be cautioned as opposed to prosecuted because they are juveniles."

There is now a real doubt as to whether the presumption referred to, albeit in negative terms, in para. 5, actually exists since the accompanying National Standards only indicate in Note 3A:

There should be a presumption in favour of not prosecuting certain categories of offender, such as elderly people or those who suffer from some sort of mental illness or impairment, or a severe physical illness;

no mention of "the young". Thus, after a long period of officially encouraged growth in the use of cautions, particularly for young offenders, diversionary policies appear, with the publication of Home Office circular 18/1994, to have shifted significantly away from approval for the use of cautions in all appropriate cases. The indications are that cautioning policies in individual police forces are currently in a state of uncertainly and flux which may, despite exhortations in the circular, lead to even more disparate practice as between police forces than in the past (Cavadino, 1995). The shift, which is line with other recent policy developments in regard to the trial and sentencing of offenders, appears to be grounded on the perceived overuse of repeat cautions (para. 8 of the circular refers to 8% of a sample of offenders cautioned in 1991 who had already received two or more cautions), and, according to Home Office research, the inappropriate administering of cautions for very serious offences in a few police forces (Evans, 1994).

2–013 **Guidance and National Standards for the Cautioning of Offenders**
National Standards for the cautioning of offenders were introduced in 1990 and revised in 1994 (18/1994). The purposes of a formal caution are set out in para. 1 of the National Standards:

"the purpose of a formal caution is:

- to deal quickly and simply with less serious offenders
- to divert them from the criminal courts
- to reduce the chances of their re-offending".

The basic requirements for the administration of a formal caution have remained constant and are reiterated in the new National Standards:

" * there must be *evidence of the offender's guilt* sufficient to give a realistic prospect of conviction;

* the offender must *admit the offence*;

* the offender (or, in the case of a juvenile, his parents or guardian) must understand the significance of a caution and give *informed consent* to being cautioned." (para. 2.)

2–014 Despite a short period between abolition of the principle of *doli incapax* by the Divisional Court (*C v. DPP* [1994] Crim.L.R.523) and its reinstatement by the House of Lords [1995] 2 W.L.R. 383, a child under the age of 14 years cannot be cautioned unless it can be established that he knew that what he did was seriously wrong, and that he had the necessary intent to commit the offence. Given concerns expressed in the past when the *doli incapax* principle was unquestioned, that 10 to 13 year olds may as a result of 'net widening' have been inappropriately drawn into the formal criminal justice system, through being cautioned rather than no further action being taken by the police (Mott, 1983), Note 2D of the National Standards is of particular importance:

"In practice consent to the caution should not be sought until it has been decided that cautioning is the correct course. The significance of the caution must be explained: that is, that a record will be kept of the caution, that the fact of any previous caution may influence the decision whether or not to prosecute if the person should offend again, and that it may be cited if the person should subsequently be found guilty of an offence by a court. In the case of a juvenile this explanation must be given to the offender in the presence of his parents or guardian, or other appropriate adult ..."

Where a caution had been administered in clear breach of the guidelines, the Divisional Court may exercise its supervisory jurisdiction to review the legality of the caution (*Commissioner of Police of the Metropolis, Ex p.P, The Times*, May 24, 1995). In that case the police had neither ensured that the 12 year old they cautioned for theft had admitted the offence, nor that he understood that what he was alleged to have done was **2–015** seriously wrong.

Public interest factors
The factors which have to be taken into consideration when a decision is reached as to whether administering a caution is in the public interest were spelt out in detail in circular 59/1990 as:

"– the nature of the offence

– the likely penalty if the offender was convicted by a court

– the offender's age and state of health

– his previous criminal history

– his attitude towards the offence, including practical expressions of regret."

Clear guidance was given that, regardless of the age or previous record of **2–016** the offender, the most serious offences (including those triable only on indictment), would not be suitable for a caution, nor would those where the victim had suffered significant harm or loss. Racial motivation for an offence was considered likely to aggravate seriousness, although it did not mean that prosecution should automatically follow (Note 3B). In current guidance repeat cautioning is specifically discouraged:

Paragraph 8.

"Research into a sample of offenders who were cautioned in 1991 indicates that 8 per cent had already received two or more cautions. Multiple cautioning brings this disposal into disrepute; cautions should not be administered to an offender in circumstances where there can be no reasonable expectation that this will curb his offending. It is only in the following circumstances that more than one caution should be considered:

– where the subsequent offence is trivial; or

– where there has been a sufficient lapse of time since the first caution to suggest that it had some effect."

The guidance suggests that where there is a doubt about the propriety of administering a caution the case should be referred to the Crown Prosecution Service at an early stage for a decision as to whether prosecution would be more suitable. If this happens the CPS will reach its decision in the light of the Code for Crown Prosecutors 1994. Prior to June 1994 the previous (1991) Code had encouraged prosecutors to consider a caution:

"The stigma of a conviction can cause irreparable harm to the future prospects of a young adult, and careful consideration should be given to the possibility of dealing with him or her by means of a caution." (para. 8 (iii))

The equivalent 'public interest' paragraph in the 1994 Code demonstrates a familiar shift of emphasis:

"Crown Prosecutors must consider the interests of a youth when deciding whether it is in the public interest to prosecute. The stigma of a conviction can cause very serious harm to the prospects of a youth offender or a young adult. Young offenders can sometimes be dealt with without going to court. But Crown Prosecutors should not avoid prosecuting simply because of the defendant's age. The seriousness of the offence or the offender's past behaviour may make prosecution necessary." (para. 6.8)

2-017 The administering and citation of cautions
The National Standards require that a formal caution should be administered in person by an officer in uniform (the rank may vary according to force practice) and at a police station where practicable. A juvenile must always be cautioned in the presence of a parent, guardian or other appropriate adult (art.5).

Formal cautions are recorded and cited in court if they are relevant to the offence under consideration. Note 6A to the national standard suggests that in order to ensure that sentencers distinguish between cautions and convictions the former should be listed on a separate sheet of paper.

2-018 Informal cautions
The 1993 Home Affairs Select Committee on Young Offenders sounded a note of warning regarding the use of informal cautions in regard to more serious offences (House of Commons 1993). Evidence put before the Committee suggested that, in direct contrast to the National Standards for Cautioning set out in paragraph 5 of HOC 85/1990, not only was there no standard national policy, but more than half of police forces did not have an internal policy on informal cautions. In the 1990 circular an informal warning by the police, administered on the spot was, confusingly, referred to as an 'informal caution' and evidence was given to the Committee that in some areas informal cautions were not only being recorded but also cited in subsequent proceedings. Circular 18/1994 seeks to clarify the difference between an informal warning and a formal caution by discouraging the use of the term 'informal caution' in any circumstances.

2-019 A statutory framework for cautioning?
Police cautioning of offenders has historically been the subject of guidance, but has had no statutory status. The report of the Royal Commission on Criminal Justice (1993) recommended that procedures concerning police decisions to divert offenders from court proceedings should be governed by statute, under which national guidelines, drawn up in consultation with the CPS and police service should be laid down in regulations. This recommendation was endorsed by the Home Affairs Committee in its report 'Juvenile Offenders' in which they considered

numerous issues regarding diversion from prosecution and cautioning (House of Commons, 1993).

The need for a statutory framework is born out by consideration that,   **2-020** despite the serious consequences for the individual of a decision to prosecute instead of administering a caution, or of agreeing to a caution without fully understanding the consequences of that decision, it is almost impossible for an aggrieved person to challenge the exercise of police and CPS discretion in this area. While cautioning remains an administrative act, the propriety of a decision to caution, or to prosecute instead of administering a caution, can only be challenged by judicial review. The decisions in *Chief Constable of Kent, ex p. L.* and *Director of Public Prosecutions, ex p. B* (1991) 93 Cr.App.R. 416 (heard together by agreement) demonstrate the difficulties inherent in seeking to challenge the validity of an administered caution, provided that the basic conditions set out in paragraph 2 of circular 18/1994 have been complied with (Uglow, *et al.*, 1991). In these cases juveniles were seeking to challenge by way of judicial review police and CPS decisions to prosecute instead of administering cautions. Both cases appeared to come within the criteria set out in current guidance, which suggested that a caution would be appropriate. The court accepted that the decisions were subject to judicial review, but held that, since there was no evidence that those responsible for making the decisions had acted improperly, refused the applications. The implications of the decision in the Kent case are discussed in some depth by Uglow, *et al.* (1991) in regard to the relationship between the police and the CPS and the role and relative powerlessness of multi-agency juvenile liaison groups when cautioning decisions are made.

What if the challenge is not to the failure to caution instead of   **2-021** prosecuting, but to the caution itself? There may be circumstances, particularly in relation to certain types of employment, that agreement to being cautioned may be given without a juvenile being fully informed of the implications of the caution. Whilst it is publicised in guidance and possibly generally understood that cautions remain on police files for three years, and may be cited in subsequent criminal proceedings, the duty of the police to inform certain professional bodies of cautions administered for certain categories of offence is less well known. Under Home Office Circular 45/1986, for instance, all registered medical practitioners, nurses, and teachers in any type of school or further education institution who are formally cautioned for offences involving violence, indecency, dishonesty, drink or drugs will (the wording is mandatory) have their professional governing bodies informed of the existence of the caution. As Tregiglas-Davey (1993) points out there is no corresponding duty on the police to inform the individual that they have to pass on the information. This, he suggests, makes it possible that an individual, thinking that accepting a caution would spare a stressful and possibly damaging court appearance, might agree to the procedure in circumstances in which, if guilt was in doubt, it could be better to defend the case in court. The author questions whether a consent to a caution in such circumstances can amount to informed consent, as has been required under successive guidance.

2–022 The cautioning of 17 year olds

Implementation of the Criminal Justice Act 1991 in October 1992 brought 17 year olds within the jurisdiction of the youth court for purposes of trial and sentence, but for the purposes of pre-trial decision making they are still treated as adults. National Standards for cautioning set out in Home Office Circular 59/1990 encouraged police forces to consider the use of cautions across all age groups. The extent to which the disparity between the national rates of cautioning of 16 and 17 year olds has narrowed since publication of 59/1990 and accelerated as a result of 17 year olds coming within the jurisdiction of the youth court, following implementation of the 1991 Act in October 1992, is apparent from statistics published by the Home Office in September 1993 (Government Statistical Service). These show that whilst previously a 17 year old was four times less likely to receive a caution than a 16 year old, during the first three quarters of 1992 the cautioning rate for 17 year olds rose from 35 per cent to 41 per cent, and in the last quarter reached 47.5 percent. There is some indication that cautioning rates are starting to decline as police forces alter their policies on cautioning in order to comply with the guidance in Home Office circular 18/1994 (See Table 2, para. 2–009).

2–023 The history of the diversion of offenders from the criminal process through use of cautioning procedures provides a clear example of the vulnerability of non-statutory schemes not only to widely discrepant practice but also to policy shifts, based on perceived problems but no research evidence, which are not subject to parliamentary scrutiny. The case for putting the cautioning of offenders on a statutory footing was well made out before circular 18/1994 turned existing policy in relation to the cautioning of juveniles on its head.

PART II THE YOUTH COURT

Chapter 3

Origins and Development

A study of magistrates' special jurisdiction in regard to young offenders **3–001**
reveals the erratic and somewhat patchy development of a separate, and
to a greater or lesser extent child welfare oriented forum with, until very
recently, a concurrent civil and criminal jurisdiction. Since 1992 the
jurisdiction, the framework of statute and guidance within which it
operates, and judicial attitudes, appear to have moved in a markedly
different direction. Shifts in youth justice policy represented by
provisions in the Criminal Justice Act 1991 and the Criminal Justice
and Public Order Act 1994, as well as the changed composition of the
magistrates youth court, have had the possibly unintended effect of
substantially reducing the previous, albeit patchily established, child
welfare orientation of the former juvenile court (Ball, 1992). Its
successor, the youth court, appears whether by design or default to have
become much more closely equated with the adult courts. This chapter
traces the rise and current decline of that special jurisdiction.

A separate court for children **3–002**
The origins of a separate youth court, located between adult criminal
justice and child welfare, are bound up with the public health, education
and child protection reforms introduced throughout the nineteenth
century. These reforms sought to address, both as a matter of
philanthropy and social control the threat posed to an ordered society by
the extremes of poverty, ill health, and poor housing caused by the rapid
growth of towns and cities during the industrial revolution (Parsloe,
1978; Harris and Webb, 1987; Morris and Giller, 1987). In living
conditions graphically described in a report of Lord Ashley to the House
of Commons in 1948 (see Parsloe, 1978, p. 106), and brought to the
attention of their contemporaries by Dickens and other writers, crime
was rife and revolution, endemic in the middle of the century in much of
Europe, only just below the surface. As Parsloe suggests:

> "Like their contemporaries in the United States, middle class **3–003**
> Britons were moved by pity and fear, by evangelical urges and those
> of self interest, to improve the lot of the masses. The impetus
> underlying innovations in the treatment of criminal and destitute
> children came from these ambivalent motives, so that genuine
> concern for the welfare of children mingled with a wish to control

them and prevent their developing into adult criminals or paupers."
(*ibid*. p. 107)

3–004 The introduction of separate courts for young offenders and of
institutions to avoid the imprisonment of children with adults were
innovations founded on this ambivalence. Not only founded on it, but
demonstrating it in a variety of guises throughout its development to
the present day (Anderson, 1978; Parker, *et al.*, 1981 and 1989; Bailey,
1987; Brown, 1991). Throughout the century whilst generally the
history of former juvenile court has been one of a developing special
jurisdiction with an ethos quite different from the adult court, it has also
demonstrated a marked diversity of interpretation of procedural rules,
sentencing practice and general ethos (Anderson, 1978; Priestley, *et al.*,
1980; Parker, *et al.*, 1981 and 1989; Ball, 1983). In many juvenile courts it
was an ethos which truly reflected the statutory duty of the juvenile
court when reaching its decisions 'to have regard to the welfare of the
child' (Children and Young Persons Act 1933, s.44), in others one which
"... can appear to operate against both the best interests of the child and
the principles of natural and criminal justice simultaneously' (Parker, *et
al.*, 1989 at p. 243).

3–005 Early developments
By the end of the nineteenth century initially tentative attempts to
increase the use of magistrates' summary jurisdiction for juvenile
offenders had culminated in the provisions of the Summary Jurisdiction
Act 1879 under which juveniles under the age of 16 could be tried
summarily for nearly all indictable offences, thus keeping them away
from the more serious adult criminals at quarter sessions and the assize
courts. A number of separate juvenile courts had also been set up in
Birmingham and other cities through the initiative of local magistrates
(Parsloe, 1978). Concurrent with these reforms were two other
important developments: the introduction of some rudimentary child
protection legislation, and the setting up of reformatories and industrial
schools. These institutions accommodated large numbers of children,
from what a leading reformer, Mary Carpenter, described as the
"dangerous and perishing classes" (1851), thus substantially reducing
the incidence of child imprisonment. Whether the creation of a separate
jurisdiction to deal with young offenders, and the creation of forms of
residential containment separate from the prison system were reforms
motivated by philanthropy or an essentially authoritarian and coercive
response to a period of rapid, possibly unprecedented, social change, or a
mixture of the two, is an issue which has long occupied and continues to
fascinate commentators. (Platt, 1978; Foucault, 1977; Morris and Giller,
1987).

3–006   The Children Act 1908, one of the cluster of criminal justice related
reforms introduced by the Liberal government during the first decade of
the century, provides the first example of what can be identified as a
recurrent phenomenon throughout the century. Piecemeal juvenile
justice reforms, begun on local initiatives, which then require

mandatory legislation to achieve their implementation on a national basis. Partly consolidating and partly reforming, the 1908 Act built on earlier statutes which had extended summary jurisdiction over juveniles and local initiatives which had sough to separate juvenile from adults in the summary courts. By making separate courts for the hearing of most criminal proceedings against juveniles—as well as all child protection and vagrancy cases—mandatory throughout England and Wales, the Children Act 1908 Act provided a foundation for future reforms. It also, by uniting in the new court the twin jurisdictional strands one relating to young offenders and the other to children in need of protection, according to the commentators perspective, either institutionalised ambivalence or provided an underpinning legitimacy for a welfare approach to young offenders (Anderson, 1987; Parsloe, 1980, Morris and Giller, 1987; Platt, 1990).

Towards a specialist court   **3–007**
The 1908 Act established separate courts for juveniles, but it was not for another quarter century that there was statutory recognition of the need for specially qualified magistrates to adjudicate in the new courts. The distinctive feature of the juvenile or children's courts introduced by the 1908 Act was the fact that hearings had to be held in a separate building or at a different time from adult courts, and that public access was restricted. Apart from this they were criminal courts of due process indistinguishable from other magistrates' courts. The development of a court for dealing with children that was not only separate, but also presided over by magistrates of both sexes theoretically selected on the basis of their interest in and experience of children, proved to be a slow process.

Both during and after the first World War, when there was a rapid increase in the incidence of recorded juvenile offending, concerns were voiced regarding wide variations in the working of juvenile courts and the suitability of many of the (male only) magistrates making decisions regarding children and young people. For example in the 1920 report of the influential Juvenile Organisations Committee, drafted by a sub-committee of which the pioneering metropolitan police magistrate William Clarke Hall was a leading member detailed the Committee's concerns:

> "The neglect of the opportunities afforded by the Probation of Offenders Act 1907, for the rehabilitation of juvenile offenders without conviction, the loose procedure in so many so-called 'Children's Courts'; the failure to observe the various sections of the Children Act 1908, relating to the conduct of juvenile courts and the conditions under which children, and particularly girls, are called upon to give evidence; the ignorance of Circulars and Instructions issued from the Home Office to justices and justices' clerks, are all difficulties which would never arise if the magistrate had a sympathetic understanding of child life, and was keen to avail himself of the many facilities for considerate treatment of young

people which existing statutes and regulations already place at his disposal." (See Bailey, 1987, p.22)

3–008 The first substantial reform came, appropriately enough, in the year of the appointment of the first women magistrates, when the Juvenile Courts (Metropolis) Act 1920 provided for police (stipendiary) magistrates to be nominated by the Secretary of State to sit as presidents of juvenile courts on the basis of their previous experience and special qualifications. The Act stipulated that the stipendiaries should sit with two justices, one of whom should be a woman, chosen from a panel nominated for the purpose by the Secretary of State. Outside London official guidance (Home Office Circular dated April 1921), recommending the trial of juveniles by specialist magistrates sitting in separate courts, met with varied response. Evidence gathered by the Children's Branch in 1925 and referred to in the report of the Committee on the Treatment of Young Offenders (Home Office, 1927) suggested that it

"revealed a wide diversity of practice and afforded ample ground for reviewing the whole system in the light of the experience which has been gained in the last 18 years." (Home Office 1927, at p. 17)

The Committee under its chairman, Sir Thomas Molony, had been set up in 1925 to

"inquire into the treatment of young offenders and young people who, owing to bad associations or surroundings, require protection and training, and to report what changes, if any, are desirable in the present law or its administration."

3–009 The Committee was urged by many witnesses to abandon the magistrates' jurisdiction and adopt a radical shift towards the social welfare orientation of the American juvenile courts. Had this happened the embryonic juvenile courts in England and Wales would at this stage have ceased, like those in the United States of America, to be courts of due process, instead adopting an entirely welfare approach. Despite their sympathies with many of the arguments presented, the Committee were not prepared to go as far as recommending that juveniles should be dealt with outside the criminal jurisdiction. They reasoned that there was:

"some danger in adopting any principle which might lead to ignoring the offence on which the action of the juvenile court in dealing with delinquents must be based. It is true that in many instances the offence may be trivial and the circumstances point to neglect rather than delinquency; but there remain cases where serious offences are committed, and neither in the public interest nor for the welfare of the young offender is it right they should be minimised. Two considerations presented themselves strongly to our minds. In the first place it is very important that a young person should have the fullest opportunity of meeting a charge made against him ... Secondly, when the offence is really serious and has been proved it is right that its gravity should be brought home to the offender." (*ibid.* p. 19)

The first passage reflects what might be regarded as the traditional **3–010** lawyers' view of the criminal court as providing protection of the individual defendant through due process as well as dispensing punishment. Despite this essentially traditional view, the extent to which the philosophical approach to offenders was changing to one of rehabilitation, a change that would have a profound impact on criminal justice policy and legislation for the next fifty years, is apparent in another passage;

> "It may be said that the reformation of the offender has become in recent years the keynote of the administration of justice. If this is true of the adult, the same principle must be applied with even greater force to the young offender whose character is still plastic and the more readily moulded by wise and sympathetic treatment." (*ibid.* p. 5)

In achieving the hoped for rehabilitation the juvenile court was seen as **3–011** the agent of reform:

> "The juvenile court performs very important functions which are not generally realised by the public and not always appreciated to their full by the Magistrates themselves. Before it appear boys and girls under 16 who are often wayward or mischievous and in some cases serious offenders; who are sometimes dull of mind or undeveloped, but more often full of vitality and intelligence, though misdirected; who are all by youthfulness hopeful subjects for care and training. The decision of the Magistrates with regard to the immediate future of these boys and girls must to a large extent influence their whole lives." (*ibid* p. 15)

Nor was the Committee in much doubt as to the qualifications needed by those who would adjudicate:

> "The qualities which are needed in every magistrate who sits in the juvenile court are a love of young people, sympathy with their interests, and an imaginative insight into their difficulties. The rest is largely common sense." (*ibid.* p. 25)

The creation and survival of the modern juvenile court   **3–012**
Following the Molony Committee's recommendations, the Children And Young Persons Act 1932, later consolidated with much of the Children Act 1908 as well as further reforming provisions, into the Children and Young Persons Act 1933, the juvenile court continued to be a court of due process focusing on proof of criminal responsibility. The main constitutional reform introduced by the 1933 Act was intended to remedy the identified deficit in interest and expertise amongst those adjudicating in criminal and child protection

proceedings in juvenile courts. Under the new legislation only magistrates elected to the new juvenile court panel for each petty sessional division, supposedly for their special expertise and interest in young people, could adjudicate and they had to reach their decisions in criminal as well as care proceedings 'having regard to the welfare of the child' (s.44). This provision still underpins the confusion of purpose and outcome apparent throughout the next half century (Anderson, 1978; Morris and Giller, 1987) and arguably continuing today, despite the separation of the criminal and civil jurisdictions in 1992.

3–013   Going back to the newly formed specialist panels, the rules provided, that all the magistrates in the petty sessional division would elect the panel. This was in contrast to appointment being dependent on external assessment of suitability for the work—the model set up for London under the Juvenile Courts (Metropolis) Act 1920. Today there is a marked contrast between the election by peers process which is used for appointments to the youth court panel outside London in England and Wales, and the fairly rigorous selection, on the basis of suitability for the work, of members of Scottish children's panels (Ravenscroft, 1987). Some indication of reason for doubt as to whether those elected rather than selected, were always suitable, may be gained from the fact that it was not until 1936 that an age limit of 70 years for membership of the panel was introduced. Prior to that time magistrates of any age could be elected as members of the juvenile court panel; an analysis of panel membership published in 1936, revealing that of approximately 10,000 members of juvenile court panels 1,284 or nearly 13 per cent were aged between 70 and 80 years and 130 were over 90 years (Elkin, 1938). In 1954, following the introduction of compulsory retirement for magistrates at the age of 70 years under the Justices of the Peace Act 1949, the age limit for membership of the juvenile court panel was reduced to 65 years where it remained until 1991 when, with little consultation, but with the active support of the Magistrates' Association Annual General Meeting (*The Magistrate*, December 1990, p. 229), it was again raised to the general retirement age of 70 years. A recent study suggests that currently more than 8 per cent of youth panel magistrates are over the age of 65 (Ball, 1995).

3–014 Proposals for abolition of the juvenile court
The fact that magistrates still retain, albeit now in separate courts, jurisdiction over both young offenders and children in need of care and protection reflects the resilience demonstrated in the 1960s, by those with a vested interest in the courts. Faced with determined attempts to bring the jurisdiction to an end and replace it with a more welfare oriented family council with a wider and possibly more expert membership (Longford, 1964; Home Office, 1965)—a reform which found favour in Scotland—magistrates, lawyers, and the probation service united in opposition (Bottoms, 1974; Harwin, 1981). The onslaught on the existence of the juvenile court had been preceded by the raising of the age of criminal responsibility from eight to ten years.

This was a compromise measure in response to the Report of the Committee on Children and Young Persons, chaired by Lord Ingleby (Home Office, 1960) which had recommended an initial rise to 12 years. (Children and Young Persons Act 1933, s.50 as amended by Children and Young Persons Act 1963).

The Labour government which came to power in 1964 had much **3–015** more radical changes than the age of criminal responsibility in mind. Proposals for reform of the treatment of juvenile offenders, as part of a wholesale reorganisation of the social services and the creation of a family service, were high on the agenda, having already been worked on by the party's policy makers. A party committee on criminal policy, chaired by Lord Longford, had perceived juvenile delinquency to be caused primarily by a breakdown in the family for which the juvenile was not responsible. The committee concluded that such delinquency could be better remedied by the child, the family, and a social worker agreeing what had gone wrong and the measures needed to resolve the problem, rather than involving the child in the (essentially stigmatising) criminal process. Only if the facts were in dispute or where agreement could not be reached was the case to come to court. For this purpose a more socially representative 'family court', would replace the juvenile court, thus, it was argued, avoiding the stigma of criminality for offending children and allowing

> "... every family to provide for its children the careful nurture and attention to individual and social needs that the fortunate majority already enjoy" (Longford, 1964, p. 1)

The White Paper *The Child, the Family and the Young Offender* (Home **3–016** Office 1965) based on the Longford committee's report, replaced the notion of a family service with a family council consisting of 'social workers of the children's service and other persons selected for their understanding and experience of children'. Predictably opposition to the somewhat vague proposals was intense amongst magistrates, justices clerks and the probation service. A resolution

> "That in the opinion of this Association the judicial functions of magistrates in Juvenile courts should be retained in preference to all-purpose Family Courts."

was carried by 269 votes to 38 at the Magistrates' Association's 1965 Annual General Meeting) (*The Magistrate*, 1965, p. 168). Nor were those with a vested interest in the courts alone. Academic commentators questioned the validity of the theoretical base on which the proposals were grounded (Downey, 1966 and Cavenagh, 1966) and Home Office officials were unsympathetic to them. These reservations coincided with the views of a new Home Secretary and plans for legislation to implement the 1965 White Paper proposals were shelved (Bottoms, 1974; Harwin, 1981).

The commitment to reform was still powerful and in 1968 the **3–017** apparently less radical and certainly more tightly reasoned White Paper,

Children in Trouble which formed the basis for the Children and Young Persons Act 1969 made proposals for reform of the treatment of young offenders, without actually abolishing the juvenile court. In contrast to the more radical reforms introduced north of the border by the Social Work (Scotland) Act 1968, the intention was to totally transform the functioning of the juvenile court in England and Wales, whilst leaving the structure of the court intact (Pitts, 1988).

Retention of the juvenile court appeased some opponents of reform, despite the fact that the detail of what was proposed was radical both in regard to the changed role of the court and in regard to sentencing (see Chapter 8). So far as the court was concerned:

* The juvenile court would be decriminalised for children under 14 years who would only be brought before the court as being in need of care and protection, which they would not receive without an order, rather than punishment for the offence committed.

* The presumption was for informal rather than formal proceedings and for civil rather than criminal proceedings, if matters could not be resolved informally.

* There was, in line with this, a substantial restriction on the bringing of criminal proceedings against older children, in that prosecution would have to be preceded by mandatory consultation between the police and the local authority children's department.

3–018 Why these proposals emerged and found so much support at this particular time, in the face of a swing, following the landmark Supreme Court judgment in *Re Gault* 387 US 1 1967, away from the procedural informality of a social welfare of treatment approach in the United States, is an issue discussed by many commentators including Parsloe (1980), Morris and Giller (1985) and Thorpe *et al.* (1980). Both the White Paper proposals and parallel, even more radical, developments with a very different legislative outcome in Scotland (Parsloe 1980, Morris and Giller 1987, Chap. 3) were grounded in the treatment approach. In England and Wales, lawyers opposed what they saw as a flawed conceptual framework which moved away from the safeguards of due process towards an administrative and consultative decision making process heavily reliant on the expertise of professionals, and in particular local authority social workers (Harwin, 1981). Even though the sort of coherent, orchestrated, opposition that might have been expected from lawyers, magistrates, justices clerks and the probation service, to proposals which clearly threatened vested interests, was missing, the Bill did not have an easy passage (Bottoms 1974, Harwin 1981). On the contrary it was opposed by the Conservatives at every stage, as Morris and Giller (1987) comment:

3–019 "They argued that the Bill was the product of inadequate preparation and consultation, it was unjust (and class-biased) as between different juveniles, it gave insufficient recognition to the constructive role of the juvenile court and it interfered with police work with juveniles especially in regard to more serious offences. They also objected to state intervention in a juvenile's life through an executive rather than a judicial body." (p. 89)

After the abortive efforts of reformers to abolish the juvenile court, or when that failed to decriminalise it, despite recurrent attempts by reform groups to arouse interest in the overtly welfare oriented children's hearings in Scotland (see for instance McCabe and Treitel, 1984), there have been no significant threats to the continued existence of magistrates' jurisdiction over young offenders since the 1960s.

The consequences of the partial implementation of the 1969 Act, and **3–020** the ensuing anger and frustration of juvenile panel magistrates, have been well documented (Webb and Harris, 1987; Morris and Giller, 1987; Pitts, 1990). A period during the 1970s of dramatic increase in the use of custody was followed through the 1980s and up to 1991 by a discernable decline (Table 3).

Table 3

Males aged 14–16 years sentenced to custody for indictable offences

1971	3,200
1975	5,900
1981	7,700
1985	5,900
1991	1,400

(Source: Criminal Statistics, Home Office, HMSO)

During this time, some juvenile courts developed a distinctive non-custodial ethos, often associated with a good working relationship between magistrates on the juvenile panel and local youth justice teams. These local initiatives both informed and were encouraged by deliberate policies, underwritten by provisions in the Criminal Justice Act 1982, amended and strengthened by the CJA 1988, to avoid the use of custody for young defendants (Bowden and Stevens, 1986; NACRO, 1987; Gibson, *et al.*, 1994).

The youth court—and the retreat from welfare   **3–021**
Recently provisions in the Children Act 1989 and the Criminal Justice Act 1991 have, arguably, and possibly unintentionally, reversed that process and altered the composition and ethos of the former juvenile court, in many cases beyond recognition. Why has this happened? At least part of the explanation may stem from the transfer of the care jurisdiction, and hence many magistrates with an interest in child welfare, from the juvenile court to the family proceedings court on implementation of the Children Act 1989 in October 1991. This

substantial reduction in both the workload and the perceived status of the juvenile court was closely followed by the transfer of 17 year old defendants to the renamed youth court under the Criminal Justice Act 1991, so that the composition and morale of the panel and the age profile of defendants changed at a stroke (Ball, 1992). This would inevitably make an impact on the ethos of some courts. What could not have been anticipated was that these changes would coincide with a period of intense public concern about youth crime and persistent young offenders (Cavadino, 1994; Hagell and Newburn, 1994) to which the government responded with a variety of seemingly unrelated initiatives. These ranged from guidance reversing previous well-established policy which encouraged diversion from the courts through cautioning with new guidance aimed at limiting the use of cautions to one for each offender (Home Office Circular 18/94) (See Chapter 2), to legislation which, by offering the courts an increased range of sentences for 10–17 year olds (Criminal Justice and Public Order Act 1994), may further erode the differences between adult and youth courts (Ashworth, 1994; Gibson, *et al.*, 1994; Gibson, 1995, Ball, 1995).

3–022   One consequence of the new cautioning guidance and the new Code for Crown Prosecutors (1994), is likely to be a substantial increase in the workload of the youth court and a shift downwards of the age profile of those appearing; the 10–13 year old offenders being those who were formally only exceptionally prosecuted under previous guidance (See Table 2, para. 2–009). If the increase in defendants requires the enlargement of youth panels, the only magistrates available to undertake this work may well be those who are retired, who may have no previous experience of adjudicating on young offenders. All this, combined with evidence of current considerable frustration of youth panel justices with the powers available to them may militate towards the youth court becoming more rather than less like the adult court (Ball, 1995).

Chapter 4

Constitution

The youth court panel

4–001

A youth court is a magistrates' court especially established for the purpose of dealing with criminal proceedings against those under the age of 18 (Children and Young Persons Act 1933, s.45). Almost every case against a person of that age will start and finish in the youth court. The exceptions to this are set out in Chapter 5 (see para. 5–002). The only magistrates who may sit in a youth court are those who are members of a youth court panel (1933 Act, Sched. 2, para. 2).

For the area comprising Inner London (as defined in Justices' of the Peace Act 1979, s. 2) and the City of London (together called the Metropolitan area) there is a single panel (CYPA Act 1933, Sched. 2, para. 14). Outside that area each petty sessional division must form a youth court panel, although this may be a combined panel with another or other petty sessional divisions (for rules regarding combined panels, see below, para. 4–005, *et seq.*).

The youth court panel for the Metropolitan area consists of **4–002** Metropolitan Stipendiary Magistrates and lay justices especially selected by the Lord Chancellor for this purpose. It sits in places specified in the Youth Courts (London) Order 1975 (as amended) under the chairmanship of a person selected from a panel constructed in accordance with the Inner London Juvenile Courts (Selection of Chairmen) Order 1990 (S.I. 1990 No. 1265). It will normally sit as a court of three justices. Where that is not possible without an adjournment of the court and where that adjournment would not be in the interests of justice, the court may be constituted by two persons or, if the justice is a metropolitan stipendiary magistrate, then that stipendiary magistrate may sit alone (CYPA Act 1933, Sched. 2, paras. 15 to 18).

Outside the Metropolitan area, the justices for each petty sessional division elect a panel every three years. The election takes place at the October meeting of the justices and the panel members are appointed for three years from the following January 1 (Youth Courts (Constitution) Rules 1954 rr. 1, 4). Elections were held in October 1994 and will be held every three years thereafter. Any vacancy that arises within the life of the panel may be filled by the justices for the petty sessional division at any time and the person appointed will serve until the end of the tenure of the panel (1954 Rules, rr. 6, 7). In selecting a panel, justices must appoint those 'especially qualified' for dealing with juvenile cases (1954 Rules, r.1).

No further guidance is given; youth panel justices are elected triennially by all the members of the bench without any scrutiny of the extent to which they are 'especially qualified' for the work of the youth court. This is in marked contrast to the position in Scotland, where applicants to join the Children's Panel undergo a rigorous selection process to determine their suitability for making decisions in the interests of the welfare of the children and young people appearing before the hearing (Ravenscroft, 1987).

4–003 From 1954 until 1991 the age of retirement from the juvenile panel was set at 65, rather than the general retirement age from the bench of 70 years. There is now some concern regarding the extent to which the age of the majority of youth panel justices distances them from the problems and lifestyles of defendants. Recent evidence suggests that with nearly 70 per cent of justices appointed to the youth panel for the first time within the last five years being over 45, and 13 per cent over 55 years, the age profile of newly appointed youth panel justices may be such as to at least question whether due attention is being paid to the requirement for members of the panel to be 'especially qualified'in this respect (Ball, 1995).

A provincial stipendiary magistrate is an automatic member of the panel for any area in which he or she exercises jurisdiction, regardless of any requirement to be 'especially qualified' for the work of the youth court. He or she may, if to convene a full bench would cause delay, adjudicate alone (Youth Court (Constitution) Rules 1954, rr. 2, 12(2)).

4–004 The size of the panel

In deciding on the number to be appointed to a youth court panel the justices for an area are directed to ensure that there are sufficient members to provide for enough courts to deal expeditiously with the business of the court. Outside Inner London—where special arrangements exist for the allocation of justices to the youth court panel—it is considered important that justices do enough youth court work to maintain and develop expertise, but without such sittings becoming so predominant that individual justices cannot maintain and develop their experience of other work. The Lord Chancellor has indicated that it is desirable that each panel member should complete at least 13 sittings a year in the youth court in order that they may obtain, retain, and develop a proper understanding of the special work, powers and responsibilities of the panel (LCD Circular AC(92)5). In practice, wide fluctuations exist in the number of sittings undertaken. Data from a recent survey of over 450 justices on 20 panels of various sizes from throughout England and Wales demonstrates the extent of these variations. At one extreme, on one panel 18 per cent of magistrates sit for more than 35 half days in a year, whilst in another almost a quarter of all panel members managed fewer than the required 13 sittings. Even on those panels where the average sittings exceed 12, there are often individual members who sit significantly less often than the approved minimum. At the other extreme individual justices recorded more than 60 half days (Ball, 1995). The Lord Chancellor has indicated that he expects that a magistrate will not be a member of both youth court and family panels unless there are insufficient justices on a bench to form an appropriately sized panel without such duplication (Mackay, 1994). In practice the recent survey suggests that nearly a third of all youth court panel justices are also members of the family proceedings panel (Ball, 1995).

Combined panels   4–005
No panel can operate effectively with fewer than six members. This is because of the risk of a justice being disqualified in an individual case, through having heard convictions during a remand application, and therefore being unable to deal with the determination of guilt if a not guilty plea is entered (Magistrates' Courts Act 1980, s. 42). In practice, any panel of fewer than eight members will prove very difficult to work. If there is insufficient work for eight panel members to complete at least 13 sittings, then the panel may find it necessary to combine with another. In the past, despite Home Office guidance (HOC 138/79) urging panels to combine in order that justices "obtain sufficient experience of this important and specialized work", there was considerable resistance to amalgamation from small panels reluctant to lose their identity. For instance a survey undertaken in 1981 showed large numbers of juvenile courts serving rural areas were held only monthly and staffed by such large panels that individual justices often only sat once or twice a year (Ball, 1983b).

Panels' reluctance to amalgamate (in 1981 only 10 per cent of panels 4–006 in England and Wales were combined panels) provoked the editor of the Justice of the Peace to complain about the prevalence of 'narrow parochial pride' (Harris, 1978). Many small divisions have amalgamated or disappeared since 1980, resulting in fewer small divisions, and the proportion of combined panels has more than doubled (Ball, 1995).

If justices cannot appoint sufficient panel members from their own number, they may seek combination with an adjoining panel or they may appoint a justice assigned to another petty sessions area in the same county who is especially qualified for dealing with juvenile cases. (Youth Court (Constitution) Rules 1954, r. 1(4)). There seems no reason why a youth court panel member should not form part of a youth court sitting in a different petty sessions area, but in the same commission area, since the Children and Young Persons Act 1933, Sched. 2, para. 2, specifies qualification as membership of *a* youth court panel.

The procedure for combination of a panel allows a magistrates' courts 4–007 committee to make a recommendation to the Lord Chancellor that he make an order forming a combined panel to cover two or more petty sessions areas within the same County or Outer London Borough (1933 Act, Sched. 2, para. 4). Before submitting a recommendation to the Lord Chancellor, a magistrates' courts committee must consult:

(a)   The justices for any petty sessions area involved in the proposed
      combination which is in the area covered by the magistrates'
      courts committee;

(b)   Any other magistrates' courts committee covering a petty
      sessions area to be involved in the combined area (1933 Act,
      Sched. 2, para. 10).

When the recommendation is submitted, the magistrates' courts
committee must give notice to those described in (a) and (b) above (1933
Act, Sched. 2, para. 10). If the Lord Chancellor proposes to make an order
different from that recommended to him notice must be given to any
magistrates' courts committee concerned and to the justices for any
petty sessions area involved who have a maximum of one month to
respond (1933 Act, Sched. 2, paras. 11 and 12). The Lord Chancellor may
also direct a magistrates' courts committee to review the function of
youth courts in its area and make a report containing recommendations
for combination orders or justifying the lack of such a recommendation
(1933 Act, Sched. 2, para. 5). This elaborate procedure should be
compared with the simpler speedier process for combination of family
panels (Family Courts (Constitution) Rules 1991, para. 11). There
appears to be no benefit to be gained by involving the Lord Chancellor in
the process of combination and the procedure could, with advantage, be
allied to that applicable to family panels.

4–008 The conduct of panel business
Each youth court panel must meet at least twice a year to discuss and
consider matters of relevance to its business (Youth Courts
(Constitution) Rules 1954 (as amended), Rule 10), which should involve
contact with others involved in juvenile justice, such as the probation
service, social services departments and voluntary organisations (Home
Office, 1992). The report of a nationwide study of the workings of youth
court related inter-agency co-operation, funded by the Home Office and
undertaken by researchers at the Institute of Criminology at
Cambridge, is due for publication.

4–009 THE YOUTH COURT

A youth court should be made up of three justices from the panel,
including a man and a woman. There is no exception to the maximum of
three justices, but:

*   if, due to circumstances unforeseen when the rota was drawn up,
      no man or no woman is available and the other panel members
      present consider it inexpedient in the interests of justice to
      adjourn (Youth Court (Constitution) Rules 1954, r. 12), a bench
      may be properly constitued without a gender mix.

* If a stipendiary magistrate is the only panel member present and thinks it inexpedient in the interests of justice to adjourn, he or she may adjudicate alone. (1954 Rules, r. 12 (2)).

* Tasks which a single justice may perform in the adult court—for example remands and committals for trial—may be undertaken by a single justice within a youth court even though the court will not consist of a man and a woman (r. 12 (4)).

Chairmanship 4–010

The youth court must sit under the chairmanship of a chairman or deputy chairman elected by the panel members. This election should take place as soon as practicable after the election of the panel; nominations are not excluded but any voting must be by secret ballot. Additional or replacement chairman or deputy chairmen may be elected at any time (r. 9). If no elected chairman or deputy chairman is available at the time of the court, the other panel members present may choose one of their number to preside (r. 13 (2)). If a chairman or deputy chairman is present but considers it appropriate for another member of the court to act as chairman, he or she may nominate that member to act as chairman providing that the elected chairman or deputy chairman continues to sit throughout the court (r. 13 (1A)).

Those who undertake the task of chairman of a panel, a role which, it is suggested, requires an important combination of communication and organisational skills have little or no guidance from The Magistrates' Association or other sources beyond that intended for adult court chairman (Ralphs and Norman, 1992). Although many panels have adopted a practice whereby the chairman does not seek to continue after a certain time in office, generally not exceeding six years, at the present time this is a voluntary arrangement.

Inner London rules for the appointment of chairmen 4–011

In contrast to the lack of guidance regarding the role, and the somewhat haphazard election of chairmen in the rest of England and Wales, within the Metropolitan area, a statutory procedure (the Inner London Juvenile Courts (Selection of Chairmen) Order 1990), provides for the Lord Chancellor to nominate as a court chairman a justice who:

(a) Has undergone the chairmanship course provided by the Inner London magistrates' courts service;

(b) Has served for at least six years as a justice of the peace, including at least five years in a juvenile court (not necessarily in Inner London).

(c) Has successfully completed a special course, and

(d) has thereafter sat as a chairman under training on at least six occasions (for a total of not less than 20 hours), on each occasion with and at the request of a court chairman (who should not always be the same one) approved for this purpose by the chairman of the panel.

4–012   Such nominations will follow a recommendation made by a selection committee. This committee has as its chairman the chairman of the Inner London youth court panel. Further members will be the Chief Metropolitan Stipendiary Magistrate (or a stipendiary magistrate nominated by him), the vice chairman of the Inner London youth court panel, the chairman of each of the rota groups into which the panel is divided and four justices who are not and have not been court chairmen. One of these four justices must be elected by each rota group once every three years. It is not permitted for all the elections from the rota groups to be held in the same year (article 9). This committee will have as its secretary the senior chief clerk for the Inner London youth courts (article 10). When the committee meets it has as a quorum the chairman of the committee who will be the chairman of the panel, the stipendiary magistrate, two rota group chairmen and two other members (article 12). In reaching its decision the committee is required to take into account the personal qualities of the candidate, the performance of the candidate and the potential of the candidate to undertake the duties of a court chairman (article 13). No member of the selection committee who is in the final category (those who are not and have not been court chairmen) may be recommended for nomination as a court chairman within one year after the end of their service on this committee. The special course referred to in article 3(c) is a special course of youth court chairmanship training and any justice who has undergone the ordinary chairmanship course provided by the Inner London magistrates' courts service and has been a justice of the peace for at least six years, which includes a minimum of five years on a youth court, may take this course if he or she wishes to do so providing a course is available for the purpose (article 4).

4–013   Article 3(c) requires successful completion of that course which must be adjudicated upon by a course assessment panel (article 5). This panel has as its chairman a stipendiary magistrate nominated by the Chief Metropolitan Stipendiary Magistrate and includes also one court chairman from each rota group elected by the members of that group and either the senior chief clerk of the youth courts in Inner London or a clerk not below the rank of senior deputy chief clerk nominated by that senior chief clerk. Again elections from the rota groups must be held once every three years but not all rota groups may elect in the same year. When the panel meets, its quorum is the chairman, two court chairmen and the clerk member (article 7). It is not possible for an individual to be a member of both the course assessment panel and the selection committee at the same time (article 19).

4–014   A court chairman may be re-nominated if he or she is a serving or a former court chairman, providing they have completed either a refresher course in youth court chairmanship or the special course within the previous six years. The selection committee may only re-nominate such a person if satisfied that the individual is suitable for further service as a court chairman. A decision not to recommend for re-nomination must be preceded by the selection committee first telling that individual the grounds of the committee's doubts as to his suitability and then giving that individual the opportunity to be heard by the committee on those grounds and any other matters which the individual wishes the committee to take into account (article 16). Any individual who is a court chairman who is considered no longer to be suitable for whatever reason may be subject to a recommendation from the selection committee to the Lord Chancellor that that persons nomination be suspended or revoked (article 17).

Training   4–015
When a justice is appointed to a youth court panel there is an obligation to undertake training, the content of which is currently determined by justices' clerks in consultation with training officers. It typically consists of an introduction to the powers and practice of youth courts supported by an observation of such courts in operation and visits to establishments responsible for the accommodation of children where the court removes them from their home surroundings. There is currently, contrary to the position for family proceedings panels, no detailed syllabus for youth panel training; the most recent guidance being that provided by the Judicial Studies Board immediately following implementation of the CJA 1991 in 1992.

The Courtroom and Care of Young People   4–016
A youth court may not sit in a room in which another type of court has sat in the hour preceding the commencement of the youth court or will sit within an hour of the sitting of the court (1933 Act, s.47). Arrangements must be made to prevent a person under 17 years from associating with an adult who is not a relative but who is charged with any offence (unless jointly charged with the person under 17) whilst being conveyed to or from a criminal court by the police or whilst waiting before or after attending such a court (see above, Chap. 1). If the person under 17 is a girl, then arrangements must be made for her to be in the care of a woman whilst being conveyed to court or waiting before or after attendance in court. (1933 Act, s. 31).

Presence in the Courtroom   4–017
There are severe restrictions on those who may be in a youth court while the court is sitting.

The court may not allow to remain,

*   members of the public with no connection with the case; or (as in the adult court) anyone under 14 years (except an infant in arms) unless they are the defendant or a witness or their presence is otherwise needed for the purposes of justice (1933 Act, s. 3)

The court may allow to remain,

*   members and officers of the court;

*   parties to the case before the court;

*   solicitors and counsel acting for the parties to the case before the court (note that solicitors and counsel in other cases have no right to be present in the courtroom);

*   witnesses and other persons directly concerned with the case— this will include social workers, probation officers or members of other similar agencies with an interest or potential interest in the case: *Southwark Juvenile Court* [1973] 3 All E.R. 383;

*   bona fide representatives of newspapers and news agencies;

*   such other persons as the court may specifically authorise to be present—this will allow justices under training, trainee social workers and others with a bona fide interest to be allowed to attend (1933 Act, s. 47(2)).

The small amount of research that has been published regarding the perceptions of juveniles and their families involved in court proceedings, suggests that even when the numbers of people in the courtroom are kept to a minimum, and considerable care is taken to explain the roles of those present, there is confusion as to who people are and their role in the proceedings (Morris and Giller, 1977; Parker, *et al.,* 1981; Ball, 1981). Good practice would suggest and magistrates' training encourages the chairman to greet the defendant and those accompanying him by name, and to explain to them in very simple terms the identity and role of the various people in court.

4–018 The courtroom layout

Courtroom fittings very often leave little choice about where people will sit, but in a youth court there are important considerations regarding communications which need to guide the use of any flexibility that can be introduced into even the most formal courtroom. It is suggested that these include:

*   the defendant being seated both so that he or she is the centre of attention, but also near to a parent or other supportive adult and an advocate (if there is one);

*   the defendant being so positioned so as to allow eye contact with the bench without being so close as to allow intimidation in either direction;

*   care being exercised to ensure that witnesses can be seen and spoken to by all in the court, without being sufficiently close to the defendant or his supports to allow intimidation.

*   sufficient flexibility in the layout to allow for sole or multiple defendants.

Recording of Decisions   **4–019**
By Magistrates' Courts Rules 1981, r. 66, the clerk of every magistrates'
court must keep a register recording matters prescribed by that rule. By
Magistrates' Courts (Children and Young Persons) Rules 1992, r. 25,
that part of the register that relates to proceedings in a youth court must
be kept in a separate book. This register has to record the adjudications
of the court, comments of the accused and reasons for the decision to
impose custody and to not make a compensation order (Magistrates'
Courts Rules 1981, r. 66). The register is open to inspection at any
reasonable hour by any justice of the peace or by anyone authorised to
inspect the register by a justice or by the Lord Chancellor (1981 Rules, r.
66(12)). The Home Secretary, by letter of February 9, 1893, requested
that police officers be allowed access to the registers (57 *JP Journal* at
105). It was at that time that the Home Secretary decided that
responsibility for collecting information to create criminal statistics
should be with the police rather than with the courts.

Chapter 5

Jurisdiction

5–001 The basic rule is that all those under 18 prosecuted for criminal offences are dealt with by a youth court (C&YPA 1933, s. 46(1)). The age of the juvenile is that which appears to the court to be his age after considering any available evidence (MCA 1980, s. 150(4)). Age changes at the commencement of the anniversary of the date of birth (Family Law Reform Act 1969, s. 9). The procedure to be adopted where a juvenile becomes 18 after committing the offence but before the proceedings are concluded is described below at para. 5–003.

5–002 There are five exceptions to this basic rule.

    (a) **The juvenile is charged with homicide** (MCA 1980, s. 24). Although there is no definition of homicide, it is likely to include any offence in which it is alleged that the juvenile caused death, for example, murder, manslaughter and including, commentators suggest, causing death by dangerous driving (Draycott and Baker, 1994).

    (b) **Remand.** An adult or youth court has equal power to remand a juvenile whether bail is granted or refused (C&YPA 1933, s. 46(2)). An adult court remanding to the care of a local authority may also grant a secure accommodation order at the same time (Criminal Justice Act 1991, s. 60(3)). (See Chapter 6, para. 6–025, *et seq.* for the criteria for making secure accommodation orders, and jurisdiction to renew them).

    (c) **Connection with an adult.** If a juvenile

      (i) is **jointly charged with an adult** (1933 Act, s. 46(1)(a));

      (ii) **has an adult charged as an aider and abettor** to the offence committed by the juvenile (1933 Act, s. 46(1)(b));

      (iii) **is charged as an aider and abettor to an adult** (1963 Act, s. 18(1)(a));

      (iv) **is charged with an offence arising out of the same circumstances as those giving rise to proceedings against an adult** (C&YPA 1963, s. 18(1)(b));

5–003 then the adult court may also deal with the juvenile. There are

52

restrictions on the sentences that can be imposed on the juvenile by the adult court (see Chapter 12). Where an adult court is dealing with a juvenile because he is jointly charged with an adult, and the adult pleads guilty and the juvenile pleads not guilty, the adult court may remit the juvenile to a youth court for trial (1980 Act, s. 29). Similarly, where the justices decide to commit the adult for trial (or to discharge him) but to proceed to summary trial of the information against the juvenile. There is no appeal available to the juvenile against the order of remittal (1980 Act, s. 29(4)). The court may remit the juvenile to a youth court that acts either for the same place as the remitting court or for the place where the young person habitually resides. The remitting court may make any necessary directions regarding custody or bail until the juvenile can be brought before the youth court (1980 Act, s. 29).

(d) **Crown Court.** This court has power to deal with a juvenile committed for trial or sentence. For consideration of committal for trial, see below (para. 5–016). For procedure on committal for sentence, see Chapter 12.

(e) **Where a court other than a youth court has started to deal with a person believing them to be an adult but then discovers they are under 18,** the court may continue to deal fully with the offender, if it thinks fit (1933 Act, s. 46(1)(c) and s. 46 (1A)). For restrictions on sentence, see Chapter 8. There is also the reverse power for a youth court to continue to deal with a person discovered to be 18 or over (1933 Act, s. 48(1)).

Reporting of Youth Court Proceedings   **5–004**
There are restrictions on what may be reported of proceedings:

(a) before youth courts,

(b) before magistrates' courts that are not youth courts when they are dealing with an application to vary or discharge a supervision order in accordance with the C&YPA 1969, s.15 or 16, or,

(c) on appeal (including case stated) from those courts.

Section 49 of the Criminal Justice and Public Order Act 1994 substitutes **5–005** a new section 49 in the 1933 Act. As before, no newspaper, sound or television report of any proceedings in a youth court may reveal the name, address or school of anyone under 18 nor may it include anything likely to lead to the identification of the person under 18. This applies whether the person under 18 is the defendant, a witness or the person in respect of whom the proceedings are brought. No picture may be published of such a person under 18. The maximum penalty is a fine up to level 5 (presently £5,000). A court (or single justice (s.49(8)) may relax or remove these provisions in any particular case:

" (a) … if it is satisfied that it is appropriate to do so for the purpose of avoiding injustice to the child or young person; or" in the case of a child or young person charged with or convicted of a violent or sexual offence (as defined in the Criminal Justice Act 1991, s.31(1)), or one punishable in the case of a person aged 21 years or over with 14 imprisonment for years or more (s.49(6)):

> (b) "that, as respects a child or young person to whom this paragraph applies who is unlawfully at large, it is necessary to dispense with those requirements for the purpose of apprehending him and bringing him before a court or returning him to the place in which he was in custody" (1994 Act, s.49(5)).

A court may only exercise its powers under section 49(5)(b) on an application by the Director of Public Prosecutions who must give notice to any legal representative of the young offender (section 49(7)). In exercising its powers the extent to which the order applies must be specified by the court (or single justice) (section 49(5) and (11)).

5–006   The prohibition on publishing the identity of defendants applies only to youth courts. However, by virtue of Children and Young Persons Act 1969, s. 10(1)(b) it is extended to magistrates' courts that are not youth courts when they are dealing with an application to vary or to discharge a supervision order in accordance with Children and Young Persons Act 1969, s. 15 or s. 16, that is where the supervised person has attained the age of 18 (Children and Young Persons Act 1969, s. 15(11)) or the matter is being heard on appeal.

In order for the prohibition to be extended, the court *must* announce that section 49 extends to the proceedings; if it does not, the prohibition does not apply (Children and Young Persons Act 1969, s. 10(2)). Other courts have the power to impose such a restriction by making an order under Children and Young Persons Act 1933, s. 39.

5–007   The restrictions on the reporting of proceedings involving a juvenile which are contained in the 1933 Act, s. 49 apply only to proceedings in a youth court. Where a person under 18 appears in an adult court (including the Crown Court), the press has the same right to report what happens as with an adult unless the court makes an order under the 1933 Act, s. 39(1). Under this section, a court has power to prohibit newspaper, sound or television reports from revealing the name, address or school of the juvenile or any particulars likely to lead to his or her identification. This power extends to any juvenile involved in proceedings either as the person by whom, against whom or in respect of whom the proceedings are being taken or as a witness in the proceedings. The court may also prohibit the publication of a picture of such a juvenile. These prohibitions may be complete or may permit use of the information in circumstances prescribed by the court (1933 Act, s. 39(1) and 1963 Act, s. 57(4)). The maximum penalty for a breach of this prohibition is a fine of level 5, presently £5,000 (1933 Act, s. 39(1)).

5–008   There has been a tendency for an adult court to make this order automatically whenever a defendant is under 18. Whilst it will usually be right to make the order, on each occasion the court should consider the situation before it and balance the need to protect juveniles against the legitimate interest of the public in knowing the identity of those who commit criminal offences. In *Crown Court at Leicester, ex p. S (a minor)* [1992] 2 All E.R. 659 a twelve year old boy was charged with arson, having set fire to an ambulance station causing damage to both the station and ambulances estimated at £2.5m. The Divisional Court decided to overturn a decision of the trial Judge to allow the identity of the child to be disclosed. In the judgment, Watkins L.J. described the way to consider such decisions:

> "... the correct approach to the exercise of the power given by section 39 is that reports of proceedings should not be restricted unless there are reasons to do so which outweigh the legitimate interest of the public in receiving fair and accurate reports of criminal proceedings and knowing the identity of those in the community who have been guilty of criminal conduct and who may, therefore, present a danger or threat to the community in which they live. The mere fact that the person before the court is a child or young person will normally be a good reason for restricting reports ... and it will, in our opinion, only be in rare and exceptional cases that directions under section 39 will not be given ...".

In reaching a conclusion that this case was not rare and exceptional, the **5–009** Divisional Court took into account:

(a) The effect on the child of the reactions of others who lived in the same community home if they were to discover the nature of the allegations against him;

(b) The effect on the family of the child;

(c) The passing of 18 months from the date of offence to the date of appearance in the Crown Court;

(d) The fact that the child would not be released into the community for some time.

No application for an order is needed but one will often be made by the **5–010** court clerk, although it may be made by any person involved in the proceedings. Indeed, it has been suggested that the prosecutor should be expected to remind a court of the need to consider making an order where it appears that the need may be overlooked: *Crown Court at Southwark, ex p. Godwin* [1991] 3 All E.R. 818 at 820c, per Glidewell L.J. If a representative of the press wishes to object to the order being made, that representative should be allowed to be heard. Indeed, a court has complete discretion to hear representations from parties that the court considers to have a legitimate interest in whether or not an order should be made: *Central Criminal Court, ex p. Crook and Godwin* 159 J.P. 295; [1995] F.C.R. 153. If the order is made, it can only be in the terms of the section but it must be in terms that are clear and readily ascertainable by those affected by it. Ideally, the order will be reduced to writing especially where there was any possibility of doubt as to the extent of the order (*ex p. Crook and Godwin*). It will then be for a publisher to decide whether the information intending to be published would be likely to lead to a breach of the section. One consequence of making an order may be that it will effectively prevent the identifying of the defendants who are adults since identifying the defendants may inevitably identify the child. In such circumstances there is no power under section 39 to specifically prohibit the publication of the details of an adult. Any publisher will need to make his own decision knowing that prosecution may follow if that decision is wrong. In *Crown Court at Southwark, ex p. Godwin* two (adult) defendants appeared at the Crown Court charged with acts of indecency on two young children who belonged to the same close knit community. At the time of the offences one of the defendants lived next door to the children and used to act as child minder for them. Defence counsel successfully argued that the close knit nature of the community to which both children and defendants belonged meant that naming the defendants was likely to have the effect of naming the children and the trial Judge added to the section 39 order a prohibition against the revealing of the names and addresses of the defendants. The Court of Appeal confirmed that this order was outside the scope of the section and could not be imposed. The issue of naming defendants was part of the practical application of the order and was for potential publishers to consider. Additional controls are contained in Contempt of Court Act 1981, s. 4 (power to postpone reporting of proceedings) and s. 11 (prohibiting publication of matters withheld from the public during the course of proceedings).

5–011 Location and Time Limits

Territorially, the court has the same jurisdiction as with an adult. Similarly, with the time during which proceedings can be started. Thus:

Nature of Offence	*Proceedings to be Commenced Within*	*Territorial Limits*
1. Summary	six months unless offence extension or restriction	County, London, Commission Area City of London (but see MC.A 1980, s. 2(6) allowing court dealing with a person for an offence committed within a County, London, Commission Area or City of London to deal also with any other summary offence for which he could be tried by a magistrates'

court for any other
area).

or

2. Indictable   No limit   No limit
    (including those
    triable either way)

Proceedings commence by way of information, that is a document **5–012**
describing the specific offence in ordinary language avoiding as far as
possible the use of technical terms and giving such particulars as
necessary to give reasonable information of the nature of the charge
(Magistrates' Courts Rules 1981, r. 100). A written information is laid
when it is received at the office of the clerk to the justices for the area
(*Manchester Stipendiary Magistrate, ex p. Hill* [1982] 2 All E.R. 963).
This is so even where the information is a letter from the Crown
Prosecution Service informing the clerk to the justices of an intention to
charge and providing enough detail to satisfy 1981 Rules, r. 100, even
though neither the prosecutor nor the clerk regarded the letter as an
information (*Kennett Justices, ex p. Humphrey and Wyatt* [1993] Crim.
L.R. 787).

The time limits given are the maximum periods and are subject to the **5–013**
line of authorities regarding abuse of the process of the court. These give
to the court power to dismiss proceedings where there has been
inordinate delay and prejudice to the defence (*Gateshead Justices, ex p.
Smith* [1984] 184 JP 609). Delay due merely to the complexity of the case
or contributed to by the actions of the defendant will not found relief
(*AG Reference (No. 1 of 1990)* [1992] 3 All E.R. 169). The defendant must
show on the balance of probabilities that, owing to the delay, he would
suffer serious prejudice to the extent that no fair trial could be held. In
addition, practitioners should be aware of the national guidelines
introduced as a result of the report of the Working Group on Pre-Trial
Issues (Home Office, 1990). This report made a number of
recommendations regarding times within which various stages of the
proceedings prior to sentence should be concluded. As regards juveniles,
recommendation 28 states that if a case is referred to a juvenile liaison
panel, the period between completion of an investigation or reporting
for process and the laying of an information should not exceed four
weeks. In other circumstances, the national guideline of three weeks
contained in recommendation 27 should apply. Recommendation 33
provides that in cases involving young people there should be a national
guideline of three weeks between the laying of informations and first
court listings. In custody cases, recommendation 68 sets a national
guideline of 14 days for the period between initial appearance and mode
of trial and plea. Whilst these guidelines do not yet have the force of law,
youth courts are likely to become increasingly keen to ensure that they
are adhered to.

The purpose of the time limits is to enable proper consideration to be **5–014** given to a case against a juvenile whilst ensuring that each case comes before the court as quickly as possible and, once before the court, is concluded rapidly (Magistrates' Association, 1993). Excessive and unproductive delay is generally accepted as harmful in all criminal proceedings. This is particularly true of people under 18 for whom either the impact of court proceedings will diminish the further away they are from the events which led to them, or the anxiety generated by the wait is likely to be disproportionate to the need for time for preparation.

5–015 Attainment Of Age 18
A young person who becomes 18 between the date of the offence and the first court appearance will be dealt with by an adult court. A young person who becomes 18 after the first hearing may continue to be dealt with in the youth court (1963 Act, s. 29). If the offence is triable either way, the court will have to determine the mode of trial if a decision for summary trial is not taken before the 18th birthday and in those circumstances the young person will have the right to refuse to consent to summary trial. If a young person appearing before a youth court has further offences preferred against him after he becomes 18 these new cases can only be dealt with in the adult court even if they were committed whilst the offender was under 18. In *Chelsea JJ., ex p. DPP* [1963] 3 All E.R. 657 a juvenile was charged with wounding with intent and appeared before the juvenile court. After he became 17 (then the age at which juveniles became adult) a further charge of attempted murder was preferred against him on the same facts as the wounding charge. The Divisional Court held that the juvenile court had no power to deal with the later charge.

5–016 Committal For Trial and Transfer
General
This section needs to be read bearing in mind the procedural changes provided for in Criminal Justice and Public Order Act 1994, s. 44. Where a person under 18 is charged with an indictable offence, whether or not it is capable of being tried either at the Crown Court or in the magistrates' court, a magistrates' court may commit the juvenile to the Crown Court for trial in two circumstances:

1. If the young person is aged 10 to 17 inclusive and the offence is punishable in the case of an adult with 14 years imprisonment or more, or with indecent assault on a woman, or causing death by dangerous driving, the magistrates' court may commit the young person to the Crown Court for trial if it believes that it is likely that it will wish to use the power of long term detention available under 1933 Act, s. 53(2) (MCA 1980, s. 24(1)(a)). For circumstances in which long term detention is appropriate see Chapter 24, paras. 24–037–24–083. The power to use long term detention is only available where the young person is *committed for trial*; committal for sentence is not sufficient (1933 Act, s. 53(2)(a) provides "where a young person is *convicted on indictment* ...").

2. If a person under 18 is charged jointly with a person aged 18 or **5–017**
    more and the court considers it necessary in the interests of
    justice to commit them both for trial (1980 Act, s. 24(1)(b)). This
    discretion must be exercised when both the juvenile and the
    adult are before the court; if a decision is to commit for trial, the
    actual committal may take place on different occasions for the
    juvenile and the adult (*Crown Court at Doncaster, ex p. CPS*
    [1987] Crim. L.R. 395).

Once a court has considered the matter and ordered summary trial, **5–018**
another court may reconsider that decision only if there has been a
change of circumstances or there are new or additional facts to be
brought to the attention of the court. It is not acceptable for a court to
examine a case afresh on the same material if another court has made
the decision for summary trial (or committal) after proper enquiry and
consideration of all relevant factors (*Newham Juvenile Court, ex p. F*
[1986] 3 All E.R. 17). However, in this case the Divisional Court seemed
prepared to accept that serious offences committed whilst on bail after
the decision for summary trial could be a sufficient change of
circumstances, as may greater detail of the defendants character (*per*
Steven Brown L.J., p.22J). These elements are, of course, relevant at this
stage in a youth court since the purpose of committal for trial will be to
enable consideration to be given to detention under the C&YPA 1933, s.
53(2), a power which is only available after conviction at the Crown
Court. If the juvenile is committed for trial on only some of the matters
against him, it is only in exceptional circumstances that the youth court
should sentence him on the other matters before the Crown Court
matter is resolved (*Khan (Abdul)*, *The Times* March 24, 1994). If a
defendant aged 15–17 years pleads guilty in the youth court, it may be
possible to commit him or her to the Crown Court for sentence (1980
Act, s.37 and Criminal Justice Act 1967, s.56). The limit will be a
maximum of twenty four months detention in a young offender
institution (Criminal Justice Act 1982, s.1B as amended by Criminal
Justice and Public Order Act 1994, s.17) or up to the maximum for the
offence, if lower.
   At the time of committing for trial, if the offence is triable either way,
the court may also exercise the powers under Criminal Justice Act 1988,
s.41 to commit other summary offences to the Crown Court for trial
providing those summary offences are punishable with imprisonment
or involve obligatory or discretionary disqualification from driving and
arise out of circumstances appearing to the court to be the same or
connected with those giving rise to the offence triable either way.
   Once the court has begun to try the information summarily, the MCA **5–019**
1980, s. 25(5) and (6) permits the court to discontinue the summary trial
at any time before the conclusion of the evidence for the prosecution
and proceed as examining justices. This power is therefore not available
where the defendant pleads guilty. If a court has determined for trial on
indictment, a court may revert to summary trial if at any time during

the enquiry the court considers after all that the case is suitable for summary trial (1980 Act, s. 25(5) and (7)). If a juvenile is charged jointly with an adult and the court determines to commit the adult for trial or discharge the adult but to deal summarily with the juvenile and the juvenile intends to plead not guilty, then the court may remit that juvenile to a youth court to be dealt with (1980 Act, s. 29).

5–020 There have been a number of guidelines from the Court of Appeal and from the Divisional Court on the circumstances where magistrates should not accept jurisdiction:

Billam [1986] 1 All E.R. 985

> "A charge of rape should always be committed for trial.
> 'The judgment of the Court of Appeal given by Lord Lane C.J. states In the case of a juvenile the court will in most cases exercise the power to order detention under C&YPA 1933 s. 53(2) ... It is important that a magistrates' court dealing with a juvenile charged with rape should *never* accept jurisdiction to deal with the case itself ...'"

Corcoran [1986] Crim. L.R. 568

> "The defendant should have been committed for trial. He was charged with two charges of robbery, 13 of burglary, two of taking a vehicle, one of going equipped and two of failing to surrender. He asked for 52 other offences to be taken into consideration (including four attempted robberies)."

Metcalfe [1986] Crim. L.R. 569

> "The defendant received a three year term of detention for attempted robbery. He had broken into the home of a man aged 69 wearing a hood and carrying an axe. He also pleaded guilty to two offences of burglary and had several previous convictions for burglary."

Learmonth (1988) 153 J.P. 18

> "Committal appropriate where the charge was assault with intent to rob and there were four other offences of burglary.
> In this case the defendant crept up behind a woman in the dark, put a dog chain around her neck, pulled it tight and robbed her. He had also committed four offences of burglary. It was agreed that three years detention was richly deserved."

5–021 Note should be taken of the anomalies created or perpetuated by the Criminal Justice Acts 1991 and 1993 highlighted by the decision in *Nagar* [1994] Crim. L.R. 136 and in the illustrative commentary that follows that report at pp. 136 and 137. Since burglary of commercial premises now carries a maximum of only ten years imprisonment for an adult, a juvenile may not be committed to the Crown Court for trial. As the commentary points out, he may be committed for handling stolen goods (maximum 14 years) but not unlawful wounding (maximum five years). He may be committed for causing death by dangerous driving or by careless driving whilst under the influence of drink or drugs but not for causing death by aggravated vehicle taking.

Procedure   5–022

The procedure to be followed by a magistrates' court during and after committal for trial is much the same as for an adult. These procedures are set out in the 1980 Act, ss. 4–8 and 1981 Rules, rr. 5–11. [These provisions are substantially amended by the Criminal Justice and Public Order Act 1994, s.44 and by rules when in force. The amending provisions will not affect proceedings where the court has begun to inquire into the case as examining justices before the amending provisions come into force (1994 Act, s.44 (4)).] The differences are:

(a) The restrictions on reports of proceedings contained in the 1980 Act, s.8 apply, although these can be extended by the court making a prohibition under the 1933 Act, s. 39 (see above para. 5–007).

(b) After the committal, the clerk of the court must display a public notice giving details of the defendant and the charge (MCA 1980, s. 6(5)). If the defendant is under 17, his name and address must not be in the notice unless the justices have directed that it should be in order to avoid injustice to him, the defendant. Use of the power under the 1933 Act, s.39 (see above para. 5–006) can extend this protection to 17 year olds.

(c) If the defendant was remanded on bail, the clerk of the court must notify the governor of the remand centre to which he would have been committed if bail had been refused as well as the governor of the prison to which he would have been committed if over 21 (1981 Rules, r. 9).

(d) The clerk of the court must send to the Crown Court a statement 5–023 indicating whether an order has been made under C&YPA 1933, s. 39(1), 1981 Rules, r. 11(2)(m).

(e) When the 1994 Act, Sched. 4 is in force, a defendant aged under 17 whose case is transferred to the Crown Court may not consent to an order that he remain in custody being made in his absence (amended 1980 Act, s.8(4)).

Chapter 6

Commencing Proceedings

6–001 There are no limitations restricting the institution of proceedings against a person under 18. However, anyone who decides to lay an information against a person they have reason to believe to be under 18 must notify:

(a) The local authority for the area in which the person under 18 resides (if the prospective defendant does not appear to reside in the area of any local authority, notice must be given to the local authority in whose area it is alleged that the offence (or one of the offences) was committed, Children and Young Persons Act 1969, s. 5(8)). Residence is defined as the usual home of the prospective defendant—where he lives and has his meals (*Stoke-on-Trent Corporation v. Cheshire County Council* [1915] 3 K.B. 699, *South Shields Corporation v. Liverpool Corporation* [1943] 1 All E.R. 338).

(b) If the prospective defendant is under 18 but 13 or over, a probation officer for the area covered by the court (1969 Act, s.34(2) as amended by the Criminal Justice & Public Order Act 1994, Sched. 9, para. 9).

6–002 If the local authority (including the local education authority) institutes the proceedings or is notified of the bringing of the proceedings, it is under a duty, unless the local authority considers it unnecessary, to investigate and provide to the court information about the home surroundings, school record, health and character of the defendant that, in the opinion of the local authority, is likely to assist the court (1969 Act, s. 9(1)). However, in practice a local authority will only provide such information at this stage where the child is already being looked after by them. In other circumstances, the information will not be provided until after the juvenile has been found guilty (Chapter 11, para. 11–001). Where the defendant is 13 or over but under 18, the local authority need not investigate or provide information to the court about the defendant's home surroundings if arrangements exist for that information to be supplied by a probation officer. The arrangements can be made as a result of the direction of the justices or of the Probation Committee for the area (1969 Act, s. 34(3)). It appears that the local authority is still obliged to provide information that it *already possesses* about the home surroundings, school record, health and character, since 1969 Act, s. 34(3) applies only to exempt local authorities from making investigations or from providing information which it does not already possess. Information in the possession of the local authority which appears to a local authority likely to assist the court, must be provided to the court, unless the local authority considers it unnecessary to do so (1969 Act, s. 9(1) and s. 34(3)). Research evidence suggests these provisions are subject to immensely diverse interpretation, and that in many instances whether or not courts receive such information will vary infinitely from one local authority to another (Parker, *et al.*, 1983 and 1989; Brown, 1991; Ball, 1983 and 1995).

If the court does not receive sufficient information it may request the **6–003** local authority to provide information, or further information, regarding home surroundings, school record, health and character. It is the duty of the local authority to comply with that request (1969 Act, s. 9(2)). The court may also require that information from a probation officer who is obliged to enquire into the circumstances or home surroundings of any person in accordance with directions of the court and to make reports in those matters to assist the court to identify the best way to deal with the case (Powers of Criminal Courts Act 1973, Sched. 3(para. 8)). Standards are set out nationally for the probation service to assist in ensuring the consistent provision of high quality information to assist those passing sentence. These were introduced in 1992 and recently revised (Home Office, 1995).

A common response to the notification requirement is now to consider in a multi-agency forum whether there is a better alternative to court proceedings (see Chapter 2). In accordance with the guidelines established by the Working Group on Pre-Trial Issues (Home Office, 1990) this consideration must not delay the commencement of court proceedings by more than four weeks (recommendation 28).

The conduct of proceedings **6–004**
The Director of Public Prosecutions is the head of the Crown Prosecution Service and it is through that service that prosecutions are conducted. Any person or body, except a police force, instituting proceedings (see definition below), may continue to conduct those proceedings subject to the right of the Director of Public Prosecutions to take over the conduct at any stage (Prosecution of Offences Act 1985, s. 6).The Director is obliged to take over all criminal proceedings instituted on behalf of a police force other than specified proceedings. This obligation extends to all binding over proceedings instituted on behalf of a police force and all proceedings begun by way of a summons for the forfeiture of obscene articles issued under Obscene Publications Act 1959, s. 3 (Prosecution of Offences Act, s.3(2)).

6–005 Proceedings are instituted:

(a) Where the proceedings are begun by way of summons,
at the time when the information for the offence is laid before the
person who issues the summons.

(b) Where proceedings are begun with the issue of a warrant on an
information being laid,
at the time that the information for the offence is laid before the
person issuing the warrant.

(c) Where a person is charged with an offence after having been taken
into custody without a warrant,
at the time when the offender is informed of the particulars of the
charge.

(d) Where a bill of indictment is preferred under Administration of
Justice (Miscellaneous Provisions) Act 1933, s. 2(2)(b),
at the time when the bill of indictment is preferred before the
court.

Where as a result of these provisions there is the potential for there being
more than one time for the institution of the proceedings, the time to be
used is the earliest possible (1985 Act, s. 15(2)).

6–006 Specified proceedings
Proceedings are specified when they come within the Prosecution of
Offences Act 1985 (Specified Proceedings) Order 1985. Even if included
within that order, proceedings are only specified if the defendant is
given the opportunity to plead guilty by letter and they will cease to be
specified if that opportunity is not taken up. Common offences coming
within this definition likely to be committed by persons under 18 are
fixed penalty offences within the meaning of Road Traffic Offenders Act
1988, s.51, and other relatively minor road traffic offences. Since
implementation of the CJA 1991 16 and 17 year old defendants have
been able to plead guilty by post under MCA 1980, s.12. Where the
opportunity to plead guilty without attending court is accepted by the
defendant, it is the responsibility of the clerk of the court to read out the
statement of the facts of the offence and any written mitigation
submitted (Magistrates' Courts Act 1980, s. 12(4)). The definition of a
police force includes not only the normal constabulary—a police force
maintained by a Police Authority—but also other specified forces
including the Metropolitan Police, the City of London Police, the
British Transport Police, various Docks Police, the Mersey Tunnel Law
Enforcement Officers, the Ministry of Defence Police, the Royal Parks
Constabulary (England) and the Atomic Energy Authority Constabulary
(1985 Act, s. 3(3) and (S.I. 1985/1956)).

6–007 The rôle of the Crown Prosecutor in instituting proceedings
The Crown Prosecutor decides:

(a) Whether proceedings should be instituted,

(b) Whether, having been instituted, they should be discontinued,

(c) What charges should be preferred.

Their powers are delegated from the Director of Public Prosecutions and are guided by a code, the most recent version of which was published in June, 1994. They may be exercised only by a crown prosecutor not by another member of the staff of the Director (*DPP, ex p. First Division Association* (1988) New L.J. 158).

The code provides for two main criteria: evidential sufficiency and **6–008** public interest. Additional provisions are included relating to juveniles which confirm the requirement for the crown prosecutor that in deciding whether or not the public interest requires a prosecution, the interests of the young person should be fully considered: paragraph 6.8. This code refers to juveniles substantially less than the previous code published in January 1992. The earlier code emphasised the need to consider that there might be positive advantages both for the potential defendant and for society in using prosecution as a last resort for most offenders, and that this presumption should be even stronger for offenders under the age of 18. There was also an emphasis that prosecution should never be used solely to secure access to the welfare powers of the court. Instead, where the crown prosecutor thought that there may be grounds for some welfare initiative which may better serve the public interest, the code recommended that the police should be invited to put this possibility to the local authority. The changes between the two codes reflect the swing of the pendulum towards prosecution reflected in the new guidance to chief officers of police regarding cautioning contained in Home Office Circular 18/1994 (see Chapter 2 above). Reported incidents of multiple cautioning, not substantiated by Home Office research, and of cautioning for very serious offences appear to have influenced both the new guidance on cautioning (Home Office, 1994) and the new Code for Crown Prosecutors (Ball, 1994; Evans, 1994; Stone, 1994b). The new code draws attention to the serious harm that the stigma of a conviction can cause to the prospects of a young offender (whether a youth or a young adult) but requires that to be balanced against the seriousness of the offence and the past behaviour of the young person (paragraph 6.8). The guidelines issued by the Home Office to guide the police in deciding whether to issue a caution rather than prosecute will also be used by Crown Prosecutors who will tell the police if they think a caution to be more suitable than prosecution (paragraph 6.9).

REMANDS OF DEFENDANTS   **6–009**

Whenever a case is adjourned, a youth court will consider whether or not to remand the defendant. There is no obligation to remand as there is for certain offences for which a person over 18 appears before a court

(1980 Act, s. 18(4)), however note the requirement not to grant bail in certain circumstances (CJPOA 1994, s. 25) (below). If a young person who has not been bailed to attend does not appear but is represented by a legal representative, then he is deemed not to be absent (1980 Act, s. 122). Generally, the powers of adjournment and the restrictions on the lengths of remands on bail are the same as in an adult magistrates' court. However, the power to adjourn after conviction for the purpose of obtaining information about the offender is affected by the Children and Young Persons Act 1933, s.48(3). After conviction, a court may adjourn for no more than four weeks to enable inquiries to be made or to determine the most suitable way of dealing with the case (1980 Act, s.10(3)). If the court remands the accused in custody, the limit becomes three weeks (*ibid.*). By 1933 Act, s.48(3), a youth court remanding a juvenile for information to be obtained about him, must ensure that the juvenile appears before a court at least once in every twenty one days. No distinction is drawn between remands before or after conviction. As mentioned, there is no obligation to remand a person under 18 when a case is adjourned. Simple adjournment may, therefore, avoid the potential difficulty where a four week adjournment is required. 1980 Act, s.10(3) refers to adjournment time limits, 1933 Act, s.48(3) refers to remand time limits. If there is a conflict, it is resolved in favour of the 1933 Act by 1980 Act, s.152.

6–010 Grant of Bail

The provisions relating to the granting of bail are similar to those that apply to an adult and therefore appear only in summary. For a detailed exposition see *Archbold* (1995, Section 1, Chap. 3). In addition to those powers, the court may require a parent or guardian who appears with a person under 18 to attend (see Chapter 7).

Unless charged with treason, any person charged with an offence shall be granted bail unless one of the exceptions to this right applies (1980 Act, s. 41, Bail Act 1976, s. 4) or the charge is one of murder, attempted murder, manslaughter, rape or attempted rape and the person charged has previously been convicted of any of these offences or of culpable homicide. If the previous conviction was for manslaughter or culpable homicide the sentence must have been imprisonment or long term detention (Criminal Justice & Public Order Act 1994, s.25).

6–011 (a) If the defendant is charged only with offences that are *not* imprisonable:

Bail may only be refused if the defendant has previously failed to surrender to bail and, in view of that failure, the court believes that the defendant would fail to surrender if released on bail on this occasion (1976 Act, Sched. 1, Part II, para. 2).

The defendant need not be granted bail:

* if the court is satisfied that he should be kept in custody for his own protection, or, if he is a child or young person, for his own welfare (1976 Act, Sched. 1, Part II, para. 3); or

* if he is in custody in pursuance of a sentence of a court or of any authority acting under any of the Service Acts (1976 Act, Sched. 1, Part II, para. 4); or

* if, having been released on bail in or in connection with proceedings for an offence, he has been arrested under 1976 Act, s.7 for failing to surrender to the custody of the court or as being in breach of conditions of bail or likely to be in breach of such conditions (1976 Act, Sched. 1, Part II, para. 5).

(b) If the defendant is being proceeded against for at least one offence **6–012** punishable with imprisonment in the case of an adult,
Bail may be refused only if the court is satisfied that there are substantial grounds for believing that the defendant would:

* fail to surrender to custody, or

* commit an offence while on bail, or

* interfere with witnesses or otherwise obstruct the course of justice, whether in relation to himself or any other person (1976 Act, Sched. 1, Part I, para. 2).

The defendant need not be granted bail **6–013**

* if charged with or convicted of an indictable offence (whether or not triable either way) committed whilst on bail in criminal proceedings (1976 Act Sched. 1, Part I, para. 2A); or

* if the court is satisfied that he should be kept in custody for his own protection, or if he is a child or young person, for his own welfare (1976 Act, Sched. 1, Part I, para. 3); or

* if he is in custody in pursuance of a sentence of a court or of any authority acting under any of the Service Acts (1976 Act, Sched. 1, Part I, para. 4); or

* where the court is satisfied that it has not been practicable to obtain sufficient information for the purpose of taking the decisions required regarding bail because of lack of time since the proceedings started (1976 Act, Sched. 1, Part I, para. 5), or

* if, having been released on bail in or in connection with proceedings for an offence he has been arrested under 1976 Act, s. 7 for failing to surrender to the custody of the court or as being in breach of conditions of bail or likely to be in breach of such conditions (1976 Act, Sched. 1, Part I, para. 6); or

* where his case is adjourned for enquiries or for a report to be prepared, if it appears to the court impracticable to complete the enquiries or make the report unless the defendant is kept in custody (1976 Act, Sched. 1, Part I, para. 7).

(c)   The only variant in these restrictions between a person under the age of 18 and a person over that age is the additional ground that bail may be refused if it is necessary to keep the defendant in custody for his own welfare (1976 Act, Schedule 1, Part II, para. 3).

(d)   Bail granted in respect of an indictable offence (whether or not triable either way) may be reconsidered by the court on application by the prosecutor. This application can only be made if based on information not available to whoever granted bail (1976 Act, s.5B).

6–014 Requirements of bail
A grant of bail will require the defendant to attend court on the date, at the time and at the place set. Failure to do so without reasonable cause is an offence punishable by fining up to level 5 (currently £5,000 for an adult, £1,000 for a young person aged 14–17 and £250 for a child aged 10–13) and/or up to three months custody in a magistrates' court or up to 12 months custody and/or a fine in the Crown Court if committed to that court either because the defendant is committed for trial or because the magistrates' court feels the defendant requires greater punishment than it has the power to impose (1976 Act, s. 6(1), (5–7)). A person who fails to surrender at the right time and place and also fails to surrender to the court as soon as reasonably practicable after that time, also commits an offence punishable as above (1976 Act, s. 6(2)). In addition, a person likely to breach a condition of bail or in breach of such condition is liable to arrest (1976 Act, s. 7).

6–015   A defendant prosecuted for failing to surrender without reasonable cause has the burden upon him to prove that reasonable cause on the balance of probabilities. In *Laidlaw v. Atkinson* [1986], *The Times*, August 2, 1986 a defendant, having handed his charge sheet to his solicitor without making a note of the date of hearing, mistakenly formed the opinion that he was to surrender to custody on a later date than the due date. This was not capable of being a reasonable cause for failing to surrender even though his solicitor had given him a date for formal consultation after the hearing date and the defendant had other matters before the same court on different days. It was accepted that the failure to surrender was not deliberate. In the judgment, it was said

> "the learned magistrate was of the opinion that this was not a matter of mere confusion on the part of the defendant but that those extraneous factors caused the confusion to arise ... No doubt the reasons outlined played a part in the defendants confusion and could be said to amount to mitigation but there was no question of anything having arisen to prevent the defendants attendance. He had been told when bailed of the date on which he was to surrender to custody and been given a signed copy of the bail form. If he was going to part with it he should have made a note of the date. The error was his responsibility and it could not be said that those reasons could amount to a reasonable cause."

Bail granted must be without conditions unless the court believes those conditions to be necessary to prevent a failure to surrender to custody, the commission of an offence whilst on bail or the interference with witnesses or other obstruction of the course of justice. Further conditions may be imposed if they are necessary for the purpose of enabling enquiries to be made or a report to be made to assist the court in dealing with the offence (1976 Act, Sched. 1, para. 8). No condition may be imposed on anyone other than the defendant and each condition must be necessary for the purposes provided, thus it will rarely be lawful to impose a condition of reporting to a police station on a person where the court is satisfied only that a condition is necessary to prevent the commission of further offences whilst on bail. A surety may be taken where necessary to avoid the non-attendance of the defendant.

A young person granted bail may be required to reside where the local **6–016** authority directs, if that condition is considered necessary in accordance with 1976 Act, Sched. 1. In those circumstances, the young person is being looked after by the local authority which may, therefore, apply for a secure accommodation order (*Re C (a Minor) (Secure accommodation order: Jurisdiction)* [1994] 2 F.C.R. 1153). However as a remand to local authority accommodation does not confer parental responsibility on the local authority no compensation order can be made against the authority even though the offence was committed whilst the young person was on remand to the local authority accommodation (*North Yorkshire County Council v. Selby Youth Court* [1994] 1 All E.R. 991).

Breach (or anticipated breach) of conditions may lead to immediate arrest (1976 Act, s. 7(3)) whereupon the person arrested must be brought before a justice for the Petty Sessions area in which he was arrested, unless arrested within 24 hours of the time at which he was due to surrender to the court, and may be remanded otherwise than on bail (see below).

Appeal against refusal of bail   6–017
A right of appeal against the refusal of bail exists allowing a defendant to seek bail in the High Court or the Crown Court. The right to apply to the High Court is in every case. The procedure is contained in R.S.C. 1965, Ord. 79, r. 9. The right to apply to the Crown Court exists where the defendant is committed for trial to the Crown Court or where the magistrates' court has issued a Certificate of Full Argument (1976 Act, s. 6). The procedure is contained in Crown Court Rules 1982, rr. 19 and 20.

Appeal against the granting of bail
Where bail is granted by a magistrates' court for certain offences despite objections by the prosecutor, an appeal by the prosecutor may be made to a Judge of a Crown Court (Bail (Amendment) Act 1993). The conditions to be satisfied apply to those under 18 years in the same way as to adults, except that if oral notice of appeal is given, the court must remand a person under 17 to local authority accommodation unless the appeal is disposed of.

6–018 Remands when bail is refused

Two different sets of provisions apply to persons under 18. One set applies to those aged 17, another to those under that age. Within the latter category there are further variants for those at the younger end of the age spectrum.

(a) Defendants aged 17 years

A person of this age who is refused bail will be remanded to prison custody in the same way as a person over that age, since the 1969 Act, s. 23 which deals with alternative places of remand is restricted to those under 17 years: see definition of young person in 1969 Act, s. 23(12). The normal maximum period of remand is eight clear days, that is with eight days elapsing between the date of remand and the date of next appearance excluding both those days (1980 Act, s. 128(6)). This period may, however, be extended to up to 28 clear days in accordance with the 1980 Act, s. 128A if the following conditions are met:

1.   The defendant has previously been remanded in custody for this offence (*i.e.* this is at least the second appearance)

2.   The defendant is before the court.

3.   The court can set a date on which the next stage of the proceedings can take place after hearing any representations that the parties to the proceedings wish to make.

A further hearing simply for a remand in custody or on bail is not a further stage of the proceedings—it would be expected to be, for instance, mode of trial, entry of plea, committal for trial or hearing of a contested case. A defendant remanded under this provision may apply for bail during the period of remand (1980 Act, s. 128A(3)).

6–019   If a court wishes to extend the period of remand beyond eight clear days but cannot use the provisions of section 128A—either because it is the first remand or it is not able to fulfill one of the other conditions—it may seek the consent of the defendant to up to three remands taking place in the absence of the defendant (1980 Act, s. 128A(3)). For a defendant aged 17, the court also has the power, as with an adult, to transfer the remand hearings to a court nearer to the remand prison (1980 Act, s. 130).

As an alternative to remand to prison, a defendant aged 17 may be remanded to police custody for a maximum of three clear days (1980 Act, s. 128(7)). Such a remand may only be for the purpose of enabling enquiries to be made into other offences. Once that need ceases the defendant must be brought back before the court even if that is before the end of the remand period (1980 Act, s.128(8)).

6–020 (b) Defendants aged under 17 years

The position is made more complex by the existence of two sets of provisions, the transitory provisions, in force now, the other to come into force when sufficient local authority provided secure accommodation exists (Criminal Justice Act 1991, ss.60—62).

Transitory provisions.
Where a person under 17 is refused bail, he will normally be remanded to accommodation provided by a local authority designated by the court (1969 Act, s. 23(1)). The maximum period before conviction is eight clear days (1980 Act, s.128(6)) and cannot be extended by agreement under section 128(3A) or by virtue of section 128A since they only apply to defendants aged 17 or over. This is the case even where the defendant is subject to a secure accommodation order granted under the Children Act 1989, s.25 prior to the remand to local authority accommodation for the offence, or during the remand period but unconnected with the alleged offending. Neither is it possible to transfer the remand hearing to a court nearer the place where the defendant is accommodated since the power to transfer remand hearings applies only to those aged 17 or over (1980 Act, s.130). The scarcity of secure accommodation results in some juveniles being transported long distances to appear before courts momentarily for formal remands, often in circumstances in which all participants know that no progress can be made. It may, therefore, be advantageous in certain circumstances to remand a juvenile on bail with a condition of residence where the local authority directs. This allows the local authority to apply for a secure accommodation order (*Re C* [1994] F.C.R. 1153).

Currently if certain conditions (see below) are met a 15 or 16 year old **6–021** boy may be remanded to a remand centre or prison (1969 Act, s. 23(4)). In addition, a person under 17 may be remanded to police custody under 1980 Act, s. 128(7) (see above) but for no more than 24 hours (1969 Act, s. 23(14)(b)). Further, if committed to the Crown Court for sentence under 1980 Act, s. 37 (see Chapter 12) and refused bail, the defendant will be remanded to a remand centre or prison (1980 Act, s. 37(2)).

In designating the local authority, the court must select the authority already looking after the defendant if he is already being looked after by a local authority. A person under 18 is being looked after by a local authority if he is in their care or is provided with accommodation for a continuous period exceeding 24 hours by the authority in the exercise of certain of its statutory functions (Children Act 1989, s. 22(1)).

If the defendant is not being looked after by a local authority, the court **6–022** must designate either the authority for the area in which the defendant resides or the area in which one of the offences was committed (1969 Act, s. 23(2)). The remand grants authority to detain the defendant to any person acting on behalf of the authority to which he is remanded (1969 Act, s. 23(3)). The local authority is obliged to receive and provide accommodation for any person remanded under the 1969 Act, s. 23(1) (1989 Act, s. 21(2)(c)).

Where a 16–year–old defendant becomes 17 during a period of remand, he will remain in local authority accommodation until the next remand takes place. On that occasion, as he is 17, refusal of bail will lead to a remand in prison custody (see above).

In remanding to local authority accommodation, the court has additional powers to impose conditions on both the defendant and the local authority:

(a) *Defendant:* Having first consulted the local authority—and this consultation means such as is reasonably practicable in the case (1969 Act, s. 23(13)(b))—a court may impose on the person remanded to local authority accommodation such conditions that could have been imposed if bail had been granted which appear to the court to be necessary to secure the surrender to custody of the defendant, to prevent the commission of further offences, to prevent the obstruction of the course of justice or to ensure availability to assist in the preparation of a report for the court (1969 Act, s. 23(7)). The court may not require a defendant remanded to local authority accommodation to reside in a specific place: *Cleveland C.C. v. D.P.P.* L.S.Gaz. 92/06, February 8, 1995. There is no power to impose obligations on the parent or guardian of the defendant.

(b) *Local authority* After consultation with the local authority, the court may impose requirements on the authority to secure compliance with the bail type conditions by the defendant (1969 Act, s. 23(9)(a)). These conditions may be imposed at the time of the remand, or between remands, on application of the local authority (1969 Act, s. 23(10)). A court may also stipulate that the local authority shall not place the defendant with a person named in the order (1969 Act, s. 23(9)(b)). Subject to this, the local authority has discretion as to the accommodation it provides for the defendant. The court may not require the local authority to accommodate the defendant in specific accommodation: *Cleveland C.C. v. D.P.P.*

6-023 Any of these conditions may be varied or revoked by the court at any time on application of either the local authority or the defendant (1969 Act, s. 23(11)). In this context "court" includes a single justice (1969 Act, s. 23(12)). If the court utilises this power to impose conditions on a defendant it must give its reasons in ordinary language in open court and those reasons must be included both in the warrant of commitment and in the court register (1969 Act, s. 23(8)).

The Criminal Justice and Public Order Act 1994, s.23 adds a new section 23A to the 1969 Act giving the police powers to arrest a child or young person who breaches a condition of remand to local authority accommodation. Prior to this there was no sanction against an accused person who broke conditions attached to a remand to local authority accommodation since the powers of arrest under Bail Act 1976, s.7 relate to a person released on bail. The exception was that if the condition breached was one of residence in local authority accommodation, there was a power of arrest under the 1969 Act, s.32.

Secure accommodation

6–024

The local authority is governed by the 1989 Act, s. 25 in its use of secure accommodation, that is, accommodation provided for the purpose of restricting liberty. Although authority for use of such accommodation for more than 72 hours is normally sought from a family procedings court, power is given to a youth court or a magistrates' court remanding or committing a person under 17 to local authority accommodation also to grant this authority (Criminal Justice Act 1991, s. 60(3)). It need not necessarily be the court that ordered the remand that considers the application for a secure accommodation order. In *Liverpool City Council v. B., The Times*, February 8, 1995, a juvenile had been remanded into the care of Liverpool City Council by a court sitting outside its boundary. The council could apply under section 25 to the Liverpool Youth Court since the wording of section 60(3) ("In the case of a ... young person remanded ... to local authority accommodation by a youth court ..., any application under section 25 ... shall ... be made to that court") was used in a generic sense meaning a youth court rather than a family court. The application should be made to the appropriate youth court and it was said to be clearly appropriate for the Liverpool City Council to apply to the Liverpool Youth Court. The Crown Court does not have power to grant such an order and application must be made to any family proceedings court (1991 Act, s.60(3) and Children (Allocation of Proceedings) Order 1991, art. 3(1)(a)) once the Crown Court itself remands to local authority accommodation. Until that time, the committal from the magistrates' court or youth court subsists and application will need to be made to a court of the same type as the committing court. The application, however, must be made by the local authority (Children (Secure Accommodation) Regulations 1991, reg. 8). The following important provisions relate to an application for such an order:

1. A local authority that can prove the grounds for an order is 6–025 entitled to receive an order (1989 Act, s. 25(4)) (*M. v. Birmingham City Council* [1995] 1 F.C.R. 50)

2. An order may not be made if the defendant is not legally represented unless he has been given the opportunity to apply for legal aid and has not done so (1989 Act, s. 25(6)).

3. The criteria vary depending on the nature of the offence or the offender—
   (a) If there is a charge of a violent or sexual offence, or
   (b) If there is a charge for an offence punishable with 14 years imprisonment or more in the case of an adult, or
   (c) If the offender has a recent history of absconding whilst remanded to local authority accommodation and is charged

with an offence said to have been committed whilst on remand to local authority accommodation,

then the local authority may not use secure accommodation unless it appears that any accommodation other than that provided to restrict liberty is inappropriate because either the defendant is likely to abscond from any other type of accommodation or is likely to injure himself or other people if kept in any other type of accommodation (1989 Act, s. 25(1) as modified by the 1991 Regulations, reg. 6).

6-026   If the defendant does not meet (a) to (c) above, the secure accommodation may only be used or authorised if it appears that the defendant has a history of absconding, is likely to abscond from any other type of accommodation and, if he does so, is likely to suffer significant harm or if it appears that if he is kept elsewhere he is likely to injure himself or other people (1989 Act, s. 25(1)).

The interaction of 1989 Act, s.25 with the welfare principle contained in section 1 of that Act was considered in *M. v. Birmingham City Council* [1995] 1 F.C.R. 50. This was a civil case. It was held that the welfare of the child was a relevant but not the paramount consideration and the criteria in section 1 were not applicable. As was pointed out, the power to make an order under section 25 could arise on the ground that the child was likely to injure others rather than himself. Use of the power in such circumstances might be inconsistent with the child's welfare being paramount. The same approach was adopted in relation to an application in criminal proceedings in *AE v. Staffordshire County Council* [1995] 2 F.C.R. 84.

Applications for orders are governed by provisions contained in Magistrates' Courts (Children and Young Persons) Rules 1992, Part III which provide for a simpler, speedier procedure than that contained in the equivalent rules governing applications made to family proceedings courts. Thus there is no requirement to give reasons (since that is contained in the Family Proceedings Courts (Children Act 1989) Rules 1991 which do not apply) but there is the obligation to invite representations and to explain the nature and effect of the order contained in Magistrates' Courts (Children and Young Persons) Rules 1992, r.22. The rules as to notice must be strictly complied with and require the applicant to send a notice to the clerk of the court giving the grounds for the proceedings and the names and addresses of the persons to whom a copy of the notice is sent. The categories of person are described in rule 14(2) and rule 14(3), as the defendant, unless that is inappropriate because of his age and understanding, and the defendants' parent or guardian if their whereabouts are known to the applicant or can readily be ascertained by him.

6-027   Parent or guardian includes a person who is the father of the child although not married to the mother at the time of birth but who has applied under the 1989 Act for acquisition of parental responsibility but whose application has not yet been determined. There is no power to appoint a guardian ad litem in these proceedings and the rules provide for the defendant to have the case conducted on his behalf by his parent or guardian in the absence of any request from him to the contrary unless he is legally represented. The court is also entitled to allow some other person to represent the defendant and present his case in certain circumstances (1992 Rules, r. 18(2)). There is an obligation on the court to arrange for copies of any written report to be made available before the hearing as far as practicable to the applicant, the defendant's legal representative, the parent or guardian of the defendant and the defendant except where it is impracticable to disclose the report or undesirable in the case of the defendant (1992 Rules, r. 21(1)). Any written report can be received and considered by the court without being read aloud (1992 Rules, r. 21(3)).

Since provisions controlling the previously unrestricted powers of **6–028** local authorities to keep children for whom they were responsible, whether under a court order or not, in accommodation intended to restrict liberty were first introduced by the Criminal Justice Act 1982 the law in this area has become increasingly complex. Many of those who have wrestled with the labyrinthine twists of the law and procedure in regard to secure accommodation, whether as judges, magistrates, their clerks, or legal or social work practitioners, will sympathise with Hollis J.'s comment in *Re C. (Secure Accommodation Order: Bail)* [1994] 2 F.L.R. 922 that it was a pity that Parliament had not taken the opportunity to spell out local authorities' powers over bailed children in the Children Act 1989. Most would probably go further and suggest that a careful review and revision of the whole of primary and delegated legislation relating to the use of secure accommodation, both for offenders on remand and children looked after by local authorities under other responsibilities, is long overdue.

Remands to prison or a remand centre
The normal consequence of refusal of bail to a person under the age of 17 **6–029** is remand to local authority accommodation. The two exceptions to this, namely remand to the custody of a constable and committal in custody to the Crown Court for sentence where the committal will be to a remand centre or prison, are referred to above. In addition, if a 15 or 16 year old male is remanded to local authority accommodation, that local authority may ask the court to declare him to be a person to whom the 1969 Act, s.23(5) applies. Under the transitional provisions currently in force, if the court makes that declaration, the young man ceases to be remanded to local authority accommodation and must be remanded to a remand centre or prison (1969 Act, s.23(4)). The criteria to be fulfilled before the court may make the declaration are:

(a) that only such a remand is adequate to protect the public from serious harm from him and,

(b) he is charged with a violent or sexual offence (for definition of violent offence and sexual offence, see Criminal Justice Act 1991, s.31), or

(c) He is charged with an offence for which an adult could be sent to prison for 14 years or more, or

(d) He has a recent history of absconding whilst remanded to local authority accommodation and is charged with an imprisonable offence said to have been committed during such a remand (1969 Act, s. 23(5)) and

(e) He is legally represented in the court or he has had legal aid refused on grounds of means or, knowing that he could apply for legal aid and having had the chance to do so, he has not applied for it (1969 Act, s.23(4A)).

The nature of the phrase "serious harm" in (a) above was considered in *Croydon Youth Court, ex p.G. (a minor), The Times,* May 3, 1995. It is not sufficient simply that the offence is one for which an adult could be sent to prison for 14 years or more. Handling stolen goods, for instance, it was said, did not necessarily cause any direct harm, serious or otherwise, to the public. There does not need to be a risk of death or serious personal injury being caused, but the court must be satisfied that the young person was liable to cause harm that could sensibly be described as serious. There has been no interpretation of the phrase "recent history". Under the sentencing provisions enacted in the Criminal Justice Act 1982 (as amended) and superseded by those in the Criminal Justice Act 1991, the phrase "history of failing to comply" was judicially interpreted as requiring one previous instance, though for other reasons, the use of this limb to justify custody required two previous penalties (*Southwark Crown Court, ex p. Ager* [1990] Crim. L.R. 531).

6-030   If the court utilises the power to remand to prison or remand centre it must give its reasons in ordinary language in open court and those reasons must be included both in the warrant of commitment and in the court register (1969 Act, s. 23(6)). When sufficient local authority secure accommodation is available remands to prison or remand centre for those under the age of 17 years will be replaced by remand to local authorities with a 'security requirement'. The Criminal Justice and Public Order Act 1994, s.20 extends the age range of children on whom the courts will be empowered to impose a 'security requirement'—a requirement that the person in question 'be placed and kept in secure accommodation' (1969 Act, s.23(5) as amended by Criminal Justice Act 1991, s. 60)—to include 12–14 year olds. This provision will be brought into force progressively for children aged 14, 13 and 12 after implementation of the powers in respect to 15 and 16 year olds. Costs incurred by local authorities in complying with court ordered remands will be defrayed by central government (1994 Act, s.21).

6-031 **Time limits**
As with an adult, where a person under 18 is refused bail in respect of an indictable offence, a time limit applies within which the court must

complete preliminary stages of the case (Prosecution of Offences Act 1985, s. 22 and Prosecution of Offences (Custody Time Limits) Regulations 1987). Each offence attracts its own time limit (*Wirral District Magistrates' Courts, ex p. Meikle* [1990] Crim. L.R. 801). These restrictions apply to any custodial remand by a magistrates' court whether to police custody, to remand centre or prison or to local authority accommodation (1985 Act, s. 22(11)). Where a defendant spends periods on bail and in custody, all the custodial periods must be added (1985 Act, s. 22(12)). The limits provided are—

(a) *Either Way Offence*

1. If the court decides for summary trial in the first 56 days in custody, the trial must commence within 56 days.

2. If not, the commencement of trial must take place or the committal to the Crown Court must take place within the 70 days.

(b) *Indictable only offences*—committal within 70 days (1987 Regulations, reg. 4).

For the purpose of calculation, the day on which custody commences is not included (1987 Regulations, reg. 2(4)). Where a time limit would expire on a Saturday, Sunday, Christmas Day, Good Friday or Bank Holiday, it is deemed to expire on the preceeding day not one of those days (1987 Regulations, reg. 2(5)).

Since a youth court determines under Magistrates' Courts Act 1980, s. **6–032** 24 whether to deal with all matters against persons under 18, all the above time limits apply subject to the right of the court to grant an extension where satisfied that there is good and sufficient cause and that the prosecution has acted with appropriate speed (1985 Act, s. 22(3)). That the views of the courts are hardening on this issue is illustrated by the case of *Central Criminal Court, ex p. Behbehani* [1994] Crim.L.R. 352 where the Divisional Court quashed an extension of a custody time limit for committal proceedings in a case of blackmail. In the judgment, it was stated

> "Once the prosecution judged that a piece of evidence is likely to be **6–033** of real importance in the defence's conduct of the pre-trial stages of the case, they must make shift to see that it gets into the defences hands swiftly."

Where a young person is committed to the Crown Court, a limit of 112 days in custody is provided in respect of certain places of sitting of the Crown Court as the period between committal and arraignment (1987 Regulations, reg. 5).

The provisions governing the procedure relating to committal to the Crown Court for trial will be affected by the Criminal Justice and Public Order Act 1994, s.44 when in force.

6-034　Use of Custodial Remands since the 1991 Act

Despite the commitment to phasing out the remand of juveniles to prison custody, the number of boys aged 15 and 16 remanded to prison has increased substantially since the implementation of the CJA 1991(ACOP/NACRO, 1995). Over the 12 month period October 1, 1993 to September 30, 1994, 1,478 boys in this age group were remanded in custody. While admissions for the six month period April to September 1992 totalled 440, the number for the same period in 1994 totalled 820, an increase of 86 per cent. The number of juveniles held in prison establishments awaiting trial, measured on the last working day of each month, has risen even more. Whereas the average end of month occupancy figure between April and September 1992 was 57, the average figure for the same period in 1994 totalled 145, an increase of 154 per cent. The average length of time held on remand has increased from 26 days in the six months prior to implementation of the Act to 47 days in the six months April to September 1994.

Not surprisingly, there are substantial disparities between different courts and local authority areas. For example, in 1994 variations ranged from a use of custodial remands in 129 per 10,000 of the 15–16 year old male population in Sunderland to no custodial remands in St Helens. Low use of custodial remands does not reflect high use of remands to secure accommodation; while a number of areas have low rates for both, others show high rates in both respects. The factors which enable some areas to use community-based bail services and facilities to good effect deserve closer study and promotion.

While national figures showed that 80 per cent of remanded juveniles were white, there were large regional variations. Of receptions to Feltham, Remand Centre for the London region, 53 per cent of juveniles were Afro-Caribbean or Asian, while 51 per cent of males remanded from the Birmingham court were classified as 'black' or 'other non-white', figures which suggest a disproportionate use of remands to custody for black young people.

6-035　Mentally disordered offenders

A remand to a hospital may be made under Mental Health Act 1983, s.35 or (Crown Court only) under Mental Health Act 1983, s.36 in the same way as for a person over 17 who fulfills the necessary criteria (Stone, 1995).

Chapter 7

The Trial Process

In the youth court the normal procedure of a criminal trial is followed, **7–001** with the prosecution having to satisfy the court of the defendant's guilt beyond reasonable doubt. Procedures in the youth court are governed by the Magistrates' Courts (Children and Young Persons) Rules 1992.

Capacity **7–002**
Children under the age of 10 years are below the age of criminal responsibility. This is an irrebutable presumption. Children under the age of 10 years who commit offences may in certain circumstances be the subject of care proceedings under the Children Act 1989, s.31, but can never be the subject of criminal proceedings. Recently, the principle, recognised in common law for at least 200 years, that a child under the age of 14 was presumed to be *doli incapax*, or incapable of forming criminal intent, was unexpectedly abolished by the Divisional Court when dismissing an appeal by a 13 year old boy against his conviction for interfering with a motorcycle with the intent to commit theft or of taking and driving away without consent, on the grounds that there was no evidence before the magistrates that he knew that what he had done was "seriously wrong" (*C. (A Minor) v. Director of Public Prosecutions* [1994] 3 All E.R. 190). That decision was overturned by the House of Lords ([1995] 2 All E.R. 43). The position is restored to one in which children aged 10 to 13 years have to be shown to have known that what they have done, or are alleged to have done, was seriously wrong (*JM. (A Minor) v. Runeckles* (1984) 79 Cr. App. Rep. 255).

In *Runeckles* a girl of 13 had stabbed another girl with a broken milk bottle. She had immediately run away, had hidden when she saw the police coming and then made a coherent statement under caution with the caption in her own handwriting. She was convicted and appealed on the ground that there was need for the prosecution to show the defendant believed her actions to be morally wrong. The Divisional Court considered that was not the correct test—the presumption was rebutted if it was shown that the defendant appreciated that she had done something "seriously wrong" of which there was ample evidence in regard to the defendant. In contrast an 11 year old boy was charged with another with criminal damage to a motor van—the windows of the van were smashed, paintwork scraped and the van pushed into a post.

The defendant admitted pushing the van and knowing that damage would be caused. The defendant did not give evidence and the prosecutor submitted that the type of activity was such that any child of this age would know that it was wrong and there was, therefore, sufficient evidence to rebut the presumption.

7–003   The Divisional Court disagreed. Whilst it was not necessary in all cases to call positive evidence to show that a youngster is a normal child of his age, the manner in which a child behaves when confronted may itself indicate that the child knew that what he was doing was seriously wrong. In this case, the boy's answers to the police showed that he appreciated the consequence of his conduct—pushing the van—but not that it was seriously wrong (*IPH v. Chief Constable of South Wales* [1987] Crim. L.R. 42; see also *JBH. and JH. v. O'Connell* [1981] Crim. L.R. 632; *A. v. DPP* [1992] Crim L.R. 34). The older a child is, the weaker the presumption that he did not know that what he was doing was seriously wrong. In calling evidence relevant to this presumption, the prosecution may make use of all relevant evidence including that of previous findings of guilt , although care had to be taken because of the potential risks of influencing any decision over whether the defendant committed the offence (*B, A* [1979] 3 All E.R. 460).

7–004   When the Divisional Court took the "momentous step" of abolishing the presumption of *doli incapax* on the basis of social arguments (Ashworth, 1994), the reasoning spelt out by Laws J. suggested that:

"The case law demonstrated that if the presumption were to be rebutted there had to be clear positive evidence that the defendant knew his act was seriously wrong not consisting merely in the evidence of the acts amounting to the offence itself.

Whatever had been the position in an earlier age when there was no system of universal compulsory education and when children did not grow up as quickly as they did nowadays, the presumption at the present time was a serious disservice to the law.

It meant that a child over 10 who committed an act of obvious dishonesty or even grave violence was to be acquitted unless the prosecution specifically proved by discrete evidence that he understood the obliquity of what he was doing.

Such an approach was unreal and contrary to common sense. Aside from anything else, there would be cases where evidence of the kind required could not be obtained but, quite apart from pragmatic considerations, the presumption was in principle objectionable.

It was no part of the general law that a defendant should be proved to appreciate that his act was seriously wrong; that additional requirement where the presumption applied was out of step with the general law.

7–005   The requirement was, furthermore, conceptually obscure. The cases indicated that the presumption might be rebutted by proof that the child was of normal capacity for his age. If that was right the underlying premise was that a child of average or normal development was in fact taken to be *doli incapax*. There could be no respectable justification for such a bizarre state of affairs.

The rule was also divisive because it attached criminal consequences to the acts of children coming from what used to be called good homes more readily than to the acts of others. It was perverse because it tended to absolve from criminal responsibility the very children most likely to commit criminal acts.

The youngster whose understanding of the difference between right and wrong was fragile or non-existent was more likely to get involved in criminal activity, yet the outdated and unprincipled presumption was tailored to secure his acquittal.

The prosecution were in effect required to prove as a condition of his guilt that he was morally responsible; but it was because he was morally irresponsible that he had committed the crime in the first place.

It was not surprising that the presumption took root in an era when the criminal law was altogether more draconian but the philosophy of criminal punishment had obviously changed out of all recognition since those days. The presumption has no utility whatever in the present era and ought to go.

In the circumstances, the presumption relied upon by the appellant was no longer part of the law of England and the appeal would therefore be dismissed."

The decision was extraordinary, not so much because it called into 7–006 question the presumption of *doli incapax*, but, as a leading criminal justice academic has suggested, because the matter is one of "policy in dealing with young harmdoers rather than of technical criminal law ... the issue should not be treated in isolation from other aspects of juvenile policy and a court is in no position to conduct a policy review" (Ashworth 1994).

In his judgment reversing the Divisional Court's decision, Lord Lowry drew attention to the fact that, whatever the admitted shortcomings of the principle in practice, particularly in regard to discrepant interpretation, it had been considered and confirmed as government policy in the White Paper *Crime, Justice and Protecting the Public* (Home Office, 1990) which, as his Lordship pointed out, said:

" ... between the ages of 10 and 13 a child may only be convicted of a criminal offence if the prosecution can show that what he did was seriously wrong. The Government does not intend to change these arrangements which make proper allowance for the fact that children's understanding, knowledge and ability to reason are still developing."

7–007 In view of this, the conclusion was that, whatever the substance of the imperfections in the principle listed by Laws J., they could not provide justification for saying that presumption was no longer part of English law and that "to sweep it away under the doubtful auspices of judicial legislation was impracticable."

The presumption that a person under 14 is physically incapable of committing rape has been abolished by Sexual Offences Act 1993, s.1.

7–008 **The trial process**

Parents are generally expected to attend hearings where the defendant is under the age of 16, and may be required to do so if they are aged 16 or 17, the court having the power to compel that attendance where necessary (Children and Young Persons Act 1933, s. 34A and Magistrates' Courts (Children and Young Persons) Rules 1992, r. 26). Evidence given in the youth court on oath, or by a person under 18 in another court, will require the form of oath prescribed by Children and Young Persons Act 1963, s. 28(1): "I promise before Almighty God to tell the truth, the whole truth, and nothing but the truth". If the wrong form of oath is used the evidence is not invalidated (1963 Act, s. 28(2)).

Before taking a plea the court must explain to the defendant in simple language suitable to his age and understanding the charge and the nature of the proceedings (1992 Rules, r. 6). The rule does not impose a duty on the court to give a detailed or elaborate explanation of charge, but the court should ensure that the essential legal elements are explained, in order that the defendant can make an informed plea (*Blandford Justices, ex p. G. (an infant)* [1967] 1 Q.B. 82).

If the child is not legally represented, the court must allow his parent or guardian to assist in conducting the case (1992 Rules, r. 5(1)). If the parent or guardian cannot be found or cannot reasonably be required to attend, the court may allow any relative or responsible person to take the parent's role (1992 Rules, r. 5(2)). If the defendant is not supported as allowed by Rule 5, and in seeking to question a witness, makes assertions, the court may convert those assertions into questions as necessary and, in order to do so, may question the defendant to clarify or develop the assertions (1992 Rules, r. 8).

When all the prosecution evidence is heard, the court must decide if a prima facie case is made out. If so, the defence will have the right to give and call evidence. If the defendant is not legally represented it must be explained to him that he may give evidence or address the court and any other witnesses must be heard (1992 Rules, r. 9).

The powers to deal with a juvenile found to be in contempt of court are limited. The power of magistrates' courts is contained in Contempt of Court Act 1981, s.12 which gives power to commit the offender to custody for up to one month or impose a fine. However, the power to commit to custody is subject to the statutory restrictions prohibiting committal of a person under 17 to custody: see Criminal Justice Act 1982 and *Selby Justices, ex p. Frame* [1991] 2 All E.R. 344. Nor is there power to make a probation order: *Palmer* [1992] 3 All E.R. 289. The same result obtains in use of the powers of the Crown Court: *Byas* [1995] Crim.L.R. 439. The only available sanction is a fine.

A CHILD OR YOUNG PERSON AS A WITNESS 7–009

Where the attendance at court of a person under 18 to give evidence in respect of an offence under the 1933 Act, Sched. 1 would involve serious danger to his life or health, a justice of the peace may take a deposition from that person if satisfied on the evidence of a duly qualified medical practitioner that such danger would be involved (1933 Act, s. 42). Such a deposition is not admissible *against* the defendant unless it is proved that reasonable notice of the intention to take the deposition had been served on the defendant and that he (or his legal representative) would have had an opportunity to cross examine the witness making the deposition (1933 Act, s. 43).

This very limited protection was substantially extended by the 7–010 Criminal Justice Acts 1988 and 1991 which built upon recommendations contained in the report of the advisory group on video evidence chaired by Judge Pigot (Home Office, 1989). The Pigot report identified as major concerns:

(a) The need to provide the court with the most reliable evidence available;

(b) The need to bring to justice those who commit offences against very young children;

(c) The stress suffered by children giving evidence in the traditional setting;

(d) The effect of stress in reducing ability to recall and describe;

(e) The possibility that the way in which that stress manifests itself may create the wrong impression.

The evidence of a person under 14 in criminal proceedings may not be 7–011 given on oath and a deposition of that evidence may be taken, where necessary, as if it had been given on oath (1988 Act, s. 33A). A child's evidence is to be received unless it appears to the court that the child is incapable of giving intelligible testimony (1988 Act, s.33A (2A)). There may be advantage in the court reminding the child in age appropriate language of the need to tell the truth. The Pigot Report (5.15) suggested "Tell us all you can remember of what happened. Don't make anything up or leave anything out. This is very important." If the trial is in the Crown Court, there is no longer a requirement for the jury to be warned about convicting on the uncorroborated evidence of a child (1988 Act, s. 34).

Where a magistrates' court is inquiring into an offence as examining justices (*i.e.* to determine whether or not to commit the case to the Crown Court for trial) and the offence is

1.   one involving assault on or injury or threat of injury to a person;

2.   an offence of cruelty to a person under 16 under Children and Young Persons Act 1933, s. 1;

3.   an offence under the Sexual Offences Act 1956;

4.   an offence under the Indecency with Children Act 1960;

5.   an offence under the Sexual Offences Act 1967;

6.   an offence under Criminal Law Act 1977, s. 54 (incitement to incestuous sexual intercourse);

7.   an offence under the Protection of Children Act 1978;

8.   an offence of attempting or conspiring to commit any of the above;

9.   an offence of aiding, abetting, counselling, procuring or inciting the commission of the above,

then a person under 14 is not to be called as a witness for the prosecution but any statement made is admissible in the committal proceedings to the same extent as oral testimony would have been. The only exceptions to this are where the prosecutor needs the child to attend to establish the identity of any person; where the court is satisfied that it has not been possible to obtain a statement from the child; or where the court had started to hear the case summarily, had heard the evidence of the child and subsequently changed to committal proceedings (1980 Act, s. 103 and 1988 Act, s. 32(2)). The functions of a magistrates' court as examining justices are abolished by Criminal Justice and Public Order Act 1994, s.44(1) when in force. In those circumstances, committal proceedings will be replaced by transfer for trial during which oral evidence will not be given (see 1980 Act, s.6 as amended by 1994 Act, Sched.4 when in force.

7–012   In proceedings before a youth court, or on appeal to the Crown Court from such proceeding, or on indictment—or on appeal from such hearings—for any of the types of offences listed in 1 to 9 above, if the witness is a child, with the leave of the court, evidence may be given by live television link, that is with the witness outside the courtroom but able to be seen and heard by those in the courtroom by means of a television link. Note that this power does not apply to a magistrates' court other than a youth court (1988 Act, s. 32(1A)).

7–013   Any party may seek the leave of the court by giving notice to the clerk of the court with a copy to every other party to the proceedings (1992 Rules, r. 23(2) and (4)). The notice must be in the prescribed form (Form 51 in 1992 Rules, Sched. 2) or in a form to the like effect (1992 Rules, r. 2) and must be given within 28 days of the first time a defendant appears before the court (1992 Rules, r. 3). This period may be extended (whether or not it has already expired) by written application to be dealt with in the same way as an application for leave (1992 Rules, rr. 8 and 9). Any party who receives such a notice has fourteen days in which to object. Written notice of objection must be given to the clerk of the court and the applicant, and must give the reasons for the opposition (1992 Rules, r. 5).

If an application is made, a single justice will decide whether to grant **7–014** it. That decision can be made without a hearing unless the justice directs otherwise, in which case the clerk will notify the parties of the time and date of the hearing (1992 Rules, r. 6). A decision whether or not to grant leave must be communicated to all parties and to the person who will accompany the witness if that person is known. If leave is granted, the notification must include the court location and, where the witness is to be called by the prosecution, the name of the witness, and if known, the name, occupation and relationship to the witness of the person who is to accompany the witness. The person to accompany the witness must be acceptable to a justice of the peace and no other person may accompany the witness except with the leave of that justice (1992 Rules, r. 10). For these purposes a child is a person under 14 years of age for offences falling within categories 1 and 2 above or a person under 17 years of age for offences falling within 3 to 7 above. Offences under 8 or 9 above are defined by reference to the principal offence, *i.e.* the definition of a child is a person under 14 if the offence is aiding and abetting an assault (1988 Act, s. 32A(7) as applied by s. 32(6)). If a youth court does not have access to the facilities to allow this to be done, it may sit to hear the proceedings at another place which does have those facilities providing the place is formally appointed for this purpose by the justices for the petty sessions area for which the youth court acts (1988 Act, s. 32(3A)). This may include places outside the normal jurisdictional limits of the youth court (1988 Act, s. 32(3B)).

The phrasing of this 'formal appointment' requirement seems to **7–015** indicate that the decision be made by the whole bench for the area of the youth court, presumably at one of its normal business meetings. Such a procedure appears unnecessarily cumbersome; it is imperative that cases involving young people are dealt with very quickly—this is likely to be even more necessary if the sensitivity of the witness requires the use of a television link. It would appear perfectly adequate for the court which is to hear the case to designate the place of hearing taking into account all the needs of the participants which would allow the maximum flexibility in selecting the most readily available convenient location at the time needed. Similar criteria already have statutory precedent in guiding magistrates' courts as to the Crown Court to which to commit a defendant for trial (Magistrates' Courts Act 1980, s. 7).

A youth court dealing with an offender will be sitting in a "petty sessional courthouse" (1980 Act, s. 121(3)). Such a courthouse is defined as,

(a) a courthouse or place at which justices are accustomed to assemble for holding special or petty sessions or for the time being appointed as a substitute for such a courthouse or place, including, where justices are accustomed to assemble for either special petty sessions at more than one courthouse or place in a petty sessional division, any such courthouse or place;

(b) a courthouse or place at which a stipendiary magistrate is authorised by law to do alone any act authorised to be done by more than one justice of the peace (Justices' of the Peace Act 1979, s. 70).

7–016 No procedure is established to govern the appointment of petty sessional courthouses and it would not seem inappropriate for the youth court to exercise this power where necessary. This is particularly attractive since a justice for any area may act as a justice for that area in any commission area which adjoins his own (1979 Act, s. 66(1)). If the justices are appointed to the Surrey or Kent Commissions they may hold courts for their county anywhere in Greater London (1979 Act, s. 66(2)). Also, if the courthouse is provided by a local authority, even if it is outside the jurisdiction of the justices, it is deemed to be within it (1979 Act, s. 55(3)). Crown Court centres equipped with live television link facilities are listed in Practice Note, [1992] 3 All E.R. 927.

7–017 Extra Statutory Developments
Much attention has rightly been paid to problems encountered by witnesses waiting to go into court. It is unacceptable:

(a) For a prosecution witness (particularly the alleged victim) to be put in an area where they come into contact with the defendant;

(b) For a witness not to be properly prepared for what will happen in the courtroom with an understanding of what is expected, who will be present and what they will be expecting from the witness;

(c) For those conducting the questioning to be untrained in the best ways of handling a child witness;

(d) For judges, magistrates and their clerks to be unaware of the needs of child witnesses and possible reactions to the stress of a court experience.

For a general analysis of the current provisions, see Birch (1992).

PART III THE SENTENCING PROCESS

Chapter 8

Sentencing Juveniles: The Historical Context

Principles and issues regarding the sentencing of young offenders **8–001**
mirror, though often in a more extreme form, those informing policies
and practice in regard to adults. The exaggerations reflect both society's
'care' or 'control' ambivalence in regard to juveniles who commit
offences (Morris and Giller, 1987; Harris and Webb, 1987; Parsloe, 1978),
and the impact that cyclical panics about perceived rises in youth crime
have on sentencing policy (Newburn and Hagell, 1994; Cavadino, 1994;
Gibson, *et al.*, 1994). This chapter attempts, within the context of the
recurring themes of disparity, deprivation and persistence, to provide an
historical overview of the consequences of the shifts in the ideological
underpinning of youth justice sentencing policies which have taken
place throughout the century.

Disparity   8–002

> "The symbiotic relationship of local courts, local prosecution
> services and local probation and social services departments is the
> core factor which transmutes any statutory change in the criminal
> justice system into a variegated pattern taking its colour scheme
> from local systems." (Burney, 1985 90)

Since the time that details of each petty sessional division's sentencing
were first available, the disparities as between courts with similar
catchment areas and offenders from similar socio-economic
backgrounds committing similar offences have been manifest (Hood,
1972; Burney, 1979; Tarling and Wetherett, 1980; Parker, *et al.*, 1981).
But it is not, as Burney identifies, only the courts. The whole system
through which the offender of any age, and more so for the young
offender for whom there are more variables within the system, must
travel between suspicion and eventual sentence is vulnerable to
discrepant, possibly even idiosyncratic, interpretation of policy,
guidance and legislation, which may profoundly alter the outcome of
proceedings at the end of the day (Anderson, R., 1978; Hilgendorf, 1978;
Priestley, *et al.*, 1977; Ball, 1983; Parker, *et al.*, 1981 and 1989; Burney,
1985). Any real reform of the legislative and practice guidance
framework of court proceedings and work with young offenders requires
legislation guidance and that removes, in so far as is possible,
discretionary interpretation.

8–003 Social deprivation

The consistency of research findings regarding the association of clusters of factors such as low family income, poor housing, unemployment, low educational attainment, harsh and erratic discipline within the home, drugs, and early experience of violence or abuse with juvenile crime cannot be ignored. From original large cohort research (Farrington and West, 1973) and detailed studies of young offenders in institutions (Milham, *et al.*, 1976; Cawson 1980) undertaken in the 1960s and 70s, through to recent immensely detailed reviews of research findings across a quarter century,(Farrington, 1994, Henricson, 1994), to a reworking of a vaste wealth of data from a 1950s study in the United States (Sampson and Laub 1993), and, closer to home, a recent study of more than 300 persistent young offenders (Hagell and Newburn, 1994), the message is identical. Economic, family, educational and employment disadvantage and deprivation do not *cause* delinquency but the strengths of the association between the two are overwhelming.

8–004 Persistence

The phenomenon of public concern about a hard-core of young offenders responsible for large numbers of offences, with whom the criminal justice agencies are powerless to deal, is not new. It recurred on a regular basis throughout the nineteenth century (Pearson, 1983), and has continued to do so. In living memory it manifested most clearly during the first world war (Bailey 1987), in the mid 1930s following implementation of the Children and Young Persons Act 1933, in the 1950s with 'Teddy Boys', and the late 1970s. The most recent episode, beginning in 1992 was, according to a Policy Studies Institute research report, fuelled by very specific factors. The authors identify these as:

* the well publicised urban disturbances of 1991, which, although they were not on the scale nor the character of the riots of the early 1980s, attracted unprecedented media attention to the activities of joy-riders and their supporters in conflict with the police in geographically distanced areas (Oxford, Tyneside and Cardiff);

* press stories about juveniles the police were powerless to control—believed to be so involved in crime that one or two individuals accounted for a significant proportion of crime in any one area;

* and the extent to which these concerns were acted on by the then Home Secretary Kenneth Clarke who in October 1992 indicated publicly in a speech to the Federated Ranks of the Metropolitan Police what he had already had in mind for some months, not only that the government was

   "taking a long hard look at the options which are available to the courts in dealing with serious offenders of this age" but that

> "If court powers need to be strengthened or new institutions created, then they will be".

The chance element which enabled the Home Secretary to get approval **8–005** for the huge expenditure necessary to establish his 'new institutions', without waiting for the White Paper on young offenders—then at an early stage of production, so that he was able to announce in the House of Commons on March 3, 1993 that he had decided that although supervision orders were

> "necessary and sensible for the great majority of juvenile offenders ... they are insufficient to deal effectivley with that comparatively small group of very persistent offenders whose repeated offences make them a menace to the community. For such persons a secure training order would be added to the sentencing powers of the courts". (*Hansard*, March 13, 1993)

—was the public furore which followed the death of two year old James Bulger and the arrest of two ten year olds for his murder. The fact that the Bulger case was irrelevant in so far as youth court powers were concerned, since the boys would be tried and sentenced under the provisions of the Children and Young Persons Act 1933, s.53(1) (see paras 2–037–24–083 below) was not a matter of interest to the public, nor apparently to the Home Secretary (Hagell and Newburn, 1994).

The myth of a clearly identifiable small minority of persistent young **8–006** offenders, recognisably different from the general run of offending youngsters for whom existing provisions are deemed adequate, dies hard. They figured largely in public and judicial reaction to the perceived softness of the new juvenile courts set up under the 1933 Act (Bailey, 1986) and in magistrates' and others reactions to to implementation of the Children and Young Persons Act 1969 (Berlins and Wansell, 1974). What has never been satisfactorily established is the criteria by which 'persistence' can be defined. The Policy Studies Institute was charged by the government with this task. Their researchers conclude from a detailed study of a total sample of 531 young offenders from two geographical areas, arrested three or more times in 1992, that:

> "the distribution of offences across reoffenders did not suggest a distinct group of very frequent offenders. Very few reoffenders were identified, and fewer still whose frequent offending continued over an extended period of time. Few juveniles appeared to offend very frequently for more than short periods."

The researchers applied three definitions of persistence and found not **8–007** only that a very small percentage of the sample came within any of the definitions, but that there was very little overlap between the criteria with only eight youngsters out of the total sample satisfying all three. Nor were any striking differences identifiable between the offenders who met any of the criteria for persistence and the total sample, except for the frequency of offending. Those who offended persistently were not disproportionately engaged in serious crime. All the rest of the PSI study's findings mirrored those of previous researchers in regard to the chaotic family lives, low school achievement, poor housing, alcohol and drug abuse problems and social isolation of the majority of young offenders (Hagell and Newburn, 1994).

> "Interviews with these persistent offenders gave an impression of a mixture of chaos, sadness and boredom". (Hagell and Newburn, 1994)

The themes of disparity, disadvantage and persistence are threaded through the history of sentencing theory and practice throughout the twentieth century.

8–008 Historical overview: in search of welfare
As we have seeen, the juvenile court established under the Children Act 1908 was a court of due process, physically separated from the adult court. It had its own range of disposals which included—as well as fines, birching and the alternative of making a probation order—the power to commit to industrial and reform schools, or a higher court for a sentence of Borstal training. For those considered too unruly to be otherwise dealt with imprisonment remained available. As with adult offenders at the time, pre-sentence information on defendants was rarely provided in juvenile courts. After the first war, in keeping with growing concern public concern regarding the physical and mental health of children, certain more enlightened juvenile courts routinely required medical reports on defendants (Bailey, 1987). From here it was a short step to demands for centres where delinquents could be assessed and their needs identified, and then to the statutory endorsement of a 'treatment' model of juvenile justice recommended by the Committee on the Treatment of Young Offenders (Home Office 1927, see para. 3–009 above).

8–009   Under the reforming 1933 Children And Young Persons Act, although the juvenile court continued to be a court of due process, focusing on proof of criminal responsibility, at the sentencing stage the emphasis shifted towards the choice of a disposal which would most nearly meet the treatment needs of the defendant. To this end the newly constituted court was given a statutory mandate to reach its decisions 'having regard to the welfare of the child' (Children and Young Persons Act 1933, s.44). With the hindsight of history, the Act can be seen to represent the statutory birth of the ideological confusion that forced a dilemma on the juvenile courts which still continues in the youth court, albeit in a more symbolic and less practical sense than in previous decades:

> "The elision of punishment with protection, the interest of society with that of the individual, and control with care..." (Anderson, 1978)

Despite the welfare rhetoric, the changes introduced by the 1933 Act in **8–010** regard to juvenile courts sentencing powers were not great:

* the distinction between industrial and reformatory schools was removed and they became known as approved schools.

* the power to place children who were in need of care and control in the care of a local authority, as a 'fit person' was extended to include offenders (section 57), thus allowing a placement in a foster home or with relatives as well as in an approved school;

The attempt to introduce what at the time was seen as radical reform, by abolishing corporal punishment in the form of birching for offenders under 14 years, failed as a result of pressure on the government by members of the House of Lords to whom

> "the fight to retain corporal punishment as a weapon in the penal armoury represented a last stand against the contagion of leniency and sentimentality which was said to have juvenile justice in its grip".(Bailey, 1987, p. 114)

Pre-war developments
The debate which followed implementation of the 1933 Act took place **8–011** in one of the times of cyclical concern about youth crime referred to above. The numbers of juveniles found guilty of indictable offences rose during the late 1920s from 11,017 in 1921 to 12,198 in 1930, and at an accelerated pace after implementation of the new Act to 22,393 in 1935 (Source: Criminal Statistics quoted in Elkin, 1938). Responses to the rise varied. The police and some magistrates were quick to blame what they perceived as 'sentimental justice', administered by the new 'drawing room' courts, for the rise in delinquency. As Elkin robustly pointed out, this could hardly be the case since sentencing powers were little altered by the 1933 Act, and sentencing patterns hardly varied between 1925 and 1935 (Elkin, 1938, p. 132). The Home Office Children's Branch publicly adhered to the view that the rise simply reflected a greater enthusiasm for taking cases to court so that juveniles could benefit from the court's expertise, whilst privately, along with reforming magistrates, social workers and some academic commentators, senior civil servants were more likely to blame economic factors, especially unemployment (Bailey, 1987; Elkin, 1938). At the same time the part played by disturbed family relationships in the making of delinquents, brought to public attention by the work of Sir Cyril Burt in this country and the criminologist William Healy in the United States, was becoming more widely accepted. As Bailey concludes:

> "It should be evident that the most accepted explanation of delinquency in the 1930s was one which emphasised unsatisfactory home conditions, psychological as well as material. Clearly, too, this explanation attracted the support of the 'reactionaries' as much as the reformers; the defective family, after all, incorporated the

absence or laxity of parental discipline which the police and magistracy were wont to stress. The essential difference between the two approaches to the problem of juvenile crime was in the conclusions drawn from the evidence about unsuitable home environments. Whereas the reformers looked to the provision of improved conditions of family life, whether in the natural, a foster, or a residential home, the reactionaries put their faith in the reanimation of the legal substitutes for parental discipline." (*ibid.* p. 128–9)

8–012   **The changing nature of the 'short, sharp, shock': birching and beyond**
The debate over corporal punishment continued to rage, despite the set-back of the 1933 Act. The professional judiciary were predominently anti-abolitionist, and, although the Magistrates' Association joined the abolitionist lobby, individual magistrates were deeply divided, many juvenile courts declining to order birching on principle. Others, particularly in northern towns, as revealed in evidence to the Departmental Committee on Corporal Punishment favoured retention. One witness taking the view that

> "the birch is felt by the offender himself, and it inflicts no hardship on his family.",

while others

> "suggested that, at a time when juvenile delinquency appeared to be growing to an alarming extent, every possible expedient should be tried to check the increase and no existing method of dealing with young offenders should be discarded" (Home Office, 1937, p. 26).

8–013   It was in his oral evidence to this Committee that Basil Henriques, Chairman of Toynbee Hall Juvenile Court and himself a supporter of abolition, but also a believer in deterrent punishment, introduced a concept which has found support in successive youth justice debates from that day to this:

> "What is needed is some new form of punishment which will be short, sharp and unpleasant, but will leave its spiritual mark on the mind of the offender rather than the physical mark ... I want to see established a special place of detention to which boys could be sent for a period not exceeding one month ..." (*ibid.* p. 32).

This concept was taken up by the Committee which recommended:

> "Some form of short sharp punishment which will pull him up and give him the lesson which he needs." (*ibid.* p. 46)

Provisions to abolish judicial birching for both adults and juveniles were included in the 1938 Criminal Justice Bill. They attracted such fierce opposition from Conservatives, particularly in regard to adult offenders, that it seemed likely that the government's measure would be lost in a free vote. In the event the whole Bill was abandoned at the outbreak of war.

Parallel to the campaign to abolish birching, the search for a sentence to fill a tariff position between probation supervision and approved school continued, as did renewed demand for specialist observation homes to which those children regarded as problem cases could be sent for a period of assessment.

Criminal Justice Act 1948   8–014

As during the first world war, juvenile crime rose steeply during the years 1939–1945. This was attributed to the closing of schools and youth clubs, evacuation, blackout and air-raid shelter life, and most of all, echoing a familiar theme, to the way in which war conditions aggravated the lack of home life and parental control (Bailey). Parallel to the rise in crime came increased demand for criminal justice reform. It was envisaged that immediately after the war there would be legislation based on the 1938 Bill, although in the social reforming climate of the immediate post-war years it was inevitable that at least some of the earlier proposals would need to be reconsidered. Although the opposition view of the need for reform did not appear differ significantly, in that a Conservative party report *Youth Astray* (1946) suggested that delinquency

> "is mainly the outcome of conditions, social and economic, and to some extent hereditary, for which they themselves cannot be blamed. The blame … rests largely upon society".

in the event, as with most criminal justice legislation, competing **8–015** interests resulted in penal reforms being introduced at the price of other more punitive measures. In this instance the introduction of detention centres for offenders aged 14–20 proved to be the price for the abolition of birching. Some commentators, with scant regard for the historical context of the legislation, have interpreted the introduction of detention centres as being the raison d'etre for the whole Act (Parker, Sumner and Jarvis, 1989). The reality, reflected in many Criminal Justice Acts since, was a climate of reform which did not extend quite as far into the judiciary and the House of Lords as the reformers would have wished.

The 1948 Act was reforming in that it:

* abolished birching;

* introduced attendance centres as a mild punitive measure designed to deprive the less serious young offender of leisure time;

* further restricted the use of prison for juveniles, both on remand and as a sentence; and

* encouraged courts to use Borstal training instead of imprisonment for older juvenile and young adult offenders.

8–016 Other provisions contrasted with the reforms. At the insistence of the judges, supported by many magistrates:

* the new short-term punitive detention centre order was introduced for offenders aged 14 and under 21 years.

This new order, intended for those for whom longer term training was not considered necessary, but for whom non-custodial measures were deemed inappropriate, was heralded by a leading juvenile court chairman as "a short sharp punishment to bring the offender to his senses and act as a deterrent in the future" (Watson, 1942). Despite a consistently poor record in terms of reconviction rates, faith in the efficacy of the short, sharp shock, provided by a dention centre sentence, proved durable—at least amongst Conservative Home Secretaries. It continued until the use of custody for young offenders went into a brief period of decline in the late 1980s (Allen, 1991) and the detention centre order was abandoned as a separate sentence (Criminal Justice Act 1988).

8–017 Rising crime and conflicting responses
Throughout the 1950s juvenile crime rose seemingly inexorably, as did the demand for stiffer penalties and more restrictive regimes in approved schools and Borstals (Millham, *et al.*, 1978, Cawson and Martell, 1979). At the same time an increasingly articulate lobby of child care social workers were demanding a shift of resources away from residential institutions towards preventative work with families, including those whose children were at risk of coming before the juvenile court (Packman, 1981).

In 1956 a Committee chaired by Lord Ingleby was required, amongst its other breathtakingly broad terms of reference, to inquire into, and make recommendations on the law:

"relating to proceedings, and the powers of the courts, in respect of juveniles brought before the courts as delinquent or as being in need of care or protection or beyond control;" (Home Office 1960)

8–018 Considering that there was no social work representation on the Committee, its recommendations reflected to a surprising degree contemporary demands for policies to reduce the numbers of children in residential care (Packman, 1981). Having singled out the lack of a satisfactory home as the primary cause of juvenile crime and of neglect, the committee supported the provision of the whole range of welfare services to families at risk, in order, wherever possible, to support the child within the home and prevent the need for court orders, whether in care or criminal proceedings (Home Office, 1960). Apart from this significant shift towards preventative work and their radical recommendations for raising the age of criminal responsibility, the significance of the Ingleby report lies in its identification of the dilemma posed by the courts' conflicting due process and welfare functions under the Children and Young Persons Act 1933:

"The combined effect of these changes has been to produce a jurisdiction that rests, at least in appearance, on principles that are hardly consistent. The court remains a criminal court in the sense that it is a magistrates' court concerned with trying offences, that is its procedure is a modified form of ordinary criminal procedure and that, with a few special provisions, it is governed by the law of evidence in criminal cases. Yet the requirement to have regard to the welfare of the child, and the various ways in which the court may deal with an offender, suggest a jurisdiction that is not criminal. It is not easy to see how the two principles can be reconciled: criminal responsibility is focused on an allegation about some particular act isolated from the character and needs of the defendant, whereas welfare depends on a complex of personal, family and social considerations." (Home Office, 1960, para. 60)

The Committee went on to identify the consequences of this ambiguity   **8–019** and the sense of injustice it could engender in children effectively deprived of their liberty for petty offending:

"The weakness of the present system is that a juvenile court often appears to be trying a case on one particular ground and then to be dealing with the child on some quite different ground. This is inherent in combining the requirement for proof of a specified event or condition with a general direction to have regard to the child's welfare. It results, for example, in a child being charged with petty theft or other wrongful act for which most people would say that no great penalty should be imposed, and the case apparently ending in disproportionate sentence. For when the court causes inquiries to be made, if those inquiries show seriously disturbed home conditions, or one or more of many other circumstances, the court may determine that the welfare of the child requires some very substantial interference which may require taking the child away from home for a prolonged period." (*ibid.* para. 66)

The Children and Young Persons Act 1963, apart from raising the age of criminal responsibility to 10 years, and including the keeping of juvenile offenders out of court amongst local authorities' new preventative duties set out in section 1, made few other changes in respect of young offenders.

The search for radical reform   **8–020**

As we have seen (Chapter 1), the Labour government which came to power in 1964 already had the radical reform of the treatment of juvenile offenders high on its agenda, and after two White Papers and a struggle through the legislative process the Children and Young Persons Act 1969 eventuallly reached the statute book. The philosophy underpinning the sentencing reforms contained in the Act was elegantly, and relatively uncontentiously, set out in the White Paper, Children in Trouble:

"Juvenile delinquency has no single cause, manifestation or cure. Its origins are many, and the range of behaviour which it covers is equally wide. At some points it merges almost imperceptibly with behaviour which does not contravene the law. A child's behaviour is influenced by genetic, emotional and intellectual factors, his maturity, and his family, school, neighbourhood and wider social setting. It is probably a minority of children who grow up without ever misbehaving in ways which may be contrary to the law. Frequently such behaviour is no more than an incident in the pattern of a child's normal development. But sometimes it is a response to unsatisfactory family or social circumstances, a result of boredom in and out of school, and indication of maladjustment or immaturity, or a symptom of a deviant, damaged or abnormal personality." (Home Office, 1968, para. 33)

8–021 Had the 1969 Act been fully implemented, Borstal training for juveniles would have been abolished and detention centre and attendance centre orders replaced by a supervision order with "intermediate treatment"—a term used to encompass a spectrum of social work intervention in the lives of offenders and non offenders:

"Existing forms of treatment available to juvenile courts distinguish sharply between those which involve complete removal from home and those which do not. The juvenile courts have very difficult decisions to make in judging whether circumstances require the drastic step of taking a child away from his parents and home. The view has often been expressed that some form or forms of intermediate treatment should be available to the courts, allowing the child to remain in his own home but bringing him into contact with a different environment." (Home Office, 1968, 9)

The 1969 Act was overtly decriminalising in its intent. As well as replacing probation orders for juveniles with supervision orders, with or without intermediate treatment, it removed from juvenile courts the power to make approved school orders in care or criminal proceedings. The only order available under the Act which could result in a defendant being removed from home, was one placing the child in the care of the local authority until the age of 18 (unless a court discharged the order). Once made the care order gave local authorities total discretion regarding almost all aspects of the child's life. Further provisions abolished Borstal sentences, detention and attendance centre orders for juveniles.

8–022 A change of government in 1970 led to the Act being only partially implemented. Far from courts being decriminalised and their powers curtailed, the effect was that from 1971, in addition to discharges and fines, the court's range of available orders amounted to a wide ranging tariff:

* supervision orders (1–3 years) with or without a requirement to participate in 'intermediate treatment';

* attendance centre orders (12–24 hours);

* care order to the local authority;

* detention centre (Boys 14–16, 3–6 months);

* committal for Borstal training (15 and 16 years)

Apparently unaware of the breadth of their sentencing powers, magistrates were deeply resentful of the change as regards approved school orders and the care order. Almost as soon as it was implemented the Act was blamed for increases in juvenile crime and senior magistrates were railing publicly about the extent to which their powers had been curtailed, with some juvenile panel members resigning in protest (Berlins and Wansell, 1974).

The perception of reduced powers was exacerbated by the effect of the **8–023** wholescale reorganisation of the personal social services following the Seebohm report of 1968. The absorbtion of the former children's committees' functions within the new generic local authority social services departments dissipated the social work expertise in dealing with difficult adolescents, on which the 1969 Act was predicated. This, together with the much diminished role of probation officers in the juvenile court, fuelled frustration, particularly in regard to care and supervision orders. Before the Act had been in force for a year there were demands for a thorough review of its working. These demands focused on those identified as persistent young offenders whom magistrates would previously have been able to sentence directly to approved schools.

> "What is abundantly clear to me, and I think to most people now, is that it is the failure to deal with the hard core of young offenders— that is to say the offenders in the very youngest age group—that is resulting in the very serious incidence in crime in the 15—17 year old groups." (Sir William Addison, Chairman of the Magistrates' Association giving evidence to the House of Commons Expenditure Committee 1974) (House of Commons 1975 HC 534—ii, p. 130).

The Labour government, in the introduction to its White Paper in response to the Expenditure Committee report, was generally robustly optimistic:

> "As regards these statutory arrangements, the Government's broad conclusion, which is in line with the Expenditure Committee's, is that although much remains to be done to make the Act fully operative and effective, and although a small number of highly publicised cases have given cause for concern, the framework provided by the Act for dealing constructively and humanely with children in trouble remains a fundamentally sound one." (Home Office, 1976, para. 3)

8–024 Regardless, however, of official optimism, the Act was not fully implemented, and the perception of powerlessness amongst magistrates and the police remained. The myth that children placed at home under care orders committed further offences with impunity, in contrast to the 'good old days' of the approved school order (when the same children were sent a long way from home) died hard. Neither research evidence regarding the low level of reoffending by children on care orders placed at home as compared with those in community homes (Zander, 1975), nor the routinely high reconviction rates following both approved school and community home placements (Cornish and Clarke, 1976; Millham, *et al.*, 1978; Cawson, 1981), appeared to make any impact on these perceptions.

8–025   There is no doubt that magistrates did not at the time recognise the extent to which provisions underpinned by a social welfare ideology but with, in the event, a wide range of punitive orders in place for courts to use, gave the juvenile courts unprecedented powers to intervene in the lives of offenders appearing before them. Whatever the perception of powerlessness, throughout the decade, as more places became available in detention centres and attendance centres, the numbers of young people aged 14 to 16 sentenced to attendance centres and custody rose and the use of community based sentences declined (See Table 4).

Table 4
14–16 year olds sentenced for indictable offences 1971–1981
(thousands)

Year (and pop under 18 years)		Total	Dis-charge or fine	Super-vision	At-tend-ance centre	Care	Cus-tody
1971	(13,666.1)	53.1	30.8	10.4	3.4	4.2	3.4
1972	(13,722.3)	55.0	32.5	9.9	3.7	3.9	3.8
1973	(13,755.2)	57.4	33.1	10.5	4.0	4.2	4.4
1974	(13,698.1)	67.8	39.3	12.3	5.2	4.4	6.0
1975	(13,598.8)	67.0	38.8	11.6	5.2	4.3	6.0
1976	(13,455.0)	67.7	39.5	11.0	5.7	3.7	6.7
1977*	(13,271.6)	67.4	42.4	11.4	6.4	3.4	7.0
1978*	(13,093.2)	72.7	43.4	10.7	7.2	3.3	7.4
1979*	(12,935.9)	63.4	34.9	10.7	7.2	2.7	7.0
1980**	(12,775.6)	71.0	38.1	12.3	9.3	2.8	7.5
1981**	(12,591.5)	69.4	35.9	12.3	10.0	2.5	7.8

* Not adjusted to take account of the Criminal Damage Act 1971
** Adjusted to take account of the Criminal Damage Act 1971

Sources: Criminal Statistics 1992, Home Office, HMSO, and OPCS Population Estimates Unit.

Moving away from custodial solutions   8–026
By the late 1970s large numbers of young offenders were in custody
(Table 4), and the juvenile justice scene bore almost no resemblance to
the decriminalised non-custodial approach to juvenile offending which
the 1969 Act was intended to achieve. By 1979, 11 per cent of offenders
aged 14 to 16 years sentenced for indictable offences were made the
subject of custodial sentences, and a further 4 per cent were placed in the
care of a local authority—an order usually involving removal from
home. Indeed the use of care and custody had increased so dramatically
that in that year Leon Brittan, then a Minister of State at the Home
Office, pointed out that in a decade that had seen a reduction by half of
the proportion of adults received into custody, the proportion of
juveniles receiving custodial sentences had more than tripled (Morris
and Giller, 1987). Was the explanation that partial implementation,
having left the police with their powers to prosecute unfettered, and
magistrates, whatever their perceptions of powerlessness, with a range
of sentencing options, they were deliberately exercising those powers to
avoid sentences for which social workers were responsible?
Or was the explanation less predictable, involving magistrates not in 8–027
avoiding social workers recommendations, but following them too
trustingly? The conclusions reached by Thorpe, *et al.* on the basis of
research into local juvenile justice systems suggests the latter. Their
work provides convincing evidence that, far from a deliberate move by
magistrates to defy social workers, it was in many cases the social
workers who were themselves partly responsible for juvenile
defendants' swift rise up the sentencing tariff towards custody. Studies
showed that supervision or care orders made at an early stage in the
juvenile's offending career, an intervention often out of all proportion to
the offences committed, were made in response to the contents and
recommendations in social workers' reports, or, possibly under the
influence of very negative information regarding the child's educational
circumstances presented in reports from schools. (Thorpe, *et al.*, 1980;
Burney, 1979; Ball, 1981 and 1983). When the juvenile reoffended
supervision was perceived as having failed, and a move to care or
custody was often the next step (Thorpe, *et al.*, 1979 and 1980).
    The later years of the decade saw the start of two developments which
were to influence a shift away from the use of care and custody through
the 1980s and into the 1990s as dramatic as the unpredicted rise of the
1970s had been. Findings from research studies undertaken at the
Centre for Youth Crime and Community at the University of Lancaster,
based on detailed monitoring of juvenile justice systems in several local
authorities, demonstrated the adverse consequences for young
offenders, in terms of their swift rise up the sentencing tariff, of
welfare-based intervention in the form of supervision orders (Thorpe, *et
al.*, 1979).
    The active dissemination in local authorities of their findings by 8–028
Thorpe and his colleagues and the subsequent setting up of rigorous
monitoring and gatekeeping procedures by juvenile justice teams,

99

played a significant part in promoting a marked shift of support away from belief in the 'treatment' model of juvenile justice. Social workers and probation officers working with young offenders came to acknowledge that treatment oriented intervention, such as that encouraged by many early intermediate treatment schemes (Thorpe, 1978), could well be responsible for many of the unintended consequences of the 1969 Act. They consequently rejected treatment and switched allegiance to the alternative of the alluringly entitled 'justice' model which achieved a vogue in the early 1980s (Morris and Giller, 1980). Although derided for being conceptually unsound, in that it was in no sense a model and was capable of almost infinitely varying interpretation according to the user's position on the crime and punishment spectrum—from radical non-intervention to the "law and order" right, (Bottoms, 1980),—the "justice" approach had wide appeal. Its adherents were, and still are, at least united in their opposition to the medical or treatment model. In direct contrast the "justice model" requires a general acceptance that intervention in the form of a court imposed sentence should be proportionate to the offence committed, and should never, regardless of the motives of the report writer or sentencer, be increased in effective severity, in terms of intervention in the offender's life, because of the offender's social, personal or educational circumstances.

8–029   Initially this approach underpinned moves to develop intermediate treatment programmes targeted solely at young offenders at risk of a custodial sentence (Morris and Giller, 1987), and in the late 1970s a number of imaginative initiatives by local authority social workers and probation officers resulted in community based intermediate treatment schemes for the sort of young offenders who were at real risk of a custodial sentence.

Unpromisingly, for those seeking to reduce the use of custody for juveniles, the late 1970s also saw yet another explosion of concern about law and order issues. The Thatcher government came to power in 1979 with William Whitelaw promising the party conference that 'young thugs' would be sent to detention centres for a "short, sharp shock", the number of secure places for juveniles would be increased, and that more places would be made available in "compulsory attendance centres for hooligans". (Morris and Giller, 1987, p. 114). Consequently the new government's White Paper, *Young Offenders*, which preceded the Criminal Justice Bill—a "bran tub of largely unrelated small items buried in a sawdust of cross-referencing to previous legislation" (Burney, 1985, p. 1) was ideologically confused. It looked, as most Criminal Justice Acts do, in more than one direction:

8–030   *   it sought to encourage courts to make greater use of supervision and the more structured programmes offered by social workers and probation officers working with young offenders through the introduction of powers for courts to make detailed directions about participation in programmes of specified activities as a requirement of a supervision order.

At the same time

* the Bill was substantially oriented towards the structure of custodial sentences for juveniles and young adults rather than encouraging the use of community sentences.

During the Bill's passage through Parliament it was considerably altered **8–031** and substantially increased in size, and the ideological confusion was increased rather than resolved. As well as replacing the indeterminate sentence of Borstal training with youth custody for a determinate period, and a new minimum sentence of three weeks in a detention centre, additional "tough" supervision requirements such as night restriction (curfew) were added. They were the price that had to be paid for the important introduction by the Parliamentary All Party Penal Affairs Committee, against the wishes of the government, of statutory criteria relating to the individual offender and the seriousness of the offence which had to be satisfied before a custodial sentence could be imposed on an offender aged 14–20 years (section 1(4)).

Unsurprisingly this substantial and somewhat contradictory **8–032** legislative package produced variable results. The government had hoped, against all available evidence, that their response to the call for more effective sentencing, and especially the re-introduction of "short, sharp shock" regimes in detention centres, would reduce recidivism. Careful monitoring of reconviction rates showed beyond argument that it did not (Home Office, 1984). At the other end of the spectrum criminal justice pressure groups, hoping that the statutory criteria in section 1(4), combined with courts greater confidence in supervision orders with court specified activities would result in a dramatic reduction in the custodial sentencing of juveniles, were disappointed. Largely because of courts' failure to apply the criteria for custody properly, this did not occur (Burney, 1985). Indeed, so far as juvenile courts were concerned, there was a rise in the use of youth custody over previous committals to the Crown Court for Borstal sentencing (NACRO 1984). This appears to have been due partly to removal of the constraint on magistrates of having to commit to Crown Court with a recommendation for a Borstal sentence, and also in part to magistrates' belief that the remedial value of training, available in youth custody but not at detention centres justified the longer sentence. Sentencers were thus not only in some cases ignoring the criteria in section 1(4), but were also imposing longer periods of custody than were warranted by the offence. (Burney 1982; Parker, *et al.*, 1989).

From the mid 1980s levels of custody began to decline, at first slowly **8–033** and, after the Criminal Justice Act 1988 introduced stiffer criteria into section 1(4) of the 1982 Act, at an accelerated rate. Several interlinked factors, in addition to the increased use of cautions and the demographic phenomenon of a 25 per cent decrease in the number of juveniles in the population between 1979 and 1989 contributed to the reduction. A combination of legal constraints on the courts and the provision, by local authorities, the probation service and volutary agencies, of an increasing range of community based programmes offering an alternative to custodial sentences can be identified as key factors (NACRO 1991). So far as the legal constraints on magistrates' sentencing was concerned, several of the leading juvenile justice organisations developed a robust policy of encouraging young offenders, whom they considered to have been improperly given custodial sentences, to appeal. This policy also enabled the appeal courts to take some steps to define key phrases in section 1(4). (See for example: *Bradbourn* (1985) 7 Cr. App.R (S.) 180; *Murray* [1987] Crim. L.R. 213; *Stanley* [1987] Crim. L.R. 214; *Hayes* [1987] Crim. L.R. 789.)

8–034   Concurrently, the number of community-based alternative to custody schemes continued to grow. In those areas in which the juvenile panel magistrates, often as a result of a chance combination of dedicated individuals on the juvenile panel and within the relevant agencies, were convinced of the potential of such schemes to deal effectively with the majority of relatively serious offenders, the new statutory provisions reinforced existing initiatives and encouraged their spread (Rutherford, 1992). However, the patchy development of community based schemes, and in some areas courts' determined preference for custody, resulted in such marked disparities in the sentencing of young offenders from similar offending backgrounds committing identical offences as to justify the allegation that the system allowed "justice by geography" (Children's Society, 1988; Richardson 1989). The need was identified for measures which would encourage provision in those areas without adequate community based schemes, and also to encourage courts with a custody ethos to use available community based programmes.

One followed the other. In 1983 a Department of Health and Social Security initiative provided the encouragement needed for extension of the number of programmes, by making up to £15 million available to voluntary organisations working in partnership with local authorities to provide alternatives to custody with new, intensively supervised, community-based projects for juvenile offenders. This productive move resulted in many courts, which had not previously had suitable programmes in which they could order an offender to participate as a requirement under a supervision order available to them, making use of the new facilities as a direct alternative to custody. As a NACRO policy paper comments:

8–035   "Magistrates were closely involved in the development and management of projects under the DHSS initiative and witnessed first-hand their capacity to work constructively with young offenders to reduce their re-offending and at the same time offer adequate levels of public protection." (NACRO 1991)

8–036 The combined effects of demographic factors, revised cautioning guidance and policies (Home Office, 1985), more community based projects and the custody restrictions of the 1982 Act was that by 1988 the custodial sentencing of juveniles was very substantially reduced. Further legislation was needed to bring down the continuing disproportionate use of custody by a few juvenile courts. In order to achieve this amendments to section 1(4) of the 1982 Act were introduced by the Criminal Justice Act 1988, which further tightened the criteria for passing any custodial sentence on a juvenile or young adult offender. This combined with increased sanctions for breach of requirements in supervision orders imposed as an alternative to custodial sentences, introduced at the same time, resulted by 1990 in a further substantial drop in custodial sentencing of juveniles which far exceeded the the concurrent change in the demographic profile of the population (Table 4). The 1988 Act also replaced the separate custodial sentences of detention centre and youth custody by the current single sentence of detention in a young offender institution.

Juvenile Justice in the 1990s: Contradiction and Confusion

In the autumn of 1992 David Faulkner, one of the architects of the Criminal Justice Act 1991, in its original form, wrote:

"The 1991 Act and its companion the Children Act 1989 were the   8-037
outcome of a number of important developments which had taken place over the last 10 or 12 years. Belief in the effectiveness of an early severe sentence had given way to an approach based on 'minimum intervention'—an important theme of the Children Act and consistent with the new sentencing principles set out in the Criminal Justice Act (1991). Intermediate treatment had proved itself to be an effective means of dealing with juvenile offenders, and was an important influence on the provisions for community sentences in the Criminal Justice Act. There had been a dramatic fall in use of custody for juveniles—sentences in 1990 were less than a quarter of the number in 1981—accompanied by a significant fall in known juvenile offending (the numbers cautioned or sentenced, although the reasons are complicated and may have included an increase in informal action by the police. The success of juvenile courts in dealing with 15 and 16 year olds was one of the reasons for the extension of their jurisdiction to 17 year olds in the new youth court." (Faulkner, 1992)

In contrast to the relative affluence and calm of the mid to late 1980s,   8-038
the first four years of the last decade of the century have seen deep recession and unprecedented levels of public concern about perceived "persistent young offenders". The response has been frenetic legislative activity, much of it overtly punitive, and much that is in direct conflict with local authorities' powers and duties under the Children Act 1989 (Cavadino 1994). At the present time it is difficult to make sense of what is happening, though what is clear is that recent Home Office policies not only reverse well established trends, and are in conflict with those of the Department of Health, but they fly in the face of such research

evidence as there is regarding both the causes of youth crime and the effectiveness of sentencing.

Chapter 9

Sentencing Juveniles: General Considerations

Young offenders or children in trouble? This familiar question poses the **9–001**
overarching dilemma for sentencing in juvenile justice. Is the juvenile
law breaker to be regarded essentially as an offender to be held
responsible for his or her actions and punished accordingly, albeit with
some concessions to youth, or in a fundamentally different way, giving
wide consideration to their problems, personality and potential? Is the
juvenile or youth court simply a junior criminal court or a welfare
tribunal which happens to be triggered by an offending event?

Since the welfarist vision of the White Paper *Children in Trouble*
(Home Office, 1968), the direction of the tide towards penalty has been
clear, pointed up in *Young Offenders* (Home Office, 1980) and *Crime,
Justice and Protecting the Public* (Home Office, 1990). Under the
framework of sentencing introduced by the Criminal Justice Act 1991,
the youth court clearly shares the same broad approach as the adult
courts, namely that "the severity of the sentence ... should be directly
related to the seriousness of the offence" (Home Office, 1990, para. 1.6).
We have thus become familiar with the following four "sentencing
bands" related to the seriousness of the offence and the commensurate
restriction of liberty.

Discharge   **9–002**
Appropriately used where it is unnecessary to impose any sanction on
the offender but, when used conditionally, a discharge leaves open the
possibility of later punishment if the offender commits a further offence
during the specified period and thus holds the promise of corrective
restraint. Though not addressed by the White Paper or regulated by the
1991 Act, this measure has a clear and possibly expanded role in the new
sentencing structure in cases where prosecution and the necessity to
appear in court may be regarded as sufficient mark of the public
disapproval of the offence. A discharge can readily be combined with a
compensation order, thus allowing some making good of any harm
caused, without additional penalty.

Fine   **9–003**
"Most offenders can be punished by financial penalties ..." (Home
Office, 1990, para. 1.6).

"The fine has great advantages for the public as well as the offender. It involves the offender actually paying back to the community something in return for the damage he has done, rather than requiring society to spend even more money upon him so that he can repay that debt. A fine, if properly assessed, can punish the offender without damaging his opportunities for employment or his responsibilities towards his family."

The fine should reflect the seriousness of the offence. Though the Act does not refer to the fine in terms of "restriction upon liberty", it clearly has that capacity, because of its impact upon spending power. The fine is also very flexible, both in the range of offences for which it may be suitable in its own right and in its use in tandem with a more restrictive sentence such as a community order.

9–004 **Community Sentence**
When the offence is too serious to be properly punished with financial penalties alone, the punishment should be partial "restriction on liberty" and freedom of movement. The White Paper makes clear that, before making a "community order" which restricts an offender's liberty in this way, a court should be satisfied that it is justified by the seriousness of the offence (the threshold criterion is that the offence is "serious enough") and that the degree of restraint, intruding on normal freedom, is also justified. The punishment lies in the loss of liberty and in the enforcement of the order, not in the activities carried out during the order. Courts must look at the overall effect of the sentence on the offender. How much time will he or she have to give up to comply with the order? How does the order match the characteristics of the offender? Courts must be realistic as well as demanding, taking into account that some offenders lead a disorganised and impulsive lifestyle and thus have difficulty in complying, and that "a comparatively short order may make more severe demands on some offenders than more severe orders would on others" (Home Office, 1990, para. 4.9).

9–005 **Custody**
"The deprivation of liberty through a custodial sentence is the most severe penalty available to the courts and the proper punishment for the most serious crimes" (Home Office, 1990, para. 2.11). The sentence

"removes an offender from home, determines where he or she will live during sentence and decides how and where he or she will spend every hour of each day."

Custody "is likely to diminish an offender's sense of responsibility and self-reliance", "provides many opportunities to learn criminal skills", "can have a devastating effect on some prisoners and on their families" and it is unrealistic to expect persons so sentenced "to emerge as reformed characters" (Home Office, 1990, para. 3.1–3.2). Given this bleak official perspective, the White Paper noted the widespread view that, "so far as possible, young offenders should not be sentenced to custody since this is likely to confirm them in a criminal career", welcomed the drop in 1989 in the number of young adults aged 17–20 sentenced to custody and anticipated that the 1991 Act could similarly restrict the use of custody for adults. Thus the Act introduced a common custody threshold for all offenders, the primary criterion being that the offence is "so serious" that only a custodial sentence can be justified. A second criterion, available only in respect of violent or sexual offences, permits custody in the very exceptional instance where only a custodial sentence would be adequate to protect the public from serious harm from the offender.

Assessing Seriousness 9–006
Offence seriousness is thus the key conceptual building block of sentencing and though ultimately this rests on a subjective judgement the 1991 Act provides a degree of assistance in making that assessment.

(i) The Circumstances of the Offence

A not surprising starting point is for the court to:

> "take into account all such information about the circumstances of the offence or (as the case may be) of the offence and the offence or offences associated with it (including any aggravating or mitigating factors) as is available to it."

This is the common wording of both CJA 1991, s. 3(3)(a) and s. 7(1)(a) in regard to forming an opinion:

(a) whether a custodial sentence is justified and, if so, for what term, or

(b) whether a community sentence is warranted and, if so, what restriction on liberty would be commensurate.

CJA 1991, s. 18, as originally enacted, also used this formula in determining unit fines but in the revised version of the section, introduced by CJA 1993, s. 65(1), the wording is omitted and s. 18(2) now refers simply to reflecting the seriousness of the offence.

Associated Offence 9–007
By CJA 1991, s. 31(2) an offence is associated with another on quite straightforward grounds, if—

(a) the offender is convicted of it in the proceedings in which he is convicted of the other offence or (although convicted of it in earlier proceedings) is sentenced for it at the same time as he is sentenced for that offence; or

(b) the offender admits the commission of it in the proceedings in which he is sentenced for the other offence and requests the court to take it into consideration in sentencing him for that offence.

Thus if a sentencer dealing with an offence committed during the operational period of a conditional discharge also opts to impose a sentence for the offence in respect of which the discharge was granted, that earlier offence is an associated offence. If, however, no penalty is imposed for that earlier offence it does not rank as an associated offence (*Godfrey* (1993) 14 Cr. App. R.(S.) 804). Similarly, if a probation order, community service order or combination order is revoked and a fresh sentence is passed for the offence for which the order was made, that offence is "associated" with any fresh offence for which the court is also passing sentence.

9–008   Despite the White Paper's approval and proposed emulation of the erstwhile restrictions governing the use of custody for young offenders under the Criminal Justice Act 1982, s. 1(4A) (as amended by CJA 1988, s. 123), subsequent statutory provision has diluted the impact of the "seriousness" criterion for all age groups of offenders. The 1988 version of the criterion, as interpreted by the Court of Appeal (*e.g. Thompson* (1989) 11 Cr. App. R.(S.) 235, *Davison* (1989) 11 Cr. App. R.(S.) 570), required the court to look individually at each offence which a young person had committed. If none of the offences taken individually was "so serious that a non-custodial sentence cannot be justified" (CJA 1982, s. 1(4A)(c)), the court could not sentence the offender to custody on the grounds that the combined seriousness of their offences justified custody. This interpretation meant that an offender convicted of a number of offences, each of a relatively minor nature, could not be sentenced to custody on the strength of the aggregate of their offending. However, this attracted a degree of criticism that to look at each offence individually was unduly narrow and artificial. The 1991 Act thus modified the position by introducing the "two offence" rule, a compromise allowing the court to consider the combined seriousness of two offences (*i.e.* the two most serious) when determining whether custody was justified or a community sentence warranted. The two offence rule proved short-lived and was amended by CJA 1993, s. 66 to allow the courts to take into account all of the offences for which the offender has been convicted or for which he or she is being dealt with. Thus, for young offenders facing sentence for a number of offences, the clock has been wound back in many respects to a position less advantageous than under the 1982 statutory provision.

9–009   *Aggravating and Mitigating Factors*
The 1991 Act does not specify how aspects of the offence and its surrounding circumstances shall be weighed, with one exception, introduced into the Act by the Criminal Justice Act 1993, s. 66(6), placing on a statutory basis what had already been made clear by the Court of Appeal. By section 29(2) as amended, the court shall treat the fact that an offence was committed while the offender was on bail as an aggravating factor. Note that this is mandatory rather than merely discretionary. The subsection does not differentiate between bail imposed by the police under PACE 1984, Part IV and bail imposed by a court, nor between bail imposed prior to conviction and bail following conviction. In other respects, the court must fall back on conventional

considerations in assessing culpability, assisted by reference to guidance from the Court of Appeal, the *Mode of Trial Guidelines* [1990] 1 W.L.R. 1439 (updated 1995) and the Magistrates' Association Sentencing Guidelines (1992, updated 1993).

(ii) Previous Convictions   **9–010**

One of the most controversial aspects of the 1991 Act as originally enacted was the provision of section 29(1) that:

> "an offence shall not be regarded as more serious for the purposes of any provision of this Part (of the Act) by reason of any previous convictions of the offender or any failure of his to respond to previous sentences."

Many sentencers felt that this provision prevented the taking into account of proper and natural considerations in passing sentence. However, the White Paper (Home Office, 1990, para. 2.18) had sought to emphasise that offenders could properly be dealt with by repeated financial or community penalties and should not receive custodial sentences purely on the basis of some incremented upward drift. The Court of Appeal's comments in *Queen* (1981) 3 Cr. App. R.(S.) 245 were cited with approval:

> "... an offender should not be sentenced for the offences which he has committed in the past and for which he has already been punished. The proper way to look at the matter is to decide a sentence which is appropriate for the offence ... before the court."

Though some critics of the original subsection suggested that the effect **9–011** was to treat the recidivist and the first time offender on an equal footing, it was clear that having few or no previous convictions could be taken into account and be the basis for mitigation under CJA 1991, s.28(1) (see para. 9–014). The Court of Appeal has often indicated that a first time offender is entitled to significant "discount" or reduction in sentence and that there is a progressive loss of such credit in the event of further offending. The principle was well illustrated in *Reynolds* [1983] Crim. L.R. 467, in which two co-offenders convicted of domestic burglary were differentiated on the basis (inter alia) that one had previous convictions for that kind of offence. He received a custodial sentence while his co-offender received a community service order.

The wording of section 29(1) as amended by CJA 1993, s. 66(6) now reads:

> "In considering the seriousness of any offence the court may take into account any previous convictions of the offender or any failure of his to respond to previous sentences."

It is unclear at the time of writing whether this change restores the **9–012** pre-1991 Act position or makes it more easy for persistent minor offenders to receive sentences out of proportion to their present offence. There is certainly evidence that custodial sentences were being imposed routinely upon repeating adult offenders prior to 1991 (*e.g. Bailey* (1988) 10 Cr. App. R.(S.) 231). The real question posed to the sentencer is the extent to which previous offences or "failure to respond" can heighten the seriousness of the present offence. Seriousness remains the crucial consideration. The existence of previous offences may well throw doubt on present claims by the offender that the current offence was an isolated lapse or was committed on a spur of the moment impulse or that they are genuinely remorseful for their behaviour. Previous convictions may point to an element of planning, deliberation or targeting or otherwise disclose aggravating features of the presnt offence. Failure to learn from the experience of earlier prosecutions is not inherently aggravating and may, on the contrary, point to the existence of greater difficulties in coping with life in a conventional way, the absence of legitimate life opportunities and the decreased likelihood of a rational response to deterrent sentencing.

9–013   As regards "failure to respond", this clearly affects "suitability" for a particular community sentence but the relationship with "seriousness" is less apparent. It is unclear whether "failure" means non-compliance (*e.g.* with the requirements of a community order) or re-offending during the course of a previous order or re-offending after the completion of a previous order or sentence. In regard to the latter, what passage of time should elapse after which re-offending should not be regarded as a "failure"? In other words, what do we count as "success"? Presumably re-offending on a lesser scale of seriousness is success of a kind. Should past sentences be regarded differently in terms of the success or failure that should be expected of them? How should we weigh "response" to an earlier custodial sentence, given the official pessimism voiced in the 1990 White Paper about the prospects of rehabilitative success and the recognition of the disadvantages faced by those seeking to resettle on release? For an argument that section 29(1) does not confer wide discretion or permit "cumulative" sentencing see Wasik and von Hirsch (1994) who contend that the subsection is best understood as giving continued statutory force to the principle of progressive loss of mitigation, permitting aggravation of sentence on account of record only in narrowly construed instances. The authors suggest, for instance, that "a sentence shall not be seen as a directive to behave well, valid indefinitely". "The principal relevance of an offender's failure to comply with the requirements of a community sentence should lie elsewhere, in assisting the court to determine, under section 6 of the 1991 Act, the offender's 'suitability' for a particular form of community sentence on a future occasion", and should not bear upon the severity of the sentence.

9–014 *(iii) General Scope for Mitigation*

By CJA 1991, s. 28(1), "nothing ... shall prevent a court from mitigating an offender's sentence by taking into account such matters as, in the opinion of the court, are relevant in mitigation of sentence". This provision gives wide discretionary scope to take account of any factor which the court views as material and relevant. This clearly enables the sentencer to go beyond the circumstances of the offence to encompass other matters in the offender's circumstances and background, arising both before and after the offence itself, and including the merits and attractions of any proposals for dealing with the offender in a constructive way as put forward, for example in a pre-sentence report. The 1991 Act does not offer any pointers as to what should be considered relevant. The following factors are conventionally considered:

(a) early admission of offence and co-operation with the police;   **9–015**

(b) age;

(c) state of health/exceptional strain or adversity prior to offence;

(d) meritorious conduct in another sphere of life;

(e) educational/employment/sporting record and prospects;

(f) adverse effects of prosecution and prospective sentence on third parties, particularly the family of the offender;

(g) "natural" punishment suffered by the offender as a result of the offence or prosecution;

(h) extent of remorse and any attempt to make good the harm or loss caused;

(i) attempts by the offender to change their lifestyle and habits since the offence;

(j) the likely adverse effects upon the offender of a custodial sentence;

(k) previous good character.

As made clear in *Cox* [1993] 1 W.L.R. 188:   **9–016**

> "Although an offender may qualify for a custodial sentence by virtue of CJA 1991, s. 1(2), the court is still required to consider whether such a sentence is appropriate having regard to the mitigating factors available and relevant to the offender, as opposed to such factors as are relevant to the offence."

In *Cox*, a sentence of four months detention imposed upon an 18 year old offender who pleaded guilty to reckless driving of a motor cycle was quashed in favour of a probation order in the light of his age, antecedent history and the attractions of the proposals in the pre-sentence report. By the same reasoning, section 28(1) could permit sentence to be mitigated from a starting point of a community sentence to a financial penalty or a discharge. What limits are there to the scope for section 28(1) considerations to mitigate? Some clues are provided by the decisions of the Court of Appeal following two recent referrals by the Attorney-General on grounds of undue lenience of sentence.

In *Attorney-General's Reference No. 8 of 1992* (1993) 14 Cr. App.   **9–017**

R.(S.) 739 the Court of Appeal overturned a probation order imposed on a young offender for manslaughter by stabbing during a street argument and held that a substantial custodial sentence is essential in such cases, despite various mitigating circumstances arising from the defendant's youth, his previous good character, as well as an element of self-defence. In *Attorney-General's Reference No. 3 of 1993* [1993] Crim. L.R. 472 the Court overturned a supervision order with an additional requirement of a specified activities programme, imposed on a 15 year old youth for rape and indecent assault of a girl of the same age, and imposed a sentence of CYPA 1933, s. 53(2) detention, despite the offender's previous good character and family background, his educational prospects, the strong proposals for a community sentence in the pre-sentence report and the likelihood that he would be exposed to criminal influences while in custody. In both cases a non-custodial sentence "was simply not tenable", irrespective of the section 28(1) considerations, because of the very serious nature of the offences. Similarly, in *Attorney-General's Reference No. 13 of 1993* [1993] Crim. L.R. 892, the Court of Appeal felt under a duty to impose a custodial sentence for unlawful sexual intercourse with a very young girl and that mitigation did not justify a probation order (see para. 23–041). In *Baxter* (1994) 15 Cr. App. R.(S.) 609, (outlined at para. 24–051), the Court of Appeal declined an invitation to make a supervision order for an offence of buggery committed without force or bribery and upheld sentence of two years

9–018 section 53(2) detention.

(iv) Totality of Sentence

CJA 1991, s. 28(2) seeks to embody in statute the principle that the court should consider any penalty it proposes in the light of the overall sentence it intends to pass.

> "Without prejudice to the generality of s. 28(1), nothing … shall prevent a court
>
> (a) from mitigating any penalty included in an offender's sentence by taking into account any other penalty included in that sentence; or
>
> (b) in a case of an offender who is convicted of one or more other offences, from mitigating his sentence by applying any rule of law as to the totality of sentences."

This is a discretionary invitation rather than a requirement. The effect is to enable the sentencer to consider the overall effect of different penalties within a single sentence or of different sentences for offences dealt with on the same occasion, lest otherwise the combined impact proves disproportionate to the overall gravity of the offender's behaviour.

(v) Guilty Plea

It has long been a principle of sentencing that a plea of guilty is a mitigating factor, normally entitling the defendant to a "discount" in sentence of between one-quarter and one-third, depending on the strength of the evidence against the defendant and the promptness of plea. This has been in recognition of the defendant's remorse or at least a preparedness to accept responsibility, and also the time and expense saved. Previously without statutory recognition except as a factor within CJA 1991, s.28(1), this principle is now given explicit weight (but not mandatory application) by CJPOA 1994, s.48:

"(1) In determining what sentence to pass on an offender who has pleaded guilty to an offence in proceedings before that or another court a court shall take into account—

(a) the stage in the proceedings for the offence at which the offender indicated his intention to plead guilty, and

(b) the circumstances in which this indication was given.

(2) If, as a result of taking into account any matter referred to in subsection (1) above, the court imposes a punishment on the offender which is less severe than the punishment it would otherwise have imposed, it shall state in open court that it has done so."

Note that subsection (1) turns upon an indication of intention, not upon the moment of plea. See also the discussion at para. 24–005 *et seq.*

Special Considerations for Youth   **9–019**
Though youthful offenders broadly stand to be sentenced according to the same principles and ground-rules that govern adult sentencing, a number of special factors apply:

(i)   the welfare principle

(ii) youth as mitigation

(iii) parental responsibility

(iv) youth and custody.

(i) The Welfare Principle

CYPA 1933, s. 44(1) enshrines a principle that:

"Every court in dealing with a child or young person who is brought before it, either as an offender or otherwise, shall have regard to the welfare of the child or young person, and shall in a proper case take steps for removing him from undesirable surroundings and for securing that proper provision is made for his education and training."

This bold statement of guiding purpose reflects the spirit of the juvenile **9–020** court's dual jurisdiction in delinquency and child protection and has the confident ring of child-saving entrepreneurship (Platt, 1977). What continuing relevance can it have for the new era of youth justice or is it merely a residual or redundant totem of little or no practical bite and significance?

Clearly it should not be confused or considered on a par with the Children Act 1989, s. 1 which makes the child's welfare the paramount consideration when a court determines any question with respect to the upbringing of a child or the administration of a child's property or income. In the criminal jurisdiction, the welfare of the juvenile is an obligatory consideration but not the sole or paramount consideration. If that were so, it would be hard to imagine circumstances in which the court could validly impose custody upon a juvenile.

Secondly, it is clear that the principle of commensurability or proportionality promoted by the 1991 Act cannot be outweighed by welfare-based arguments for heavier intervention seeking to promote the future good and rehabilitation of the offender. Rehabilitation and welfare cannot justify a more substantial or restrictive penalty than is commensurate with the seriousness of the offence. Now that the court no longer has the power to make a "criminal care order" previously available under CYPA 1969, s. 7(7) but abolished by the Children Act 1989, this risk of rampant welfarism has markedly receded but there is residual scope for the sentencer determined to remove the juvenile from "undesirable surroundings" to make inappropriate use of residential requirements in supervision or probation orders or to retain pious hopes of the training potential of secure training centres or young offender institutions.

9–021   Thirdly, the principle clearly invites the court to depart from commensurability by giving extra weight to mitigating factors such as the negative consequences of a custodial sentence or the need wherever possible to deal constructively with the juvenile. This interpretation of the welfare principle as one of "restraint" is dealt with further in the context of youth as mitigation (see para. 9–023).

Overall, it may be said that section 44 has received no judicial interpretation breathing active life and meaning into its presence as a day-to-day working rule. What is also missing is some explicit bridge between the criminal jurisdiction of the youth court and the family and child jurisdiction of the domestic proceedings court. The youth court (or the Crown Court) could, and some believe should, have been given a power similar to that provided by the Children Act 1989, s. 37 requiring a local authority to undertake an investigation of the juvenile's circumstances and to consider whether they should make an application for a care or supervision order in the civil court, or provide services or assistance for the young person or his family or take any other appropriate action with respect to the juvenile (Children's Society, 1993).

9–022   Section 44(1) can be contrasted with principles adopted by the United Nations in developing international law on the administration of juvenile justice, principally in the Convention on the Rights of the Child, adopted in November 1989 and entering into force in September 1990. The Convention defines a child as anyone under the age of 18 (unless majority is attained earlier under national legislation). The

Convention (article 40) establishes as the aim of child penal justice the entitlement of children to be treated in a manner consistent with:

"the child's age and the desirability of promoting the child's reintegrtion and the child's assuming a constructive role in society."

"Reintegration" is identified as a preferable concept to "rehabilitation" which can be the basis for the removal of children as a heavy-handed form of institutional quarantine. Deprivation of liberty through detention "shall be used only as a measure of last resort and for the shortest appropriate period of time" (article 37(b)). As yet, the Convention does not incorporate any system for individual children to challenge national legislation before the UN Committee on the Rights of the Child (see van Bueren, 1992).

(ii) Youth as Mitigation   9–023

To what extent should youth be treated as an intrinsic mitigating factor? Children and young persons have some degree of built-in protection from the full severity of adult sentencing by being subject to a distinctive spectrum of penalties, either peculiar to their age such as the attendance centre or modified versions of adult penalties. But there is a broad expectation that the courts should also deal less severely with the young. As Walker (1985, 51) has remarked, the underlying reasoning is hardly ever made clear. The rationale appears to draw upon the following considerations, some of which relate to moral culpability and some to the impact of penalty.

Reduced Culpability   9–024

*   The young are not so culpable because they have not had the experience and have not acquired the capacity to realise as fully as adults the consequences of their actions for themselves or others. Their ability to appreciate the pain and distress they are causing to others lacks adult capacity for empathy and sensitivity.

*   Young people have less capacity to resist temptation and peer group pressure.

*   The young should be accorded a greater degree of tolerance and latitude to allow for a greater degree of self-expression and experimentation in adolescence. They should be given more scope to learn from their mistakes without undue penalisation or stigma.

*   By reason of their youth, adolescents are more likely to be able to claim credit for previous good character or the absence of serious offending in their records.

*   Young people tend to have less stake in society with reduced benefits and recognition and thus their communal liabilities and

sense of responsibility or obligation should be correspondingly reduced.

* Young people appearing before the courts have often been subject to poor, disadvantaged or disrupted upbringing, featuring abuse, loss, lack of parental care and example, a negative experience of schooling or ineffective state care, and have not yet had time to distance themselves from such experiences (Hagell and Newburn, 1994; Farringdon and West, 1990 and 1993; Stewart and Stewart, 1993). However, note the comments of the Court of Appeal in *Hart* (1983) 5 Cr. App. R.(S.) 385:

"There are gaps in the social services through which these men have fallen or have thrust themselves. But it is not the task of the courts to remedy those deficiencies. The court must take the offenders ... as they find them."

* With certain crimes, for example more complex regulatory offences, the young person's ability to understand the wrongness of that behaviour is still undeveloped.

9–025 It is not suggested that the juvenile's cognitive abilities, life experience and capacity for discernment should be evaluated by case-by-case individual assessment but that the notion of reduced culpability can be adopted as a broad normative principle that it is appropriate to make less societal demands of youth. This can be viewed as a sliding scale so that, as the young person approaches adulthood, a greater degree of responsibility can be expected of them, possibly analogous with the capacity to take greater personal responsibility for decisions regarding medical treatment (*Gillick v. West Norfolk and Wisbech Area Health Authority and the D.H.S.S.* [1986] A.C. 112)

9–026 *Reduced Penalty*

* Young people's offending is frequently a "passing phase" and reactions to their transient misbehaviour should thus be kept in check in order to avoid counter-productively alienating them from society.

* Punishment which may damage young people's prospects and opportunities should be kept to a minimum and should seek as far as possible to integrate young people and promote their future citizenship.

* Punishment impacts more heavily upon young people, for example two years loss of liberty in the life of an adolescent is of greater significance than the same penalty for an adult. The principle of equal impact (Ashworth 1983, 277) would thus require us to take into account differing sensibilities.

* Young people may be more receptive to learning the error of their ways and thus more open to rehabilitative or constructive

sentencing options. Thus in *Seymour* (1983) 5 Cr. App. R.(S.) 85, May L.J. commented:

"A sentence other than a custodial one is perhaps justified, particularly in the case of a young offender, if there is any indication that he is beginning to realise the extent of his past criminality and the situation to which offences of a similar nature will take him if they are persisted in."

* Young people are more likely to be vulnerable to contaminating influences if exposed to incarcerating or segregating penalties and are thus likely to become more entrenched in offending ways. We must on no account persuade ourselves that custodial sentences are justified to meet a need for "training in a contained environment" (*Hart and Hart* [1984] Crim. L.R. 189).

Though these principles may operate widely but usually implicitly, **9–027** there are clearly instances of serious crime where the court has had to balance "on the one hand the need for punishment, expiation and deterrence and, on the other hand, the interests of the offender, his educational prospects and his future in general" (*Forshaw* (1984) 6 Cr. App. R.(S.) 413). In *Stewart* (1985) 7 Cr. App. R.(S.) 33, Lord Lane C.J. stated:

"There are occasions when the duty of the judge to pass a sentence as short as possible upon a young man must give way to the corresponding duty to see that the public is protected so far as the court can from the activities of a person who has displayed himself to be as merciless and as unrepentant as this appellant had."

Sentence of 12 years youth custody was upheld on a 19 year old who had pleaded guilty to grievous bodily harm with intent (blinding an elderly woman in one eye with a pair of scissors), robbery and malicious wounding, having been previously convicted of stabbing a person in the course of a robbery. As Walker (1985, p. 51) notes, "if violence of a kind regarded as pathological and dangerous is manifested early, this is regarded as especially alarming, and the person may be detained for a very long period."

The recent case of *Powell* (1994) 15 Cr. App. R.(S.) 611, where a 16 year **9–028** old with a previous conviction for indecent assault received six years section 53(2) detention for rape of a 15 year old girl, nicely illustrates the courts' attempts to balance the various considerations posed by the very serious youthful offender. Stating that age was not so much a mitigating factor in such instances and upholding sentence, Macpherson J. commented that the offender:

"must be able to see light at the end of the tunnel but in those circumstances the tunnel should be a long one so that as much attention can be given to this man as is possible during the ensuing years during his teens".

9–029 *(iii) Parental Responsibility*

As the White Paper (Home Office, 1990, Chap. 8) was at pains to point out, the parental context of young offenders' lives can hardly be left out of the reckoning, but how much responsibility should be placed on parents and how does this dovetail with the personal responsibility of the juvenile? The White Paper envisages a sliding scale of parental responsibility between age 10 when parents continue to have "a very real measure of responsibility" for their children up until "the age at which they can begin making their own decisions". By age 16 and 17, young people "are at an indeterminate stage between childhood and adulthood" when they "should begin to take more responsibility for the consequences of their own decisions and actions".

These broad brushstrokes translated into some rather limited practical initiatives:

(a) a revised version of parental responsibility for financial penalties which in fact reduces the scope to hold parents responsible for juveniles aged 16 or over;

(b) a strengthened requirement upon courts to bind over the parents or guardian of offenders aged under 16. Though the White Paper's single big idea on the parental responsibility front, the proposal attracted widespread criticism for its questionable touch with the reality of difficult family circumstances and likely counter-productive consequences (see para. 14–002) but has susbsequently been extended to encompass compliance with a community sentence (see para. 14–003).

9–030 Ultimately it has proved extraordinarily difficult if not futile to devise powers of sentence to promote parental responsibilities. The courts' powers to provide alternative sources of influence through the supervision of social workers and probation officers are properly limited by considerations of seriousness and restriction upon liberty and it is somewhat questionable to what extent a court should regard poor parenting as a mitigating factor under CJA 1991, s. 28(1). In a survey of magistrates and other criminal justice practitioners following implementation of the 1991 Act, the Home Office found that only 40 per cent of magistrates thought that the Act's provisions regarding parental responsibility were working well, compared with 39 per cent who considered that they were working either badly or not at all and five per cent who felt that they had achieved no change. Among other practitioners there was a clear tendency to think that the Act's provisions in this respect were working badly/not at all (Mair and May, 1995). In prospect there is more promise in the duty placed upon local authorities by the Children Act 1989 to take reasonable steps to reduce the need to bring criminal proceedings against children, to encourage children not to commit criminal offences (Sched. 2, para. 7(a)(ii) and (b)) and to provide advice, guidance and counselling for children and their families (Sched. 2, para. 9).

Effective exercise of parental responsibility can be marked in **9–031** mitigation of sentence upon the juvenile. If a parent, out of consideration for their child, believes that it is in the public interest to report the child to the police, this responsible action should be taken into account and credit given in passing sentence, said the Court of Appeal in *Catterall* (1993) 14 Cr. App. R.(S.) 724 where a father had told the police that his son had been abusing drugs, leading to his arrest for possessing and supplying Class A and B drugs, principally ecstasy.

> "The appellant's father cares so much about his future that he was prepared to disclose the offences to the police. He and the appellant's mother are likely to support the appellant's attempts to give up his habit and it was to this end that they brought the position to the notice of the police."

(iv) Youth and Custody: Retreat or Advance?   9–032

A widespread retreat from inappropriate use of custodial sentencing powers for young people was clearly articulated in the White Paper (Home Office, 1990, para. 8.24, *et seq.*). Noting that the number of juveniles under 17 given custodial sentences had fallen by more than 50 per cent since 1981, the Government reported that "there is no evidence that the reduction in the use of custodial sentences has resulted in increases in juvenile crime" and commented that "in all parts of the country there are good, demanding and constructive community programmes for juvenile offenders who need intensive supervision. These programmes are capable of dealing with all but the most serious offenders". The White Paper went so far as to question "whether it is necessary to keep the sentence of detention in a young offender institution for girls under 18", feeling that they could almost always be dealt with in the community, except in the rare instances where CYPA 1933, s. 53 detention is required.

The 1991 Act ultimately opted to treat young males and females equally and raised the minimum age for YOI detention to 15 for boys, placing all 15 to 17 year olds on a common footing. In the wake of this legislation the united voice of the penal reform lobby argued that the minimum age for YOI detention should be raised to 16 (Penal Affairs Consortium, 1992).

> "Holding juveniles in the prison system has no place in a civilised society. It is a recipe for intimidation, criminal contamination and suicide attempts. As a way of reducing crime it is spectacularly ineffective, as over 70 per cent of juveniles are reconvicted within two years of release. The small number of juveniles for whom detention in a secure establishment is necessary should be held in local authority secure accommodation."

Apart from the concern about the custodial experience of bullying, self-harm, and the cultivation of criminal techniques, attention was also drawn to the likelihood of young people becoming isolated, often serving sentence far from home, creating real difficulties for visits from families and the social workers or probation officers who have to plan and supervise their resettlement.

9–033   Within a fortnight of the implementation of the Act, however, the Home Secretary was signalling an intention to increase court powers "to lock up, educate and train" a small number of offenders who are said to be committing a disproportionate number of crimes. Subsequently, in March 1993, plans were announced for a new sentencing power, the secure training order, now enacted in the Criminal Justice and Public Order Act 1994 and detailed in Chapter 19. The same legislation raised the maximum term of detention in a young offender institution (YOI) from 12 months to 24 months and also reduced the minimum age for detention under CYPA 1933, s.53(2) from 14 to 10.

Though sentenced young offenders are held predominantly in separate establishments, the system has difficulties in making safe, positive provision for the under–18s. A Commission of Inquiry into violence in penal institutions for young people (Howard League, 1995) has concluded that "the prison system is unable to protect young people or address the problems of damaged and troubled teenagers". Although sentenced juveniles are supposed to be separated from older youths, the policy is not consistently applied and staff reported that "the younger ones are much calmer with the older ones around". The Commission's report identifies the dangers of bullying, assault, 'taxing', area or racial rivalry and self-harm to which the under–18s are particularly exposed and proposed that legislation should be introduced to end the use of prison custody for all young persons. A survey by the charity Kidscape (1994) of 79 young offenders in two YOI establishments, Onley and Glen Parva, reported that all respondents admitted being involved in bullying in some way, 85 per cent as bullies or bystanders. In 1993–94 there were 907 incidents of deliberate self-harm in Young Offender establishments (House of Commons Parliamentary Answer, January 30, 1995).

The most recent (provisional) figures (House of Commons Parliamentary Answer, March 17, 1995) indicate the rising number of receptions of sentenced 15 year olds into custody 1990–94:

	1990	1991	1992	1993	1994
males	436	509	465	549	709
females	11	12	6	25	31

In 1994, 191 (27 per cent) of male receptions were for theft/handling and 261 (37 per cent) for burglary. Violence or sexual offences constituted 10 per cent of receptions, with robbery adding a further 11 per cent.

9–034   The perceived threat created by young people's offending clearly has the capacity to generate major and rapid swings of policy and the commitment of enormous resources. The most recent government initiative to achieve a renaissance in the use of custodial sentencing, allied to a renewed faith that "prison works", demonstrates how vulnerable juvenile justice sentencing policy is to ideological shifts in disregard of both informed opinion and clear research evidence, as detailed in Chapters 8 and 24.

Chapter 10

Considerations Prior to Sentence

10–001 **Statements by the Offender and Parent(s)**
Where a juvenile offender has been found guilty of an offence in the youth court, whether on a plea of guilty or after trial, the Magistrates' Court (Children and Young Persons) Rules 1992, r. 10(2)(a) require that the juvenile and their parent or guardian, if present, "shall be given the opportunity of making a statement". This should be given irrespective of whether the offender is legally represented.

The scope for direct communication between sentencer and defendant or their parent may well be inhibited by the formality of the occasion but it has been suggested that magistrates find it valuable to gain impressions by this means. Based on her research and observations in juvenile courts, Brown (1991, 72) reports that magistrates seek clues from the appearance and presentation of parents and defendants in the following respects:

10–002 (a) moral character and "decency" of the parent;

(b) evidence of an affective bond between parent and offender;

(c) ability of the parent to control their offspring, *e.g.* whether the parent is over-protective or indulgent, whether care is backed with structure and discipline, whether the parent is able to be assertive towards the child or is "at the end of their tether";

(d) signs of the juvenile's malleability and deference as opposed to a lack of respect for authority.

10–003 The obvious risks are that misleading impressions may be gained based on stereotypical assumptions and limited perceptions. Brown suggests that the defendant and their parent are disadvantaged by their lack of familiarity with court routines and conventions and are likely to confine themselves to "compliant utterances appropriate to the vocabulary of integration and control", avoiding challenge to "the logic of the magistrate or the smooth running of court business", delay in proceedings and embarrassment to the Bench. The potential for good effective dialogue within the conventions and timetable of the court is very difficult to achieve and requires skill, sensitivity and clarity of expression by the Chair.

Previous Cautions 10–004

Among the available information to be taken into consideration by the youth court about the juvenile's "general conduct", in furtherance of MC(C & YP) Rules 1992, r. 10(2)(b), cautions previously administered by the police may be cited. Despite the major role played by cautioning in juvenile justice (see Chapter 2), its legal basis remains non-statutory and consequently somewhat imprecise. The most recent Circular on the cautioning of offenders (HOC 18/1994) contains revised "National Standards for Cautioning" in which Note 6A states:

> "Formal cautions should be cited in court if they are relevant to the offence under consideration. In presenting antecedents, care should be taken to distinguish between cautions and convictions, which should usually be listed on separate sheets of paper."

Argument about the justification for citation has contrasted the importance for magistrates to have the fullest information about young offenders to reach the best decision with doubts about whether a caution constitutes a criminal record to be treated on a par with a previous conviction. It had been suggested (NACRO, 1989) that a caution should not be cited in court because it might have been administered following an inappropriate admission of guilt and may have been given to a child aged under 14 in instances where the *doli incapax* rule would have prevented a finding of guilt in court. NACRO (1992) subsequently concluded that the controversy would be largely resolved by CJA 1991, s. 29(1), as originally worded, greatly reducing the importance attributable to previous cautions. The impact of previous cautions under the new wording of s. 29(1) (para. 9–011), remains to be seen.

Explanation of Proposed Sentence or Order 10–005

A youth court has a duty to explain the manner in which it proposes to deal with the case and the effect of any order to be made and, in regard to the former, must allow opportunity for representations or comment to be made.

Magistrates' Courts (C & YP) Rules 1992, r.11

"(1) Before finally disposing of the case or before remitting the case to another court in pursuance of CYPA 1933, s. 56, the court shall inform the relevant minor and his parent or guardian, if present, or any person assisting him in his case, of the manner in which it proposes to deal with the case and allow any of those persons so informed to make representations; but the relevant minor shall not be informed as aforesaid if the court considers it undesirable so to do.

(2) On making any order, the court shall explain to the relevant minor the general nature and effect of the order unless, in the case of

an order requiring his parent or guardian to enter into a recognisance, it appears to it undesirable so to do."

10–006 Remittal to Another Youth Court
Instead of sentencing a juvenile following conviction, a youth court may instead remit the case to a youth court acting for the place where the offender habitually resides (CYPA 1933, s. 56(1), see para. 12–011). The court must inform the juvenile and their parent(s) and explain its decision in pursuance of the Magistrates Courts (Children and Young Persons) Rules, r. 11 (above). The court receiving the remittal may deal with the offender in any way in which it might have dealt with him if he had been tried and found guilty by that court.

10–007 Age and Sentencing
Given the significance of the offender's age for the court's powers of sentence, it is perhaps surprising that this is not regulated more precisely by statute. A number of ambiguities have had to be resolved on the basis of ad hoc statutory interpretation. As a broad principle, however, a court would not be acting judicially and lawfully if it adjourns a case solely for the purpose of gaining sentencing powers not presently available to it (*Arthur v. Stringer* (1987) 84 Cr. App. R. 361).

(a) Attainment of age 18 years

This affects powers to impose:

(i)   detention under CYPA 1933, s. 53(2) (in the Crown Court);

(ii) detention in a young offender institution for a period exceeding 24 months (in the Crown Court);

(iii) a supervision order;

(iv) fine exceeding £1,000 (in magistrates' courts).

CYPA 1963, s. 29

"Where proceedings in respect to a young person are begun ... for an offence and he attains the age of 18 before the conclusion of the proceedings, the court may deal with the case and make any order which it could have made if he had not attained that age."

10–008 The scope of section 29 appears extremely broad but has been qualified by the decision of the House of Lords in *Islington North Juvenile Court, ex p. Daley* [1983] 1 AC 347 in regard to mode of trial. However, it appears to have clear application where a juvenile pleads guilty or is found guilty while aged under 18 but attains the age of 18 prior to sentence. This interpretation was accepted by the Divisional Court in *St. Albans Juvenile Court, ex p. Godman* [1981] Q.B. 964 and approved in *Lewes Juvenile Court, ex p. Turner* [1984] 149 J.P. 186.

In regard to power to impose a sentence of detention in a young offender institution, the relevant date is the date of conviction (CJA 1982, s. 1A(1)(a)). This provision was considered in *Danga* [1992] Q.B. 476 in respect of a young offender aged 20 at the time of conviction but aged 21 at the time of sentence. The Court of Appeal held that the offender was not eligible to receive a sentence of imprisonment and the proper sentence was therefore detention in a young offender institution. CJA 1982, s. 1B which sets a maximum YOI sentence available for offenders aged 15–17 does not expressly indicate that date of conviction is the relevant date but the Court of Appeal has interpreted this to be the case, thus limiting the powers of the court in respect of a young offender who attained the age of 18 between committal for sentence and appearance for sentence in the Crown Court (*Starkey* (1994) 15 Cr. App. R.(S.) 576. Note, however, that if a court is re-sentencing an offender upon revocation of a community order, it may pass an sentence which it could pass if the offender had just been convicted.

In regard to powers of CYPA 1933, s. 53(2) detention, the relevant date for the purpose of determining the age of the defendant for the purpose of sentence is the date of conviction (*Robinson* [1993] 1 W.L.R. 168).

(b) Attainment of age 16 years   **10–009**

This affects the powers of the court to impose:

(i)   a probation order;

(ii) a community service order;

(iii) a combination order;

(iv) a curfew order;

(v)   binding over of parent or guardian;

(vi) an attendance centre order exceeding 24 hours.

The relevant age in instances (i)–(v) is that of "conviction" (PCCA 1973, ss. 2(1) and 14(1), CJA 1991, ss. 11(1), 12(1) and 58(1)). It seems clear that the date of conviction is the date of the finding of guilt or plea of guilty (*T* [1979] Crim. L.R. 588 where it was held that a juvenile aged 14 when found guilty but aged 15 when the juvenile court purported to commit him to Crown Court with a view to a sentence of borstal training, which was then available for 15 year olds, was not eligible to be dealt with in that manner). Thus a young offender who attains their 16th birthday during an adjournment for a pre-sentence report would not be eligible to receive any of the community orders (i)–(iii) above.

In regard to an attendance centre order exceeding 24 hours, the relevant statutory provision (CJA 1982, s. 17(5)) appears to refer to age at the date of sentence.

(c) Attainment of age 15 years   **10–010**

This primarily affects the power of the court to impose a sentence of detention in a young offender institution. As the relevant age is the date of conviction (CJA 1982, s. 1A(1)(a)), the logic of *Danga* [1992] Q.B. 476 in respect of the upper age limit for this sentence would appear to apply regarding the minimum qualifying age (see also *T* [1979] Crim. L.R. 588).

The age of 15 is also relevant for the purposes of the upper age limit for a secure training order. CJPOA 1994, s. 1(1) makes clear that the young person must be "under 15 years of age" at the time of their conviction.

(d) Attainment of age 12 years

This affects the power to impose a secure training order. CJPOA 1994, s. 1(1) specifies that the child must be not less than 12 at the point of conviction and s. 1(5)(a) qualifies this by stipulating that the child must also have been not less than 12 when the offence was committed.

10–011   DEFERMENT OF SENTENCE

Power to Defer Sentence

Power to defer the passing of sentence following a finding of guilt, under PCCA 1973, s.1, is intended to enable the court which eventually passes sentence to have regard to:

(a)   the offender's conduct after conviction, or

(b)   any change in the offender's circumstances.

The court must be satisfied that, having regard to the nature of the offence and the offender's character and circumstances, deferment would be in the interests of justice.

Length: The date to which sentence is deferred is fixed at the time of deferment and the period of deferment shall not exceed six months (section 1(2)). The offender is released without being bailed.

Consent: The offender must consent to deferment and this should be sought in open court.

10–012   Appropriate Use of Deferment

"(Deferment) may be summarised as an agreement between the court and the defendant that if the defendant does what is expected of him during the deferment, he will not receive the severe sentence—normally one of custody—which the offence might otherwise warrant." *Sentence of the Court* (1990), para. 3.24

Power to defer sentence was recommended by the Advisory Council on the Penal System (ACPS, 1970, Chapter 4) which felt that it would sometimes be advantageous for the court to

"see how in fact the offender does behave. If the offender has shown by his conduct that he genuinely intends to try to make a fresh start, the court can then more readily gauge the right penalty for his offence. Thus the deferment of sentence has the merit of involving sentencers in the reformative effect of the criminal process." (para. 72)

The Council anticipated two distinct categories of cases where power of **10–013** deferment would be helpful:

" (a) to ensure future good conduct or to enable the court to await the happening of an event, *e.g.* the obtaining of specific employment or the return of the offender to his family home; and

(b) to await the outcome of the offender's undertaking to make reparation to his victim." (para. 70)

"We are firmly of the opinion that there is a definite place in the penal code for the deferment of sentence to provide an opportunity for the offender to show good behaviour, to repay money which he has acquired dishonestly, to pay compensation for damage which he has caused maliciously, or to perform some other act which would indicate ability to stay out of trouble." (para. 81)

Deferment is thus a means of allowing the offender additional time to earn specific post-offence mitigation (now under CJA 1991, s. 28(1)), knowing that the court will give due credit if that time is put to good use and expectations are fulfilled. The principal concerns arising from deferment designed to promote "good conduct" have been, firstly, whether the defendant is clear what conduct is expected of him or her and, secondly, whether the desired conduct could be better promoted by other means, for example by a probation order, perhaps containing specific additional requirements.

Following a number of appeals by dissatisfied defendants, coupled **10–014** with research evidence that deferment was being used in some cases simply as a compromise where a court was reluctant to follow the advice given in a probation report (Corden and Nott, 1980) or even as a device to side-step difficult cases, the Lord Chief Justice gave a guideline judgement in *George* [1984] 1 W.L.R. 1082 C.A. Lord Lane C.J. made clear that the expectations of the sentencer should be clearly spelt out at the time of deferment and that deferment should be reserved for cases which cannot be dealt with in any other way.

"In many cases a short probation order may be preferable to a deferment of sentence. Such an order enables the defendant's behaviour to be monitored by the probation officer; it ensures that formal notice of the requirements of the court are given to the defendant.

On the other hand a deferment of sentence will be more appropriate **10–015** where the conduct required of the defendant is not sufficiently specific to be made the subject of a condition imposed as part of a probation order without creating uncertainty in the mind of the probation officer and the defendant as to whether there has been a breach of the order; for example, where the defendant is to make a real effort to find work, or where the sentencer wishes to see whether a change in the defendant's attitude and circumstances, which appears to be a possibility at the time of deferment, does in fact come about. Again, deferment may be the appropriate course where the steps to be taken by the defendant could not of their nature be the subject of a condition, for example where he is to make reparation, or at least demonstrate a real intention and capacity to do so.

These are only examples. It is unnecessary and undesirable to attempt an exhaustive definition of the circumstances in which the procedure should be employed. It is sufficient to say that it should not be adopted without careful consideration of whether the sentencer's intentions could not best be achieved by other means, and that if deferment is decided upon, care must be taken to avoid the risk of misunderstanding and a sense of injustice when the defendant returns before the court."

10–016 *Skelton* [1983] Crim. L.R. 686 C.A. presents an example of circumstances where a short probation order would have been more appropriate. The basis of the deferment was that the offender should fulfil his undertaking to receive voluntary in-patient treatment at a psychiatric hospital. The Court of Appeal said that the purpose of deferment is to see if the offender is capable of behaving himself, not to impose some form of discipline, residence or treatment. There is not, however, a neat dividing line between legitimate and improper expectations during deferment. Take, for example, an offender who is repeatedly offending because of drug dependency and who is now indicating the intention to seek the assistance of a specialist clinic and advisory centre. Though a condition of attendance at such a project could be a requirement of a probation order (under PCCA 1973, Sched. 1A, para. 6), deferment has the advantage of giving the offender the responsibility and incentive to seek help on a flexible and voluntary basis, without involving the project in any formal supervisory responsibilities.

Within the framework of sentencing under CJA 1991, deferment will probably be most appropriate where the offence is of sufficient seriousness to be at least at the threshold of custody but the court is minded to pass a non-custodial sentence if the offender takes advantage of an opportunity which holds real promise of diversion from further offending. Deferment may also give important clues about the suitability of the offender for alternative community sentences.

10–017 **Procedure When Deferring Sentence**
To avoid lack of clarity and subsequent understandable sense of grievance for the defendant, Lord Lane proposed the following guidelines in *George* [1984] 1 W.L.R. 1082:

1.   The court should make it clear to the defendant what particular purposes of deferment it has in mind and what conduct is expected of him or her and what steps, if any, he or she is expected to take during deferment.

2.   It is essential that the deferring court should make a careful note of what has been said to the defendant.

3.   Ideally, the defendant should be given notice in writing of what he or she is expected to do or refrain from doing, so that there can be no doubt in his or her mind.

Sentencing at the End of the Deferment Period   **10–018**

Court Composition: Where possible, the court should have the same composition as the deferring court. If this is not possible, it should be fully appraised of the reasoning of the deferring court (*Gurney* [1974] Crim. L.R. 472). Counsel who appeared for the defendant at the time of deferment should regard themselves as bound to appear when the defendant returns for sentence (*Ryan* [1976] Crim. L.R. 508).

Task: As outlined by Lord Lane C.J. in *George* [1984] 1 W.L.R. 1082:

> "The task of the court which comes to deal with the offender at the expiration of the period of deferment is as follows. First the purpose of the deferment and any requirement imposed by the deferring court must be ascertained. Secondly the court must determine if the defendant has substantially conformed or attempted to conform with the proper expectations of the deferring court, whether with regard to finding a job or as the case may be. If he has, then the defendant may legitimately expect that an immediate custodial sentence will not be imposed. If he has not, then the court should be careful to state with precision in what respects he has failed.
>
> If the court does not set out its reasons in this way, there is a danger, particularly where the sentencing court is differently constituted from the deferring court, that it may appear that the former is disregarding the deferment and is saying that the defendant should have been sentenced to immediate imprisonment by the latter: see *Glossop* [1981] 3 Cr. App. R.(S.) 347."

As Lane C.J. indicates, the offender who conforms to stated expectations can legitimately expect a non-custodial sentence. Mere avoidance of further offending will not, however, suffice. In *Smith* (1976) 64 Cr. App. R. 116, a defendant convicted of burglary was expected to work regularly and reduce his alcohol consumption during deferment. The Court of Appeal upheld his eventual custodial sentence because he had failed to achieve either objective. If the offender has substantially conformed but has failed to meet expectations in some minor respect, a custodial sentence would not be justified.

In *Smith* (1979) 1 Cr. App. R.(S.) 339 the defendant convicted of social **10–019** security fraud had been expected to stay in work, behave sensibly, see a probation officer and try to repay the dishonestly obtained sum. He had failed only in the latter respect and had a good excuse for the default. His eventual custodial sentence was quashed.

Reports: In deciding whether and to what extent an offender has conformed or complied, a pre-sentence report (or an update on any such report available at the time of deferment) will very probably be sought. To avoid unnecessary delay, this should be requested at the time of deferment.

Delay of Date: A defendant under a deferred sentence should be dealt with as nearly as possible on the due date to which the sentence was deferred (*per* Lord Lane C.J. in *Anderson* (1983) 78 Cr. App. R. 251) but if sentencing takes place on a later date for some exceptional reason the court is not deprived of jurisdiction (see *Ingle* (1974) 59 Cr. App. R. 306 and *Anderson* (1983) 78 Cr. App. R. 251). If delay does occur, this can be reflected in the sentence eventually passed. If the delay is really excessive in any particular case, it is always possible for a judge to grant an absolute discharge: Lane C.J. in *Anderson.*

10–020 *Unresolved Criminal Charges:* Offences allegedly committed during the deferment period which are not resolved by the end of that period should not influence the eventual sentence (*Aquilina* [1990] Crim. L.R. 134). Power to postpone sentence until pending proceedings have been completed should not be exercised "save where there are strong reasons which make it necessary for the judge, before deciding what he is going to do, to know the result of the trial of the other outstanding charges" *per* Roskill L.J. in *Ingle* (1974) 59 Cr. App. R. 306.

No Power to Re-Defer: The court dealing with the offender following a period of deferment does not have the option to defer sentence further (section 1(2)). If, however, that court is a magistrates' court and opts to commit the offender to the Crown Court for sentence, the Crown Court has the power to defer sentence, as if the offender has just been convicted on indictment (s.1(8A)).

Non-Appearance: If the offender does not appear on the date fixed, the court may either issue a summons requiring appearance or a warrant for the offender's arrest (s.1(5)).

10–021 Sentencing Before the End of Period of Deferment
When sentence has been deferred, an offender should not be dealt with prior to the expiry of the deferment period unless the court is empowered to do so by PCCA 1973, s. 1(4) or (4A) following conviction of a subsequent offence, even if that offence was committed prior to deferment. In essence:

(a) The deferring court is entitled to sentence forthwith for the deferment offence following conviction of a subsequent offence anywhere in Great Britain.

(b) Any court in England and Wales sentencing the offender for a subsequent offence may also sentence for the deferment offence, but a magistrates court may not sentence for an offence where sentence was deferred by the Crown Court.

(c) Where the court dealing with the subsequent offence is the Crown Court, and the deferment court was a magistrates court, the Crown Court has only the same powers as a magistrates' court.

Notice of Conviction Before Expiry of Deferment Period   **10–022**
Where a magistrates court convicts an offender of a subsequent offence during the currency of a period of deferment, the clerk of the court shall give notice of the conviction to the clerk of the magistrates court which deferred sentence or to the appropriate officer of the Crown Court, as the case may be (Magistrates' Courts Rules 1981, r. 27).

Chapter 11

Reports for the Court

PRE-SENTENCE REPORTS

11–001 Duty to Prepare Reports
PCCA 1973, Sched. 3, para. 8(1) places probation officers under a general
duty:

> "to inquire, in accordance with any directions of the court into the
> circumstances or home surroundings of any person and to make
> reports on such matters with a view to assisting the court in
> determining the most suitable method of dealing with his case."

Local authority social workers are placed under a similar duty in regard
to children and young persons by CYPA 1969, s. 9. Section 9(1) places
the local authority under a duty, where a juvenile is facing prosecution:

> "to make such investigations and provide the court ... with such
> information relating to the home surroundings, school record,
> health and character of the (juvenile) ... as appear to the authority
> likely to assist the court."

This duty is qualified by the rider "unless of the opinion that it is
unnecessary to do so". However, section 9(2) specifies that if the court
requests the authority to make investigations and provide information,
then the authority has a duty to comply with that request. CYPA 1969,
s. 34(3) provides that if the juvenile has reached the age specified by the
Secretary of State (designated as 13 by S.I. 1970, No. 1882) and the
authority does not already have information about the juvenile's home
surroundings, then the authority need not make section 9(1)
investigations if there are local arrangements for this information to be
provided by a probation officer. These provisions should now be viewed
in the context of the duty to obtain and consider pre-sentence reports as
required by CJA 1991.

11–002   Local arrangements frequently place emphasis upon partnership and
collective responsibility between the Probation Service and Social
Services in providing reports and advice to courts, in monitoring report
content and proposals and in maximising use of the range of non-
custodial sentencing measures. Thus the report presented at court may
carry the added weight of prior scrutiny and endorsement by a panel
drawn from both agencies, especially where the young offender is

132

considered at risk of a custodial sentence. In some cases multidisciplinary juvenile justice teams have been formed to specialise in statutory responsibilities for young offenders, undertaking all agency duties that would otherwise be divided between Probation and Social Services.

It should be noted that probation officers and social workers are responsible only to the court, and solicitors representing defendants should not make direct requests to those agencies for reports upon their clients. Any such requests should be made to the court (*Adams* [1970] Crim. L.R. 693).

Duty to Consider Reports **11-003**

The Magistrates' Courts (Children and Young Persons) Rules 1992, r. 10(2)(b) places a broad requirement upon youth courts, following a finding of guilt, to take into consideration:

> "all available information as to the general conduct, home surroundings, school record and medical history of the relevant minor and, in particular, shall take into consideration such information as aforesaid which is provided in pursuance of CYPA 1969, s. 9."

If such information is not fully available, the court shall consider the desirability of adjourning the proceedings for such enquiry as may be necessary (r. 10(2)(c)). Note that the court is not placed under a duty to obtain this background information but must heed it if it is available, either because the local authority or the Probation Service has supplied it, or because the court has opted to seek such information. These provisions are thus secondary to the mandatory requirements of CJA 1991.

Within the sentencing framework introduced by CJA 1991, a court must obtain and consider a pre-sentence report before reaching a sentencing decision in four important respects, three in regard to custodial sentences and one in respect of community sentences.

Custodial Sentences **11-004**

A pre-sentence report is required (s. 3(1)):

(a) Before forming the opinion that an offence is so serious that only a custodial sentence can be justified for it.

(b) Before forming the opinion in regard to a violent or sexual offence that only a custodial sentence would be adequate to protect the public from serious harm from the offender.

(c) In regard to offences where the court has formed either opinion (a) or (b), before determining the length of sentence commensurate with the seriousness of the offence or, in regard to a violent or sexual offence, before determining whether a longer sentence than is commensurate with the seriousness of the offence is necessary to protect the public from serious harm from the offender and, if so, for how long.

Note that a custodial sentence on grounds of the offender's refusal to give consent to a community sentence proposed by the court requiring that consent (CJA 1991, s. 1(3)) may be imposed without the necessity of a pre-sentence report (*Meredith* [1994] Crim. L.R. 142), though a report is very likely to be obtained in enabling the court to propose the community sentence to which consent is declined.

11–005 *Sentencing without a Report or with a Previous Report*
CJA 1991, s. 3(2), as amended by CJPOA 1994, Sched. 9, para. 39, empowers a court dealing with a defendant aged 18 or more to proceed to sentence without a pre-sentence report if of the opinion that it is unnecessary to obtain one. For younger defendants a special compromise applies (section 3(2A)).

Criminal Justice Act 1991, s. 3

"(2A) In the case of an offender under the age of 18 years, save where the offence or any other offence associated with it is triable only on indictment, the court shall not form such an opinion as is mentioned in subsection (2) above or subsection (4A) below unless there exists a previous pre-sentence report obtained in respect of the offender and the court has had regard to the information contained in that report, or, if there is more than one such report, the most recent report."

11–006 The court may thus proceed to sentence without a report where the offence or any other associated offence is triable only on indictment, if the court is of the opinion that it is unnecessary to obtain a report. This is intended to give the Crown Court the discretion to proceed without a report in very serious cases where a custodial sentence is inevitable, but it appears also to apply where a youth court is dealing with more serious offences, either one to which CYPA 1933, s. 53 does not apply (*e.g.* threat to kill, riot, attempted sexual intercourse with a girl under 13, certain offences of buggery, causing death by dangerous driving, perjury), or with a section 53(2) offence which it has opted to deal with summarily.

11–007 It seems highly unlikely that a youth court dealing with such matters would decide that a report is unnecessary. When a court is dealing with a child or young person for an either way or summary offence, the implication of section 3(2A) is that any report can serve the purpose of informing the sentencing decision, irrespective of its out-datedness or its relevance to the offence for which the juvenile has now been convicted. It is difficult to see how a past report prepared specifically for a different sentencing occasion can be reliable in understanding the young offender's current offence, their current circumstances, their response to the sentence which was passed on the earlier occasion or the current options available to the court. Changes can occur rapidly in the lives and attitudes of adolescents and also within the range of non-custodial options available under local inter-agency provisions for young offenders (Stone, 1994a). Courts may thus prefer to seek up-to-date reports as a matter of good practice even if this is no longer a formal requirement.

In the most recent relevant case on the importance of a report, **11–008** *Massheder* (1983) 5 Cr. App. R.(S.) 442, the Crown Court judge had imposed a sentence of 18 months detention under section 53(2) on a boy aged 15 for arson, without the benefit of a report, on the grounds that the offence was very serious and beyond anything in the nature of probation and because the Social Services Department requested to provide a report had not done so because of an industrial dispute. The Court of Appeal stated that a report was necessary in a case of this nature, "to give help and balance to the consideration of all available courses open to the court ... Without a report it is impossible to say categorically that this was not a case for a supervision order". A supervision order for two years was substituted. The fact that the judge had originally sought a report unsuccessfully implied that a report was considered "necessary". If a court gives indication that it would ideally have liked more information about the offender before passing sentence, this could well be incompatible with a conclusion that a report is "unnecessary".

Reports on Appeal **11–009**
CJA 1991, s. 3(4A), also introduced by CJPOA 1994, governs procedure on appeal. Though a custodial sentence imposed on grounds of the seriousness of the offence or the protection of the public from serious harm, without the benefit of a pre-sentence report, is not invalidated by that omission, a court hearing an appeal against such a sentence should ordinarily obtain and consider such a report (section 3(4)). Section 3(4A) provides that the appeal court need not obtain and consider such a report if of the opinion either that the court below was justified in its opinion that a report was unnecessary or, even if the court below was not so justified, that a report is nevertheless unnecessary. Thus if a youth court dealing with an either way offence passes a sentence of detention in a young offender institution without cosidering a pre-sentence report, it would be open to the Crown Court to deal with an appeal against sentence with the benefit only of a report prepared for an earlier sentencing occasion.

Community Sentences **11–010**
A pre-sentence report is required before forming an opinion as to the suitability for the offender of one or more of the following orders, whether for an offence triable only on indictment or otherwise (s.7(3)):

(i)   a probation order which includes additional requirements under PCCA 1973, Sched. 1A;

(ii) a community service order;

(iii) a combination order;

(iv) a supervision order which includes additional requirements under CYPA 1969, ss. 12, 12A, 12B, or 12C.

Before making a curfew order, a court is not required to consider a pre-sentence report but must obtain and consider information about the place proposed to be specified in the order, including information as to the attitude of persons likely to be affected by the enforced presence of the offender. It is unclear yet whether such advice to courts will be provided by probation and social services or by private curfew enforcement agencies.

11–011 *Sentencing without a Report or with a Previous Report*
Provisions similar to those now existing in regard to custodial sentencing apply to community sentences so that a court dealing with an adult defendant can dispense with a pre-sentence report if of the opinion that it is unnecessary to obtain one (CJA 1991, s. 7(3A)). A special compromise applies to younger defendants in regard to either way and summary offences (section 7(3B)).

Criminal Justice Act 1991, s. 7

"(3B) In the case of an offender under the age of 18 years, save where the offence or any other offence associated with it is triable only on indictment, the court shall not form such an opinion as is mentioned in subsection (3A) above or subsection (5) below unless there exists a previous pre-sentence report obtained in respect of the offender and the court has had regard to the information contained in that report, or, if there is more than one such report, the most recent report."

The comments above relating to sentencing of juveniles to custody without the benefit of a pre-sentence report applies equally in the context of community sentences.

11–012 *Reports on Appeal*
CJA 1991, s. 7(5), also introduced by CJPOA 1994, governs procedure on appeal. Though a specifically community sentence passed without the benefit of a pre-sentence report is not invalidated by that omission, a court hearing an appeal against such a sentence should ordinarily obtain and consider such a report (section 7(4)). Section 7(5) provides that the appeal court need not obtain and consider a report if of the opinion either that the court below was justified in its opinion that a report was unnecessary or, even if the court below was not so justified, that a report is nevertheless unnecessary.

11–013 **Mentally Disordered Offenders**
CJA 1991, s. 4(3)(a) mentions consideration of a pre-sentence report as one source which the court may use in fulfilling the requirement to

consider information relating to the mental condition of an offender who is or appears to be mentally disordered, before passing a custodial sentence on such an offender, whether for an offence triable only on indictment or otherwise. There is no general requirement that a pre-sentence report shall be obtained before passing sentence on a mentally disordered offender but section 4(1) requires consideration of a medical report before passing a custodial sentence upon an offender who is or appears to be mentally disordered (see para. 11–043).

Pre-Sentence Report Defined   **11–014**
A pre-sentence report, the successor to the social inquiry report under earlier legislation, is defined by the 1991 Act, s. 3(5) as:

"a report in writing which—

(a)   with a view to assisting the court in determining the most suitable method of dealing with an offender, is made or submitted by a probation officer or by a social worker of a local authority Social Services Department, and

(b)   contains information as to such matters, presented in such manner, as may be prescribed by rules made by the Secretary of State."

Within the definition it should be noted "it is for the trial judge (or the magistrates) to decide whether the report actually available to the court is adequate for sentencing purposes and constitutes proper compliance with the statute" (Lord Taylor C.J. in *Okinikan* [1993] 1 W.L.R. 173). Lord Taylor went on to state:

"Provided that the report ... gives appropriate information about the offender in relation to the offences which bring him before the court, the judge is not obliged to ensure that every detail of information put before him by counsel is checked and confirmed in a further pre-sentence report or by way of an addendum. If he considers that a further written report is required to confirm further information, he may, of course, adjourn the case, but he is not obliged to do so."

It is not necessary for the report to have addressed the particular order that the court may have in mind. The Act does not prevent oral information or opinion being offered to supplement a written report.
    Though the Home Secretary is empowered by section 3(5)(b) to make **11–015** rules regulating the presentation of reports, no rules have yet been made. Instead, the *National Standard for Pre-Sentence Reports* (revised 1995) covers the preparation and content of pre-sentence reports. The revised version (Home Office, 1995a) includes the following general requirements:

*   whenever a case is adjourned for a report, the report should be allocated immediately and an appointment date with the report writer should be set as soon as possible and in any event within

two working days, to enable the preparation to be undertaken without delay;

* all reports must be prepared within a maximum of 15 working days;

* where adjournment involves a custodial remand, the report should be prepared as expeditiously as possible; in the Crown Court a report should be prepared whenever possible on the day of request, to avoid the necessity of such a remand.

11–016 As a general principle, where a PSR is being prepared on a child or young person:

> "the report writer must take into account section 44 of the Children and Young Persons Act 1933 which requires the court to have regard for the welfare of the individual. The United Nations Convention on the Rights of the Child, to which the United Kingdom is a signatory, also requires that in all actions concerning children, *i.e.* those aged below 18 years, in courts of law the best interests of the child shall be the primary consideration. The report writer should therefore take account of the age of the young offender, his or her family background and educational circumstances." (para. 35)

It may be desirable for the parent (or person with parental responsibility) to be interviewed as well as the offender (para. 38), in which case the parent (or PR holder) should be offered at least two opportunities for an appointment to discuss the case (para. 5). The introduction to the report should indicate whether the parent has been interviewed and whether s/he has seen the report (para. 11). The section of the report addressing "relevant information about the offender" should indicate:

> whether or not any positive action has been taken by the offender (or on behalf of a young offender by the parents or local authority) since the offence was committed. (para. 21)

This is amplified by paragraph 38:

> "A PSR written on a child or young person must also take account of any care plan prepared for that individual under the Children Act 1989 and must address the child or young person's relationship with his/her parent(s) or person(s) with parental responsibility and the degree to which they are responsible for the child or young person and should be involved in any supervision."

For a more detailed analysis of the revised *Standard* as it affects pre-sentence reports, see Stone (1995b).

Adjournment for Reports 11–017

Adjournment Period

Magistrates Courts Act 1980, s. 10

"(3) A magistrates' court may, for the purpose of enabling inquiries to be made or of determining the most suitable method of dealing with the case, exercise its power to adjourn after convicting the accused and before sentencing him or otherwise dealing with him; but, if it does so, the adjournment shall not be for more than four weeks at a time unless the court remands the accused in custody and, where it so remands him, the adjournment shall not be for more than three weeks at a time."

This provision must be read subject to CYPA 1933 s.48(3) which specifies:

"(3) When a youth court has remanded a child or young person for information to be obtained with respect to him, any youth court acting for the same petty sessional division or place—(a) may in his absence extend the period for which he is remanded, so however, that he appears before a court or a justice of the peace at least once in every twenty one days; (b) when the required information has been obtained, may deal with him finally."

This requirement that the defendant must appear in person after no longer an interval than 21 days is likely to be less of a procedural burden now that the *National Standard for Pre-Sentence Reports* (Home Office 1995a, para. 52) requires reports to be prepared "within a maximum of 15 working days unless the court requires otherwise".

If the young person is remanded to local authority accommodation following a finding of guilt, the magistrates' power of remand is limited to a maximum of three weeks. A court is not obliged to sentence at the end of the first such adjournment and may further adjourn, for example if the reports required are not ready. Power of adjournment must be exercised for the purposes specified in section 10(3). Thus magistrates dealing with an offender approaching a birthday should not adjourn in order to delay sentence until the offender has attained a certain age and thus become eligible for sentencing options not currently available. It would also be in excess of jurisdiction to purport to remand the defendant to local authority accommodation or custody ostensibly to obtain a report or other information but in reality for the purpose of punishment or correction. Thus in *Toynbee Hall Juvenile Court Justices, ex p. Joseph* [1939] 3 All E.R. 16 the Divisional Court quashed the remand of a boy aged 16 convicted of travelling by railway without payment of fare where the court had indicated as the reason for remanding him that it was for his own good as he was a liar who had to learn not to defraud the railway.

11–018 *Indicating Sentence Possibilities*
When a court adjourns in order to obtain a pre-sentence report it may wish to give some indication of what issues it considers that the report may assist with. As pre-sentence reports are required by CJA 1991 either in aiding the court to determine whether only a custodial sentence is justified or adequate, or whether certain community orders are suitable for the offender, the court may be able to indicate for which purpose it seeks assistance. Clearly the court is implying by seeking a report that it does not feel that its powers of fine or discharge will be adequate. It can certainly be of assistance to the writers of pre-sentence reports to know if their report should focus primarily upon the offender's suitability for alternative community orders or should address in detail the seriousness of the offence including aggravating and mitigating factors, mitigating factors in the offender's circumstances, the likely impact of a custodial sentence on the offender and significant other people, as well as reviewing possible community penalties which could be more constructive, have some prospect of securing change in the offender and are likely to be completed satisfactorily.

There are two principal reasons why sentencers may be wary of giving an indication of their thinking at the point of requesting reports: they do not wish to make implicit promises about the likely outcome of the case and they may consider that they should not reach any expressed view of the case until they have had the assistance of a report.

11–019 *Implied Promises*
A series of cases prior to CJA 1991 illustrated the principle, first enunciated in *Gillam* (1980) 2 Cr. App. R.(S.) 267, that if the court adjourns for reports in circumstances which justifiably lead the offender to expect that the sentence will be non-custodial, provided that the report proves to be favourable, then the court is bound by the implied promise it has given.

> "When a judge ... purposely postpones sentence so that an alternative to prison can be examined and that alternative is found to be a satisfactory one in all respects, the court ought to adopt the alternative. A feeling of injustice is otherwise aroused." (*per* Watkins L.J. in *Gillam*, p.269)

In *Gillam* the judge asked that the offender's suitability for community service should be assessed. In the parallel case of *Ward* (1982) 4 Cr. App. R.(S.) 103, the adjournment was to allow a period of bail assessment at a probation hostel with a view to a requirement of residence. In *McMurray* (1987) 9 Cr. App. R.(S.) 101, the adjournment was to allow assessment of suitability for attendance at a probation day centre. The fact that the subsequent judge or bench considers a non-custodial sentence to be unacceptably lenient for the offence does not negate the implied promise at the earlier hearing. The *Gillam* principle has been held to bind the Crown Court in dealing with a committal for sentence or an appeal from a magistrates' court (*Rennes* (1985) 7 Cr. App.R.(S.) 343 and *Gutteridge v. DPP* (1987) 9 Cr. App. R.(S.) 279).

The *Gillam* principle depends upon "there having been something in **11–020** the nature of a promise, express or implied, that if a particular proposal is recommended, it will be adopted" (per Croom-Johnson J. in *Moss* (1983) 5 Cr. App. R.(S.) 209). Thus courts became accustomed to using a formula of words designed to avoid tying the hands of the sentencers at the subsequent hearing. In *Horton* (1985) 7 Cr. App. R.(S.) 299 the judge, in requesting a report as then statutorily required before passing a custodial sentence on a young offender aged under 21, stated that he regarded any form of street robbery as extremely serious and thought that a custodial sentence would be the likely conclusion, though not ruling out the possibility that something exceptional in the reports might persuade him that a non-custodial sentence was appropriate. Magistrates have often preferred to seek safety in the expansive phrase "all options are to be considered".

This line of decisions must be viewed in the light of CJA 1991. **11–021** Ashworth, *et al.*, (1992, 36) have commented:

> "Unless the court is free to indicate broad levels of seriousness/ sentence on the basis of the information available at the time of the request, then there is a real risk that the framework envisaged by the Act will be placed in jeopardy."

Sentencers may consider, however, that they are entitled to see the report before they reach any view, at least as regards whether the offence merits a custodial sentence. It has been suggested that magistrates should give some guidance as to why they are asking for a report, that these observations should be recorded by the clerk and that the following form of words should be adopted:

> "On what we have heard so far, we are considering a community sentence/custodial sentence. We must point out that the magistrates who deal with your case will not be bound by our view or any suggestion in the report about how your case should be dealt with." (Magistrates' Association, *et al.*, 1994)

It is clear from *Woodlin* [1994] Crim. L.R. 72, *Renan* [1994] Crim. L.R. **11–022** 379 and *Chamberlin* [1995] Crim. L.R. 85 that the *Gillam* principle still applies where the court on adjourning for a pre-sentence report gives a positive indication or uses words which create a justifiable expectation that a favourable report would lead to a non-custodial sentence. However, where a court adjourns for a report, there is no obligation to give a specific warning that a custodial sentence remains a possibility. While it may be desirable practice to give such a warning, mere failure to warn, even if granting bail in the interim, does not in itself justify an expectation of a non-custodial sentence. The Court of Appeal in *Renan* made clear that "Silence by the judge ... should never be taken as an indication that a non-custodial sentence will be considered appropriate" and also indicated that the defence advocate has a duty to ensure that the defendant understands the position.

11-023 *PSRs and Bail*
In cases where the court requires a pre-sentence report before deciding the appropriate sentence, the normal practice should be to grant bail unless there are exceptional reasons for denying bail. The Bail Act 1976, Sched. 1, Part I, para. 7 provides that an offender convicted of an imprisonable offence need not be granted bail where his or her case is adjourned for inquiries or a report "if it appears to the court that it would be impracticable to complete the inquiries or make the report without keeping the defendant in custody". For a child or young person under the age of 17, remand will be to local authority accommodation under the provisions of CYPA 1969, s. 23(1), unless the offender falls within the transitory provisions of CJA 1991, s. 62 (see para. 6–020 *et seq.*).

If it is considered that the offender will not voluntarily attend appointments with a probation officer or social worker, the court may consider imposing a condition of bail under the Bail Act 1976, s. 3(6)(d) to comply with such requirements as appear to the court to be necessary to secure that:

"... he makes himself available for the purpose of enabling inquiries or a report to be made to assist the court in dealing with him for the offence."

This power is qualified by the restriction contained in Sched. 1 Pt. I para. 8(1) that no condition of this nature shall be made unless it appears to the court:

"that it is necessary to impose it to enable inquiries or a report to be made into the defendant's physical or mental condition."

It is not clear to what extent the issue of "physical or mental condition" narrows the scope for use of such a bail condition. Clearly, pre-sentence reports do not necessarily address such considerations and it appears that the use of such a bail condition would only be appropriate where some medical, psychiatric or psychological dimension of the offender is in issue, *e.g.* the offender's dependency on alcohol or drugs.

11-024 Refusal of bail or the granting of bail upon a condition of co-operation with the making of reports highlight the question of the offender's willingness to be the subject of a report. The 1991 Act makes no mention of the offender's consent. The *National Standard* (1995, para. 4) specifies that if an offender withholds consent to the preparation of a report, "the report writer remains under a duty to produce the most useful report possible using the information available." Realistically, a report cannot be prepared without the offender's active participation and yet some offenders may consider that a report may be irrelevant to their sentencing prospects or may even worsen their jeopardy. Failure to co-operate with the report preparation may, of course, mean that the offender cannot be considered suitable for certain community sentences and may also indicate unwillingness to consent to a community order requiring consent, thus triggering consideration of a custodial sentence under CJA 1991, s. 1(3). In most instances, initial refusals to co-operate will be resolved when the offender has received legal advice but the offender's ultimate right to decline should be respected. Refusal to co-operate with the making of a report is not an aggravating feature but may well diminish the effect of a guilty plea or any mitigation such as remorse offered on the defendant's behalf (*Moriarty* (1993) 14 Cr. App. R.(S.) 575).

Access to Reports

11–025

The juvenile's opportunity to receive a copy of the report or to be made aware of its contents depends upon which court is exercising jurisdiction.

In the youth court, the Magistrates' Courts (Children and Young Persons) Rules 1992, rule 10 specifies as follows:

"(3) The court shall arrange for copies of any written report before the court to be made available to—

(a)   the legal representative, if any, of the relevant minor,

(b)   any parent or guardian of the relevant minor who is present at the hearing, and

(c)   the relevant minor, except where the court otherwise directs on the ground that it appears to it impracticable to disclose the report having regard to his age and understanding or undesirable to do so having regard to potential serious harm which might thereby be suffered by him.

(4) In any case in which the relevant minor is not legally represented **11–026** and where a report which has not been made available to him in accordance with a direction under paragraph (3)(c) has been considered without being read aloud in pursuance of paragraph (2)(d) or where he or his parent or guardian has been required to withdraw from the court in pursuance of paragraph (2)(e), then—

(a)   the relevant minor shall be told the substance of any part of the information given to the court bearing on his character or conduct which the court considers to be material to the manner in which the case should be dealt with unless it appears to it impracticable so to do having regard to his age and understanding, and

(b)   the parent or guardian of the relevant minor, if present, shall be told the substance of any part of such information which the court considers to be material as aforesaid and which has reference to his character or conduct or to the character, conduct, home surroundings or health of the relevant minor, and if such a person, having been told the substance of any part of such information, desires to produce further evidence with reference thereto, the court, if it thinks the further evidence would be material, shall adjourn the proceedings for the production thereof and shall, if necessary in the case of a report, require the attendance at the adjourned hearing of the person who made the report."

11–027 In the Crown Court or an adult magistrates' court, PCCA 1973, s. 46(1) states that a copy of any report by a probation officer "shall be given by the court to the offender or to his counsel or solicitor" but this is qualified in regard to juveniles by section 46(2) which states that if the juvenile is unrepresented "a copy of the report need not be given to him but shall be given to his parents or guardian, if present in court". Though the legal obligation to provide copies of reports strictly rests with the court, the provision of reports is more likely to be determined by local understandings and good practice considerations. The offender may well have had the opportunity to go through the contents of the report with the reporter beforehand. Uncertainty is frequently expressed about the retention of reports by defendants or their advocates at the conclusion of the case. This is ultimately a question for the court to decide and resolve, but it would seem perverse to argue that legal representatives are not able to retain a copy in their case papers as part of their responsibility to their client. The main fears of the Probation Service are (a) that solicitors may seek to make improper use of old reports in subsequent proceedings, and (b) that defendants may mislay or discard reports in a way which conflicts with the principles of confidentiality, contrary to the interests not just of defendants themselves but third parties about whom sensitive information may be given. It should be made clear in regard to the former concern that a report is prepared for a specific sentencing occasion only, and reports are customarily headed by a note to this effect.

11–028   Neither the provisions of section 46, the 1992 Rules nor the *National Standard* specify any scope for advance disclosure to advocates. The implication is almost to the contrary because only the court can authorise copies to be given or made available to the defence. It is thus necessary to rely upon local conventions for supplying copies to lawyers prior to the case so that they can consider them with their clients. It is customary for this to be a somewhat rushed exercise at the court on the day of sentencing immediately prior to the case being called.

Given the potential importance of report contents in the evaluation of seriousness and in making proposals for community disposal, this seems an increasingly unsatisfactory arrangement. A formal system of advance disclosure would allow more considered study of reports, the opportunity to speak to the report writer about any aspects which are considered inaccurate or which need clarification, and greater scope to request the writer to attend to be questioned about or to amplify aspects of the report.

Presentation of Reports

A pre-sentence report should be read by the court before it is addressed by the defence advocate (*Kirkham* [1968] Crim. L.R. 210).

Extraneous Use of Information in Reports   **11–030**

Pre-sentence reports are prepared for the purpose of a specific sentencing exercise and are intended to be as frank as necessary to enable the court to make an informed decision about the appropriate sentence. The question may arise whether information contained in a report can be used for tangential purposes. This issue was posed in *Lenihan v. West Yorkshire Metropolitan Police* (1981) 3 Cr. App. R.(S.) 42 where a mother's comments to the probation officer, as contained in the social inquiry report, were relied upon in making the mother responsible for payment of compensation in respect of £200 stolen by her 14 year old daughter. The Divisional Court stated that it was quite wrong for the report to be taken into account in deciding that issue and to do so would inhibit report preparation. Lord Donaldson commented:

> "... the purpose of a social inquiry report is of course to inform the court about all sorts of matters concerning the accused, usually very much for the benefit of the accused, revealing perhaps stresses and strains and difficulties which, while they do not excuse the offence or even wholly explain it, may in the interests of the accused suggest various ways of disposing of the case. Everybody knows that that is the purpose of the social inquiry report. Accordingly people are prepared to talk very frankly with probation officers, and it is in the public interest that they should do so. But if parents are faced with the possibility that, if they frankly say to a probation officer, 'Well, to some extent I was to blame for this offence, although the child was too', they are promptly going to get faced with a compensation order based on that admission made almost certainly under the cloak of confidentiality—certainly in a confidential relationship and made in the interests of the child—I think that in no time at all we shall find that parents are very much less co-operative with probation officers than they are at the moment. That would be contrary to the public interest."

The most common extraneous use of information in a report is by **11–031** prison staff who can find details of an offender's needs and problems useful in planning and supervising a custodial sentence. The *National Standard* (1995, para.42) requires reports to be supplied to the custodial institution in all such instances and this potential disclosure should be drawn to the offender's attention beforehand (para.41).

11–032 OTHER SOCIAL REPORTS

School Reports

CYPA 1969, s. 9 (see para. 11–001) also places a statutory responsibility upon Local Education Authorities (LEAs) to investigate and provide information to courts dealing with children and young persons in criminal proceedings. Section 32(1) of the Education (No. 2) Act 1986 authorises LEAs to request reports for the use of the court from maintained schools within their areas. Section 103(3) of the Education Reform Act 1988 places a similar duty on grant-maintained schools to provide LEAs with the information they require to carry out their functions. The use of school reports in youth courts, like local authority reports, is regulated by the Magistrates' Courts (Children and Young Persons) Rules 1992, s. 10(2)(b) which requires the court after a finding of guilt to

> "take into consideration all available information as to the general conduct, home surroundings, school record and medical history of the child or young person as may be necessary to enable it to deal with the case in his best interests and, in particular, to take into consideration such information as aforesaid which is provided in pursuance of CYPA 1969, s. 9".

Prior to the 1991 Act a number of research studies (Ball, 1983; NACRO, 1984; Sumner, *et al.*, 1988; Brown, 1991) had highlighted both the importance attached by magistrates to school reports, given that teachers could be considered to have far more extended and detailed knowledge of juveniles appearing before the courts, and the wide scope of the observations and remarks contained in school reports, often of a very negative or unsubstantiated nature and based on hearsay, supposition, rumour or prediction about the juvenile's behaviour or background.

11–033   With these concerns in mind the Department for Education has sought to promote greater consistency, fairness and good practice by providing guidance in *School Reports to the Courts* (Department for Education, 1992), primarily to ensure that reports "should be comprehensive, unbiased and factual. They should have a primarily educational focus and be specific to the school experience ... In the interests of justice, judgement and opinions should be substantiated" (p. 4). In a more detailed checklist of pointers, the guidance states that reports should: be balanced, describing strengths as well as weaknesses; avoid moral judgements and innuendo; not make unsubstantiated allegations; reflect the fact that the school's knowledge of the juvenile is not comprehensive; disclose any family or health information only on a strictly need-to-know basis; incorporate information from other agencies appropriately and sensitively. Matters relating to the school record are identified:

11–034   *Achievement:* Performance should be related to age and potential and compared with that of other pupils in the class of similar ability. Care should be taken to identify successes as well as failures, and positive as well as negative attributes. Application and motivation are equally important. Where a pupil has a statement of special educational needs which includes a direct reference to education, this should be mentioned in the report. Under the Education (Special Educational Needs) Regulations 1983 rule 11(a) a statement should not be disclosed without the consent of the child's parents, subject to certain exceptions including "on the order of any court for the purposes of any criminal proceedings".

Attendance: This should be factual, recording the actual number of half days attended out of a total possible. A reasonable base period should be taken, *e.g.* two consecutive terms or an academic year. The pupil's record should be set in the context of the normal pattern for the year group in the school.

Behaviour: Report writers should be able to substantiate their judgements and opinions, for example by reference to particularly serious incidents, regular occurrences of misbehaviour, any period of exclusion, temporary or permanent, or time spent in a special unit. The facts should be fairly presented and a moralistic tone avoided. Where teachers hold conflicting views, the report should attempt to provide a balanced picture by drawing attention to them. Appropriate weight should be given to strengths as well as weaknesses. Hearsay comments about behaviour out of school hours should be excluded.

As regards home surroundings, the school report should be restricted to **11–035** information which the school can verify from its own knowledge of the pupil. Relevant factual information on parental attitudes to, and co-operation with the school, including attendance at parents' evenings, ensuring that homework is completed, and co-operating in disciplinary procedures, may be useful. But schools should bear in mind that a seemingly negative or indifferent attitude may not necessarily indicate an uncaring parent. Work demands, coping as a single parent or language difficulties may inhibit parental involvement.

The report writer should ideally be a teacher with current knowledge of the pupil and the guide suggests that advice should be sought from the Education Welfare Service, the School Health Service or an educational psychologist where this would throw helpful light on the pupil's attendance, behaviour or health.

Bearing in mind that the report will be disclosed to the parent and the juvenile's legal representative and, in most cases, to the juvenile, consultation and discussion with the parent and pupil about the report's contents before it is finalised should be regarded as good practice.

The guide offers very sensible advice which should help to avoid the **11–036** submission of irrelevant or unsubstantiated material to sentencers. It is also clear that school reports should not seek to replace pre-sentence reports and that they should not contain sentencing recommendations or proposals. It is anticipated that school reports will complement pre-sentence reports. The possibility of discrepancies between school reports and those submitted by another agency is acknowledged and the advice is given that "it would be helpful to the court if discrepancies could be resolved wherever possible, whilst recognising that school reports are independent documents".

11–037   What the Department for Education guidance does not address is the crucial issue of the validity of submitting a school report to a court dealing with a criminal offence and how educational information should legitimately affect sentencing decisions. While maximum social information may be advantageous to a tribunal seeking to promote the future welfare of the juvenile, the broad requirement of CYPA 1933, s.44 upon the court to have regard to the welfare of the child or young person is now subject to the approach to sentencing introduced by the 1991 Act. This permits the court to mitigate sentence by taking into account such matters as, in the opinion of the court, are relevant in mitigation of sentence. Should juveniles be in a different position from other defendants in having their performance in an area of their lives not directly related to the offence before the court being made subject to a special and separate report simply because of their status as pupils in compulsory state education? If, say, an adult offender is serving in the Armed Forces, would it seem appropriate for the court to receive routinely a report about the individual's absentee rate, work, behaviour and disciplinary record from their commanding officer? If relevant aspects of an adult offender's life should be properly addressed in the pre-sentence report, following whatever consultation seems appropriate in the light of any views expressed by the offender, it is difficult to maintain that a young offender should be in a different position.

11–038   It should be noted that school reports can be sought and considered by the court after the young person has left school, thus making the legitimacy of such information even more questionable. The court may also receive a school report even though a pre-sentence report has not been required. As the Department for Education guidance notes, practice in this regard varies between areas, as does the availability of school reports which, a recent survey suggests, is for the most part—possibly as a result of changes in the management of schools—at a much lower level than magistrates would wish to see (Ball, 1995). The case for reviewing the anomalies of CYPA 1969, s. 9 and for placing juveniles on the same footing as adults, subject simply to pre-sentence report requirements, appears strong and urgent.

11–039   The *National Standard for Pre-Sentence Reports* (1995, para. 37) expects the report writer, in every case where the young offender is of school age, to obtain information from the school, pupil referral unit or local education authority concerning the pupil's attendance, behaviour and performance, for use in the section of the report dealing with relevant information about the offender. "In cases where the court orders additional information from the school this should be attached to the PSR."

Supervision Progress Reports

Under Probation Rules 1984, Rule 38(1) a probation officer

"shall make a report concerning the progress of any person under his supervision to the supervising court or to the court which made the order placing the person under his supervision not being the supervising court, if so requested by either court."

This power, available to both the Crown Court and youth courts, appears rarely exercised but can serve two principal purposes. Firstly, to allow information on the offender's progress under supervision to be supplied to the court in cases where the offender is denying charges or a plea has yet to be taken but it is nevertheless considered helpful to have information to hand in the event of a conviction. A report of this nature would not count as a pre-sentence report for the purposes of CJA 1991, s.3(5). Secondly, a report of this nature provides feed-back to sentencers who may opt to request such a report at the point of sentencing, indicating at what stage or stages of supervision this update would be expected.

MEDICAL AND PSYCHIATRIC REPORTS

Youth Courts   11–040

MCA 1980, s. 30 gives magistrates the power to adjourn a case to enable a medical examination and report to be made if the following conditions are met:

(a) the defendant is charged with an offence punishable, in the case of an adult, with imprisonment on summary conviction;

(b) the court is satisfied that the accused "did the act or made the omission charged" (in other words, the remand may in certain instances be ordered prior to conviction);

(c) the court is of the opinion that inquiry ought to be made into the defendant's physical or mental condition.

The defendant can be remanded in custody (for not more than three weeks at a time) or on bail (also for not more than three bail, it shall be a condition of bail that the defendant co-operates in the preparation of reports (section 30(2)).

Otherwise, magistrates may request medical opinion and adjourn after conviction "for the purpose of enabling inquiries to be made or of determining the most suitable method of dealing with the case", either for not more than four weeks, or for not more than three weeks at a time if the defendant is remanded in custody.

The Mental Health Act 1983, s. 35 makes separate provision for the court to remand a defendant to hospital for a report on his or her mental condition where the following conditions are met:

(a) Either—
  (i) the defendant has been convicted of an offence punishable, in the case of an adult, with imprisonment on summary conviction, or
  (ii) the court is satisfied that the offender "did the act or made the omission charged", or
  (iii) the defendant has consented to the exercise of this power.

11–041   (b) the court is satisfied, on the written or oral evidence of a doctor that the defendant may be suffering from mental illness, psychopathic disorder, severe mental impairment or mental impairment;

      (c) the court is of the opinion that it would be impracticable for a report on the offender's mental condition to be made if the defendant were remanded on bail;

      (d) the court is satisfied on the written or oral evidence of the doctor who would be responsible for making the report (or someone representing the hospital managers) that arrangements have been made for the defendant's admission to hospital within seven days of the date of remand.

Such a remand shall be for not more than 28 days at a time but the defendant may be further remanded, though for no longer than 12 weeks in total. Power of further remand may be exercised in the defendant's absence if he or she is legally represented and the legal representative is given an opportunity to be heard. The court may terminate the remand at any time if it appears appropriate to do so (section 35(7)). The defendant so remanded is entitled to obtain an independent medical report at his or her own expense from a doctor of his or her choice and may apply to the court on the basis of such a report for the remand to hospital to be terminated (section 35(8)).

11–042 The Crown Court
Though no specific provisions govern the obtaining of medical reports by the Crown Court, the Court may exercise its inherent power to adjourn following conviction on indictment or committal for sentence to enable a report to be prepared. The Court has the same powers as magistrates to remand the defendant to hospital for reports under the Mental Health Act 1983, s. 35, with one difference, namely that the Crown Court can also remand an accused person awaiting trial for an offence punishable with imprisonment in the case of an adult (section 35(2)(a)). The Crown Court may not exercise this power in respect of a convicted person if the sentence for the offence is fixed by law (section 35(3)).

Circumstances in which Medical Reports are Necessary   **11–043**
Reports from medical practitioners are required as follows:

(a) *Before passing a custodial sentence*
CJA 1991, s. 4(1) places a general duty upon a court to obtain and consider a medical report upon a defendant "who is or appears to be mentally disordered" before passing a custodial sentence, in any case where CJA 1991, s. 3(1) (imposing a duty to consider a pre-sentence report) applies. By CJA 1991, s. 31(1), "mentally disordered" means suffering from a mental disorder within the meaning of the 1983 Act (*i.e.* mental illness, arrested or incomplete development of mind, psychopathic disorder and any other disorder or disability of mind: MHA 1983, s. 1(2)). A medical report means "a report as to the offender's mental condition made or submitted orally or in writing by a medical practitioner approved under MHA 1983, s. 12" (CJA 1991, s. 4(5)). It does not need to be written and may be an oral report, for example by the court's duty psychiatrist, if such a scheme is in operation. This duty to obtain a report is subject to the caveat in section 4(2) that a court is not bound by section 4(1) if, in all the circumstances, the court is of the opinion that it is unnecessary to obtain a report. The court need not obtain a medical report if the offence or any other associated offence is triable only on indictment and the court is of the opinion that a report is unnecessary (section 3(2) qualifying section 3(1)).

Before passing a custodial sentence on a mentally disordered **11–044** offender for any offence, even one triable only on indictment, the court must consider (section 4(3)):

(a) any information which is before it which relates to the offender's mental condition, whether given in a medical report, a PSR or otherwise; and

(b) the likely effect of such a sentence on that condition and on any treatment which may be available for it.

A medical report is almost certainly the most appropriate way for **11–045** such issues to be addressed, though it may be that a pre-sentence report can convey the conclusions of any psychiatric assessment that has been undertaken.

If the court fails to obtain a medical report where required to do so, the Act provides the familiar safety net that sentence will not thereby be invalidated but, in any appeal against sentence, the court must obtain and consider a medical report (section 4(4)).

(b) *Before making a hospital order, interim hospital order or guardianship order*
Under the Mental Health Act 1983, ss. 37 and 38, the court must be satisfied on the oral or written evidence of two medical practitioners that the offender is suffering from mental disorder

within the meaning of the Act such as to warrant the making of an order. One of the doctors must be a psychiatrist approved by the Home Office (MHA 1983, s. 54(1)) and, in the case of an interim hospital order, one of the doctors must be employed at the hospital where the offender is to be detained. If a medical report is submitted in evidence, a copy must be given to the defence solicitor (section 54(3)(a)). In the unlikely event that the defendant is unrepresented, he or she is not entitled to receive a copy but the gist of the report should be disclosed to the defendant.

11–046   The detailed provisions relating to the requirements, duration, enforcement and discharge of hospital and guardianship orders appropriate in rare instances for mentally disordered juveniles under the Mental Health Act, and supervision and treatment orders under the Criminal Procedure (Insanity) Act 1964 are not outlined in this volume and reference should be made to Stone (1995a).

11–047 (c) *Before making a probation order or supervision order with a requirement of treatment for mental conditions*
Under PCCA 1973, Sched. 1A, para. 5 (para. 18–051), the court must have evidence from a medical practitioner approved for the purpose of MHA 1983, s. 12 that the mental condition of the offender is such as requires and may be susceptible to treatment but is not such as to warrant detention in pursuance of a hospital order. There are similar pre-conditions before a supervision order may be made with a condition of mental treatment under CYPA 1969, s. 12B (para. 17–024).

Chapter 12

Sentencing Juveniles in Adult Courts

Adult Magistrates' Court   12–001

CYPA 1969, s. 7(8) places considerable restrictions on the powers of an adult magistrates' court to deal with a juvenile offender following summary conviction.

CYPA 1969, s. 7

"(8) Without prejudice to the power to remit any case to a youth court which is conferred on a magistrates' court other than a juvenile court by CYPA 1933, s. 56(1), in a case where such a magistrates' court finds a person guilty of an offence and either he is a young person or was a young person when the proceedings in question were begun it shall be the duty of the court to exercise that power unless the court is of the opinion that the case is one which can properly be dealt with by means of—

(a) an order discharging him absolutely or conditionally; or

(b) an order for the payment of a fine; or

(c) an order requiring his parent or guardian to enter into a recognisance to take proper care of him and exercise proper control over him,

with or without any other order that the court has power to make when absolutely or conditionally discharging an offender."

Though section 7(8) refers to a "young person", the Home Secretary has **12–002** used powers of delegated legislation to order that the reference shall be construed as including a child who has attained the age of 10: *Children and Young Persons (Transitional Modifications of Part I) Order* S.I. 1970, No. 1882, art. 4. In cases proceeding by summons, the beginning of proceedings for the purposes of determining whether the offender is a "young person" is the date on which the summons was served on the defendant (*Billericay Justices, ex p. Johnson* [1979] 143 J.P. 697).

The power of fine that the adult court may impose under section 7(8)(b) is subject to the same maximum as may be imposed by a youth court. The principal additional or ancillary orders which may be made at the same time as a discharge are: endorsement of driving licence, disqualification from driving, restitution, forfeiture, compensation, costs.

If the adult court considers that its powers under section 7(8) are insufficient to deal with the case, it must remit the juvenile to a youth court for sentence under CYPA 1933, s. 56(1) (see para. 10–006) and may grant the juvenile bail or direct remand in custody or to local authority care (section 56(3)). It has no power to commit a juvenile aged 15, 16 or 17 direct to Crown Court for sentence under MCA 1980, s. 37 (para. 12–003), even where the adult court believes that a sentence exceeding six months detention is appropriate, though the youth court may exercise that option following remittal.

12–003 The Crown Court

On Committal for Sentence

Juveniles aged 15, 16 or 17 may be committed to the Crown Court for sentence, not under the usual provision for adults contained in MCA 1980, s. 38 but under a special, narrower provision under section 37.

Magistrates' Courts Act 1980, s. 37

"(1) Where a person who is not less than 15 but under 18 years old is convicted by a magistrates' court of an offence punishable on conviction on indictment with a term of imprisonment exceeding six months, then if the court is of opinion that he should be sentenced to a greater term of detention in a young offender institution than it has power to impose, the court may commit him in custody or on bail to the Crown Court for sentence."

In the light of CYPA 1969, s. 7(8) (para. 12–001), this power may only be exercised by a youth court and not by an adult magistrates, court.

12–004   A young person aged 15 or 16 who is committed for sentence and is not granted bail must be remanded to local authority accommodation unless, in the case of males only, the criteria laid down in CYPA 1969, s. 23(5) (the transitory version) are satisfied in which case the court shall remand him to a remand centre, if one is available, or to prison custody. When the transitory provision is replaced in due course, committal for boys as well as girls will be exclusively to local authority accommodation but, in cases when the section 23(5) criteria are satisfied, the court will be able to require the local authority to keep 12–16 year olds in "secure accommodation" (as defined by section 23(12)). Where the young person refused bail is aged 17, remand in custody shall be to a remand centre, if the court has been notified that a centre is available to take receptions from that court, but otherwise to a local prison establishment.

12–005   Power to commit for sentence may be exercised in respect of an offence which could have been committed for trial on indictment under the special provisions of CYPA 1933, s. 53(2) and (3) for "grave crimes". Though there is no direct authority on the use of section 37 powers in such instances, analogy with MCA 1980, s. 38 would suggest that, though committal will usually follow only when new information has been received following the decision to proceed by way of summary trial, the court is not restricted in its discretion and may nevertheless opt to commit for sentence in the absence of such information being disclosed. (*Dover Magistrates' Court, ex p. Pamment* [1994] Crim. L.R. 471 and *North Sefton Magistrates' Court, ex p. Marsh* (1995) 16 Cr.App.R. (S.)401). The use of section 37 powers may increase, following the implementation of the new maximum term for YOI. If a youth court at the time of accepting jurisdiction does not consider that section 53 powers of detention are necessary but subsequently concludes that a YOI sentence in excess of six months for a single offence (or 12 months for two or more offences) is merited, committal under section 37 would seem legitimate whether on the basis of new information or otherwise.

Where section 37 power is exercised, the court may also commit the **12–006** juvenile to the Crown Court to be dealt with for any other offences for which he or she has been convicted which the committing court has jurisdiction to deal with, under the provisions of CJA 1967, s. 56. If a youth court is dealing with a number of offences, one or more of which are committed to the Crown Court, save in exceptional circumstances the youth court should postpone passing sentence in respect of the less serious offences of which it retains jurisdiction pending the outcome of the case before the Crown Court (*Khan, The Times*, February 24, 1994).

Upon committal for sentence, the Crown Court's powers are **12–007** governed by PCCA 1973, s. 42(2).

PCCA 1973, s. 42

"(2) Where an offender is committed by a magistrates' court for sentence under section 37 of the Magistrates' Courts Act 1980 ... the Crown Court shall enquire into the circumstances of the case and shall have power—

(a) subject to CJA 1982, s. 1B(2) to sentence him to a term of detention in a young offender institution not exceeding the maximum term of imprisonment for the offence on conviction on indictment; or

(b) to deal with him in any manner in which the magistrates' court might have dealt with him."

The Crown Court is thus bound by the requirement of CJA 1982, s. 1B(2) **12–008** (as amended by the Criminal Justice and Public Order Act 1994, s. 17) which restricts the maximum term of YOI that can be imposed on 15–17 year olds to 24 months, whether the offender is to be sentenced for one or several offences. Though it has no power to impose detention under

CYPA 1933, s. 53(2), since that requires conviction on indictment, the Crown Court now has significant additional custodial power to deal with young offenders committed for sentence. Prior to the 1994 amendment the only practical advantage to be gained by committal arose where the offender was convicted of a single indictable offence and the youth court was of the opinion that six months YOI was an inadequate term. Some indication of the previously limited use of section 37 committal and the discretion of the Crown Court can be gained from the Table. The numbers committed are now likely to show a modest increase.

12–009   *Sentencing by the Crown Court on s. 37 Committal*

	Total	*Custodial Sentence*		*Non-Custodial Sentence*	
		Number	*%*	*Number*	*%*
1986	64	46	72	18	28
1987	75	42	56	33	44
1988	77	50	65	27	35
1989	45	25	56	20	44
1990	56	33	59	23	41
1991	42	23	55	19	45
1992	41	32	78	9	22

Source: Criminal Statistics, England and Wales, Home Office.

If the Crown Court decides not to impose a sentence of YOI, its powers are limited to those which could have been exercised by the youth court.

12–010 *On Conviction on Indictment*
The Crown Court can exercise all the sentences and orders statutorily provided in dealing with juvenile offenders. The powers available *only* to the Crown Court are as follows:

    (a)   Detention under CYPA 1933, s. 53.

    (b)   Detention in a Young Offender Institution under CJA 1982, s. 1A for a single offence for a period exceeding six months but not exceeding 24 months and for two or more offences for a period exceeding 12 months but not exceeding 24 months.

    (c)   Fine or compensation order without statutory limit.

12–011 *Remittal to the Youth Court*
Though the Crown Court has this breadth of powers, there is a statutory presumption that the Crown Court will remit the case (save an offence of homicide) back to the youth court for sentencing.

CYPA 1933 s. 56

"(1) Any court by or before which a child or young person is found guilty of an offence other than homicide, may, and, if it is not a youth court, shall unless satisfied that it would be undesirable to do so, remit the case to a youth court acting for the place where the offender was committed for trial, or, if he was not committed for trial, to a youth court acting either for the same place as the remitting court or for the place where the offender habitually resides and, where any such case is so remitted, the offender shall be brought before a youth court accordingly, and that court may deal with him in any way in which it might have dealt with him if he had been tried and found guilty by that court.

(3) A court by which an order remitting a case to a youth court is made under this section may give such directions as appear to be necessary with respect to the custody of the offender or for his release on bail until he can be brought before the youth court, and shall cause to be transmitted to the clerk of the youth court a certificate setting out the nature of the offence and stating that the offender has been found guilty thereof, and that the case has been remitted for the purpose of being dealt with under this section."

Upon remittal, the youth court may only exercise the powers available to that court on summary conviction. The offender has a right of appeal against sentence as if convicted by that court but there is no right of appeal against the remission order (section 56(2)).

Interpretation of the discretion given to the Crown Court to retain **12–012** sentencing responsibility for the juvenile offender where it would be "undesirable" to remit the case has varied. In *Holden* (1981) 3 Cr. App. R.(S.) 78, the Court of Appeal held that the Crown Court should remit a juvenile for sentence unless of the opinion that a more severe sentence should be imposed than the lower court had power to impose or, at the opposite extreme, felt that a very lenient disposal such as conditional discharge was appropriate, in which case remittal would unnecessarily prolong the offender's predicament. However, following the changes in the sentencing powers of the juvenile court arising from CJA 1982 which aligned the sentencing powers of the Crown court and juvenile courts to a much greater extent, the Court of Appeal gave further guidance in *Lewis* (1984) 79 Cr. App. R. 94, remarking that "the concept of the juvenile court being the sole proper forum in which to deal with juveniles now seems ... to be out of place". Lord Lane C.J. suggested possible reasons where it would be undesirable to remit, a list which he said should not be viewed as comprehensive:

(a) Where there has been a trial and the presiding judge is better informed as to the facts and circumstance.

(b) Where there are adult and juvenile co-defendants and there would be a risk of unacceptable disparity if the co-defendants are sentenced in different courts on different occasions.

(c) Where remission will cause delay, duplication of proceedings and fruitless expense.

(d) If the case is remitted, appeal against conviction would be to the Court of Appeal, whilst appeal against sentence would be to the Crown Court.

12–013 Lord Lane added that "it may become desirable to remit the case where a report has to be obtained and the judge will be unable to sit when the report becomes available" but thought that this situation should be avoided wherever possible. The effect of this guidance has been to give the Crown Court almost complete scope to justify retention of sentencing responsibility, particularly on ground (c). Thus the apparent presumption of remittal has become, in effect, a working presumption that the Crown Court will retain jurisdiction.

PART IV

Chapter 13

Discharges and Financial Penalties
POWER TO DISCHARGE 13–001

Powers of the Criminal Court Act 1973, s.1A

"(1) Where a court by or before which a person is convicted of an offence (not being an offence the sentence for which is fixed by law) is of opinion, having regard to the circumstances including the nature of the offence and the character of the offender, that it is inexpedient to inflict punishment, the court may make an order either—

(a) discharging him absolutely; or
(b) if the court thinks fit, discharging him subject to the condition that he commits no offence during such period, not exceeding three years from the date of the order, as may be specified in the order.

(3) Before making an order for conditional discharge the court shall explain to the offender in ordinary language that if he commits another offence during the period of conditional discharge he will be liable to be sentenced for the original offence."

A discharge, absolute or conditional, can be combined with the following orders in respect of a single offence: costs; compensation or **13–002** forfeiture under 1973 Act, s. 43 (s.12(4)); disqualification from driving (Road Traffic Act 1988, s.46); restitution (Theft Act 1968, s.28). If an offender is convicted of more than one offence, the imposition of a discharge for one offence does not affect the court's freedom to exercise its full powers of sentence in dealing with the other offences.

In 1993 the percentage of children and young persons sentenced for indictable offences who received an absolute or conditional discharge was as follows, the corresponding 1983 figures being in brackets:

	Males	Females
10–under 14	49 (37)	70 (47)
14–under 18	31 (17)	51 (31)

Source: Criminal Statistics for England and Wales, Home Office.

This disposal was the most frequently used outcome in the juvenile courts, despite fears that an increased use of cautioning could erode the market share of discharge powers. In a NACRO survey (1993) of sentencing in the youth courts in 15 local authority areas in the first six months following implementation of the 1991 Act, discharges were imposed in 38 per cent of the sample of 3005 cases, accounting for 50 per cent of 14 year olds dealt with, 43 per cent of 15 year olds, 35 per cent of 16 year olds and 32 per cent of 17 year olds.

13-003   Absolute Discharge
This is the lightest measure which can be ordered following conviction and implies that the process of prosecution and the effect of conviction is sufficient response to the offence for which it is made.

> "An absolute discharge ... is used where the court ... considers that no further action is required on its part beyond the finding of guilt."
> *The Sentence of the Court* (1990) 4.2

Wasik (1985) has suggested three main justifications for granting an absolute discharge: where the offence is venial; where the offender had low culpability or high motivation but the law does not provide a defence; where the offender has suffered collateral losses or indirect, non-judicial punishment as a result of the offence.

13-004   Conditional Discharge
There is no statutory minimum period of conditional discharge. It is sound practice for the court to explain the effect of a conditional discharge personally and directly to the offender to ensure that the juvenile understands its effect but in exceptional circumstances this may be delegated to the offender's advocate, provided that the court is satisfied that explanation has been given and understood before the order is made (*Wehner* [1977] 1 W.L.R. 1143). PCCA 1973, s. 11 makes provision for a conditional discharge to be made in substitution for a probation order, where it appears that the probation order is no longer appropriate but the continuing validity of this power following CJA 1991 is open to doubt (para. 22–089 *et seq.*). On making a conditional discharge, a court may, if it thinks it expedient for the purpose of the reformation of the offender, allow any person who consents to do so to give security for the good behaviour of the offender (PCCA 1973, s. 12(1)).

13-005   Commission of Further Offences
The commission of a further offence during a period of conditional discharge is commonly referred to as a breach of conditional discharge, though the term "breach" is not used in the relevant statutory provision and may cause confusion with breach of a requirement of a community order. The provisions for dealing with the original offence for which the discharge was ordered are now contained in PCCA 1973, s. 1B, introduced by CJA 1991, s. 8(3) and Sched. I but substantially reproducing the provisions of the now repealed PCCA 1973, s. 8. These provisions are somewhat complex, depending upon which court granted

the discharge and the court before which the offender is subsequently convicted of a fresh offence. The provisions can be conveniently summarised as follows:

(a) If, as is likely to be the most common instance of "breach", the **13–006** offender was conditionally discharged by a youth court and is subsequently convicted of a fresh offence by a youth court acting for the same petty sessions area, the latter court may deal with the offender for the original offence as if it has just convicted the offender of that offence (s. 1B(6)).

(b) If the offender was conditionally discharged by a youth court and is subsequently convicted of a fresh offence by a youth court acting for a different petty sessions area, then the latter court may deal with the offender for the original offence, provided that it obtains the consent of the court which made the order (s. 1B(8)).

(c) If the offender was conditionally discharged by a youth court and is subsequently convicted of a fresh offence by the Crown Court, the Crown Court may deal with the offender for the original offence in any manner in which the lower court could deal with the offender, if it had just convicted the offender of that offence (s. 1B(7)).

(d) If the offender was conditionally discharged by the Crown Court and is subsequently convicted of a fresh offence by a magistrates' court, including a youth court, the lower court may commit the offender, either on bail or in custody/local authority accommodation (depending on eligibility), to be dealt with at the Crown Court (s. 1B(5)).

(e) If the offender was conditionally discharged by the Crown Court **13–007** and is subsequently convicted of a fresh offence by the Crown Court, the Crown Court may deal with the offender for the original offence as if it has just convicted the offender of that offence.

(f) If a juvenile offender was conditionally discharged by a youth court or adult magistrates' court for an offence which, in the case of an adult, is triable only on indictment, any court which subsequently deals afresh with the offender for the original offence after the offender has attained the age of 18 may only exercise such powers as would be available for an "either way" offence being dealt with summarily (s. 1B(9)).

(g) If the offender subject to a conditional discharge is convicted of a fresh offence by a court in any part of Great Britain but is not dealt with at the same time for the original offence, then the offender may be summoned back to the court which made the conditional discharge and, if the terms of the discharge and subsequent conviction are formally proved, the court may deal with the original offence as if the offender has just been convicted of that offence by that court (s. 1B(1)).

In dealing afresh with the original offence, a court exercising its powers under section 1B(6), (7) or (8) may make a fresh conditional discharge, though this is perhaps an unlikely prospect. If a conditional discharge is made in respect of the subsequent offence, the court can still deal afresh with the original offence in any manner it sees fit (*Wilcox Current Sentencing Practice*, L2–1F04).

13–008 Limited Effect of Conviction

PCCA 1973, 1C

"(1) Subject to subsection (2) below ... a conviction of an offence for which an order is made ... discharging the offender absolutely or conditionally shall be deemed not to be a conviction for any purpose other than—

(a)   the purposes of the proceedings in which the order is made and of any subsequent proceedings which may be taken against the offender under the following provisions of this Act; and

(b)   the purposes of CYPA 1969, s. 1(2)(bb).

(2) Where the offender was of or over 18 years of age at the time of his conviction of the offence in question and is subsequently sentenced under this Part of this Act for that offence, subsection (1) above shall cease to apply to the conviction."

13–009 Subsection (1) thus affords the discharged offender a degree of protection from the consequences of having a conviction, limiting its impact primarily to subsequent criminal proceedings and the resulting exposure to being sentenced for the original offence. This protection is normally lost if the offender is convicted of a further offence and is sentenced for the original offence. As a special dispensation for youth, this loss of protection is not incurred if the offender was a juvenile at the time of the original conviction and CJA 1991 extended this advantage to 17 year olds.

FINANCIAL PENALTIES

Juveniles can be ordered to pay fines, compensation and costs in the same way as adults, with some minor differences in regard to the maximum sum that may be levied, in the scope for the court to order that the parent or guardian shall be responsible for payment and in powers of enforcement.

13–010 Powers of Magistrates' Courts to Fine

The power in MCA 1980, s. 32(1) to fine upon summary conviction of an indictable offence is restricted in respect of juveniles by MCA 1980, s.

36. If the adult court would have power to impose a fine exceeding £1,000 for that offence, the amount that may be imposed in respect of a young person under 18 shall not exceed £1,000 (section 36(1)). If the juvenile is aged under 14 and the court could otherwise have imposed a fine exceeding £250, the amount of fine shall not exceed £250 (section 36(2)). The same limitations apply also to fines imposed for summary offences though the maximum that may be imposed upon an adult offender for a summary offence under the general power of MCA 1980, s. 34(3) is the level 3 maximum of £1,000, and thus within the maximum for 14 to 17 year olds.

Powers of the Crown Court to Fine   **13–011**

PCCA 1973, s. 30

"(1) Where a person is convicted on indictment of any offence other than an offence for which the sentence is fixed by law, the court, if not precluded from sentencing the offender by the exercise of some other power ..., may impose a fine in lieu of or in additon to dealing with him in any other way in which the court has power to deal with him, subject however to any enactment ... requiring the offender to be dealt with in a particular way."

There is no statutory limit to the amount of fine which may be imposed by the Crown Court either upon an adult or a juvenile. The only exceptions arise where the Crown Court is dealing with an appeal from the lower court or a breach of a conditional discharge imposed by the lower court. In both cases the lower court's maximum powers apply. The Crown Court's normal duty under PCCA 1973, s. 31(2) when imposing a fine, to make an order fixing the term of detention to be served in default under CJA 1982, s. 9, is not exercisable where the offender is under 18.

Determining the Amount of a Fine   **13–012**

Within the maximum stated, the statutory principles to be applied by a court in fixing the amount of any fine are specified by CJA 1991, s. 18 (as amended by CJA 1993, s. 65):

1. The court shall inquire into the financial circumstances of the offender (s. 18(1));

2. the amount shall be such as, in the opinion of the court, reflects the seriousness of the offence (s. 18(2));

3. the court shall take into account the circumstances of the case including, among other things, the financial circumstances of the offender so far as they are known, or appear, to the court (section 18(3)). Consideration of the offender's financial circumstances can have the effect of both increasing or reducing the amount of the fine (s. 18(5)).

This statutory approach approximates to the principles developed by case law prior to the brief reign of the unit fines system between October 1992 and September 1993.

13–013 *Seriousness of Offence:* The court's assessment of the gravity of the offence will take account of aggravating and mitigating features of the offence, including the financial gain if any to the offender. When imposing fines for a number of offences, the sentencer should consider the total proposed aggregate sentence and ensure that this is proportionate to the totality of offending (as well as being within the offender's capacity to pay). "The total fine imposed should not exceed that appropriate to the criminal conduct seen as a whole" (*The Sentence of the Court 1990*, 5.15). This principle has been developed in case law and is also acknowledged in CJA 1991, s. 28(2)(b). Section 28(2)(a) anticipates that any penalty, including a fine, may be mitigated by taking into account any other penalty included in the sentence. Under section 28(1), the court can mitigate the amount of fine imposed by taking into account any such matters as in its opinion are relevant in mitigation of sentence.

13–014 *Financial Circumstances:* CJA 1991, s. 20(1) empowers a court to make a financial circumstances order with respect to an offender before sentence. This is an order requiring the offender "to give to the court, within such period as may be specified in the order, such a statement of his financial circumstances as the court may require" (section 20(1C)). Failure to comply with such an order without reasonable excuse renders the offender liable to a fine not exceeding level 3 on the standard scale (section 20(2)). Knowingly or recklessly making a false statement or knowingly failing to disclose any material fact in a financial circumstances order also constitutes an offence punishable in the case of an adult by a term of imprisonment not exceeding three months or a fine not exceeding level 4 on the standard scale (section 20(3)). Proceedings for this offence may be commenced at any time within two years of the commission of the offence or six months of the discovery of the offence, whichever is the sooner (section 20(4)). While the fine should be adjusted to take account of the offender's limited means, the Court of Appeal has indicated that a fine should nevertheless represent a "hardship", since "one of the objects of the fine is to remind the offender that what he has done is wrong" (*Olliver* (1989) 11 Cr. App. R.(S.) 10).

13–015   In 1993 the percentage of children and young persons sentenced for indictable offences who received a fine was as follows, the corresponding 1983 figures being in brackets:

	Males	*Females*
10–under 14	5 (17)	6 (23)
14–under 18	11 (34)	12 (37)

Compensation Orders

PCCA 1973, s. 35

"(1) Subject to the provisions of this Part of this Act and to section 40 of the Magistrates' Courts Act 1980 (which imposes a monetary limit on the powers of a magistrates' court under this section), a court by or before which a person is convicted of an offence, instead of or in addition to dealing with him in any other way, may, on application or otherwise, make an order (in this Act referred to as "a compensation order") requiring him to pay compensation for any personal injury, loss or damage resulting from that offence or any other offence which is taken into consideration by the court in determining sentence or to make payments for funeral expenses or bereavement in respect of a death resulting from any such offence, other than a death due to an accident arising out of the presence of a motor vehicle on a road, and a court shall give reasons, on passing sentence, if it does not make such an order in a case where this section empowers it to do so.

(1A) Compensation under subsection (1) above shall be of such amount as the court considers appropriate, having regard to any evidence and to any representations that are made by or on behalf of the accused or the prosecutor.
(2) In the case of an offence under the Theft Act 1968, where the property in question is recovered, any damage to the property occurring while it was out of the owner's possession shall be treated for the purposes of subsection (1) above as having resulted from the offence, however and by whomsoever the damage was caused."

An order may be made even though the injured party has not sought **13–016** compensation and even if there would not be a civil liability to the injured party. MCA 1980, s. 40(1) limits the amount of compensation that may be ordered by a magistrates' court to £5,000 for each offence. Juvenile offenders are subject to the same maximum liability. If the offender asks for other offences to be taken into consideration, the amount ordered by way of compensation for those offences shall not exceed the statutory maximum minus the amount of compensation ordered to be paid in respect of the substantive offence(s). Thus if an offender is convicted of an offence for which compensation of £500 is ordered, the court may only award a maximum of £4,500 in respect of the matters taken into consideration.

A compensation order may be made "instead of or in addition to **13–017** dealing with" the offender in any other way. Though initially introduced as an ancillary order to provide a convenient and speedy means of avoiding the expense of resort to civil litigation and thus not intended to affect the punishment imposed for the offence, PCCA 1973, s. 35 was amended by CJA 1982, s. 67 to allow the compensation order to be a free-standing disposal in its own right. Furthermore, section 35(4A) states that where a court considers it appropriate both to impose a fine and to make a compensation order but the offender has insufficient means to pay both, the court "shall give preference to compensation (though it may impose a fine as well)". This implies that a fine as the punishment of the court should be reduced or even disposed with to enable compensation to be paid.

13–018   The broad principles to be followed in making compensation orders can be summarised thus:

(i) Compensation orders are only appropriate where the case is straightforward and clear, and the amount can be readily and easily ascertained.

(ii) In the event of a failure to agree the amount of the victim's loss, the court should not make an order unless it has received evidence; merely hearing representations is not enough (*Horsham Justices, ex p. Richards* [1985] 1 W.L.R. 986). However, complex inquiries into the scale of loss are not appropriate. The standard of proof required is not specified but it would seem necessary that the court should be satisfied at least on the balance of probabilities that the particular sum is appropriate.

13–019   (iii) Where there has been no loss or damage, *e.g.* property is recovered and there is no evidence of damage, a compensation order should not be made (*Sharkey* [1976] Crim. L.R. 388).

(iv) A compensation order is not precluded by the fact that the offender has made no profit or gain from the offence.

(v) Personal injury or damage includes terror or distress directly occasioned by the offence.

(vi) The order must be precise, making clear which amounts of compensation relate to which offences. The fixing of a "global" figure is inappropriate (*Oddy* [1974] 1 W.L.R. 1212), unless the offences were committed against the same victim (*Warton* [1976] Crim. L.R. 520). Where there are co-defendants, separate orders should be made against each of them (*Grundy* [1974] 1 W.L.R. 139).

13–020   (vii) While there may be good moral grounds for requiring an offender to make good the harm done, a compensation order must be realistic and should not be oppressive in effect. While an order may be appropriately combined with a custodial sentence where the offender is clearly able to pay or has good prospects on release from custody, it is often inappropriate to combine a compensation order with a custodial sentence and it may be wrong in principle for the order to be hanging over the offender's head on release, inhibiting their resettlement and possibly increasing their likelihood of re-offending (see *Parker* [1982] Crim. L.R. 130).

The Offender's Means   **13–021**
In determining whether a compensation order should be made and the amount to be paid, the court must have regard to the means of the offender, "so far as they appear or are known to the court" (section 35(4)). The prosecution is not under a duty to establish the offender's means (*Johnstone* (1982) 4 Cr. App. R.(S.) 141). If the defence mitigates on the basis that the offender will be able to pay substantial compensation, the advocate is obliged to check to ensure that the necessary means exist (*Coughlin* (1984) 6 Cr. App. R.(S.) 102). Co-defendants can properly be required to pay different sums towards compensation if their capacity to pay is different (*Beddow* (1987) 9 Cr. App. R.(S.) 235).

Costs   **13–022**
Juveniles are liable to be ordered to pay such prosecution costs as the court considers "just and reasonable" (Prosecution of Offences Act 1985, s. 18(1)). This liability is subject to the usual limitation that where any fine imposed is for £5 or less, no order for costs should be made "unless, in the particular circumstances of the case, the court considers it right to do so" (section 18(4)). In addition, where a juvenile "is convicted of an offence before a magistrates' court, the amount of any costs ordered to be paid by the accused ... shall not exceed the amount of any fine imposed on him" (section 18(5)).

An order should be made under section 18 where the court is satisfied that the offender has the means and ability to pay (*Practice Direction (Crime: Costs)* [1989] 1 W.L.R. 625). The decision on costs must be viewed in the light of the overall financial orders made by the court (*Nottingham Justices, ex p. Fohmann* (1986) 84 Cr. App. R. 316). The order for costs should not be out of proportion to the overall penalty. Where the offender receives a custodial sentence, an order for costs should not normally be made, given that the offender has no immediate income, but this is a matter for the court's discretion.

Responsibility for Financial Penalties Imposed on Young Offenders   **13–023**

Parents or Guardians

Because juveniles may be without means to meet financial penalties, the parent or guardian may be ordered to pay fines, costs and compensation.

CYPA 1933, s. 55

"(1) Where—

(a) a child or young person is convicted or found guilty of any offence for the commission of which a fine or costs may be imposed or a compensation order may be made under section 35 of the Powers of Criminal Courts Act 1973; and

(b) the court is of the opinion that the case would best be met by the imposition of a fine or costs or the making of such an order, whether with or without any other punishment,

it shall be the duty of the court to order that the fine, compenstion or costs awarded be paid by the parent or guardian of the child or young person instead of by the child or young person himself, unless the court is satisfied—

(i) that the parent or guardian cannot be found; or

(ii) that it would be unreasonable to make an order for payment, having regard to the circumstances of the case."

13–024   Section 55(1A) makes the same provision in regard to a fine imposed under CYPA 1969, s. 15(2A) for failure to comply with a supervision order or under CJA 1991, Sched. 2 for breach of a requirement of a community service order. In the case of a young person who has attained the age of 16, the court has the power to make an order under section 55(1) or (1A), rather than a duty, reflecting the view in *Crime, Justice and Protecting the Public* that young people of 16 or 17 should, in appropriate cases, be considered to be independent and responsible for themselves (Home Office, 1990).

13–025   Despite the statutory duty to order parents of young persons aged under 16 to pay, the power has not been widely used. As the White Paper noted (para. 8.8):

"In 1988, courts ordered parents to pay in only 13 per cent of cases where juveniles were fined and 21 per cent of cases when they received compensation orders ... Some courts may take the view that it is unnecessary to make a formal order requiring parental payment since the parents will pay anyway. The Government considers the imposition on the parents of a formal requirement to pay has an important effect. It brings home to them the reality of the consequences of the children's behaviour and the implications for their own actions."

The questionable nature of this assumption is addressed in regard to the power or duty to bind over parents to ensure their children's behaviour, para. 14–002. In 1993, orders for parents to pay as a percentage of fines or compensation orders imposed on this age group were as follows:

	Males		*Females*	
	Fine	*Compensation*	*Fine*	*Compensation*
10–13 years	25	36	8	27
14–17 years	6	12	6	13
10–17 years	6	14	6	14

Right to be heard: No order should be made requiring a parent or **13–026** guardian to pay the sum in question without giving that parent or guardian an opportunity of being heard, but an order may be made against a parent or guardian who has been required to attend and be heard and fails to do so (section 55(2)).

Unreasonable to make an order: A parent or guardian may satisfy the court that it would be unreasonable to hold them responsible for the financial penalty, for example because they did not have charge or control of the juvenile at the time that the offence was committed or because the offence did not arise out of a failure to exercise due care or control of the juvenile.

Means and circumstances: Where the parent or guardian is required to pay, the amount is determined with reference to the financial circumstances of the parent or guardian, not the juvenile (CJA 1991, s. 57(3)). The lower maximum in respect of juveniles applies, however, whether the juvenile or the parent is required to pay.

Financial circumstances order: Before ordering a parent or guardian to **13–027** be responsible for a financial penalty, the court may make a financial circumstances order with respect to that person, requiring a statement of their financial circumstances to be given to the court. If the parent or guardian fails to comply or otherwise fails to co-operate with the court's inquiry, the court may make such determination of their circumstances as it thinks fit (CJA 1991, s. 18(4)(c)). Failure to comply can also render the parent or guardian liable on summary conviction to a fine not exceeding level 3 on the standard scale (CJA 1991, s. 20(2)). Making a false statement may render the parent or guardian liable to the penalties specified in section 20(3), *i.e.* imprisonment not exceeding three months or a level 4 fine.

Appeal: A parent or guardian made subject to a section 55 order by a magistrates' court may appeal to the Crown Court against the order (section 55(3)). If the order is imposed by the Crown Court, appeal lies to the Court of Appeal as if the parent or guardian had been convicted on indictment and the order were a sentence passed on conviction.

Local Authorities   **13–028**

CYPA 1933 s. 55

"(5) In relation to a child or young person for whom a local authority have parental responsibility and who—

(a) is in their care; or

(b) is provided with accommodation by them in the exercise of any functions (in particular those under the Children Act

1989) which stand referred to their social services committee under the Local Authority Social Services Act 1970,

references in this section to his parent or guardian shall be construed as references to that authority.

In this subsection 'local authority' and 'parental responsibility' have the same meanings as in the Children Act 1989".

The power to order a local authority to pay any financial penalties as a parent arises only where the local authority holds "parental responsibility", as defined by the 1989 Act ("all the rights, duties, powers, responsibilities and authority which by law a parent of a child has in relation to the child and his property": Children Act 1989, s. 3(1)). Parental responsibility is expressly devolved on a local authority in two instances:

(i)   While a care order is in force with respect to the juvenile (CA 1989, s. 33(3));

(ii) while an emergency protection order is in force with respect to the juvenile (CA 1989, s. 44(4)).

13–029 The Divisional Court has ruled that section 55(5) must be interpreted narrowly and that a youth court was in error in determining that a local authority had parental responsibility for a juvenile remanded to local authority accommodation under CYPA 1969, s. 23 and was thus liable to meet a compensation order: *North Yorkshire County Council v. Selby Youth Court Justices* [1994] 1 All E.R. 991. Laws J. found it "difficult to conceive that this bundle of legal functions could be transferred to a local authority unless statute expressly so provided".

Now that statute has reinstated local authority liability, there will be scope for authorities to seek to avoid liability by reference to the caselaw developed prior to the House of Lords ruling in *Leeds City Council v. West Yorkshire Metropolitan Police* [1983] 1 A.C. 29 that no liability lay with local authorities. An authority may thus argue that liability does not arise where the juvenile has been placed in a community home belonging to another local authority (or with an agency in the voluntary sector) and therefore not under its control (*Somerset County Council v. Brice* [1973] 1 W.L.R. 1169), or has been returned to live at the parental home (*Lincoln Corporation v. Parker* [1974] 1 W.L.R. 713), or where, in the individual circumstances of the case, the authority had exercised a proper degree of care and control (*Somerset County Council v. Kingscott* [1975] 1 W.L.R. 283 where the authority was absolved from liability because it was not guilty of neglect or breach of its duty to the public in its management of a community home. The Divisional Court acknowledged that a community home is not a secure penal institution and staff could not keep residents under perpetual supervision). The Divisional Court has recently acknowledged that a local authority is in a different position from a natural parent or a guardian and may be entrusted with the care of a young person who is already an offender or of a criminal propensity. The steps the authority can take to restrain such a young person may thus be limited. It is therefore inappropriate to impose an obligation upon the authority to bear financial responsibility for compensation to victims of crime perpetrated by young persons in its care where the authority had done everything that it reasonably and properly could to exercise its powers over the young person and protect the public from that person's offending (*D. v. Director of Public Prosecutions, The Times*, April 15, 1995).

In determining whether liability arises under section 55, the view of Widgery CJ in *Somerset County Council v. Brice* seems pertinent, that the court should give the local authority an opportunity to be represented by someone trained and experienced who is more concerned than a social worker with the primarily legal issues which arise under that section.

Where the local authority is required to pay a compensation order, the usual requirement under PCCA 1973, s. 35(4)(a) that the court must have regard to the offender's means shall not apply (CJA 1991, s. 57(4)).

Where a court has determined that it is unreasonable to order a local authority to pay compensation in respect of an offence committed by a young offender in its care, it is wrong to order the authority to pay the costs of the prosecution (*Leeds City Council* (1995) 16 Cr. App. R. (S.)362).

Paying within a Reasonable Time   **13–030**
Fines and compensation orders should be capable of being paid off within a reasonable time. What is "reasonable" will clearly depend on the circumstances. Since *Olliver* (1989) 11 Cr. App. R.(S.) 10, it is no longer correct to consider that the sum should be payable within 12 months, as was suggested in a number of earlier cases. Lord Lane C.J. stated in *Olliver*:

> "... there is nothing wrong in principle in the period of payment being longer, indeed much longer than one year, providing it is not an undue burden and so too severe a punishment having regard to the nature of the offence and the nature of the offender. Certainly ... a two-year period will seldom be too long, and in an appropriate case three years will be unassailable ..."

Whether fines and compensation orders should be regarded on an equal footing in this respect is difficult to say. Lord Widgery C.J. in *Bradburn* (1973) 57 Cr. App. R. 948 said that compensation orders "should be sharp in their effect rather than protracted" and that an order which would take four years to complete was "unreasonably long". The Magistrates Association's Sentencing Guidance (1989) stated that an offender on Income Support may find particular difficulty in sustaining a compensation order for three or even two years and that a fine should be payable within 12 months "in the normal run of cases".

13–031 Enforcement of Financial Penalties and Orders

If a parent or guardian is required to pay any financial penalty or order and fails to do so, enforcement proceedings take place in the adult court as if the sum had been ordered upon that parent or guardian's own conviction. If the sum was imposed upon the juvenile, the order is enforced, at least initially, against the juvenile.

13–032 *At the Time of Making the Order*

When the order is initially made, the youth court may:

(i)   require the money to be paid straightaway, or

(ii) require payment within a specified period of time, or

(iii) accept payment by stated instalments.

Additionally, the court may stipulate a date upon which the offender must return to court for a means inquiry if at that time any part of the financial penalty remains unpaid. The court may also make a supervision order under MCA 1980, s. 88, placing the offender under the supervision of such person as the court may appoint. This order does not require the consent of the defendant. The supervisor may be a probation officer or social worker or a fine enforcement officer attached to the court staff. The supervisor's duty is to "advise and befriend the offender with a view to inducing him to pay the sum" (Magistrates Court Rules 1981, r. 56). The supervisor is not required to collect the fine or to decide the rate of payment but simply to encourage the offender to meet their liability. This power is not normally exercised until the offender has been given the opportunity to pay and has defaulted. If a young offender aged under 21 is liable to be committed to detention in default of payment, under CJA 1982, s.9 (*i.e.* is aged 18 or over), committal may not be ordered unless the offender has first been placed under supervision, or unless the court is satisfied that supervision is "undesirable or impracticable" (s.88(4)). While subject to supervision, an offender cannot be committed to custody in default of payment unless the court has "taken such steps as may be reasonably practicable" to obtain from the supervisor "an oral or written report on the offender's conduct and means" (s.88(6)). The supervision order ceases to have effect on payment of the outstanding sum, or on the making of a transfer of fines order, so that enforcement responsibility is transferred to another petty sessions area, or when discharged by the court that made the order (s.88(3)).

13–033 *Following a Means Inquiry*

If the juvenile defaults on payment, the magistrates' court may issue a summons requiring the juvenile to appear before the court, or issue a warrant for his or her arrest, backed or not backed for bail (MCA 1980, s. 83(1)). If the offender does not answer to summons, a warrant may be issued (section 83(2)). The purpose of the inquiry is to determine why payment has not been made, to consider the offender's current means and to determine what measures are necessary to deal effectively with the outstanding sum. The powers of the court at this stage are as follows:

1. *Further Time to Pay:* The court may allow further time for **13–034** payment, either within a fixed period or, more usually, by instalment, varying where necessary the original instalment order (MCA 1980, s. 85A).

2. *Remission of Fine:* The court may remit part or the whole of any **13–035** outstanding fine, though if the fine was imposed by the Crown Court the consent of that Court is required. MCA 1980, s. 85(1) gives power to remit, "but only if (the court) thinks it just to do so having regard to a change of circumstances which has occurred ... since the date of the conviction". In addition, CJA 1991, s. 21 empowers the court to remit a fine imposed under section 18 of that Act where, in retrospect, it becomes clear that the offender's financial circumstances were not as great as originally determined.

CJA 1991, s. 21

"(2) If, on subsequently inquiring into the offender's financial circumstances, the court is satisfied that had it had the results of that inquiry when sentencing the offender it would

(a) have fixed a smaller amount, or

(b) not have fined him,

it may remit the whole or any part of the fine."

3. *Reduction or Discharge of Compensation Order:* At any time **13–036** before a compensation order has been fully complied with, the court may discharge or reduce the order under PCCA 1973, s. 37 in any of the following circumstances:
   (a) if a civil court has determined an amount of damage or loss less than that stated in the order, or
   (b) if the property (or part of it) has now been recovered, or
   (c) where the offender's means are insufficient to satisfy in full both the compensation order and a confiscation order made in the same proceedings, or
   (d) where the offender has suffered a substantial reduction in means which was unexpected at the time that the order was made, and those means seem unlikely to increase for a considerable period.

   If the order was made by the Crown Court, the consent of that Court is required if the magistrates propose to act on grounds (c) or (d).

4. *Supervision Order:* The court may make a supervision order **13–037** under MCA 1980, s. 88 (see para. 13–032).

5. *Parental Responsibility:* Where the court is satisfied that the defaulter has, or has had since the date on which the sum was ordered, the means to pay the sum or any instalment of it on which he or she has defaulted, or has refused or neglected to pay it (MCA 1980, s. 81(4)), the court may either—

   (a) order the defaulter's parent or guardian to enter into a recognizance to ensure that the defaulter pays the outstanding sum (section 81(1)(a)), provided that the parent or guardian consents (section 81(2)(a)); or

   (b) order that the defaulter's parent or guardian shall pay the outstanding sum (section 81(1)(b)), provided that the court is satisfied in all the circumstances that it is reasonable to make such an order (section 81(2)(b)).

   The parent or guardian must be given the opportunity to attend and be heard before an order transferring responsibility for payment is made but, if required to attend and they fail to do so, the order can be made in their absence (section 81(5)).

13–038   6. *Attendance Centre Order:* In circumstances where, in the case of an adult, the court could order a term of imprisonment or detention in default, it may make an attendance centre order in default. Thus, under the provisions of MCA 1980, s. 82(4)(b), the court must be satisfied that the default "is due to the offender's wilful refusal or culpable neglect". All other methods of enforcing payment must have been considered or tried and it must appear to the court that they are inappropriate or unsuccessful. The normal provisions for the making of an attendance centre order must be satisfied, including the number of hours which may be imposed for the offender's age group, the availability of a suitable centre and the avoidance of interference with school or work hours (CJA 1982, s. 17—para. 16–003 *et seq.*). Where an offender who has been ordered to attend a centre in default pays the outstanding sum, the order ceases to have effect. Part payment reduces the liability to attend on a proportionate basis. Time spent at the centre reduces the amount outstanding proportionately.

13–039   7. *Attachment of Earnings Order:* If in employment, the juvenile defaulter is in the same position as an adult and an order may be made requiring the employer to take an amount (the "normal deduction rate") out of the defaulter's pay to forward to the court. The order must take account of the defaulter's outgoings and the court will fix a "protected earnings rate", the level below which the defaulter's earnings must not fall. Clearly, the majority of juveniles appearing before the court will either not be in work or, if employed, their employment will be insufficiently stable or their earnings will not be substantial enough to make this option feasible.

8.   *Distress Warrants:* MCA 1980, s. 76 empowers the court to issue a distress warrant authorising bailiffs to seize goods to be sold, so that the proceeds can be applied towards the outstanding sum and to the bailiff's costs. In practice it is unlikely that the juvenile will have sufficient goods to make this power worthwhile. Magistrates are not likely to issue such a warrant unless satisfied that there would be sufficient goods to satisfy the sum owed (*German* (1891) 56 J.P. 358).

9.   *Deduction from Income Support:* CJA 1991, s. 24 and the Fines **13–040** (Deductions from Income Support) Regulations 1992 (S.I. 2182) provide for deductions to be made from Income Support Benefit where a fine or compensation order has been imposed and the offender is in default. However, no deductions may be made unless the offender is aged 18 or over at the time of the application. Apart from very exceptional circumstances, young people under 18 will not be in receipt of Income Support. An application should not be made in respect of a parent or guardian who has been made liable for the financial penalty of a juvenile (see HOC 74/1992, para. 12).

Chapter 14

Binding Over

14-001 BINDING OVER PARENTS AND GUARDIANS TO
EXERCISE PROPER CARE AND CONTROL

Parents and guardians of children and young persons convicted of an
offence may be ordered to enter into a recognisance of up to £1,000 to
take proper care of them and exercise proper control of them. Formerly
under CYPA 1969, s. 7(7)(c), the power is now contained in CJA 1991, s.
58. The major change embodied in the new legislation is that when the
juvenile is aged *under 16*, the court is now under a duty to bind over the
parent or guardian if satisfied in the circumstances of the case that it
would be desirable in the interests of preventing further offending by the
juvenile. This change reflects the belief of the Government expressed in
Crime, Justice and Protecting the Public (Home Office, 1990, para. 8.10)
that more routine use should be made of a previously little used power:

> "in ensuring that parents do all they can to stop their children
> reoffending. The knowledge that they may forfeit up to £1,000 if
> they fail to meet the terms of their recognisance would be a strong
> incentive to improve their supervision of their children ... The
> courts will be required to consider binding over the parents ... in
> every case unless it would be unreasonable in the circumstances to
> expect the parents to be able to exercise the required degree of
> supervision and control".

14-002 Attempts to use sanctions to oblige parents to share greater
responsibility for their children's wrongdoing have a long history. In
1890 a Bill was introduced unsuccessfully seeking to make general
negligence in the care and control of a child a statutory offence. In 1989
the Minister of State at the Home Office suggested that a new offence of
"failure to prevent child crime" might be introduced but this idea was
soon abandoned. There is little evidence that sentencers believe that
such additional powers would be helpful or that greater use of the
parental bind over would be an effective way of promoting parental
responsibility. A commonly held view maintains that bind over powers
are either superfluous and unnecessary because responsible parents will
seek to exert greater control without the need for sanctions or will prove
ineffective with families experiencing high levels of disharmony, poor

communication and strained relationships, together with the pressures of unemployment, bad housing and poor recreational amenities. At worst, such sanctions can be counter-productive so that instead of providing an incentive to parents to stand by their adolescents, they may encourage parents to cut off links with their children for fear of being punished on their behalf. As Allen (1990), a Home Office adviser, has remarked:

> "... although it is clear that the influence of the home is important in the genesis of delinquent behaviour, and many would agree that policies which encourage the development of improved parenting skills might be useful in helping to prevent it, the idea that the criminal justice system should be used to further such policies is curiously outmoded, showing a naive faith in the power of the court to influence behaviour."

Despite the intentions of the 1991 Act, the evidence to date suggests that the power has been used very infrequently since October 1992.

To Ensure Compliance with a Community Sentence   14–003
Power of parental bind over has been extended by the Criminal Justice and Public Order Act 1994, Sched. 9, para. 44 to add the following provision to CJA 1991, s. 58(2):

> "Where the court has passed on the relevant minor a community sentence (within the meaning of CJA 1991, s. 6) it may include in the recognisance a provision that the minor's parent or guardian ensure that the minor complies with the requirements of that sentence."

This power cannot be exercised in its own right but as an optional additional feature of a general recognisance to take proper care and exercise proper control. It remains to be seen whether youth courts will find this an attractive and helpful recourse in seeking to enhance the prospects of youthful compliance with court orders.

Procedural Requirements   14–004

Consent

A parent or guardian cannot be bound over unless their consent is obtained, but this is not a completely open choice because, if they refuse consent and the court considers that this refusal is unreasonable, they can be fined up to £1,000 (level 3 on the standard scale) (section 58(2)(b)).

Duration

The period of the order shall not exceed three years or until the juvenile's 18th birthday, whichever is the shorter (section 58(3)). In the case of a bind over to ensure compliance with a community order it is implicit that liability extends for the period of the order's duration.

Amount

In fixing the amount of the recognisance, the court shall take into account, among other things, the means of the parent or guardian (section 58(5)).

Appeal

The parent or guardian may appeal against the order (section 58(6) and (7)).

14–005 Role of Pre-Sentence Report

The *National Standard for Pre-Sentence Reports* (1995, para. 39) indicates that "PSRs have an important part to play in providing information and advice to courts which can help them to decide upon the desirability of proposing a bindover". The following factors are identified as of likely relevance:

*   whether the juvenile is likely to benefit from increased supervision and intervention by parents;

*   whether the parents' authority and control over the juvenile would be strengthened;

*   whether the parents are physically in a position to exercise the necessary degree of care and control (*e.g.* the juvenile may be living away from the parents);

*   the circumstances of the offence.

14–006 Forfeiture of Recognisance

MCA 1980, s. 120 applies to this kind of recognisance when made by a magistrates' court as it does to recognisances to keep the peace (section 58(3)). Under section 120(2) a recognisance can only be forfeited by an order on complaint and only the magistrates' court which imposed the bind over can order the forfeiture. The whole or part of the recognisance can be forfeited and costs can also be ordered. Forfeiture proceedings are civil in character, requiring only the civil standard of proof. The parent or guardian shall be told the nature of the alleged breach and be given the opportunity to present evidence, call witnesses or give an explanation. The complaint would normally be that their son or daughter has been convicted of a further offence committed during the period of recognisance. It is doubtful whether other behaviour indicating a lack of proper care or control would be sufficient basis of complaint. The juvenile's conviction of a further offence does not by itself amount to a breach of the order. Parents are frequently advised to deny their liability because in practice it can be very difficult to establish that they have failed to exercise proper care or control, *e.g.* if the further offence occurred while the juvenile was attending school.

14–007   The procedure to be adopted to bring the parents before the court and to enforce the recognisance, and responsibility for conduct of the case against the parents is far from clearcut. Procedure is by way of complaint

178

(MCA 1980, s. 120(2)) but the Crown Prosecution Service is under no duty to act and it would not be good practice for the justices' clerk to make a complaint, since this would entangle the separate roles of complainant and legal adviser to the court. It is also unclear whether parents should be proceeded against in the adult court or the youth court, bearing in mind that the latter normally has jurisdiction over matters specifically assigned to it.

The Home Office, Lord Chancellor's Department and Crown Prosecution Service have expressed a joint view in a letter of May 1994 to the clerk to the Leeds Justices (cited in Gibson, et al., 1994) that venue should be determined locally but encouraging choice of the youth court where magistrates are "probably better able to judge whether the parent has tried to control the child or whether the child is out of parental control". The letter also favoured the court itself instigating proceedings by way of complaint, issuing a summons to the parent to attend if need be, adding that "there seems to be no reason why the prosecutor should not point out the possible breach to the court if ... aware of it". Whether the new liability arising upon a juvenile's non-compliance with a community sentence will be any easier to enforce remains to be seen. The liability is couched in strict terms but parents may seek to establish that they have taken all reasonable steps to ensure the juvenile's compliance and should thus not be held responsible for default. The parent or guardian does not have a right of appeal against a forfeiture order (*Durham Justices, ex p. Laurent* [1945] K.B. 33).

Variation or Revocation 14–008
Under section 58(8) the court which imposed the bind over may vary or revoke the order, on the application of the parent or guardian, where in the light of the change of circumstances since the order was made, this would be in the interests of justice.

BINDING OVER JUVENILES

As a measure of "preventive justice" juveniles may be bound over to 14–009 keep the peace or to be of good behaviour, either following the full hearing in an adult court of a complaint under MCA 1980, s. 115 or of the court's own motion under common law powers pursuant to the Justices of the Peace Act 1361 at any time during the proceedings. A youth court does not have jurisdiction to deal with complaints under MCA 1980, s. 115 so may only bind over a juvenile of its own motion. As with adult defendants, this power may be appropriate for cases of minor assault where the prosecution are prepared not to proceed, provided that the defendant agrees to be bound over. However, it is more likely that such matters will be diverted from prosecution and dealt with by a police caution.

If the charge against the juvenile proceeds to conviction, it is unclear whether the offender may be bound over without the passing of some other penalty or order. The Justices of the Peace Act 1968, s. 1(7) refers to the bind over as "ancillary" to the court's jurisdiction but some courts have been prepared to bind over without additional penalty.

The bind over as a sentence has attracted a considerable degree of criticism:

> "The powers to bind an offender over at the sentencing stage are unduly wide, are productive of inconsistency and unfairness and are found unnecessary at least by some courts. They ought to be abolished at the earliest opportunity." (Ashworth, 1992, p. 248)

More recently, the Law Commission (1994) has proposed that the power to bind over to keep the peace and be of good behaviour, either without or upon conviction, is no longer defensible and should be abolished. The proposal has attracted considerable opposition from stipendiary and lay magistrates and justices clerks (Justices' Clerks' Society, 1994).

14–010 Procedural Requirements

Consent

The juvenile must consent to entering a recognisance, whether under section 115 or common law. The normal sanction for failure or refusal to enter a recognisance is imprisonment. Because a court has no power to impose imprisonment on a juvenile, a juvenile cannot be compelled to be bound over (*Veater v. Glennon* [1981] 1 W.L.R. 567) but if consent is given then the bind over can properly be ordered, despite the absence of sanction (*Conlan v. Oxford* (1983) 5 Cr. App. R. (S.) 237).

14–011 *Duration*

At the discretion of the court.

Amount

There is no fixed upper limit but it should be a reasonable sum, having regard to the juvenile's means and personal circumstances. This is not a financial liability which a parent or guardian may be ordered to pay under CYPA, 1933, s. 55.

Appeal

There is a right of appeal to the Crown Court against an order by a magistrates' court to enter into recognisances, and to the Court of Appeal where the Crown Court orders the bind over.

14–012 Forfeiture of Recognisance
Procedure upon failure to comply with the requirement of the binding over follows MCA 1980, s. 120, outlined above in regard to the enforcement of bind overs in respect of parents and guardians.

Chapter 15

Community Sentences: General

A major objective of the framework introduced by the 1991 Act was to **15–001** introduce an intermediate sentencing band, giving a new conceptual coherence to a number of existing orders and adding two new powers to the sentencer's repertoire. The White Paper *Crime, Justice and Protecting the Public* (Home Office, 1990) had signalled the Government's belief that more offenders should be punished in the community, "particularly those convicted of property crimes and less serious offences of violence" (paragraph 4.3). Much effort had been expended during the 1980s in seeking to give various penalties the de facto status of "alternatives to custody", by devising and marketing programmes to be undertaken by those placed on probation or supervision, adopting various rationing devices to ensure that these were only proposed to sentencers in social inquiry reports for offenders whose offences and previous records suggested that they were "at risk of custody" and by trying to make these programmes "credible in the eyes of the court". The White Paper concluded that talk of "alternatives to custody" was confusing and unhelpful because:

"(a) it implied that custody was the true benchmark of punishment;

(b) it was an unrealistic and unpersuasive fiction to pretend that the equivalent of custody could be achieved in the community."

The Government thus proposed that community punishment should be **15–002** recognised in its own right, bringing together penalties which combined:

"(a) partial but nevertheless substantial restriction of liberty;

(b) discipline demanded of offenders, usually extending over a number of months, requiring them to take a real measure of responsibility for fulfilling the sentence requirements;

(c) consistent enforcement so that offenders would be held to account and returned to court in the event of default."

Despite this, the 1991 Act leaves unchanged the one pre-1991 order which was statutorily prescribed as an alternative to custody, namely a supervision order with a requirement of activities under CYPA 1969, s.

181

12A(3)(a) and s. 12D (para. 17–015). This is thus a somewhat anomalous exception to the new framework.

The existing measures incorporated in this new overarching identity of "community orders" are (CJA 1991, s. 6(4)):

(a) attendance centre order;

(b) supervision order;

(c) probation order;

(d) community service order.

To these have been added:

(d) combination order (a single order combining probation supervision and community service requirements);

(e) curfew order (an order confining offenders to their homes for specified periods, optionally reinforced with electronic monitoring).

Orders (c)—(e) may only be imposed on young persons aged 16 or over.

15–003   A "community sentence" is a sentence which consists of or includes one or more community orders (section 6(1)). Thus the 1991 Act empowers courts to combine different available orders into a sentence, thus enabling combinations of order for a single offence that were not previously permissible. There is only one explicit exception to this facility (sometimes referred to somewhat pejoratively as the "pick 'n' mix" approach): "a community sentence shall not consist of or include a probation order and a community service order" (section 6(3)). This restriction is imposed to ensure that probation and community service are only combined as a combination order under CJA 1991, s. 11. The scope for combining orders is considered in the separate chapters detailing the provisions for the individual community orders. There has, for instance, to be considerable doubt about the desirability of combining community service with a supervision order for a single offence (para. 17–009).

15–004 Restrictions on Imposing Community Sentences

CJA 1991, s. 6

"(1) A court shall not pass on an offender a community sentence, that is to say, a sentence which consists of or includes one or more community orders, unless it is of the opinion that the offence, or the combination of the offence and one or more offences associated with it, was serious enough to warrant such a sentence.

(2) ... where a court passes a community sentence—

(a)   the particular order or orders comprising or forming part of the sentence shall be such as in the opinion of the court is, or taken together are, the most suitable for the offender; and

(b) the restrictions on liberty imposed by the order or orders shall be such as in the opinion of the court are commensurate with the seriousness of the offence, or the combination of the offence and one or more offences associated with it."

"Serious Enough" 15–005
The Act thus creates an entirely new threshold, between community sentences and financial penalties, in the interpretation of which little help is forthcoming from previous Court of Appeal guidance. The challenge to courts, as spelt out in the White Paper, is "to be satisfied that the offence ... was so serious that restrictions on liberty were justified, but not serious enough to deserve a custodial sentence" (para. 4.6). Offence seriousness is the sole criterion for imposing a community sentence. Of the existing orders brought into the community sentence fold, the community service order is the one which lends itself most closely to the new framework, being a relatively straightforward, restrictive punishment but there has been little principled guidance on its use prior to the 1991 Act. Thus in *Cordner* (1992) 13 Cr. App. R.(S.) 570, an appeal against a 100 hour order imposed for theft of 50 pence from a London Underground ticket machine was dismissed. The extent to which guidance will now be more forthcoming will depend on the preparedness of the defence to appeal against community sentences.

It may be that the Court of Appeal will suggest a version of the 15–006 *Bradbourn* test (para. 23–004), *i.e.* the kind of offence which would make right-thinking members of the public, knowing all the facts, feel that justice had not been done by the passing of any sentence less than a community one. There will, of course, be cases where, notwithstanding that the offence itself passes the custody threshold, there is sufficient mitigation to lead the court to impose a community sentence (*Oliver* [1993] 1 W.L.R. 177). Similarly, there will also be cases where the offence passes the community sentence threshold but there is sufficient mitigation to lead the court to impose a financial penalty alone or even a conditional discharge, though it is less likely that illustrations of this mitigation at work will be provided by the Court of Appeal.

In a number of recent instances the Attorney-General has successfully referred community sentences to the Court of Appeal on grounds of undue leniency. In *Attorney-General's Reference No. 8 of 1992* (1993) 14 Cr. App. R.(S.) 729, a probation order imposed on an offender aged under 21 for manslaughter by stabbing during a street argument was replaced by a custodial sentence despite various mitigating circumstances including his youth, previous good character and his intentions to train for a professional career. See also *Attorney-General's Reference No. 27 of 1993* [1994] Crim. L.R. 465 (detailed at para. 23–040). The offender's good response to the community order is not likely to influence the Court of Appeal's assessment (but see

Attorney-General's Reference No. 15 of 1994 (1995) 16 Cr. App. R.(S.) 619 (detailed at para. 18–023).

Restriction on Liberty

15–007 The White Paper implies that there is gradation of community orders within the community sentencing band, taking account of the extent to which liberty is restricted. This is not addressed by the legislation which thus leaves it to sentencers to work out for themselves. Is "restrictiveness" based on a simplistic calculation of time demand or on a more complex assessment of the time-effort nexus? Ultimately, it is impossible to rank logically such diverse demands as:

(i) a probation order of 12 months with a requirement of residence in a probation hostel for nine months;

(ii) a combination order consisting of 100 hours community service and two years probation;

(iii) a supervision order with a requirement of psychiatric out-patient treatment.

15–008 Commensurability is further complicated by the subjective element acknowledged by the White Paper that the same order can impact on individuals in different ways and that "a comparatively short order may make more severe demands on some offenders than more severe orders would on others" (para. 4.9). This may be because of the difficulty some offenders will find in keeping to any requirements because of their "disorganised and impulsive lifestyle" but may also be because of varying demands on their time. Thus a person with family responsibilities in full-time employment six days a week could experience 100 hours of community service as more restrictive on liberty than a 200 hour order on an unemployed person with no domestic ties. When these factors are brought into the equation a ranking of restrictiveness becomes even more problematic.

Suitability

15–009 Section 6(2) requires the court to achieve dual objectives of "suitability" (section 6(2)(a)) and "restriction" (section 6(2)(b)) in determining the actual sentence within the community sentence band. The Act does not indicate how the court should proceed in seeking to combine these two objectives which may well not sit readily together. What seems clear, however, is that the proportionality or deserts principle should set the limit on the degree of restrictiveness that is imposed and that considerations of suitability, *e.g.* the needs of the individual offender, should not lead to a more onerous burden being placed upon the offender than is justified by the seriousness of the offence. "Suitability" considerations could, however, suggest a less restrictive sentence than considerations of seriousness prima facie indicate.

15–010 In forming an opinion as to the order or orders most suitable for the offender, the court must take into account any information about the offender which is before it (section 7(2)) and must ordinarily obtain and consider a pre-sentence report before forming an opinion as to the suitability for the offender of all community orders except an attendance centre order, a probation order without PCCA 1973, Sched. 1A requirements or a supervision order without requirements (section 7(3)). Since implementation of the Criminal Justice and Public Order Act 1994 a court dealing with a juvenile for an offence triable only on indictment is not obliged to consider a report if of the opinion that a report is unnecessary. If the offence is triable either way or only summarily, the court can dispense with a report if a report prepared for a previous sentencing occasion is available to it (section 7(3B)). If there is more than one such report, the most recent report should be considered. The questionable merits of such a choice are addressed at para. 11–007.

In assessing suitability, the following factors will be relevant **15–011** considerations:

(a) the defendant's circumstances, needs, abilities, difficulties;

(b) the risk of re-offending or the potential harm to others and the kind of intervention which could reduce this risk;

(c) the demands of the order and their fit with the individual's commitments, capacities and motivation;

(d) the likelihood of successful completion in the context of competing pressures;

(e) the defendant's response to previous court orders;

(f) the willingness of the defendant to give consent and to make a commitment to the demands of the proposed order.

In attempting to match considerations of seriousness and suitability, the *National Standard for Pre-Sentence Reports* (Home Office, 1992, Annex 2.B) offered a matrix plotting seriousness against need for social work intervention:

Diagram 1

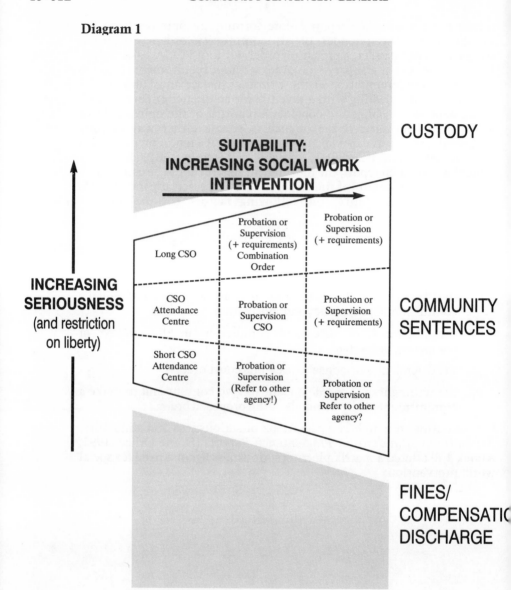

15–012 It is made clear that the model is not intended to be prescriptive but a starting point and, if used, will need to be adapted to local structures and programmes of supervision. This approach has been developed in local areas to create a matrix specifically for youth justice. The following (Hampshire Probation Service, 1992) represents the approach devised as a working tool for Hampshire, agreed between the Probation Service, the Social Services Department and the local courts.

Diagram 2

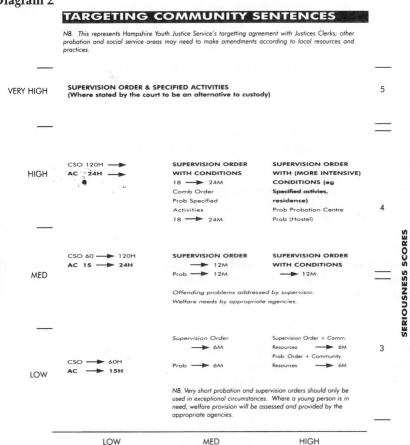

TARGETING COMMUNITY SENTENCES

NB. This represents Hampshire Youth Justice Service's targeting agreement with Justices Clerks; other probation and social service areas may need to make amendments according to local resources and practices.

RESTRICTIONS ON LIBERTY

VERY HIGH — **SUPERVISION ORDER & SPECIFIED ACTIVITIES** (Where stated by the court to be an alternative to custody)   5

HIGH
CSO 120H ➤
AC 24H ➤

SUPERVISION ORDER WITH CONDITIONS
18 ➤ 24M
Comb Order
Prob Specified Activities
18 ➤ 24M

SUPERVISION ORDER WITH (MORE INTENSIVE) CONDITIONS (eg Specified activies, residence)
Prob Probation Centre
Prob (Hostel)   4

MED
CSO 60 ➤ 120H
AC 15 ➤ 24H

SUPERVISION ORDER
➤ 12M
Prob ➤ 12M

SUPERVISION ORDER WITH CONDITIONS
➤ 12M

Offending problems addressed by supervisor.
Welfare needs by appropriate agencies.

LOW
CSO ➤ 60H
AC ➤ 15H

Supervision Order
➤ 6M
Prob ➤ 6M

Supervision Order + Comm.
Resources ➤ 6M
Prob. Order + Community
Resources ➤ 6M   3

NB. Very short probation and supervision orders should only be used in exceptional circumstances. Where a young person is in need, welfare provision will be assessed and provided by the appropriate agencies.

LOW   MED   HIGH

SERIOUSNESS SCORES

DEGREE OF PROFESSIONAL INTERVENTION REQUIRED

(*Seriousness Score:* The Hampshire Matrix adopts an offence gravity **15–013** scale ranging from five (the most serious offences, *e.g.* rape) to one (the least serious, *e.g.* common assault). In the revised *National Standard for Pre-Sentence Reports* (1995, para. 14) the Home Office has indicated that seriousness scales should not be quoted in pre-sentence reports, partly to avoid usurping the role of the sentencer and partly out of a preference for the judgement of the report-writer, taking account of all the specific circumstances of the offence. The matrix is likely to be further revised.)

15–014 Consent

The offender's consent is required before the following orders can be made:

(a) probation order (PCCA 1973, s. 2(3))

(b) community service order (PCCA 1973, s. 14(2))

(c) combination order (CJA 1991, s. 11(3) and PCCA 1973)

(d) curfew order (CJA 1991, s. 12(5))

Attendance centre order does not require consent. A supervision order requires consent only if it contains certain additional requirements, as detailed in Chapter 16.

15–015 Consent is not statutorily defined but clearly implies that the offender is given the opportunity to make a genuine, informed choice. It will not be valid consent if the offender consents having been incorrectly led to believe by the court that, failing their consent, a custodial sentence will be imposed. Thus in *Marquis* [1974] 1 W.L.R. 1087, a defendant was pressured into agreeing to a probation order for a comparatively less serious offence, making clear that she was doing this unwillingly only because she wished to avoid imprisonment. The judge had evidently wished to place her on probation and improperly sought to overcome her reluctance by giving the impression that she would otherwise lose her liberty. This was not a probable alternative and the Court of Appeal quashed the order. In *Barnett* (1986) 8 Cr. App. R.(S.) 200, the Court of Appeal reviewed a not dissimilar case where the offender claimed he had been improperly coerced to accept a probation order. In this case, the Court of Appeal considered that a custodial sentence was the realistic alternative and that consent given with this awareness was sound. If this were not the case, then a community sentence imposed in a case where seriousness considerations point to a custodial sentence would never be valid. In the words of Glidewell L.J.:

> "What is necessary is that the defendant should have full appreciation of what the realistic alternatives are, and having considered them he can decide whether or not to consent."

15–016 Taken at face value, this interpretation would require a court seeking an offender's consent to indicate what would be the alternative sentence. Courts in fact rarely make their thinking that clear, nor do defendants raise awkward questions in an attempt to gain clarification, in case they aggravate their predicament. Many defendants do continue to over-estimate the risk of custody and so may well believe that their consent saves them from that fate. What *Marquis* and *Barnett* show is that the court should not actively manipulate the defendant into believing incorrectly that a custodial sentence will result.

15–017 Under CJA 1991, s. 1(3), refusal to give consent to a proposed community sentence allows (but does not oblige) the court to pass a custodial sentence, even if custody would not be justified by one of the two criteria specified in CJA 1991, s. 1(2) ("so serious" or "protection of the public"). This subsection awaits further interpretative guidance. If, for example, an offender is willing to consent to a probation order but not to a community service order, and the pre-sentence report proposes that a probation order would be the most suitable community sentence for the offender, would a custodial sentence be upheld on appeal? If the court in the circumstances outlined would have been prepared to impose a probation order, then reluctant consent to a community service order obtained by giving the defendant the impression that, without such consent, section 1(3) powers would be exercised, would not seem valid. In more straightforward vein, refusal of consent may be a tactical option where the offender considers that a short custodial sentence would be a preferable outcome, for example following a period of remand in custody which will count towards a YOI sentence, causing their release in the near future with no continuing sentence responsibilties (other than liability to post-release supervision).

Binding Over Parent or Guardian 15–018
The Criminal Justice and Public Order Act 1994, Sched. 9, para. 44 introduced a new optional power applicable where a court passes a community sentence upon a juvenile aged under 16 and also exercises power under CJA 1991, s. 58(2) to bind over the parent or guardian to take proper care and exercise proper control of the juvenile (see para. 14–003). The court may include in the recognisance a provision that the minor's parent or guardian ensures that the minor complies with the requirements of that sentence. Little use has been made to date of the duty introduced by section 58(2) and it remains to be seen whether this additional dimension will encourage greater uptake.

Rethinking Community Sentences 15–019
In a Green Paper *Strengthening Punishment in the Community* (Cm 2780, Home Office, 1995b), the Government has announced proposals for legislation introducing "a comprehensive new framework for community sentences", replacing the present "piecemeal" provisions. There would be a single, integrated community sentence, replacing all the current orders which would become options which courts could choose to include within a community sentence, either singly or in any combination, reflecting restriction of liberty, reparation and/or prevention of reoffending. Courts would have "increased discretion to determine the content of community sentences in individual cases and to decide what restrictions and compulsions should apply to offenders in pursuance of those three principal purposes". Present requirements that offenders should give their consent to community sentences would be removed, on the basis that it is a matter for the court, not the offender, to decide on the appropriate sentence, and that the more important issue is not consent at point of sentence but the offender's willingness to comply throughout the sentence. Courts would have greater scope to require information on the progress and outcome of community sentences.

The Green Paper (Chapter 7) recognises that special provisions would be necessary for offenders aged under 18, in recognition of differentiating features of youth justice and suggests certain options:

(i) applying a modified version of the proposed model to all those under 18, including the introduction of "a more formalised reparative requirement for the entire age range";

(ii) applying the proposed adult model to offenders aged 16 or over (though possibly retaining the supervision order as a separate sentence), while either retaining the existing range of community sentences for under 16s or developing a junior version of the new integrated community sentences for that younger age group "perhaps emphasising school attendance and parental involvement";

(iii) reserving the proposed integrated model for those aged 18 and above and developing a separate new system for juveniles. A variant of this option would allow courts the option to select either adult or juvenile arrangements for 16–17 year olds, thus reflecting their transitional status.

Chapter 16

Attendance Centre Orders

First introduced by the Criminal Justice Act 1948, the attendance centre **16–001** order is now governed by the Criminal Justice Act 1982, as amended by the Criminal Justice Act 1991 which designated it as one of the "community orders" which can feature in a "community sentence" (CJA 1991, s. 6(4)). The attendance centre order is also used as a secondary penalty for non-payment of financial orders or for breach of supervision and probation orders. The requirement of the order is for the offender "to attend at such centre to be specified in the order, for such number of hours as may be specified" (section 17(1)). An attendance centre is statutorily defined as "a place at which offenders under 21 years of age may be required to attend and be given under supervision appropriate occupation or instruction": CJA 1982, s. 16(2). The Attendance Centre Rules 1995 (S.I. 1995) (replacing the 1958 Rules) provide more detailed regulations covering staffing, attendance and discipline at centres and are reinforced by a *National Standard for Attendance Centres* (1995). Though now a community sentence, the amendment, breach, revocation and discharge of attendance centre orders are not governed by CJA 1991, Sched. 2 but retain separate provisions within CJA 1982.

Powers to Make Attendance Centre Orders 16–002

As a Community Sentence: CJA 1982, s. 17

A youth court or the Crown Court can make an attendance centre order where the offender has been found guilty of an offence punishable with imprisonment (section 17(1)(a)), provided that the court is of the opinion that the offence, or the combination of the offence and one or more offences associated with it, is serious enough to warrant such a sentence (CJA 1991, s. 6(1)). An order can only be made if the court has been notified by the Secretary of State that a centre is available for the reception of persons of the offender's description. The court has to be satisfied that the centre to be specified in the order is reasonably accessible to the offender, having regard to the offender's age, means of access to the centre and any other circumstances (section 17(7)). The restriction formerly contained in section 17(3) that orders should not normally be imposed on offenders who had previously received a custodial sentence was repealed by CJA 1991, section 67(1). This reflects the emphasis in the 1991 Act on sentencing on the basis of seriousness of the current offence, though some sentencers may continue to feel that a young offender who has experienced a YOI regime is not a likely candidate for the gentler demands of an attendance centre.

16–003 *In Default of Payment of a Financial Order: CJA 1982, s. 17*

The use of what is primarily a community sentence as a penalty for non-payment of financial orders which may have been imposed for an offence not serious enough to warrant a community sentence may seem somewhat anomalous. CJA 1982, s. 17(1)(a) permits an attendance centre order to be imposed in circumstances where the court would have power in the case of an adult to commit to prison in default of payment of any sum of money "or for failing to do or abstain from doing anything required to be done or left undone". Thus the court should be satisfied that the default arises because of the offender's wilful refusal or culpable neglect (MCA 1980, s. 82(4)(b), para. 13–038). Payment of the full outstanding sum causes the order to cease to have effect (section 17(13)(a)). Part payment reduces the number of hours of attendance proportionately, "that is to say by such number of complete hours as bears to the total number the proportion most nearly approximating to, without exceeding, the proportion which the part bears to the said sum" (section 17(13)(b)). This complex calculation formula can best be illustrated by an example:

16–004   A defaulter has been made subject to a 12 hours attendance centre order for the non-payment of a fine of £90. This gives each hour a financial value of £7.50. He attends for three hours. This reduces the amount outstanding by £22.50, leaving £67.50. If he then pays £50, leaving £17.50 outstanding, he would be required to attend for a further two hours ("worth" £15 only but the hours outstanding are rounded down to the nearest complete hour).

On Breach of a Supervision Order: CJA 1969, s. 15

Youth courts and other magistrates' courts may make an attendance centre order on breach of a requirement of a supervision order (section 15(2A)). In these circumstances CJA 1982, s. 17 should apply as if its wording were amended to include attendance centre orders made in respect of breach of a supervision order (CYPA 1969, s. 16A(1)).

16–005 *On Breach of a Probation Order: CJA 1991, Sched. 2*

Youth courts and other magistrates' courts which have jurisdiction in respect of a probation order or the probation element of a combination order may deal with the breach of a requirement of either by making an attendance centre order and allowing the probation or combination order to continue in effect (Sched. 2, para. 3(1)(c)). If the probation order or combination order was made by the Crown Court, and a magistrates' court having jurisdiction to deal with the offender's breach commits the case to the Crown Court, the Crown Court may deal with the failure by making an attendance centre order and allowing the original order to continue (Sched. 2, para. 4(1)(c)). CJA 1991, Sched. 2, paras. 3 and 4(1)(c) replace PCCA 1973, s. 6(3)(c), now repealed, which previously empowered the making of an attendance centre order upon breach of a probation order.

Combining the Attendance Centre Order as a Community Sentence   **16–006**
with other Sentences or Orders
The general rule applies that "courts should avoid mixing sentences which fall into well established and different categories": *McElhorne* (1983) 5 Cr. App. R.(S.) 53. Thus an attendance centre order should not be combined with a custodial sentence. Clearly an attendance centre order and a discharge cannot be combined for a single offence, but a fine can be imposed alongside an attendance centre order for a single offence. The 1991 Act permits the combination of attendance centre orders with any other community orders for which the offender is eligible by age, either for a single offence or for separate offences dealt with on the same sentencing occasion. The scope for combining an attendance centre order with other sentences and orders on the same sentencing occasion can be summarised as follows:

Combination of attendance centre order with other penalties

	Dis-charge	Fine	Super-vision	Pro-bation Order	CSO	Com-bin-ation Order	Curfew Order	Cus-tody
Same Offence	No	Yes	Yes	Yes	Yes	Yes	Yes	No
Different Offences	Yes	Yes	Yes	Yes	Yes	Yes	Yes	No

Length of Order   **16–007**
The court shall specify the number of hours of attendance, subject to the following limits:

(a) The aggregate number of hours shall not be less than 12, except where the offender is under 14 and, in the opinion of the court, 12 hours would be excessive, having regard to the offender's age or other circumstances (section 17(4)).

(b) The aggregate number of hours shall not exceed 12 except where the court is of the opinion, having regard to all the circumstances, that 12 hours would be inadequate (section 17(5)).

(c) Where the court is of the opinion that 12 hours would be inadequate, the aggregate number of hours shall not exceed 24 where the offender is under 16, or 36 hours where the offender is not less than 16 (section 17(5)). (CJA 1991 increased the maximum number of hours for 16 year olds to place them on the same footing as 17 year olds, in accordance with their status as "near adults").

(d)　A further attendance centre order may be passed upon an offender whilst a previous order remains in effect and the number of hours to be specified shall be determined without regard to the number specified in the earlier order or to the fact that that order is still in force with hours outstanding (section 17(6)).

Age	Minimum Hours	Maximum Hours
10–11	12 (unless 12 is excessive)	24 (if 12 is inadequate)
12–15	12	24 (if 12 is inadequate)
16–20	12	36 (if 12 is inadequate)

16–008　Times of Attendance
The times of attendance shall be such as to avoid interference as far as practicable with the offender's school hours or working hours (section 17(8)). The order should specify the time at which the offender must first attend the centre. Subsequent times shall be fixed by the officer in charge of the centre, having regard to the offender's circumstances (section 17(10)). An offender shall not be required to attend the centre on more than one occasion on any day, or for more than three hours on any occasion (section 17(11)). Sessions last two hours at junior centres and three hours at senior centres. Most centres normally open on alternate Saturdays. The expectation is that even the longest orders should be completed within six months, if offenders attend regularly (*National Standard*, 1995, para. 9). Latecomers may be refused admission (ACR 1995, r.6(3)).

16–009　Availability and Accessibility of Centres
Young persons are allocated to centres according to age, sex and category of centre. Centres are categorised as "junior" and "senior". Some "junior" centres take males and females under 17 but the majority take only males. There are no junior centres for females only. "Senior" centres at present take males only, primarily those aged 17–20, but with some flexibility in regard to 16 year olds. Thus the attendance centre order is not an available sentencing option for young women aged 18–20 anywhere in England and Wales and the availability for younger girls is very limited. The Table summarises the arrangements as set out in Home Office Circular 72/1992.

In the case of males aged 16–17 receiving orders of 24 hours, "suitability" will be resolved according to the general criteria for resolving the most suitable community sentence for that age group, set out in HOC 30/1992, para. 9 (para. 17–030).

16–010　　Before making an order the court must be stisfied that the centre is reasonably accessible to the offender in all the circumstances. The *National Standard* (1995, para. 10) specifies that offenders should not normally be expected to travel for more than one hour or ten miles each

MALES

Age	Type of Centre
10–15	Junior Centre

16–17
(a) where no senior centre   Junior Centre

(b) where a choice of centre:

   (i) orders up to 24 hours   Junior or Senior Centre according to the individual's suitability

   (ii) orders 25–36 hours   Senior Centre

FEMALES

Age	Type of Centre
10–17	Junior Mixed Centre (where available)
18–20	Not available

way, whichever is the more, though "courts may consider that less demanding travelling requirements are appropriate to younger attenders". Travelling time does not count towards completion of the order.

Staffing of Centres   **16–011**
Nearly all centres are administered by police officers (with civilian support) but this is a matter of policy and convenience rather than a statutory responsibility of the police. Each centre must have an officer in charge to whom offenders must report. The officer in charge has responsibilities which include:

(a) maintaining a register of attendance, failure to attend and any breaches of the rules;

(b) informing each offender orally and in writing, before they leave the centre, of the date and time of their next attendance, unless this is impracticable;

(c) determining whether an attender is unfit for attendance by reason of illness, infection, or a condition likely to be detrimental to others;

(d) exercising discipline;

(e) making application to the relevant court for variation or discharge of the order or initiating breach proceedings.

Save in exceptional circumstances, a female member of staff should be present at a centre at which girls and young women attend and should, "so far as practicable", supervise their physical training (ACR 1995, r.4(2)).

16–012 Occupation and Discipline
The occupation and instruction given at a centre shall include a programme of group activities designed to assist offenders to acquire or develop personal responsibility, self-discipline, skills and interests (ACR 1995, r. 4(1)).
The basic requirement to attend the specified centre is supplemented by ACR 1995, r. 10:

> "Persons shall while attending at a centre behave in an orderly manner and shall obey any instruction given by the officer in charge or any other member of the staff".

16–013 Though the discipline of a centre is to be maintained primarily by the personal influence of the staff (rule 9), the Rules specify a number of sanctions which can be exercised in the event of a breach of the rules:

(a) separation from other persons attending (rule 13(a));

(b) being given an alternative form of occupation (rule 13(b));

(c) being required to leave the centre for the remainder of the session (rule 11(1) and (2)(a));

(d) where misconduct is sufficiently serious, suspension from further attendance pending court appearance for breach (rule 11(2)(b)).

Where the breach is serious, the officer in charge should interview the offender and caution him or her as to their future conduct at the centre before imposing the sanction (*National Standard*, 1995, para. 42).
   In the event of unauthorised non-attendance, a telephone call should be made, if possible, to the offender's home to find out the reason for absence. A warning letter should be sent to the offender explaining the consequences of non-attendance and giving notice of the date and time of the next session. If the offender is aged under 16, a letter should also be sent to the offender's parents advising them of the non-attendance and asking them to do all they can to ensure future attendance.
16–014   If the offender misses the next session, a final warning letter should be sent (*National Standard*, 1995, para. 43). Breach action must be instituted no later than the third consecutive unauthorised absence, though proceedings may be commenced earlier than this if the officer in charge is satisfied that the offender has no intention of obeying the sentence of the court. Where unauthorised absences are not consecutive, greater flexibility is allowed but "generally no more than four non-consecutive unauthorised absences should be tolerated" (*National Standard*, 1995, para. 44).

Rationale, Suitability and Restriction on Liberty   **16–015**

"The aims of the order are to impose, in loss of leisure over a considerable period, a punishment that is generally understood by young people and to encourage them, in a disciplined environment, to make more constructive use of their leisure time. The sentence will not normally be suitable for those who have a long record of offences or who need removal from bad home surroundings, nor can it, of itself, meet a requirement for sustained supervision. It can, however, be ordered as an alternative to custody for an offence of some gravity." *The Sentence of the Court* (1990), 8.2

This guidance pre-dates the Criminal Justice Act 1991 with its emphasis on the seriousness of the current offence and it remains to be seen how the attendance centre order will find its place as a community sentence. It is a straightforward restriction on liberty, curtailing what is likely to be premium leisure time for the offender, but will sentencers feel that, for 16 and 17 year olds, it is of lesser impact than the obvious alternative, a short community service order?

Much previous research on attendance centres focused on whether this sentence was either perceived or used by sentencers as an "alternative to custody", concluding that it has not been a high tariff disposal. However, Home Office research in 1981–82 (Mair, 1991), asking magistrates in Hampshire to rate the position of senior attendance centres in relation to other non-custodial disposals, revealed a variety of perceptions. A quarter of respondents located the attendance centre between the probation order and the community service order in severity, whilst a fifth saw it as coming between the community service order and detention. Smaller groups of respondents rated it on a par with community service, or being close to the level of a fine. There was clearly no uniform view "but a sizeable minority did perceive [the senior attendance centre order] as coming immediately before custody".

The amended CJA 1991, s.29(1) (para. 9–011) notwithstanding, the offender's record and response to previous court orders seems of less significance than before, except in helping to gauge the likelihood of their sustaining the commitment of the order. The statutory presumption that someone who had previously served a custodial sentence is normally unsuitable for the order, presumably because their experience would make them less amenable to the gentler style of centre activities, has now been removed, though whether centre staff will welcome those with youth offender institution sentences behind them is uncertain.

One unusual feature of the attendance centre order is that those who **16–016** run centres have no say in who comes their way, while probation officers and social workers who make proposals in pre-sentence reports may know little or nothing about attendance centres. An obvious aspect worth considering at the time of writing the pre-sentence report is whether the offender will be able to cope with the demands. Experience suggests that youngsters who are quite withdrawn and reluctant to tackle either new or existing commitments in their life may well find the demands of the centre very difficult to sustain and may then find themselves at risk of a custodial sentence upon revocation following breach proceedings.

16–017   The White Paper *Crime, Justice and Protecting the Public* (para. 4.19) stated that the order is useful as a punishment "when the offender does not need supervision for a long time". Nevertheless, as *The Sentence of the Court* extract suggests, it is natural for centre staff to wish to make the experience more constructive than just a "restriction on liberty". The *Attendance Centre Rules 1958* required that those attending shall be occupied "in a manner conducive to health of mind and body" (rule 2(1)). Sessions have usually combined PT with some form of craft activity or training in first aid. A Home Office questionnaire to officers in charge of senior attendance centres found that:

> "Most officers either stated that they agreed with the aims of a senior attendance centre as laid down by the Home Office or simply repeated these aims by mentioning such ideas as instilling discipline, punishing through loss of leisure and providing a constructive programme of activities. Some, however, mentioned aims which seemed to have a stronger welfare orientation and more than a hint of social work: to educate offenders in topics of social concern such as applying for a job; to allow them to discuss any difficulties they might have with the staff at the centre. At times an almost Victorian notion of self-improvement with the help of a paternalistic teacher came through: a centre could give a sense of achievement and a need to strive; it would whet appetites for a better way of life; it might induce higher personal standards. Only one officer in charge stated that an aim was to provide a further alternative to a custodial sentence. The aims mentioned by respondents thus covered a wide area from, on the one hand, punishment and discipline to, on the other, constructive social work help. There was no mention of any possible tension between such aims; perhaps officers were not aware of any such tension, or perhaps they considered that in the practice of a centre such contradictions were resolved and posed no problems." (Mair, 1991, 152)

16–018 The capacity of the attendance centre to be "all things to all people", with perceived advantages ranging from idealistic rehabilitation to economic pragmatism, has often been remarked on and this spread of perceptions will doubtless continue.

In 1993, the percentage of children, young persons and young adults sentenced for indictable offences who received attendance centre orders was as follows, the corresponding 1983 figures being in brackets:

	Males	Females
10–under 14	21 (21)	9 (4)
14–under 18	13 (12)	5 (4)

In a NACRO survey (1993) of sentencing in the youth courts in 15 local **16–019** authority areas in the first six months following implementation of the 1991 Act, the attendance centre order was used in 12.8 per cent of the sample of 3005 cases, 11 per cent of orders exceeding 24 hours. The order accounted for 20 per cent of sentences for 15 year olds, 13 per cent for 16 year olds and six per cent for 17 year olds.

Chapter 17

Supervision Orders

17–001 The power to make a supervision order was introduced in the Children and Young Persons Act 1969 to offer a distinctive form of statutory supervision for juveniles. This order, together with additional requirements broadly identified as "intermediate treatment", was originally intended to replace the punishments of attendance centre and detention centre with a new, constructive flexible range of local authority provision. This undiluted vision of the 1969 Act was not implemented but the supervision order has nevertheless been the cornerstone of developments in modern juvenile justice. The 1969 Act remains the relevant authorising statute but the supervision order was designated a community order under the 1991 Act within the middle band of community sentences. Unlike the probation order, the supervision order was not originally devised to be used "instead of sentencing" the offender and has always been a sentence in its own right. Its identity has thus not been transformed to the same extent by the 1991 Act. Though a community order, it retains its own statutory provisions governing amendment, termination and breach and is not within the general enforcement framework provided by CJA 1991, Sched. 2. There is virtually no case law guidance from the Court of Appeal regarding the use and enforcement of supervision orders (but see cases cited at para. 9–017).

17–002   The following Table shows the percentage of juveniles sentenced for indictable offences in 1993 who received supervision orders, by age and sex (1983 figures in brackets):

	Male	Female
10–under 14	23 (19)	14 (21)
14–under 18	16 (10)	19 (13)

17–002 Power to Make a Supervision Order

A supervision order can be made in criminal proceedings by a youth court or the Crown Court where a child or young person has been found guilty of any offence by or before any court, other than an offence of murder (CYPA 1969, s. 7(7)(b)). A supervision order cannot be made by an adult magistrates' court (section 7(8)). The effect is to place the young

200

offender under the supervision of a designated local authority (*i.e.* a social worker) or a probation officer (section 11). The supervisor's duty is "to advise, assist and befriend the supervised person" (section 14).

Length of Order 17–003
The order will last for three years from the date on which it is made, or for such shorter period as may be specified in the order (CYPA 1969, s. 17(a)). In common with the community orders being imposed as a community sentence, the length of the order or, in other words, the restriction on liberty imposed, should be commensurate with the seriousness of the offence or that offence combined with other associated offences, taking into account the suitability of the order for the offender. This assessment cannot be made on the basis simply of the time and effort which the order will demand but must also take account of the likely impact upon the offender in the light of their formal circumstances and characteristics. As the White Paper observed, "... a comparatively short order may make more severe demands on some offenders than more severe orders would on others" (paragraph 4.9). These are somewhat nebulous considerations which are not easily explained in distinguishing one offender from another and may cause offenders who are considered able to cope with "more severe" orders to feel an understandable grievance if their equally culpable but less resilient co-defendant receives a shorter order. In 1993 73 per cent of supervision orders supervised by the Probation Service were for one year or less. Only two per cent of orders were made for periods longer than two years (Home Office, 1994a).

Age of Offender 17–004
The upper age limit for an offender to receive a supervision order was raised a year by the 1991 Act so that it is now available to a young person aged under 18. There is thus now an overlap in eligibility for a supervision order and a probation order for offenders aged 16 and 17. This reflects the proposal in the White Paper that there should be flexibility in the sentencing arrangements for that age group, according to their "maturity" or stage of development and the arrangements available locally. The basis for this overlap of community sentencing options is considered further at para. 17–028 *et seq.*

Procedural Requirements 17–005

Pre-Sentence Report

A court is not required to consider a pre-sentence report before deciding whether an offender is suitable for a supervision order, unless the order includes requirements imposed under CYPA 1969, s. 12, s. 12A, s. 12AA, s. 12B or s. 12C (*i.e.* any additional requirement except one imposed under the general power of section 18(2)(b) to add requirements). The Judicial Studies Board has advised magistrates to obtain a PSR before making any supervision order, even where this is not a statutory requirement. Failure to obtain and consider a report where this is a mandatory requirement does not render the order invalid (CJA 1991, s. 7(4)) but such a failure could provide basis for appeal and the court considering the appeal is required to obtain and consider a report. The requirement to consider a pre-sentence report does not mean that the report has to address the possibility of a supervision order with or without additional requirements, but some sections authorising such requirements specify that the court must consult the supervisor or must be satisfied that the requirement is viable.

17–006 *Consent*

The consent of the offender is not required before a supervision order can be made but specific requirements within a supervision order may require consent either of the offender or his/her parent or guardian, as indicated in the detailed outline of requirements.

Supervising Agency

A local authority shall not be designated as supervisor unless it appears to the court that the offender resides or will reside in the authority's area or the authority agrees. If the offender is aged under 13, the supervisor must be a local authority unless a probation officer is exercising or has exercised statutory responsibilities for another member of the child's household and the relevant local authority requests that the Probation Service undertakes supervision (CYPA 1969, s. 13(2)).

17–007 For young offenders aged 13 or over, the appropriate agency to be specified in the order will depend on local agreements as to division of responsibility. Generally, those under 16 are likely to be supervised by Social Services unless there is a good reason why the Probation Service should undertake the task. Sixteen and 17 year olds are likely to be supervised by the Probation Service unless there is ongoing Social Services involvement which favours continuity. The order shall name the area of the local authority and the petty sessions area in which it appears to the court making the order that the supervised person will live (CYPA 1969, s. 18(2)(a)).

Form

The form of a youth court supervision order is specified in Form 38, prescribed by the Magistrates' Courts (Children and Young Persons) Rules 1992 (S.I. 2071/1992).

17–008 **Combining a Supervision Order with other Sentences or Orders**
The general rule broadly applies that "courts should avoid mixing sentences which fall into well-established and different categories" (*McElhorne* (1983) 5 Cr. App. R.(S.) 53). The scope for combining a supervision order with other sentences and orders in respect of either the same or different offences on the same sentencing occasion can be summarised as follows:

Combination of Supervision Order with Other Penalties

	Dis-charge	Fine	Super-vision	Pro-bation Order	CSO	Com-bin-ation Order	Curfew Order	Cus-tody
Same Offence	No	Yes	Yes	No	Yes*	No	Yes*	No
Different Offences	Yes	Yes	Yes	No	Yes	No	Yes*	No

* Appears legally permissible but probably undesirable in practice (in the case of curfew orders, given the power to make a night restriction requirement in a supervision order).

Though the 1991 Act does not prohibit combining a supervision order with a probation order, this appears to be completely contrary to the principle that an offender should be assessed as suitable for either the juvenile or the adult form of community supervision but not both. A court might wish to secure the "best of both worlds" to take advantage of local resources (*e.g.* an IT programme and a drug treatment programme) but the consequent confusion and duplication would suggest that this would be wrong in principle. For the same reasons, a supervision order should not be mixed with a combination order.

A mix of supervision order with a community service order for the **17–009** same offence is not prohibited by CJA 1991, s. 6(3) but appears to be contrary to the spirit and intentions of the Act. The combination of a supervision order and community service order for different offences was possible in law for 16 year olds prior to CJA 1991 and has not been subject to any reported Court of Appeal comment. There appears to be no inherent contradiction in this combination provided that regard is had to the offender's ability to tackle the two commitments simultaneously (see *Harkess* (1990) 12 Cr. App. R.(S.) 366, indicating that a CSO may be combined with a probation order for different offences).

Requirements in a Supervision Order   **17–010**
As indicated, the basic requirement of the "standard" supervision order is to be supervised by the designated local authority or a probation officer. To facilitate the supervisor's performance of their function, either or both of the following supplementary requirements may be inserted in the standard order (MC(C&YP)R 1992, r. 29(3)):

"(a) That s/he shall inform the supervisor at once of any change of his/her residence or employment.

(b) That s/he shall keep in touch with the supervisor in accordance with such instructions as may from time to time be given by the supervisor and, in particular, that s/he shall, if the supervisor so requires, receive visits from the supervisor at his/her home."

The form of a supervision order is prescribed by MC(C&YP)R 1992 Sched. 2 Form 38.

Nearly 76 per cent of supervision orders made during 1993, supervised by the Probation Service, contained no additional requirement (Home Office, 1994a). In a NACRO survey (1993) of sentencing in the youth courts in 15 local authority areas in the first six months following implementation of the 1991 Act, 74 per cent of supervision orders were "standard" orders.

General Power to Impose Additional Requirements

CYPA 1969, s. 18(2)(b) empowers a court to include "such prescribed provisions as the court considers appropriate for facilitating the performance of" supervisory functions, including provisions "for requiring visits to be made by the supervised person to the supervisor". This general power should not be used to side-step the provisions of the Act to impose a range of specific requirements and, in practice, little use is made of this open-ended provision. By far the most important and utilised power to impose additional requirements is in regard to intermediate treatment and specified activities under section 12(2) and section 12A(3)(a).

17–011 *Discretionary Intermediate Treatment*

CYPA 1969, s. 12

"(2) Subject to section 19(12) of this Act, a supervision order may require the supervised person to comply with any directions given from time to time by the supervisor and requiring him to do all or any of the following things—

(a) to live at a place or places specified in the directions for a period or periods so specified;

(b) to present himself to a person or persons specified in the directions at a place or places and on a day or days so specified;

(c) to participate in activities specified in the directions on a day or days so specified;

but it shall be for the supervisor to decide whether and to what extent he exercises any power to give directions conferred on him by virtue of this subsection and to decide the form of any directions; and a requirement imposed by a supervision order in pursuance of this subsection shall be subject to any such requirement of the order as is authorised by section 12B(1) of this Act.

(3) The total number of days in respect of which a supervised person may be required to comply with directions given by virtue of paragraph (a), (b) or (c) of subsection (2) above in pursuance of a supervision order shall not exceed 90 or such lesser number, if any, as the order may specify for the purposes of this subsection; and for the purpose of calculating the total number of days in respect of which such directions may be given the supervisor shall be entitled to disregard any day in respect of which directions were previously given in pursuance of the order and on which the directions were not complied with."

This constitutes the original power to impose "intermediate **17–012** treatment", and reflects the breadth of potential schemes, provisions and programmes, residential and community-based, which were envisaged in the White Paper *Children in Trouble* (1968). CYPA 1969, s. 19(12) requires the court to be satisfied that a scheme providing appropriate facilities is available in the area where the supervised person lives or will reside. The supervisor has the discretion to decide what directions shall be given and these are not specified in the order.

"Intermediate treatment" has had a somewhat erratic history; its **17–013** meaning, coherence, funding and enforcement was particularly patchy and inconsistent in its first decade of life. As a result, magistrates were not always confident that the supervised person would be required to undertake any additional demands of this nature. The Criminal Justice Act 1982 thus introduced an alternative power to impose intermediate treatment requirements, the crucial difference being that the court could specify the activities to be undertaken (CYPA 1969, s. 12A, below). At around the same time a financial initiative (usually referred to as LAC 3/83) was launched by the Department of Health to encourage the development of IT projects which could be used as community sentences as an alternative to custodial sentences or "criminal care orders" (then available under CYPA 1969, s. 7(7) and subsequently abolished by the Children Act 1989). This initiative coincided with new developments in practice which placed greater emphasis on working with juveniles on their delinquent behaviour or in making some kind of practical reparation, as well as encouraging them to pursue legitimate leisure or educational activities.

Stipulated Intermediate Treatment **17–014**

Under CYPA 1969, s. 12A (3)(a) (introduced by CJA 1982) the supervised person can be required to undertake any of the requirements which can be directed by the supervisor under section 12(2), for up to 90 days (section 12A(5)) or such lesser number of days specified in the order. Such a requirement may not be included in a supervision order which also imposes section 12(2) requirements. The two forms of intermediate treatment are thus not compatible within the same supervision order. Before including a requirement of stipulated IT the court has to follow certain procedural steps and restrictions required by section 12A(6) and

(7), including obtaining the *consent* of the supervised person (or their parent, if aged under 14).

CYPA 1969, s. 12A

"(6) The Court may not include requirements under subsection (3) above in a supervision order unless—

  (a) it has first consulted the supervisor as to—
    (i) the offender's circumstances; and
    (ii) the feasibility of securing compliance with the requirements,

and is satisfied, having regard to the supervisor's report, that it is feasible to secure compliance with them;

  (b) having regard to the circumstances of the case, it considers the requirements necessary for securing the good conduct of the supervised person or for preventing a repetition by him of the same offence or the commission of other offences; and

  (c) the supervised person or, if he is a child, his parent or guardian, consents to their inclusion.

17–015   (7) The court shall not include in such an order by virtue of subsection (3) above—

  (a) any requirement that would involve the co-operation of a person other than the supervisor and the supervised person unless that other person consents to its inclusion; or

  (b) any requirement requiring the supervised person to reside with a specified individual; or

  (c) any such requirement as is mentioned in section 12B(1) of this Act."

This form of requirement is commonly perceived to be more "intensive" and to demand a greater degree of commitment and restriction upon liberty and thus to be commensurate with a greater seriousness of offence. This status is reflected in an unusual provision of the 1969 Act (s. 12D) which allows the court in appropriate cases to impose this requirement as an explicit alternative to a custodial sentence. This provision has survived the passage of CJA 1991.

CYPA 1969, s. 12D

17–016   "(1) Where—

  (a) in pursuance of section 12A(3)(a) of this Act a court includes a requirement in a supervison order directing the supervised person to participate in specified activities; and

(b) it would have imposed a custodial sentence if it had not made a supervision order including such a requirement,

it shall state in open court—

(i) that it is making the order instead of a custodial sentence;

(ii) that it is satisfied that—
    (a) the offence of which he has been convicted, or the combination of that offence and one or more offences associated with it, was so serious that only a supervision order containing such a requirement or a custodial sentence can be justifed for that offence; or
    (b) that offence was a violent or sexual offence and only a supervision order containing such a requirement or such a sentence would be adequate to protect the public from serious harm from him; and

(iii) why it is so satisfied.

(1A) Sub-paragraphs (a) and (b) of subsection (1)(ii) above shall be construed as if they were contained in Part I of the Criminal Justice Act 1991.

(2) Where the Crown Court makes such a statement, it shall certify in the supervision order that it has made such a statement.

(3) Where a magistrates' court makes such a statement, it shall certify in the supervision order that it has made such a statement and shall cause the statement to be entered in the register."

This is the sole community order which, under the CJA 1991 **17–017** framework, can legitimately claim to be an "alternative to custody". The basis on which it may be imposed has not been the subject of any Court of Appeal guidance but it appears to apply where the offence(s) satisfy the "so serious" criterion to justify custody but the court considers that there are mitigating or other special circumstances which allow the imposition of a community sentence. This will often be the case in regard to the making of other community orders. What distinguishes the use of section 12D is that the basis of the sentence is made explicit and the consequences in the event of a breach of the order are subject to specific powers in CYPA 1969, s. 15(4) (para. 22–051).

"Intermediate treatment" in either form is by far the most prevalent form of additional requirement inserted in supervision orders. In 1993, when approximately 24 per cent of supervision orders supervised by the Probation Service contained additional requirements, 7.9 per cent specified (discretionary IT) under s12(2) and 14.7 per cent stipulated supervised activities under s. 12A(3)(a).

17–018 *Night Restriction*

Under CYPA 1969, s. 12A(3)(b) (introduced by CJA 1982) the supervised person can be required to remain for specified periods between 6.00 pm and 6.00 am either at a place specified in the order or at one of several places so specified.

17–019 This place or one of the specified places shall be where the supervised person lives (section 12A(8)). A night restriction order shall not require the supervised person to remain at a place for longer than 10 hours on any one night (section 12A(9)) and shall not be imposed for more than 30 days (section 12A(11)). For the purposes of calculating "days" subject to restriction, a period beginning in the evening and ending the following morning shall count as one day, namely that upon which the period begins (section 12A(13)). The days subject to night restriction must not fall outside the first three months of the supervision order (section 12A(10)). The supervised person is permitted to leave the place of restriction if accompanied by their parent or guardian, the supervisor or some other person specified in the order (section 12A(12)). Before including a night restriction requirement, the court must follow the same procedural steps and statutory restrictions specified in section 12A(6) and (7) as apply to stipulated IT orders (para. 17–014). The *consent* of the supervised person (or their parent, if aged under 14) is required.

17–020 This requirement has been used extremely rarely and was imposed in only four orders during 1993 where the Probation Service was the supervising agency. The 1990 White Paper (paragraph 8.11) commented that it was a "valuable but under-used power":

> "Young people who are free to come and go as they please at all hours are exposed to greater temptations and are at greater risk of getting into trouble. When they have already offended, that risk can be reduced by placing restrictions on their freedom of movement during the evening and night. One of the reasons for the under-use of the provision is the belief that it could be difficult to enforce. When a juvenile is living at home, his parents should know whether he is there in the evenings and at night. Most parents will exercise some control over their children's movements, especially at night. Combining the binding over of parents with a curfew imposed on the children will help ensure that curfews are enforced. The courts will be encouraged to make greater use of the power they already have."

Probation officers and social workers are unlikely to be persuaded by this argument. There is no statutory provision (yet) for night restriction requirements to be subject to electronic monitoring in the same way as curfew orders.

Requirement to Refrain from Activities

Under CYPA 1969, s. 12A(3)(c) (introduced by CJA 1982) the supervised person can be required "to refrain from participating in activities specified in the order" on a specified day or days occurring within the period of the order, or during the whole or a specified portion of the order. There are only two recorded instances of the use of this requirement during the period 1985—1993 in respect of supervision orders supervised by the Probation Service. Before including a refraining requirement, the court must follow the same procedural steps and statutory restrictions specified in section 12A(6) and (7) as apply to stipulated IT orders (para. 17–014). The *consent* of the supervised person (or their parents, if aged under 14) is required.

Residence Requirements   **17–021**

(i) *With a named individual*
Under CYPA 1969, s. 12(1) a supervision order may require the supervised person "to reside with an individual named in the order who agrees to the requirement" being made. Such a requirement "shall be subject to any such requirement" imposed under section 12(2) (discretionary IT), section 12A (stipulated IT, etc.), section 12B (mental treatment) or section 12C (education). This means that the demands of any of these requirements will take precedence even if this temporarily prevents adherence to the general requirement as to residence.

(ii) *In local authority accommodation*   **17–022**
Under CYPA 1969, s. 12AA (introduced by the Children Act 1989) a court has limited powers to require that a supervised person shall live for a specified period in local authority accommodation (section 12AA(1)). This was introduced when the former power to make a care order in criminal proceedings under section 7(7) was abolished. The requirement shall designate the local authority which will receive the child and this shall be the authority in whose area the juvenile resides (section 12AA(2)). The requirement shall not be made unless the designated local authority has been consulted (section 12AA(3)). The maximum period that may be specified is six months.

The power may only be exercised where the following conditions are satisfied:

(a) the offence in respect of which the requirement is being considered was *committed* during the currency of a supervision order containing either a "named person" residence requirement under section 12(1) or a section 12A(3) requirement (stipulated IT, night restriction or a "refraining" requirement);

(b) the offence is punishable with imprisonment (if committed by a   **17–023**
person aged 21 or over) and, in the opinion of the court, is serious" (section 12AA(6) (c)(iii));

(c) "the court is satisfied that the behaviour which constituted the offence was due, to a significant extent, to the circumstances in

209

which (the offender) was living" (this condition does *not* apply where the previous supervision order contained a "named person" residence requirement);

(d)   the offender must be legally represented (unless the individual has applied for but been turned down for legal aid on grounds of means or has failed to apply for legal aid despite being informed of their right to apply) (section 12AA(9)).

The residence requirement may stipulate that the juvenile shall not live with a named person. This means that the court may restrict the discretion of the local authority in placing the juvenile. Any supervision order imposing this requirement may also impose any of the requirements available under section 12(2), section 12A, section 12B or section 12C.

17–024   Residence requirements are imposed very infrequently. In 1993, of all supervision orders made specifying supervision by the Probation Service only four contained a residential requirement.

Mental Treatment Requirement

Under CYPA 1969, s. 12B, the supervised person can be required to receive treatment for his or her mental condition. The provisions are almost identical to the provisions in PCCA 1973, Sched. 1A para. 5 empowering such a requirement to be imposed in a probation order (para. 18–050). In summary:

(a)   the court must consider the evidence of a medical practitioner appropriately qualified under the Mental Health Act;

(b)   the court must be satisfied that the mental condition of the offender is such as requires and may be susceptible to treatment but not such as to warrant detention under a hospital order;

(c)   the requirement shall be that the supervised person submits to one of the following kinds of treatment—

(i)   by or under the direction of a specified medical practitioner,

(ii)   as a non-resident patient at a specified place,

(iii) as a resident patient in a hospital or mental nursing home;

17–025   (d)   the court must be satisfied that arrangements can be or have been made for the treatment in question and, in the case of treatment as a resident patient, for the reception of the patient.

Where the offender has attained the age of 14, a treatment requirement cannot be included unless the offender *consents*. Such a requirement shall not continue in force after the supervised person attains the age of 18 (section 12B(2)).

Requirements of this kind are only rarely imposed. In 1993, of all supervision orders made, supervised by the Probation Service, only six contained a treatment requirement, all non-residential.

Education Requirements

Under CYPA 1969, s. 12C(1), a supervision order other than one which specifies discretionary IT under section 12(2) may require a supervised person of compulsory school age to comply with such arrangements for his or her education as may from time to time be made by his or her parent (being arrangements approved by the local educational authority). That authority must be consulted in advance about the proposal to include such a requirement and the court must be satisfied that, in the view of that authority, "arrangements exist for the (juvenile) to receive efficient full-time education suitable to his age, ability and aptitude and to any special educational needs (the juvenile) may have" (section 12C(2)). The supervisor must also be consulted about the offender's circumstances. The court must be satisfied that the proposed requirement is "necessary for securing the good conduct of the supervised person or for preventing a repetition of the same offence or the commission of other offences" (section 12C(4)). The juvenile's *consent* is not required.

The Management of a Supervision Order   **17–026**
The administration and management of a supervision order is regulated by the *National Standard for Supervision Orders* (Home Office, 1995a) which applies to supervision exercised by Social Services Departments and by probation officers. The stated expectations and guidance follow very closely the provisions for probation orders and so are not repeated in detail here. In summary, the requirements specify:

* prompt commencement of supervision after the order is made, the initial appointment being given, whenever possible, before the offender leaves court and taking place within five working days;

* the prompt drawing up (within ten working days) of a written **17–027** supervision plan and regular review (at least every three months) of progress;

* frequent contact with the offender—a minimum of twelve appointments, normally weekly, in the first three months of an order; six in the next three months, and thereafter at least one each month to the completion of supervision;

* among "methods" of supervision utilised, at least one home visit should take place in all cases;

* if physical activities are offered, these should be "significantly more than recreation" and should not "give the impression of providing a reward for offending";

* offenders should never be sent abroad as part of their supervision;

* any apparent failure to comply should be dealt with within two working days and if the offender's explanation is not considered

acceptable, the incident should be formally recorded as an instance of failure to comply;

* if breach proceedings are not instituted, the offender should be given a formal warning, in person and confirmed in writing, the offender's response being noted on the record;

* at most, two warnings may be given before breach proceedings are instituted;

* any action taken to enforce the order should take full account of the welfare of the child or young person. The process of enforcement should encourage the juvenile to accept discipline but should retain the degree of flexibility demanded by the individual's age, stage of development and degree of responsibility for his or her actions.

17–028 At the initial meeting, the probation officer or social worker is required to ensure that "the offender is aware of what the order will entail and is able and willing to co-operate (or, if not, take appropriate action by instituting breach proceedings)".

Certain modifications arise in recognition of the offender's age and status to give appropriate regard to the offender's parents (or others who will be material to the supervision). The supervisor is required to include the parents as follows:

* at the commencement of supervision information should be provided to them about the order and their commitment to it should be sought;

* the supervision plan should be drawn up and reviewed in consultation with them, as appropriate;

* their partnership and involvement should be sought at all stages of supervision, including the process of enforcement, and they should receive a copy of any written warning given to the offender for failure to comply.

A probation officer has a duty to "advise, assist and befriend" a person placed under supervision by a supervision order (Probation Rules 1984, r. 33). The observations in regard to probation order records (para. 18–069) broadly apply also to supervision order records held by either a probation officer or a Social Services Department.

In 1993 77 per cent of terminations of supervision orders supervised by the Probation Service followed completion of their full term and a further seven per cent terminated early for good progress (Home Office, 1994a).

17–029 **The Overlap of Probation and Supervision Orders for 16–17 year olds**
In proposing that courts should have the discretion to choose either the 1969 Act regime for statutory supervision (a supervision order) or that provided by the 1973 Act (a probation order), *Crime, Justice and*

Protecting the Public (1990) was of the view that 16 and 17 year olds should be dealt with as "near adults".

"Since some 16 and 17 year olds are more mature than others ... there should be some flexibility in the sentencing arrangements ... the courts should be able to select either (juvenile or adult) disposals according to the maturity of the offender and the arrangements available locally." (paragraph 8.17)

Home Office Circular 30/1992 *Young People and the Youth Court* **17–030** (paragraph 9) sought to explain the concept of varying maturity, referring more helpfully to "stage of development", a less emotive term.

"In deciding which is the most suitable community sentence for a 16 or 17 year old, courts will need to take account both of the offender's circumstances and of the stage of his/her emotional, intellectual, social and physical development in the transition from childhood to adulthood. This decision will be a particularly difficult one to make. Factors which are likely to be relevent include:

* the offender's continuing dependence on or independence from his or her parents;

* whether he/she is leading a stable independent life, and has family responsibilities of his/her own;

* whether he/she is still in full-time education or in or seeking employment;

* the general pattern of his/her social behaviour and his/her leisure interests and activities;

* the nature of his/her relationship with friends and associates;

* whether he/she accepts personal responsibility for his/her actions;

* his/her attitude towards the offence and any victim; and

* whether he/she is intellectually impaired.

Information about and assessment of these factors in pre-sentence reports will be particularly helpful to the courts in reaching their decision."

The original *National Standard* (1992, paragraph 14) provided a clear **17–031** indication that there should be a presumption that the supervision order is more the appropriate form of supervision for this age group:

"While both a supervision order and a probation order are intended to assist an offender to become more responsible and to keep out of trouble, the clearest distinguishing feature is that the supervison order is also intended to help a young person to develop into an adult, whereas a probation order is more appropriate for someone

who is already emotionally, intellectually, socially and physically
an adult. Since many 16 and 17 year olds are still very much in the
stage of transition into adulthood, the supervision order may often
in practice be the more suitable form of supervision."

In addition to the list of factors identified in HOC 30/1992, that version
of the *National Standard* also mentioned the following considerations:

* How would the young person be influenced by other offenders
  currently subject to supervision orders or probation orders whom
  he or she may meet at group sessions?

* Is assistance currently being received or needed from Social
  Services?

17–032 The two professional associations representing Chief Probation Officers
(ACOP) and probation practitioners (NAPO) clearly favour the view that
the supervision order should be the standard order for the under 18s.
ACOP (1992) has stated:

"It can be argued persuasively that the criteria (in National
Standards) exclude all those aged under 18. All such persons require
help to develop into an adult and young persons are always at risk of
being adversely influenced by more mature offenders. We do not
believe that probation orders, and especially combination orders,
should be used for the under 18 year olds except in the most
exceptional circumstances."

NAPO has gone further and stated that "if the young person needs
assistance, there should be no occasion when a probation order is made
rather than a supervision order". The Association has cautioned against
use of the terms "maturity" and "immaturity". "Immature", it is
argued, often has negative connotations and can be discriminatory,
leading to judgements based on simplistic criteria or stereotypes
(NAPO, 1992).

17–033   One question which appears not to have been raised in the debate
about flexible sentencing for near-adults is whether the young person
makes a once-only, irreversible step across the frontier or whether it is a
reversible step, depending on the ebb and flow of circumstances in their
lives, *e.g.* into and out of the family home, employment or full-time
education. Might an offender who has been considered suitable for a
probation order later be viewed as more appropriate for a supervision
order? As the person's suitability for different community sentences has
to be considered afresh on each sentencing occasion, then it would seem
proper to conclude that the step is indeed reversible. For a review of the
application of the various criteria in determining the appropriate
sentence for near adults, suggesting that proposals in pre-sentence
reports are more likely to be influenced by considerations such as the
seriousness of the offence, the young offender's previous record and
assumptions about the way in which the order in question will be
supervised, see Stone (1994).

A thematic inspection of the Probation Service's work with young **17–034** offenders in 12 probation areas, conducted by H.M. Inspectorate of Probation (1994) in late 1993, suggests that supervisory community sentences fall to be determined primarily by the age of the offender:

Order	Age	
	16	17
Supervision	77%	23%
Probation	10%	90%
Combination	27%	73%

The Inspectorate noted that in some areas offenders were far more likely to be proposed for a probation order, regardless of their stage of development, because of staff's reluctance to propose supervison orders on the assumption that such proposals would be viewed less favourably by sentencers.

It should be noted that the demands and restrictions that can be **17–035** imposed as additional requirements in supervision orders can be greater than is lawful under the terms of a probation order, *e.g.* activities requirements under CYPA 1969, s. 12(2) or s. 12A(3) can extend for 90 days instead of 60 days as under PCCA 1973, Sched. 1A, para. 2. The discretion given to the supervisor under CYPA 1969, s. 12(2) is significantly greater than can be exercised under a probation order with PCCA 1973, Sched. 1A, para. 2 activity requirements. The offender's consent is not required before a straight supervision order can be imposed, or even with the addition of section 12(2) requirements. It would thus be wrong to regard the supervision order as intrinsically more benign. It is also quite possible for young offenders subject to supervision orders to come into contact with older offenders, either in the course of reporting or as part of their participation in activities. There is no obligation in law or *National Standards* to segregate young offenders to avoid "contamination", though good practice procedures may well seek to ensure that they receive a distinctive or separate service. The basic distinction between the probation order and the supervision order lies in the name of the order. It is advantageous for the young offender in growing out of crime that their record shows a distinctively juvenile penalty from which they can more readily distance themselves, rather than an adult-sounding penalty with the additional element of stigma attached thereto.

A NACRO survey (1993) of sentencing in the youth courts in 15 local **17–036** authority areas in the first six months following implementation of the 1991 Act showed that 110 supervision orders wre imposed compared with only six probation orders in sentencing a total sample of 754 16 year olds. In dealing with 1178 17 year olds, 103 supervision orders were imposed compared with 41 probation orders.

Chapter 18

Probation Orders

18–001 With a pedigree dating back to 1907, the probation order has been transformed under the 1991 Act from an expression of conditional liberty made "instead of sentencing" (PCCA 1973, s. 2(1), now repealed) to a "community order" within a wider framework of "punishment in the community" and restriction on liberty. The 1990 White Paper, *Crime Justice and Protecting the Public* justified this change of identity by claiming that the wording of section 2(1) reflected:

> "the original intention that probation should be used mainly for first, or relatively trivial offenders. Since then, probation orders have been used increasingly for persistent offenders and for those whose offences put them at risk of custody ... In practice, the probation order can be a penalty making significant demands on the offender."

18–002 This interpretation of the origins of the probation order is of questionable accuracy and, prior to implementation of the 1991 Act, probation was being used as a disposal flexibly in a wide range of cases where it was considered expedient to offer the offender the opportunity to demonstrate their capacity to conform, given supervisory oversight and support, while retaining the scope to impose punishment in the event of default. Those who proposed incorporating the probation order within a range of "intermediate sanctions" (Wasik and Von Hirsch, 1988; Bottoms, 1988) acknowledged the lack of conceptual fit but suggested that offenders placed on probation have customarily experienced the disposal as punitive and thus argued that such a rationalisation had a common-sense appeal. However, the fact that a measure has a demanding impact and curtails personal freedom of choice does not make it a punishment deliberately designed to cause pain, inconvenience or erosion of autonomy. Probation as classically conceived aims to enhance freedom and citizenship and is not intended to be restrictive for its own sake. Probation officers and sentencers have thus experienced some difficulty in absorbing the probation order's new identity as an exercise in both restrictiveness and rehabilitation, particularly now that the "traditional" order without additional requirements is the least restrictive community order.

216

POWER TO MAKE A PROBATION ORDER   **18–003**

PCCA 1973, S. 2

"(1) Where a court by or before which a person of or over the age of sixteen years is convicted of an offence (not being an offence for which the sentence is fixed by law) is of the opinion that the supervision of the offender by a probation officer is desirable in the interests of—

(a)   securing the rehabilitation of the offender; or

(b)   protecting the public from harm from him or preventing the commission by him of further offences,

the court may make a probation order, that is to say, an order requiring him to be under the supervision of a probation officer for a period specified in the order of not less than six months nor more than three years.

For the purposes of this subsection the age of a person shall be deemed to be that which it appears to the court to be after considering any available evidence."

A youth court or the Crown Court may make a probation order in **18–004** respect of any offender aged 16 years or over who has been convicted of any offence, whether imprisonable or not, provided that the court is of the opinion that:

(a)   the offence, or the combination of the offence and one or more offences associated with it, is serious enough to warrant such a sentence (CJA 1991, s. 6(1)), and

(b)   an order is the most suitable for the offender (section 6(2)(a)), and

(c)   supervision is desirable in the interests of either (i) securing the offender's rehabilitation, or (ii) protecting the public from harm from the offender or preventing further offending by the offender.

Though section 2(1) poses the two purposes of probation, rehabilitation or prevention, as alternatives, the court is not explicitly required to state which purpose it has in mind when passing sentence. The *National Standard* appears to expect probation officers to pursue both aims of supervision routinely. For a suggestion that courts should state which objective is considered to make supervision desirable, as this may impact upon the shape of that supervision and upon whether the supervising officer should apply for revocation if the probationer is convicted of a further offence while the order is in force, under CJA 1991, Sched. 2, para. 7, see Shelley (1993).

18–005 Length of Order
The length or, in other words, the extent of restriction on liberty imposed shall be commensurate with the seriousness of the offence or that offence combined with one or more associated offences (section 6(2)(b)). This assessment cannot be made on some objective scale of the time and effort demanded of the offender but must also encompass the anticipated impact upon the offender in the light of their personal circumstances and characteristics. Thus *Crime, Justice and Protecting the Public* (4.9) observed that "the lifestyle of many offenders, especially young adults, is often disorganised and impulsive ... A comparatively short order may make more severe demands on some offenders than more severe orders would on others". However, these are somewhat elusive considerations, not easily explained in distinguishing one offender from another, and may prove difficult to articulate in open court in a way which avoids a sense of grievance for those offenders considered suitable for or more able to tackle "more severe" orders. Courts may find it easier to opt for formal equality of sentence rather than seeking individualised equality of impact.

18–006   The average imposed length of probation orders has reduced in recent years, as the following Table (for all age groups) demonstrates:

	Under 1 Year	1 Year +	2 Years +	3 Years
1983	5%	33%	58%	4%
1993	12%	49%	38%	2%

Source: Probation Statistics 1983 and 1993, Home Office.

This reflects a changing emphasis in probation practice towards shorter, more purposeful periods of supervision, with clearer goals, rather than merely an expectation of a sustained supportive relationship.

18–007 Age of Offender
The minimum age at which an offender may be placed on probation was reduced from 17 to 16 by CJA 1991. This means that there is now an overlap in eligibility for a probation order and a supervision order to reflect the proposal in *Crime, Justice and Protecting the Public* that there should be some flexibility in the sentencing arrangements for 16 and 17 year olds, according to their "maturity" or stage of development and the arrangements available locally. This consideration is explored further in Chapter 17 on Supervision Orders. However, some indication of practice can be gained from a NACRO survey (1993) of sentencing in the youth courts in 15 local authority areas in the first six months following implementation of the 1991 Act. This showed that only six probation orders (none with a probation centre requirement) were imposed on a total of 754 16 year olds dealt with, compared with 110 supervision orders. For 17 year olds, 41 probation orders were imposed on 1178 defendants, compared with 103 supervision orders.

It is for the court to determine whether the offender satisfies the age requirement. The critical date for determining age appears to be date of conviction, *i.e.* the date of the finding of guilt or of plea of guilty (*T* [1979] Crim. L.R. 588; *Danga* (1992) 13 Cr. App. R.(S.) 408). The court may normally rely upon the age stated by the offender or his/her parents, unless there are clear indications that this is unreliable and it would be appropriate to hear evidence of date of birth (*R. v. Recorder of Grimsby, ex p. Purser* [1951] 2 All E.R. 889).

Procedural Requirements 18-008

Pre-Sentence Report

A court is not required to consider a pre-sentence report before deciding whether an offender is suitable for a probation order, unless the order includes an additional requirement authorised by PCCA 1973, Sched. 1A, but good practice discourages the making of standard probation orders (or orders which contain an additional requirement under PCCA 1973, s. 3(1)—see para. 18–019) without a PSR. The Judicial Studies Board has advised magistrates to obtain a PSR before making any probation order, even where this is not a statutory requirement, to ensure that orders are imposed only on suitable defendants where there are reasonably clear and purposeful supervisory aims for the order, agreed with the defendant beforehand. Failure to obtain and consider a report where this is a mandatory requirement does not invalidate the order so made but would be an obvious basis for appeal. The court considering such appeal is required to obtain and consider a report (CJA 1991, s. 7(4)). However, an appeal against a probation order made in such circumstances is perhaps rather unlikely.

The requirement to consider a pre-sentence report does not mean that the report has to address the possibility of a probation order with Schedule 1A requirements but in most instances of such requirements the Schedule requires either consultation with a probation officer or the consent of any third party whose co-operation is required, or both (see, for example, para. 18–041).

Explanation and Consent 18-009

PCCA 1973, s. 2

"(3) Before making a probation order, the court shall explain to the offender in ordinary language—

(a) the effect of the order (including any additional requirements proposed to be included in the order in accordance with section 3 below);

(b) the consequences which may follow under Schedule 2 to the Criminal Justice Act 1991 if he fails to comply with any of the requirements of the order; and

(c) that the court has under that Schedule power to review the order on the application either of the offender or of the supervising officer,

and the court shall not make the order unless he expresses his willingness to comply with its requirements."

18–010 Explanation should thus be given directly to the offender by the court and should not be delegated to the defence advocate or probation officer. The offender should be given a fair opportunity to make an informed choice whether to consent. The issue of consent, including reference to the pre-CJA 1991 case law concerning consent to a probation order, is detailed at para. 15–015.

Specified Area

PCCA 1973, s. 2

"(2) A probation order shall specify the petty sessions area in which the offender resides or will reside; and the offender shall, subject to paragraph 12 of Schedule 2 to the Criminal Justice Act 1991 (offenders who change their residence), be required to be under the supervision of a probation officer appointed for or assigned to that area."

18–011 The order must specify a petty sessions area and thereafter jurisdiction in regard to the enforcement, amendment or revocation of the order will be exercised by a justice or magistrates' court acting for that area. Supervision of the offender will be undertaken by a probation officer attached to that area. This is normally a straightforward matter but complications can arise if the offender lives or intends to live outside of England and Wales or is without a clear plan for their future accommodation:

(a) If the offender resides or will reside abroad, *e.g.* in the Republic of Ireland (*McCartan* [1958] 1 W.L.R. 933) a probation order should not be imposed because the English court cannot specify supervision and enforcement in a foreign jurisdiction.

(b) If the offender resides or will reside in Scotland or Northern Ireland, the court must be satisfied that suitable arrangements for the offender's supervision can be made by the Scottish Regional or Islands Council for the proposed home area or by the Probation Board for Northern Ireland. Transfer of orders to these two jurisdictions is regulated by CJA 1991, Sched. 3. The order must specify the offender's "locality" in Scotland together with the appropriate court of summary jurisdiction or the appropriate petty sessions district in Northern Ireland.

(c) If the offender is homeless or is an itinerant traveller, then there will clearly need to be particular consideration of the offender's suitability for a probation order or of the viability of supervision. The Probation Service may well be able to assist the homeless young offender to obtain accommodation. If the order is considered appropriate, then the court will specify the PSA which seems most appropriate, in the anticipation that this may need to be amended as circumstances develop.

Provision for the amendment of a probation order to substitute another **18–012** petty sessions area is contained in CJA 1991, Sched. 2, para. 12, detailed at para. 22–001 *et seq.*

Commencement and Provision of Copies of the Order

A probation order imposed by a youth court or the Crown Court comes into force on the date that the order is made. Thus an order imposed on June 13 for 12 months expires at midnight on June 12 the following year, unless revoked in the meantime.

PCCA 1973, s. 2

"(4) The court by which a probation order is made shall forthwith give copies of the order to a probation officer assigned to the court, and he shall give a copy—

(a) to the offender;

(b) to the probation officer responsible for the offender's supervision; and

(c) to the person in charge of any institution in which the offender is required by the order to reside.

(5) The court by which such an order is made shall also, except **18–013** where it itself acts for the petty sessions area specified in the order, send to the clerk to the justices for that area—

(a) a copy of the order; and

(b) such documents and information relating to the case as it considers likely to be of assistance to a court acting for that area in the exercise of its functions in relation to the order."

By analogy with *Walsh v. Barlow* [1985] 1 W.L.R. 90, considered at para. 19–014, delivery of a copy of the order to the offender is not a pre-requisite of the coming into force of the order.

Combining a Probation Order with other Sentences and Orders **18–014**
The general rule broadly applies that "courts should avoid mixing sentences which fall into well-established and different categories": *McElhorne* (1983) 5 Cr. App. R.(S.) 53. Thus the Court of Appeal has made clear that a probation order should never be imposed on the same

occasion as a custodial sentence: *Evans* [1959] 1 W.L.R. 26, even for different counts or separate indictments.

Whereas prior to CJA 1991 a probation order was not a "punishment" and thus could not be combined with any other disposal of a punitive nature, its new status under the Act removes such limitations, with one significant exception. A probation order and a community service order may not be combined for the same offence except in the form of a combination order (CJA 1991, s. 6(3)). However, prior to implementation of CJA 1991, the Court of Appeal held that the combination of probation and community service orders for different offences was lawful (*Harkess* (1990) 12 Cr. App. R.(S.) 366).

18–015   The scope for combining a probation order with other sentences and orders in respect of either the same of different offences on the same sentencing occasion can be conveniently summarised in the following Table:

Combination of Probation with Other Penalties

	Dis-charge	Fine	At-tend-ance Centre	Super-vision Order	CSO Order	Com-bin-ation Order	Curfew	Cus-tody
Same Offence	No	Yes	Yes	No	No	No	Yes	No
Different Offences	Yes	Yes	Yes	No	Yes	Yes*	Yes	No

* Appears legally permissible but probably undesirable in practice.

Though the Act does not prohibit combining a probation order with a supervision order, this appears to be completely contrary to the notion that an offender should be assessed as suitable for either the juvenile or the adult form of supervision but not both. A court might wish to secure the "best of both worlds" to take advantage of local resources but the consequent confusion and duplication would suggest that this would be wrong in principle.

A mix of a combination order with a probation order for the same offence, is not explicitly barred by CJA 1991, s. 6(3) but appears contrary to the spirit and intentions of the Act. Whilst a probation order can properly be combined with an attendance centre order, careful thought should be given to whether this is a realistic accumulation of demands upon a young offender. However, as an attendance centre order can be imposed as a penalty for breach of a probation order under Sched. 2, Pt. II, where the probation order is allowed to continue, the Act clearly envisages that the two orders can be fulfilled compatibly.

REQUIREMENTS IN A PROBATION ORDER 18–016

The Standard Requirement

PCCA 1973, s. 2

"(6) An offender in respect of whom a probation order is made shall keep in touch with the probation officer responsible for his supervision in accordance with such instructions as he may from time to time be given by that officer and shall notify him of any change of address."

This specification for the standard probation order is reproduced intact in the form of order prescribed by the Magistrates Courts (Children and Young Persons) Rules 1992, Sched. 2, Form 47. This replaces the traditional trinity of requirements including the somewhat imprecise expectation that the offender "shall be of good behaviour and lead an industrious life". "Good behaviour" primarily related to the avoidance of further offending which then constituted a breach of probation under PCCA 1973, s. 8, but could also be invoked to enforce acceptable behaviour whilst on probation premises or in contact with probation staff. Thus breach proceedings could be initiated if the probationer persisted in the use of unacceptable racist, sexist or other discriminatory language or behaviour. However, the vagueness of the requirement made such enforcement a rather uncertain process.

It could be argued that the present requirement to keep in touch in **18–017** accordance with instructions covers also an obligation to follow any reasonable rules and expectations specified by the Probation Service. Breach proceedings initiated on the basis of unacceptable or oppressive conduct might be contested on grounds that the requirement is simply "to keep in touch" as regards the time and location of appointments and does not extend to include how an offender should behave whilst keeping in touch unless instructions regarding language or behaviour are clear and explicit. It might also be argued that requirements should be express and precise if they are to command legal enforcement. As Lord Goddard indicated in a *Practice Statement* (1952) 35 Cr. App. R. 207:

"If the court simply says that it makes a probation order, the effect is an order requiring the probationer to be under the supervision of a probation officer for the period specified. If the court desires to impose other conditions, the court must specifically impose them."

It would be open to the sentencing court to impose a specific **18–018** requirement relating to the offender's conduct during the course of supervision, using the general power to impose additional requirements under PCCA 1973, s. 3(1). Failing enforcement by breach action, the alternative remedy could be to seek revocation of a standard order on the basis that the offender's attitude made the order unworkable and its objectives unattainable.

Gone too is any explicit requirement to receive visits from the probation officer at home, though this may be the basis of an instruction for keeping in touch. Contact guidance in the *National Standard* (1995, para. 15) governing probation orders identifies a home visit as a method of supervision and specifies that "at least one home visit should take place in all cases", subject to health and safety considerations. "Keeping in touch" is a somewhat casual expression which emphasises how much the spirit of the probation order is to seek to promote goodwill and co-operation rather than a climate of formality and instruction. Unlike community service, there are no statutory rules regulating lateness, disruptiveness and non-compliance, or *National Standard* guidance on standards of behaviour.

18–019 Nevertheless an offender who persistently turns up late for appointments is clearly in default of instructions and liable to breach proceedings. More difficulties apply to the offender who persistently arrives drunk and thus unable to participate in any meaningful discussion. Instruction may be given that the offender should report in a sufficiently sober state to participate but the offender may seek to establish a reasonable excuse for their failure to comply on grounds of their alcohol dependency. Here too recourse may be necessary to revocation rather than breach action. Orders including requirements as to activities, attendance at a probation centre or hostel residence have the advantage of a specific provision that the offender shall comply with instructions whilst under the authority of the person in charge.

General Power to Include Additional Requirements

PCCA 1973, s. 3

"(1) Subject to subsection (2) below, a probation order may in addition require the offender to comply during the whole or any part of the probation period with such requirements as the court, having regard to the circumstances of the case, considers desirable in the interests of—

(a) securing the rehabilitation of the offender; or

(b) protecting the public from harm from him or preventing the commission by him of further offences."

18–020 This power appears to offer considerable scope to devise bespoke requirements to match the circumstances of the individual offender but should be read subject to the following limitations:

(a) "the payment of sums by way of damages for injury or compensation for loss shall not be included among the additional requirements of a probation order" (section 3(2), though compensation can be ordered as an ancillary measure under PCCA 1973, s. 12(4)) or as a separate order under PCCA 1973, s. 35);

(b) a requirement should not be vague or unenforceable (per Lord Goddard in a *Practice Statement* (1952) 35 Cr. App. R. 207). Thus a requirement not to enter amusement machine arcades or not to associate with a named person such as a co-defendant could prove very difficult to enforce;

(c) a requirement under section 3(1) should not seek to impose a **18–021** form of demand for which there is alternative, precise and more appropriate statutory provision, *e.g.* to perform unpaid work akin to community service, to reside in a residential establishment or to take part in some form of group activity (*per* Lord Bridge in *Cullen v. Rogers* [1982] 1 W.L.R. 729);

(d) "any discretion conferred on the probation officer pursuant to the terms of the order to regulate a probationer's activities must itself be confined within well-defined limits" (*per* Lord Bridge in *Cullen v. Rogers, supra*);

(e) a requirement under section 3(1) should not "involve a substantial element of custodial punishment" (*per* Lord Bridge in *Cullen v. Rogers,* supra) (though made in the context of pre-CJA 1991 law in which the probation order was made *instead of* sentence, it is submitted that this still remains a valid limitation on the use of section 3(1) powers);

(f) the restrictions on liberty imposed by any requirement under section 3(1) must be in accordance with the general rule contained in CJA 1991, s. 6(2)(b) as regards commensurability with the seriousness of the offence(s) and suitability.

In general, additional requirements should, if possible, be devised in **18–022** accordance with those authorised and regulated by PCCA 1973, Sched. 1A (for example, a refraining order under paragraph 2(1)(b)) and ad hoc requirements should be viewed very circumspectly. A preferable option may be for the court to defer sentence, making clear its expectations of the offender (see para. 10–013). Note that a court is not required to obtain and consider a pre-sentence report before forming an opinion as to the suitability for an offender of a probation order which includes an additional requirement under section 3(1) but is almost certainly likely to seek a report in such circumstances.

The Court of Appeal has recently upheld a requirement made under section 3(1) that the offender should not commit any further offence during the currency of the order (*Peacock, The Times,* November 7, 1994). Though acknowledging that the offender would not be liable to be dealt with in breach proceedings if he further offended, because of the specific exclusion in CJA 1991, Sched.2, para.5 (1) (para. 22–025), the Court nevertheless considered that the requirement was a valid use of section 3(1) powers because, if the offender committed a further offence while on probation and was brought back before the Crown Court, the order could be revoked under Sched.2, para.8(2) (see para. 22–074) and the offender could be dealt with afresh for the original offence. It is difficult to follow what this additional requirement added to the enforcement powers of the court, since scope to exercise Sched.2, para.8 powers would apply equally to a standard order. If such a requirement was added to an order imposed by a youth court, revocation could only be considered on the application of either the offender or the supervising officer as magistrates, unlike the Crown Court, have no jurisdiction to revoke on their own initiative. Further, revocation is only possible in either the Crown Court or a youth court while the order is in force. The *Peacock* decision thus seems to confuse breach and revocation proceedings.

18–023 **Requirements as to Residence**

PCCA 1973, Sched. 1A, para. 1

"(1) Subject to sub-paragraphs (2) and (3) below, a probation order may include requirements as to the residence of the offender.

(2) Before making a probation order containing any such requirement, the court shall consider the home surroundings of the offender.

(3) Where a probation order requires the offender to reside in an approved hostel or any other institution, the period for which he is so required to reside shall be specified in the order."

This power is cast in very wide terms but tends to be used in two main instances: to require a period of residence at either a probation hostel or a rehabilitation unit run by a voluntary organisation, or to provide some role for the supervising officer in determining where the offender will live beyond that of simply being informed of any change of address. In 1993, only two per cent of probation orders contained an additional requirement of residence in an approved probation hostel (a decrease from four per cent in 1982), less than one per cent specified residence in another form of institution, and one per cent some other residential requirement.

A residence requirement has the capacity to be both a substantial restriction of liberty and an invaluable opportunity for rehabilitative initiatives. The Court of Appeal has not given any general guidance on the appropriate use of this measure but *Attorney-General's Reference No.15 of 1994* (1995) 16 Cr. App. R.(S.) 619 suggests the potential of this community sentence for serious offences in some instances. The offender aged 17 had attacked a 60 year old man with a piece of wood, fracturing his skull. For causing grievous bodily harm with intent, he received a probation order with a requirement of residence at a semi-secure children's centre. Though the Court of Appeal accepted that this sentence was unduly lenient, the probation order was allowed to continue in the light of the offender's age and plea, his experience of disadvantage, his progress and increased self-discipline at the centre in the ten months on remand and six months since sentence, and the nature of the centre's "very stiff regime" (residents were not allowed out unaccompanied and had only one accompanied outing per week). It was thus not considered in the public interest to disturb this opportunity.

Residence in an Approved Hostel   **18–024**

Approved hostels may be run either directly by probation committees (or boards, as they will become) or by voluntary management committees. Both kinds of establishment are subject to the Approved Probation and Bail Hostel Rules 1995 (S.I. 1995/302) and to the *National Standard for the Management of Approved Probation and Bail Hostels* (Home Office, 1995a).

Purpose of Hostels: The *National Standard* (1995, paragraphs 5–7) indicates that the purpose of approved hostels is "to provide an enhanced level of supervision to enable ... offenders to remain under supervision in the community" and shall not be seen as simply a means of providing accommodation. They should provide a structured and supportive environment which will seek to:

(a) ensure that the requirements of the court are met;   **18–025**

(b) promote a responsible and law-abiding lifestyle and respect for others;

(c) create and maintain a constructive relationship between staff and residents;

(d) facilitate the work of the probation service and other agencies aimed at reducing the risk that residents will offend or re-offend in future;

(e) assist the residents to keep or find employment and to develop their employment skills;

(f) encourage and enable residents to use the facilities available in the local community and to develop their ability to become self-reliant in doing so;

(g) enable residents to move on successfully to other appropriate accommodation at the end of their period of residence;

(h) establish and maintain good relations with neighbours and the community in general.

Given the substantial commitment that hostel residency requires, it is not easy to locate this form of community order in some rising scale of restriction on liberty. All seem agreed that it constitutes "a very great restriction" (Magistrates Association, *et al.*, 1993), perhaps the greatest form of restrictiveness possible within a community sentence, and thus should not be considered unless the offence is of a degree of seriousness on the threshold of custody. The implication is that rather fewer offenders will be proposed for this disposal and that probation hostels will increasingly serve a bail function rather than a statutory supervisory role.

18-026 *Suitability for Admission:* The *National Standard* (1995, paragraph 12) indicates, firstly, that priority should be given "to those who both require and will benefit from the structured and supportive environment provided" and, secondly, that the following categories of offender should not be accepted:

(a) those convicted of offences too minor to justify hostel placement (this reflects the wish to avoid imposing considerable restrictions upon liberty upon minor offenders);

(b) those whose sole need is accommodation and who do not need the level of supervision provided by an approved hostel;

(c) those whose admission would present an acceptable risk of serious harm to the staff, other residents, or those in the immediate community;

(d) those whose admission might place them at risk from other residents.

18-027 Each hostel is required to adopt an admissions policy, notified to the courts for the area in which the hostel is situated (APHR 1995, r.10(2)). An offender who is being considered for a condition of hostel residence is usually required to undertake a trial period of residence on "bail assessment", normally for 28 days, to gauge their suitability and attitude and to give them the opportunity to decide if they wish to make a longer term commitment. At the conclusion of that period the warden or their deputy will normally provide a report to the court indicating whether a requirement of residence appears appropriate and, if so, for what duration. Sched. 1A, para. 1 does not explicitly require the agreement of the hostel or institution to receive and accommodate the offender before the making of a residence requirement but the requirement would clearly be unworkable without such agreement. No hostel shall refuse to accept a person who is required by a probation order to reside therein, except with the consent of the Secretary of State (APHR 1995, r.10(1)).

18-028 The reduction in the minimum age for a probation order to 16 has made it necessary to re-consider the suitability of youths under 18 for a requirement of residence in approved hostels. Home Office Circular 44/1993 suggests that residence is not appropriate for many 16 and 17 year olds and indicates that all such referrals will have to be made to an Assistant Chief Probation Officer for approval, taking the following factors into consideration:

(i) Is the young person concerned still at school?

(ii) In the case of 16/17 year old girls, does a mixed hostel have living accommodaton for the sexes which is quite distinct and separate?

(iii) Hostels do not provide secure or intensively supervised accommodation, so failure of juvenile establishments to hold young offenders or control their behaviour should not be a reason to consider the adult alternative.

(iv) The *National Standard for the Management of Approved Probation and Bail Hostels* requires that the risk posed to any potential resident by other residents is a factor which must be considered. Other residents could present a real risk to young offenders of injury, intimidation and contamination. This is especially true where hostels already accommodate sex offenders.

(v) Hostels are required to prepare residents to move on to independent living as soon as possible. This may not be appropriate for 16 and 17 year olds who are not sufficiently mature or financially independent.

Length of Residence: The period of residence should be specified in the **18–029** order. It is questionable whether a form of wording which refers to "a period of up to x months" would be sufficiently precise. It is open to the supervising officer to seek to amend the order if residence becomes unnecessary or inappropriate prior to the end of the specified period. Except with the consent of the Chief Probation Officer, no person under the supervision of a probation officer shall reside in a hostel for any longer than the period specified in the probation order (APHR 1995, r. 11(a)). A resident shall not be required to cease to reside at the hostel before the expiry of the term of residence specified in the probation order (or of the remand period, if on bail assessment), except in case of emergency. In the event of such emergency, the hostel shall give reasonable notice to the supervising officer (if that is not the warden) or to the court which granted bail (if the resident is on bail assessment) (APHR 1995, r. 12(2)).

Place of Residence: The wording of Sched. 1A, para. 1 (unlike PCCA **18–030** 1973, s. 2(6), now repealed) is not explicit that the requirement should specify the particular hostel or institution but a requirement which simply refers to "an approved hostel" (thus leaving it to the supervising officer to allocate the offender) is both undesirable in practice and probably void for lack of certainty. The same objection would probably apply to a requirement "to reside at a hostel to be determined by the probation officer", a format which confers undue discretion upon the probation officer, contrary to the principle stated by Lord Bridge in *Cullen v. Rogers* (see para. 18–021). Given the careful discretion to be exercised in the placing of young persons, such imprecise requirements are highly unlikely.

18–031 *Rules of the Hostel:* An approved hostel (and doubtless any residential institution) will have a set of rules detailing the requirements and restrictions on residents. Paragraph 1 is silent as regards the residents' compliance with rules, unlike the provision in the Bail Act 1976, s. 3(6A) which states that a defendant with a bail condition of residence at a hostel "may also be required to comply with the rules of the hostel". A requirement that the resident on probation should comply with the rules of the hostel is arguably within the ambit of "requirements as to residence", as a matter of commonsense. It would certainly be an unfortunate omission if such a power was held to be outside of the scope of sub-paragraph (1). For an example of an instance in which an offender was placed on probation with a requirement to abide by the rules of the hostel, see *Powell* (1992) 13 Cr. App. R.(S.) 202. The offender subsequently absconded and so was clearly in breach of his residence requirement but the Court of Appeal did not criticise the requirement format. If a power to impose a requirement as to compliance with the rules does exist, it does not follow that the hostel has total discretion as to the nature of those rules. Rules should be reasonably related to the viability of residence. For example, a rule prohibiting consumption of alcohol in the hostel addresses a legitimate issue of residence but an alternative rule prohibiting residents from drinking alcohol in public houses exceeds that ambit. If breach proceedings are initiated for non-compliance then the offender may seek to challenge the rule in question as gratuitously controlling and unrelated to the essentials of residence. The *National Standard* (1995, paras. 17–19) specifies the following rules for hostels:

18–032 (a) payment by residents of the agreed weekly charge, unless this has been waived;

  (b) a requirement that residents should return to the hostel by a fixed time, by 11.00 pm at the latest, though this may exceptionally be extended to 11.30 pm, and remain there until 6.00 am, unless a dispensation has been granted in certain circumstances, *e.g.* if the resident is employed on shift work;

  (c) prohibition of (i) violent, threatening or disruptive language or conduct; (ii) disorderly, threatening or abusive behaviour as a result of alcohol or drug abuse; (iii) the use of controlled drugs, other than on prescription and following notification to staff; (iv) language or conduct that might reasonably give serious offence to others; (v) theft or damage to the property of the hostel, staff or other residents.

18–033 A common rule requirement specifically affecting residents under 18 is that they should participate in a government scheme of youth employment training. This is necessary to ensure that they qualify for state benefit entitlement and are thus able to pay their weekly residence charge. This is thus a rule relating to viability of residence rather than an extraneous or gratuitous demand.

Specified PSA and Supervising Officer: The petty sessions area specified in the order shall be the area in which the hostel or institution is situated. If the establishment is an approved hostel run by a probation committee or board with probation officers acting as warden and deputy warden, then the supervising officer will be one of those officers. In other instances the supervising officer will be a local probation officer assigned to undertake that role.

Supervision Programme: Residents should be offered support to address **18–034** their personal needs (*National Standard* 1995, para. 14). Hostel staff should work with the resident and the supervising officer to put together a programme for the duration of the period of residence which complements supervision of the probation order and plans for the resident's eventual discharge, provided that this does not conflict with the resident's employment, education, training or religious observances (*National Standard* 1995, para.22). Facilities should be available for the provision of any necessary medical and dental treatment (APHR 1995, r.17(1)(a)).

Absconding: Where a resident absconds from the hostel, the warden or **18–035** manager shall immediately notify the supervising probation officer (if the warden does not hold that responsibility personally) if the resident is on probation (or the relevant court and the police, if the resident is on bail) (APHR 1995, r.14). The requirement in the 1976 Rules that next of kin should be notified if the resident is aged under 18 has not been retained.

Breach of Requirement: Breach of the rules of the hostel constitutes a breach of supervision requirements and should be dealt with in accordance with the *National Standard* for probation orders. In certain instances breach may be initiated even though the offender is able to continue residence but disciplinary action is felt appropriate to indicate the unacceptability of their behaviour. If the nature of the alleged breach is considered so serious that continued residence is considered to be unacceptable, the question arises whether the hostel should await the outcome of court proceedings before resolving the resident's future status so that, if breach is denied, the resident will have the opportunity to contest the allegation without incurring loss of residency in the meantime.

Immediate eviction might seem contrary to justice, yet in the **18–036** circumstances the offender's continued residence may well be untenable in practice. In many instances the alleged misconduct may be difficult to substantiate, for example bullying or intimidation of another resident where the victim is unwilling to give evidence yet it is considered essential to remove the perpetrator. If the individual cannot be transferred to another hostel, the question arises whether, on eviction, breach proceedings could be initiated on the ground not of a failure to abide by the rules but of their 'failure to reside' at the hostel.

This is common practice but illustrates the difficulties which can occur in the practical management of hostel life within a statutory framework.

18–037 *Residence as Directed by the Supervising Officer*

A requirement sometimes proposed or felt desirable for offenders whose living arrangements have been very unstable or otherwise a cause of concern is the very open-ended format: "to reside where directed by the probation officer". This appears to place the onus upon the probation officer to choose where the offender should live. It would be objectionable to use this power to direct residence in an "institution" as this should properly be specified in the order and thus subject to paragraph 1(3) (see HOC 137/1949). Nevertheless, some independent or voluntary agencies offering residential services stipulate that they will only accept a resident as a requirement of probation where that requirement is drafted flexibly to reside where directed by the probation officer. If the resident then opts to leave or is required to leave the programme, a return to court is neither the inevitable next step nor the agency's direct responsibility. It could be argued that this broad wording confers undue discretion upon the probation officer, contrary to Lord Bridge's dictum in *Cullen v. Rogers* (see para. 18–021). An alternative format, "to reside where approved by the probation officer" appears to give the probation officer less power and discretion but a right to be consulted and of veto in regard to arrangements proposed by the offender. Even here, there could be considerable problems in seeking to establish breach of the requirement if the offender argues that their circumstances changed for reasons beyond their control, rendering them homeless and needing urgent alternative accommodation, the probation officer being either unavailable or unable to offer more appropriate housing resources.

18–038 *Other Residence Requirements*

A requirement that the offender shall reside at an establishment or institution other than an approved probation hostel, *e.g.* a drug rehabilitation unit, operates in a similar way to residence in an approved, hostel, albeit without being regulated by the APBH Rules 1995 or the *National Standard*. For issues concerning the length and place of residence, rules and the relevant petty sessions area, see 18–029 *et seq.* The supervising officer will normally be a probation officer designated as the liaison officer for that establishment.

An order may require the offender to live with a specified person, *e.g.* a relative. Schedule 1 paragraph 1 does not explicitly require the agreement or consent of the person to accommodate the offender but the requirement would clearly be an unworkable nonsense unless such agreement was clearly forthcoming.

Requirements as to Activities or Attendance at a Probation Centre
The clear majority of additional requirements in probation orders are of this nature and used to be well known as "Schedule Eleven" conditions,

in reference to CJA 1982, Sched. 11 which introduced PCCA 1973, s. 4A and s. 4B, now repealed but almost entirely re-enacted in Sched. 1A, paras. 2–4. Such requirements can now be conveniently referred to as "probation programmes". The broad purpose is to require the offender to participate in a programme of education, therapy, group activities or training intended to rehabilitate but also requiring a greater commitment of time and effort than the standard probation order and thus appropriate where the offence merits additional restriction on liberty. There are broadly three forms of the "programme" requirement:

(a) to report to a particular person at a specific place and comply with **18–039** instructions;

(b) to participate in specified activities;

(c) to attend a probation centre.

Each of these requirements may not extend beyond 60 days of attendance. There is thus scope to tailor the particular requirement flexibly to suit the available facility. Thus it may be more appropriate to draft the requirement in terms of the place(s) to be attended, the person who will be responsible or the activity to be undertaken, depending on what is proposed and how it is organised. There is, however, a widespread belief that the probation centre requirement is likely to be the most sustained, "intensive" and demanding experience on offer within this range and that attendance at a centre is particularly appropriate "for some of the most serious offenders given a community sentence" (*National Standard*, 1992, Annex 3A, para. 3). Centres have thus acquired an identity as the "top of the range" flagship of the Probation Service and subject to particular attention in the 1992 *National Standard* (not repeated in the 1995 revised version) in regard to the length of the day of attendance. They also have to be specifically approved by the Secretary of State and thus should meet criteria of consistency and quality. In 1993, seven per cent of probation orders contained a requirement of centre attendance, 13 per cent required participation in specified activities and only two per cent required reporting to a specified person/place.

Specified Place or Specified Activities Requirement　　　　**18–040**

PCCA 1973, Sched. 1A, para. 2

"(1) Subject to the provisions of this paragraph, a probation order may require the offender—
　(a) to present himself to a person or persons specified in the order at a place or places so specified;
　(b) to participate or refrain from participating in activities specified in the order—
　　(i) on a day or days so specified; or

(ii)   during the probation period or such portion of it as may be so specified.

(5)   A place specified in an order shall have been approved by the probation committee for the area in which the premises are situated as providing facilities suitable for persons subject to probation orders."

18–041 Though the two kinds of requirement are posed as alternative possibilities, they are not mutually exclusive and it would be possible to require an offender to undertake requirements of both kinds, though this would appear subject to the limitation under paragraph 2(4) and (6) that the total number of days of attendance required by an order should not exceed 60 days in aggregate (see below). Paragraph 2 is specific in regard to consultation, feasibility and the consent of other persons whose co-operation is essential for the requirement to be viable:

PCCA 1973, Sched. 1A, para. 2

"(2)   A court shall not include in a probation order a requirement such as is mentioned in sub-paragraph (1) above unless—
(a)   it has consulted a probation officer; and
(b)   it is satisfied that it is feasible to secure compliance with the requirement.

(3)   A court shall not include a requirement such as is mentioned in sub-paragraph (1)(a) above or a requirement to participate in activities if it would involve the co-operation of a person other than the offender and the probation officer responsible for his supervision, unless that other person consents to its inclusion."

The maximum duration of an activities or "place" requirement and the obligations upon an offender are specified as follows, having regard to the offender's work or educational commitments:

18–042   **PCCA 1973, Sched. 1A, para. 2**

"(4)   A requirement such as is mentioned in sub-paragraph (1)(a) above shall operate to require the offender—
(a)   in accordance with instructions given by the probation officer responsible for his supervision, to present himself at a place or places for not more than 60 days in the aggregate; and
(b)   while at any place, to comply with instructions given by, or under the authority of, the person in charge of that place.

(6)   A requirement to participate in activities shall operate to require the offender—
(a)   in accordance with instructions given by the probation officer

responsible for his supervision, to participate in activities for not more than 60 days in the aggregate; and

(b) while participating, to comply with instructions given by, or under the authority of, the person in charge of the activities.

(7) Instructions given by a probation officer under sub-paragraph (4) or (6) above shall, as far as practicable, be such as to avoid any interference with the times, if any, at which the offender normally works or attends a school or other educational establishment."

No mention is made of avoiding a clash with religious or cultural **18–043** commitments but this would be an obvious anti-discriminatory consideration in practice and an issue that could be raised in answer to a breach allegation. "As far as practicable" suggests that work or education cannot claim an absolute priority but if it is not possible to make arrangements which avoid such interference then there would clearly be doubts in the first instance as to the offender's suitability for this form of order and, if these commitments arise during the course of the order, then an application for revocation might be the most appropriate course.

There is one significant exception to the normal maximum duration of the commitment. An offender convicted of a sexual offence (as defined by CJA 1991, s. 31(1)) may be ordered to participate for "such greater number of days as may be specified" (Schedule 1A, paragraph 4). This allows longer term attendance, *e.g.* at a sexual offending therapy group, up to the total length of the order.

Probation Centre Requirement   **18–044**

PCCA 1973, Sched. 1A, para. 3

"(1) Subject to the provisions of this paragraph, a probation order may require the offender during the probation period to attend a probation centre specified in the order.

(3) A requirement under sub-paragraph (1) above shall operate to require the offender—

(a) in accordance with instructions given by the probation officer responsible for his supervision, to attend on not more than 60 days at the centre specified in the order; and

(b) while attending there to comply with instructions given by, or under the authority of, the person in charge of the centre.

(5) References in this paragraph to attendance at a probation centre include references to attendance elsewhere than at the centre for the purpose of participating in activities in accordance with instructions given by, or under the authority of, the person in charge of the centre.

(7) In this paragraph "probation centre" means premises—
- (a) at which non-residential facilities are provided for use in connection with the rehabilitation of offenders; and
- (b) which are for the time being approved by the Secretary of State as providing facilities suitable for persons subject to probation orders."

18–045 On the commencement of the Act, all existing "day centres" under PCCA 1973, s. 4B automatically became probation centres (CJA 1991, Sched. 12, para. 3). This requirement cannot be imposed in respect of an offender who resides or intends to reside in Scotland (CJA 1991, Sched. 3, para. 1(3)(c)). If the offender resides or intends to reside in Northern Ireland, the equivalent facility is a "day centre" as defined by the Probation Act (Northern Ireland) 1950, s. 2B (Sched. 3, para. 2(3)(c)). As in the case of para. 2 requirements, Sched. 1A para. 4 permits one exception to the normal maximum duration of attendance. An offender convicted of a sexual offence (as defined by CJA 1991, s. 31(1)) may be ordered to attend for "such greater number of days as may be specified". This allows longer term attendance up to the total length of the order.

Prior consultation and the need to clarify that the proposed arrangements are feasible are specified as follows:

PCCA 1973, Sched. 1A, para. 3

"(2) A court shall not include such a requirement in a probation order unless—
- (a) it has consulted a probation officer; and
- (b) it is satisfied—
  - (i) that arrangements can be made for the offender's attendance at a centre; and
  - (ii) that the person in charge of the centre consents to the inclusion of the requirement."

18–046 As in the case of paragraph 2 requirements, instructions to attend a probation centre "shall, so far as practicable, be such as to avoid any interference with the times, if any, at which the offender normally works or attends a school or other educational establishment" (paragraph 3(4)). The observations in regard to paragraph 2 (para. 18–043) apply also here.

Regime: Though the 1990 White Paper indicated that the Government would introduce a *National Standard* for probation centres to promote standardisation, including a core curriculum to be provided by every centre, no separate Standard for centres has been introduced to date. The 1992 *National Standard for Probation Orders* provided an Annex stipulating the expectations of the Secretary of State in approving centres. This made clear that the offender will be expected to attend a programme for 20 or more full days attendance (or 40 or more half days) and that a day's attendance shall comprise at least six hours (at least three hours for a half day). A broad ranging programme should be provided, "addressing offending behaviour, personal difficulties relevant to offending and constructive use of leisure time". If these expectations are not met, specific justification will be necessary in seeking approval. The Secretary of State may make rules regulating centres and attendance by offenders, the reckoning of days of attendance and the keeping of records (Schedule 1A, paragraph 3(6)).

Some probation centre programmes have devised activities which **18–047** require attenders to undertake practical "reparation", by working alongside offenders undertaking community service orders. This would seem questionable both in practice and in law as it blurs the distinction between two different kinds of community orders. Community service can be imposed as a penalty for failure to comply with the requirement of a probation order (CJA 1991, Sched. 2, paras. 3(1)(b) and 4(1)(b) and should not be an informal ingredient of the requirement of a probation order.

Sentencing Guidance: Reported appeal cases provide little useful gui- **18–048** dance on the appropriate use of the probation centre. In regard to the "day training centre", the probation centre's early predecessor under pre-CJA 1982 legislation, the Court of Appeal in *Cardwell* (1974) 58 Cr. App. R. 241 stated that this kind of requirement was to be used for "a limited class of offender, the socially inadequate pest" and should not be routinely "tacked on to a probation order of the ordinary kind". This is clearly a dated interpretation, albeit a useful reminder that the power should not be exercised without careful thought both as to suitability and seriousness. In more recent cases such as *Adamson* [1989] Crim. L.R. 79 the Court of Appeal has demonstrated a willingness to take a calculated risk and impose a probation order with a requirement of day centre attendance as a "last chance" attempt to prevent the offender from becoming institutionalised, even though his offences were regarded as meriting a custodial sentence. In very serious cases, an order of this nature may prompt reference to the Court of Appeal by Attorney-General (*e.g. Attorney-General's Reference No. 8 of 1992 (1993)* 14 Cr. App. R.(S.) 739).

Requirement to Refrain from Activities   **18–049**

Under PCCA 1973, Sched. 1A, para. 2(1)(b) (see para. 18–040) a probation order may require the offender to "refrain from participating in activities specified in the order on a day or days specified or during the probation period or such portion of it as may be specified. This so-called "negative" requirement or "refraining order" is not subject to the usual 60 day limit and so could be ordered to run for the duration of the order. There are obvious problems in regard to such a prohibiting condition. Firstly, how feasible is it to secure compliance? A court is unlikely to favour the imposition of a requirement which the offender could ignore with impunity. Secondly, a requirement which imposes considerable restraint upon the offender's liberty (*e.g.* by requiring a curfew) might offend the dictum of Lord Bridge in *Rogers v. Cullen* opposing quasi-custodial impositions (para. 18–021). Thirdly, a requirement which gives wide discretion to the supervising officer (e.g. to refrain from taking part in a specified activity without the prior permission of the supervising officer) could also be said to offend against the principles of *Rogers v. Cullen*. If, for example, the court wished to impose a requirement that the offender should keep away from football grounds following an offence of football related violence, or from licensed premises, it would probably be preferable to exercise specific powers to make exclusion orders under the Public Order Act 1986, s. 30 or the Licensed Premises (Exclusion of Certain Persons) Act 1980 (see para. 25–010). Very few orders containing an additional "negative" requirement have been made since this power became available in 1982. Only 7 orders of this nature were imposed in 1993.

18–050 Treatment of Mental Condition

Schedule 1A, para. 5 (amended by CJPOA 1994, Sch. 9, para. 10) re-enacts the provisions of PCCA 1973, s. 3 permitting a requirement of treatment for the offender's mental condition. The court must be satisfied, on the evidence of a qualified medical practitioner (approved for the purpose under the Mental Health Act 1983, s. 12) that the mental condition of the offender:

(a) is such as requires and may be susceptible to treatment; but

(b) is not such as to warrant the making of a hospital order or guardianship order within the meaning of the Mental Health Act.

"Mental condition" is not defined but is not restricted to the four forms of mental disorder specified by the Mental Health Act 1983, s. 37 for the making of a hospital order (mental illness, psychopathic disorder, severe mental impairment or mental impairment). The 1994 Act's amendment allows treatment to be directed by a chartered psychologist, defined as a person listed on the register maintained by the British Psychological Society.

18–051   **PCCA 1973, Sched. 1A, para. 5**

"(2) The probation order may include a requirement that the offender shall submit, during the whole of the probation period or during such part or parts of that period as may be specified in the order, to treatment by or under the direction of a duly qualified medical practitioner or a chartered psychologist (or both, for different parts) with a view to the improvement of the offender's mental condition.

(3) The treatment required by any such order shall be such one of the

following kinds of treatment as may be specified in the order, that is to say—

(a)   treatment as a resident patient in a mental hospital;

(b)   treatment as a non-resident patient at such institution or place as may be specified in the order; and

(c)   treatment by or under the direction of such duly qualified medical practitioner or chartered psycholigist (or both) as may be so specified;

but the nature of the treatment shall not be specified in the order except as mentioned in paragraph (a), (b) or (c) above.

(4)   A court shall not by virtue of this paragraph include in a probation order a requirement that the offender shall submit to treatment for his mental condition unless it is satisfied that arrangements have been made for the treatment intended to be specified in the order (including arrangements for the reception of the offender where he is to be required to submit to treatment as a resident patient)."

The court must thus phrase the requirement carefully within the range **18–052** of options specified in sub-paragraph (3). It would not, for instance, be lawful to stipulate "such medical treatment as may be directed by the probation officer". In 1993 two per cent of all probation orders made contained a requirement of non-residential treatment or treatment 'as directed' whilst less than one per cent (only 53 orders) specified residential mental treatment. Treatment "under the direction of" a medical practitioner may extend to treatment undertaken by others such as a community psychiatric nurse, a psychologist or perhaps a probation officer, provided that this is clearly authorised and overseen by a responsible doctor.

Residential Treatment: In this instance the statutory role of the **18–053** supervising probation officer is limited by paragraph 5(5) to undertaking what "may be necessary for the purpose of the revocation or amendment of the order". As the Butler Committee on Mentally Abnormal Offenders pointed out (1975), this curtailment should not be read literally to mean an absence of involvement and good practice may well require liaison, joint work, preparation for discharge, contact with relatives, etc.

Flexibility and Discretion: It is clearly not possible for the court imposing the requirement to anticipate how treatment will proceed and the offender-patient's response. Scope for flexible discretion without the need for referral back to court is given by paragraph 5(6).

"(6) Where the medical practitioner or chartered psychologist by whom or under whose direction an offender is being treated for his mental condition in pursuance of a probation order is of the opinion that part of the treatment can be better or more conveniently given in or at an institution or place which—

(a) is not specified in the order; and
(b) is one in or at which the treatment of the offender will be given by or under the direction of a duly qualified medical practitioner or chartered psychologist,

he may, with the consent of the offender make arrangements for him to be treated accordingly.

(7) Such arrangements as are mentioned in sub-paragraph (6) above may provide for the offender to receive part of his treatment as a resident patient in an institution or place notwithstanding that the institution or place is not one which could have been specified for that purpose in the probation order.

(8) Where any such arrangements as are mentioned in sub-paragraph (6) above are made for the treatment of an offender—

(a) the medical practitioner or chartered psychologist by whom the arrangements are made shall give notice in writing to the probation officer responsible for the supervision of the offender, specifying the institution or place in or at which the treatment is to be carried out; and
(b) the treatment provided for by the arrangements shall be deemed to be treatment to which he is required to submit in pursuance of the probation order."

18–055 This informal amendment without referral back to the court in the normal manner requires the consent of the offender and, in the event of any subsequent enforcement proceedings, the issue could be raised whether the offender gave valid, informed consent to the change in treatment. This illustrates the difficulties of seeking to regulate the doctor-patient relationship by sentencing in criminal proceedings.

Sentencing Guidance: A number of cases have indicated the Court of Appeal's preparedness to endorse the making of "psychiatric probation orders" where the offender has committed a serious offence and or represents a real risk to the public, *e.g. Hoof* (1980) 2 Cr. App. R.(S.) 299 (arson with intent to endanger life) *McDonald* (1983)5 Cr. App. R. (S.)419 (indecent assault) *Cartwright, The Times,* April 18, 1989 (reckless driving), *Jones* (1992) 13 Cr. App. R. (S.) 275 (robbery). However, this course is likely to be adopted only where there is a reasonable prospect that such an order will have a beneficial effect upon the offender and that this outweighs the element of risk to the public.

Treatment for Drug or Alcohol Dependency 18–056

Schedule 1A, para. 6 introduces a new power to require the offender to submit to treatment for their drug or alcohol dependency. This was proposed by the 1990 White Paper which noted a frequent "link between drug misuse and offences such as burglary and theft committed in order to gain money to buy drugs. Similarly, alcohol is implicated in a wide variety of crimes, drunken driving, offences of public disorder and domestic violence" (paragraph 4.14). The court must be satisfied as to the following pre-conditions:

(a) the offender is dependent on drugs or alcohol;

(b) the offender's dependency caused or contributed to the instant offence;

(c) the offender's dependency is such as requires and may be susceptible to treatment.

The paragraph does not specify on what basis or evidence the court must **18–057** be satisfied of the above. There is no requirement that there should be evidence from a medical practitioner. 'Dependency' is defined as including the offender's "propensity towards the misuse of drugs and alcohol" (paragraph 6(9)) and so is open to quite wide interpretation. The offence for which an order containing such a requirement may be imposed need not have been directly drug or alcohol related nor need the offence have been committed under the influence of drugs or alcohol. It is enough that the "dependency" contributed in some degree towards the offence.

PCCA 1973, Sched. 1A, para. 6

"(2) The probation order may include a requirement that the offender shall submit, during the whole of the probation period or during such part of that period as may be specified in the order, to treatment by or under the direction of a person having the necessary qualifications or experience with a view to the reduction of elimination of the offender's dependency on drugs or alcohol.

(3) The treatment required by any such order shall be such one of the following kinds of treatment as may be specified in the order, that is to say—

(a) treatment as a resident in such institution or place as may be **18–058** specified in the order;

(b) treatment as a non-resident in or at such institution or place as may be so specified; and

(c) treatment by or under the direction of such person having the necessary qualifications or experience as may be so specified;

but the nature of the treatment shall not be specified in the order except as mentioned in paragraph (a), (b) or (c) above.

(4) A court shall not by virtue of this paragraph include in a probation order a requirement that the offender shall submit to treatment for his dependency on drugs or alcohol unless it is satisfied that arrangements have been made for the treatment intended to be specified in the order (including arrangements for the reception of the offender where he is to be required to submit to treatment as a resident)."

18–059 The provisions of paragraph 6 closely resemble those of paragraph 5 (treatment for mental condition) but the person responsible for the treatment does not have to be medically qualified. There is no yardstick by which to determine whether the responsible person is adequately qualified or experienced. Thus that person might be a probation officer, though this would not in itself be a sufficient qualification. The White Paper had in mind "specialised local services, including the National Health Service". In addition to legal aspects of this power, there are resource implications if drug or alcohol agencies choose to work within this framework. Will agencies be able to cope with referral under relatively tight court deadlines, particularly if the offender is remanded in custody or the agency offers a residential facility a long distance away? Does the agency have sufficient staff to give a firm commitment to work with a client on probation? Will the agency expect additional funding to be available to meet the expenses of assessment or treatment? In 1993 three per cent of all probation orders specified drugs/alcohol treatment, one per cent being for residential treatment.

Residential Treatment: Provision for programmes of this nature may be better made as a "requirement as to residence" (see para. 18–023 *et seq.*). If made under paragraph 6, the statutory role of the probation order is limited by paragraph 6(5) to carrying out what "may be necessary for the purpose of the revocation or amendment of the order", though, as in the case of psychiatric probation orders, this may seem a highly artificial restriction in practice.

18–060 *Non-Residential Treatment:* Community drug or alcohol treatment agencies may prefer the least restrictive form of requirement, *e.g.* preferring to limit the length of period for which the requirement is imposed, which need not run for the full length of the order. Agencies may be very reluctant to enter into relationships with clients on coercive-sounding terms for fear of compromising their non-controlling ethos and differentiating inappropriately between voluntary and directed clients. Some may refuse to enter into arrangements of this nature. Others may be willing to support a requirement that the offender shall attend the agency but may reserve the nature of any subsequent treatment or counselling to be negotiated privately between the agency and the client. The agency may have concerns about client confidentiality and may make clear that information to the probation service will be limited to stating whether the client has attended or not. The agency may seek to place all statutory responsibility upon the probation officer by proposing a requirement "to receive treatment as directed by the probation officer". This does not, however, seem to be a legal option within sub-paragraph (3) and thus no more lawful than such a requirement would be under paragraph 5.

Flexibility and Discretion: As in the case of psychiatric treatment as a **18–061** requirement of probation, paragraph 6 gives scope for flexibility and discretion in respect to treatment without having to refer the matter back to court for amendment.

PCCA 1973, Sched. 1A, para. 6

"(6) Where the person by whom or under whose direction an offender is being treated for dependency on drugs or alcohol in pursuance of a probation order is of the opinion that part of the treatment can be better or more conveniently given in or at an institution or place which—
  (a) is not specified in the order; and
  (b) is one in or at which the treatment of the offender will be given by or under the direction of a person having the necessary qualifications or experience,

he may, with the consent of the offender, make arrangements for him to be treated accordingly.

(7) Such arrangements as are mentioned in sub-paragraph (6) above may provide for the offender to receive part of his treatment as a resident in an institution or place notwithstanding that the institution or place is not one which could have been specified for that purpose in the probation order.

(8) Where any such arrangements as are mentioned in sub-paragraph **18–062** (6) above are made for the treatment of an offender—

  (a) the person by whom the arrangements are made shall give notice in writing to the probation officer responsible for the supervision of the offender, specifying the institution or place in or at which the treatment is to be carried out; and

  (b) the treatment provided for by the arrangements shall be deemed to be treatment to which he is required to submit in pursuance of the probation order."

As in respect of psychiatric probation orders (para. 18–054), this scope for informal amendment may subsequently give rise to the challenge that the offender did not give informed, valid consent.

THE MANAGEMENT OF A PROBATION ORDER

The administration and management of a probation order is largely governed not by statute or statutory instrument but by a *National Standard for Probation Orders*, introduced in 1992 and revised in 1995 as a means of achieving greater consistency and rigour in the supervision of offenders in the community. However, the Probation Rules 1984 (S.I. 1984/647), r. 33(a) specifies that it shall be part of the duties of a probation officer:

"... to undertake the supervision of a person who has been placed under supervision by a probation order ... and to advise, assist and befriend such a person."

18–063 The *National Standard* (1995, para. 4) identifies the following broad objectives for probation supervision:

* confronting offending behaviour, challenging the offender to accept responsibility for his or her crime and its consequences;

* making offenders aware of the impact of the crimes they have committed on their victims, the community and themselves;

* motivating and assisting the offender towards a greater sense of personal responsibility and discipline, and to aid his or her re-integration as a law-abiding member of the community;

* intervening to remedy practical obstacles preventing rehabilitation (*e.g.* education, training, skills needed for employment and action to counter drug or alcohol misuse, illiteracy or homelessness) and to help the offender acquire relevant new skills; and

* ensuring that the supervision programme for the offender is demanding and effective.

18–064 Commencement (*National Standard*, 1995, paras. 10–11)

The initial appointment between the supervising officer and the offender should be made, where possible, before the offender leaves court and should take place within five working days of the making of the order. Local arrangements may require the offender to see the duty probation officer pending the allocation of a supervising officer. There is no automatic presumption that the writer of the PSR subsequently will undertake supervisory responsibility. At the first meeting, the offender should be clearly informed of their obligations and responsibilities under the order. This procedure includes:

18–065   * confirming the offender's co-operation and compliance with the order; if the offender indicates withdrawal of co-operation, breach proceedings should be instituted;

     * giving the offender *written information* (in languages other than English where this would be helpful and is practicable) setting

out what is expected of the offender and what s/he can expect from the probation service.

* serving the offender with a copy of the order to keep (if this is already available, or otherwise at the earliest opportunity) and requiring the offender to sign a copy for retention on file, as demonstration that the offender is fully aware of its contents and obligations.

* issuing a copy of instructions setting out the required standards of behaviour that apply during the period of supervision, together with a statement explaining breach action that may be taken if the offender fails to comply, the offender signing an acknowledgement of receipt;

* making clear both procedures for revocation or amendment (including the offender's right to apply) and the procedure for complaints about treatment under the order.

The emphasis is thus upon clarification so that the offender knows **18–066** where he or she stands and the probation service in any subsequent breach proceedings will be able to demonstrate that the offender understood their obligations. The *National Standard* of 1992 also stated that the probation officer should establish whether the offender has given informed consent to the order: "If not, ... (the officer should) take appropriate action, if necessary by returning the offender to court". Though the 1995 revised *Standard* is silent on the issue, if there is doubt about the offender's informed consent in court, the matter should be referred to the offender's solicitor because there may well be grounds for a challenge of a magistrates' court sentence either by judicial review or an appeal against sentence or by seeking a variation under the Magistrates' Courts Act 1980, s. 142(1), or an application to the Crown Court in the case of a Crown Court order for variation of sentence under the Supreme Court Act 1981, s. 47(2). This is likely to be an extremely rare occurrence. In the relatively more likely event that the offender has now decided against compliance with the order, the most appropriate course would be to test that refusal by seeking to persevere with supervision and then initiating breach proceedings in the event of non-compliance. If the offender's refusal arises out of changed circumstances since the time of sentence, then an alternative option might be to seek a revocation of the order on the grounds that this would be in the interests of justice, having regard to circumstances which have arisen since the order was made. If the court agrees to the application, the order can be revoked and the offender can then be dealt with in some other manner.

Where the probation order contains a requirement of residence at a **18–067** probation hostel, the *National Standard* for the Management of Approved Probation and Bail Hostels makes separate provision for the induction of new residents by confirming that they understand the

rules, give their agreement to abide by those rules and understand what action will follow if the rules are broken (1995, para. 13).

18–068 Supervision Plan (*National Standard*, 1995, paras. 12–17)

An initial supervision plan should be drawn up in writing in consultation with the offender, within ten working days of sentence. This should be signed by both the offender and the supervising officer, and a copy given to the offender. The plan should be reviewed, progress recorded and amendments made after every three months (or more frequently, if appropriate), with a final review on the completion of the order.

Frequency of Contact (*National Standard*, 1995, para. 21)

"The most frequent contact should generally be made early in an order as a basis for a prompt and concerted effort to secure lasting change. The offender should attend a minimum of twelve appointments—normally weekly—with the supervising officer (or a person operating under his or her direction) in the first three months of an order; six in the next three momths, and thereafter at least one each month to the completion of supervision."

At least one home visit should take place in all cases (para. 15).

18–069 Records

A probation officer is under a general duty to keep an up to date record concerning each person under supervision (Probation Rules 1984, r. 31(1)). This is amplified by the *National Standard* requiring up to date records of appointments and contact with the offender during the order, the supervision plan and of any other information material to effective supervision. The General Introduction to *National Standard*s (1995, para.12) adds:

"Information held on an individual should be shared with him or her, unless there are good reasons for not doing so. It should be borne in mind that social services records may be disclosed to the individual under the provisions of the Access to Personal Files Act 1987. In the case of a young person, information should normally be shared with his or her parent(s) if, in consultation with the offender, that is considered appropriate. Confidentiality of records and all other information about the offender should otherwise be maintained having regard to the need to protect the public and the need to co-operate with other criminal justice services."

Access to records can be summarised as follows:

(a) Access to probation records shall be allowed to persons authorised by the probation committee or to one of HM Inspectors of Probation, but to no other person (Probation Rules 1984, r. 22(3)).

(b) Police access to Probation or Social Services records will need to **18–070**
be authorised by a circuit judge under Police and Criminal
Evidence Act 1984, Sched. 1.

(c) If the offender has a right of access to the relevant part of their
record and wishes their legal representative to see the record, this
would seem a logical extension of the client's access.

(d) Right of access does not include a right to a copy of that record
either to the offender or their legal representative but if the
pertinent material does not contain confidential information
about third persons, then it may be appropriate to provide such
information as disclosure may help to avoid unnecessary
contested legal proceedings.

(e) If a probation officer is giving evidence in court proceedings,
reference may be made to records to refresh the memory,
provided that the entries were made contemporaneously (*i.e.*
when the matters were fresh in the mind of the record maker).
Such a use of records requires the permission of the court and the
witness may be asked when the record was made. The court and
the advocate may be entitled to inspect the section of the record
from which the memory is being refreshed, so care should be
taken with regard to the confidentiality of the material therein.

(f) If a probation officer is required to give evidence about aspects of
an offender's supervision, confidentiality does not automatically
mean that records are privileged and entitled to absolute
immunity from disclosure. The witness can ask the court to
extend privilege to the document. The court should then weigh
the competing claims of immunity on the one hand and fairness
to the party seeking disclosure on the other.

Apparent Default (*National Standard*, 1995, paras. 22–24)   **18–071**
Any apparent failure to comply with requirements should be dealt with
as soon as possible and in any event within two working days, seeking
an explanation from the offender. If the explanation, or lack of one, is
not considered acceptable, the incident must be formally recorded as an
instance of failure to comply. Breach proceedings should be taken at any
stage in the order and without prior warning "if the failure to comply is
serious, such as an attempt to avoid its completion or serious
misconduct". Where breach action is not taken, the offender should be
given a formal warning, in person and confirmed in writing, with a note
on the record of the offender's response, but a maximum of two
warnings may be given before breach proceedings are instituted. Once a
decision is made to take breach action, proceedings should be instituted
within ten working days.
    In 1993, 80 per cent of probation orders imposed on young offenders
aged 16–20 for one year or under ran their full course, the same rate as for
all age groups. For orders of all lengths, 69 per cent of orders upon this

age group ran their full course, only two per cent less than the rate for all age groups (Home Office, 1994a).

Chapter 19

Community Service Orders

First introduced by the Criminal Justice Act 1972, the community **19-001**
service order is now governed by the Powers of Criminal Courts Act
1973, as amended by the Criminal Justice Act 1991 which designated it
as one of the "community orders" which can feature in a "community
sentence" (CJA 1991, s. 6(4)). The community service order may also be
used as a penalty for breach of the community orders governed by
Schedule 2 of the 1991 Act.

COMMUNITY SERVICE ORDER AS A COMMUNITY SENTENCE

PCCA 1973, S. 14

"(1) Where a person of or over sixteen years of age is convicted of an
offence punishable with imprisonment, the court by or before
which he is convicted may, (but subject to subsection (2) below)
make an order (in this Act referred to as "a community service
order") requiring him to perform unpaid work in accordance with
the subsequent provisions of this Act.

The reference in this subsection to an offence punishable with
imprisonment shall be construed without regard to any prohibition
or restriction imposed by or under any enactment on the
imprisonment of young offenders."   **19-002**

A youth court or the Crown Court may make a community service order
in respect of any offender aged 16 years or over who has been convicted
of an offence punishable with imprisonment (s. 14(1)), provided that the
court is of the opinion that the offence, or the combination of the offence
and one or more offences associated with it, is serious enough to warrant
such a sentence (CJA 1991, s. 6(1)). The order requires the offender to
perform unpaid work in accordance with the provisions of the Act. If the
offence is imprisonable only upon sentence at Crown Court, it would
appear that a youth court could not impose a community service order.

Length of Order

19–003   PCCA 1973, s. 14

"(1A) The number of hours which a person may be required to work under a community service order shall be specified in the order and shall be in the aggregate—

    (a)   not less than 40; and

    (b)   not more than 240.

(3) Where a court makes community service orders in respect of two or more offences of which the offender has been convicted by or before the court, the court may direct that the hours of work specified in any of those orders shall be concurrent with or additional to those specified in any other of those orders, but so that the total number of hours which are not concurrent shall not exceed the maximum specified in paragraph (b) of subsection (1A) above."

19–004 The number of hours which an offender may be required to work must be specified in the order and, in aggregate, shall be:

    (a)   not less than 40

    (b)   not more than 240.

Prior to implementation of CJA 1991 the maximum number of hours that a 16 year old could be required to work was 120 hours but this lower ceiling was removed by CJA 1991, s. 10(2). This followed the proposal in the 1990 White Paper that 16 and 17 year olds should be regarded as 'near adults' and the Government's belief that the varied maximum "will give courts greater flexibility in using the order for 16 year olds who have been convicted of more serous offences and should encourage its use for some who might otherwise be at risk of a custodial sentence" (para. 8.18). The old maximum of 120 hours remains for 16 year old offenders living or intending to live in Northern Ireland (CJA 1991, Sched. 3, para. 4(1)(a)). In a NACRO survey (1993) of sentencing in the youth courts in 15 local authority areas in the first six months following implementation of the 1991 Act, orders exceeding 120 hours constituted 17.5 per cent of orders for 16 year olds and 16 per cent for 17 year olds.

19–005   As the minimum length of 40 hours applies to the aggregate of hours under more than one order, this appears to suggest that consecutive orders could be made for less than 40 hours duration each. However, this is generally considered to be undesirable practice to be avoided. There would, for instance, be an obvious problem if some orders were set aside on appeal leaving one or more orders which amount in aggregate to less than 40 hours.

Where orders are imposed to run consecutively, this can create potential problems in the event of breach proceedings. Though 240 hours is the maximum that can be imposed on a single sentencing occasion, section 14(3) does not prohibit different courts on different occasions from making orders which in aggregate exceed 240 hours (*Siha* (1992) 13 Cr. App. R.(S.) 588). In *Siha* the offender was sentenced to work 180 hours community service. Six months later he received a further order for 90 hours. Though the Court of Appeal indicated that this was a valid additional order, "it is highly desirable that there should not be in existence at the same time orders which cast upon the offender a liability to perform more than a further 240 hours consecutively" (citing *Evans* (1976) 64 Cr. App. R. 127). Because information was not available to the Court of Appeal about the number of hours already worked or outstanding under his initial order of 180 hours, the Court reduced his second order from 90 hours to 60 hours to ensure that the consecutive total still to be worked did not exceed 240 hours. There is thus a firm expectation that the court should respect the 240 hour ceiling intended by the legislature as the maximum commitment to which an offender should be subject at any time.

A further instance of the complexity of consecutive orders arose in **19–006** *Meredith* [1994] Crim. L.R. 142, with the additional complication which arises where orders are imposed by courts at different levels of jurisdiction. The offender had been sentenced to an order for 80 hours by a magistrates' court and was subsequently sentenced to a further 160 hours by the Crown Court. Though the aggregate did not exceed 240 hours, the offender contended that the Crown Court subsequently had no power to deal with his non-compliance when he had failed to work as instructed after completing only 14 hours. Dismissing his claim that he was in breach of only the first of the two orders, the Court of Appeal stated that "once two community service orders are made, they are for all practical purposes one order" and he was thus in breach of both and could be dealt with by the Crown Court. This is addressed further in Chapter 22 on breach of community orders.

The length of a community service order should reflect the **19–007** seriousness of the offence and the appropriate restriction on liberty commensurate with that offence, taking into account the suitability of the offender to undertake the order. This is pursued below. The length of orders as a percentage of orders made in respect of all age groups in 1993 was as follows:

	40–99	100–149	150–199	200–240
Male	29	36	21	14
Female	44	33	14	9
All persons	30	36	20	13

Source: Home Office (1994a)

19–008 Procedural Requirements

Suitability and Pre-Sentence Reports

PCCA 1973, s. 14(2)

"(2) A court shall not make a community service order in respect of any offender unless the offender consents and the court, after hearing (if the court thinks it necessary) a probation officer or social worker of a local authority social services department, is satisfied that the offender is a suitable person to perform work under such an order."

The requirement of "suitability" under section 14 (2) should be read in conjunction with CJA 1991, s. 6(2)(a) which requires the court to pass the community sentence "most suitable for the offender" (see para. 15–004). The pre-1991 Act requirement provision in section 14(2) continues that a court should "hear" a probation officer or social worker, if it "thinks it necessary", but before deciding that the offender is suitable for a community service order, the court is ordinarily required to consider a pre-sentence report (CJA 1991, s. 7(3)), subject to the new provisions of section 7 (3A) and (3B) permitting a court to dispense with a report in the case of indictable only offences, or to refer to an earlier report (see para. 11–011). An order made without obtaining or considering a report is nevertheless a valid order (s. 7(4)) but failure to consider could be a basis for appeal. The court considering an appeal is required to obtain/consider a report (s. 7(4)) subject to the "get out" provisions of section 7(5).

19–009   Neither the requirement to consider a report nor the scope to hear a probation officer or social worker means that the pre-sentence report has to address the possibility of a community service order or that the probation service/local authority has to be consulted on that precise prospect before an order can be made. An order can validly be imposed against the clear advice of the report writer or agency representative in court, albeit that frequent disregard of professional opinion is likely to lead to urgent out-of-court dialogue to resolve the obvious difficulties. In practice, the court will almost certainly wish to give the probation service the opportunity to assess the offender's suitability for community service where this is not addressed in the PSR. A court adjourning a case for a pre-sentence report may specifically indicate that it is seeking advice on the suitability of the offender for a community service order and has that disposal provisionally in mind.

19–010   Probation practice in assessing an offender's suitability for community service varies. In some areas the pre-sentence report writer will make the assessment, consulting the relevant officer where serious doubts arise; in other areas there may be an expectation that the offender will be separately assessed by a specialist community service officer before a clear proposal for community service can be put forward in the report.

Availability of Work

PCCA 1973, s. 14

"(2A) Subject to paragraphs 3 and 4 of Schedule 3 to the Criminal Justice Act 1991 (reciprocal enforcement of certain orders) a court shall not make a community service order in respect of an offender unless it is satisfied that provision for him to perform work under such an order can be made under the arrangements for persons to perform work under such orders which exist in the petty sessions area in which he resides or will reside."

The one inescapable requirement is for the court to be satisfied that arrangements can be made to provide work for the offender. If the probation service feels strongly that an individual offender could not be safely placed on any available work task or project then that would appear to block the making of an order.

Consent **19–011**

An order must not be made unless the offender gives consent (s. 14(2)), a reflection of the prohibition of "forced or compulsory labour" under the European Convention on Human Rights, Article 4.2. The Green Paper *Strengthening Punishment in the Community* (Home Office, 1995b, para.4.20) re-examines the effect of Article 4 and suggests that the requirement of consent is an over-cautious interpretation of its ambit, given that the convention specifically creates an exception for "any work required to be done in the course of detention imposed according to the provisions of Article 5". It is argued that as a community service order is imposed under due process of law, is less restrictive than "detention", is not oppressive and does not involve avoidable hardship, the current requirement of consent could be properly dispensed with.

Explanation

PCCA 1973, s. 14

"(5) Before making a community service order the court shall explain to the offender in ordinary language—

(a) the purpose and effect of the order (and in particular the requirements of the order as specified in section 15 of this Act);

(b) the consequences which may follow under Part II of Schedule 2 to the Criminal Justice Act 1991 if he fails to comply with any of those requirements; and

(c) that the court has under Parts III and IV of that Schedule the power to review the order on the application either of the offender or of a probation officer."

19–012 *Specified Petty Sessions Area and Relevant Officer*

PCCA 1973, s. 14

"(4) A community service order shall specify the petty sessions area in which the offender resides or will reside; and the functions conferred by the subsequent provisions of this Act on the relevant officer shall be discharged by a probation officer appointed for or assigned to the area for the time being specified in the order (whether under this subsection or by virtue of Part IV, Sched. 2 to the Criminal Justice Act 1991), or by a person appointed for the purposes of those provisions by the probation committee for that area."

19–013 The appointed "relevant officer" is a pivotal figure in the administration and enforcement of the order and, by virtue of CJA 1991, s. 15(3)(b), is the 'responsible officer' for the purposes of CJA 1991, Sched. 2 where the relevant community order is a community service order (or the community service element of a combination order).

Commencement and Provision of Copies of the Order

PCCA 1973, s. 14

"(6) The court by which a community service order is made shall forthwith give copies of the order to a probation officer assigned to the court and he shall give a copy to the offender and to the relevant officer; and the court shall, except where it is itself a magistrates' court acting for the petty sessions area specified in the order, send to the clerk to the justices for the petty sessions area specified in the order a copy of the order, together with such documents and information relating to the case as it considers likely to be of assistance to a court acting for that area in exercising its functions in relation to the order."

19–014 A community service order comes into force as soon as the court has pronounced sentence and the offender is immediately subject to it. In *Walsh v. Barlow* [1985] 1 W.L.R. 90, an offender argued unsuccessfully that a community service order imposed on him by a magistrates' court was ineffective as no copy of the order had been delivered to him. The Divisional Court held that such delivery is "not a pre-requisite of the coming into force of the order".

19–015 **Requirements of the Order**
The core requirements are as specified by PCCA 1973, s. 15(1).

PCCA 1973, s. 15

"(1) An offender in respect of whom a community service order is in force shall—

(a) keep in touch with the relevant officer in accordance with such instructions as he may from time to time be given by that officer and notify him of any change of address; and

(b) perform for the number of hours specified in the order such work at such times as he may be instructed by the relevant officer.

(3) The instructions given by the relevant officer under this section shall, so far as practicable, be such as to avoid any conflict with the offender's religious beliefs and any interference with the times, if any, at which he normally works or attends a school or other educational establishment."

The court may not specify the dates or times when community service **19–016** work shall be performed, nor the type of work to be undertaken, though this may be indicated in the pre-sentence report and may be a factor in assisting the court to decide whether to impose community service. The wording of section 15(1) was amended by CJA 1991, s. 10(4) so that an offender can be required to report at any stage during the order when the responsible officer considers this necessary to receive the offender's compliance with the order (rather than merely at the beginning of the order as was the implication of the previous wording). This enables the offender "to be interviewed and warned of the consequences of failure to comply and helped with any difficulties which are preventing the satisfactory completion of the order" (*Crime, Justice and Protecting the Public*, para. 4.15). The requirement to "keep in touch" could also be argued to require the offender to supply medical notes, employment details and other evidence to support a claim of "reasonable excuse" for unavailability for work.

The basic requirement to perform work is expanded by the Community Service and Combination Order Rules 1992, r. 4(1) (see para. 19–030) which requires the offender to comply with reasonable directions as to the manner in which the work should be undertaken and rules reasonably imposed in the interests of the health, safety and well-being of others present.

The form of a magistrates' court community service order is specified by Form 43 in the Magistrates' Courts (Children and Young Persons) Rules 1992, Sched. 2 (S.I. 1992/2071).

Combining Community Service with other Sentences or Orders **19–017**
The general rule broadly applies that "courts should avoid mixing sentences which fall into well-established and different categories": *McElhorne* (1983) 5 Cr. App. R.(S.) 53. Thus the Court of Appeal has stated that it is wrong to make a CSO and impose a custodial sentence

on the same occasion, even though (in the Crown Court) the sentences relate to different counts or separate indictments.

19–018 CJA 1991 has removed the former requirement of PCCA 1973, s. 14(1) that a community service order should be made "instead of dealing with (the offender) in any other way", thus allowing the sentencer to combine a community service order with another form of sentence or order for the same offence. At the same time, the Act restricts the mixing of community service and probation orders so that they can be imposed for the same offence only in the form of a combination order (s. 6(3)). Though a supervision order can be equated with a probation order in many respects, the Act is silent in regard to the mixing of supervision and community service orders in respect of the same offence. By analogy, however, this combination may be considered inappropriate, albeit lawful. Prior to implementation of CJA 1991 the Court of Appeal held that the combination of probation and community service orders for different offences was proper (*Harkess* (1990) 12 Cr. App. R.(S.) 366). Combining a community service order with a combination order for a single offence is not expressly prohibited but appears contrary to the spirit of section 6(3), as it would blend a community service order with the probation element of a combination order. It is submitted that such a combination is not permissible even if the aggregate number of community service hours does not exceed 100, though the aim of such a combination would presumably be to secure a greater number of hours than a combination order permits. The scope for combining sentences and orders either in respect of the same or different offences on the same sentencing occasion can be conveniently summarised in the following Table:

19–019 *Combination of CSO with Other Penalties*

	Dis-charge	Fine	At-tend-ance Centre	Super-vision Order	Pro-bation Order	Com-bina-tion Order	Cur-few Order	Cus-tody
Same Offence	No	Yes	Yes	Yes*	No	No	Yes	No
Different Offences	Yes	Yes	Yes	Yes	Yes	Yes*	Yes	No

> * Appears legally permissible but may well be regarded as undesirable in practice.

The court imposing a community service order may also make ancillary orders, including disqualification from driving, endorsement of driving licence, compensation order, costs, forfeiture.

19–020 Sentencing Practice and Principles
When initially proposing community service orders as a new sentence, the Advisory Council on the Penal System (1970, para. 33) recognised

their broad appeal, offering an attractive blend of retribution, reparation and rehabilitation:

> "To some, it would be simply a more constructive and cheaper alternative to short sentences of imprisonment; by others it would be seen as introducing into the penal system a new dimension with an emphasis on reparation to the community; others again would regard it as a means of giving effect to the old adage that the punishment should fit the crime; while still others would stress the value of bringing offenders into close touch with those members of the community who are most in need of help and support."

Community service rapidly and not surprisingly became established as a major sentencing option, particularly for males aged 17 and under 21, and in 1992 approximately one in seven (15 per cent) males in that age group sentenced for indictable offences received this sentence. In 1993 eight per cent of males and four per cent of females aged 14—under 18 sentenced for indictable offences received community service. When introduced as an option for 16 year old juveniles by CJA 1982, an early attempt (Lacey, 1984) to locate it as a complement rather than a rival to existing supervision order powers suggested a CSO's particular appropriateness in three instances:

(a) where a young person has committed a fairly serious offence **19–021** which seems "out of character", as the intensity of a full intermediate treatment programme might be counter-productive;

(b) where a young person already subject to intermediate treatment commits a further offence and can complete a community service order concurrently, thus avoiding a custodial sentence;

(c) where the young person's employment or educational commitments make it unrealistic to expect them to tackle an intensive intermediate treatment programme yet their offence is serious and merits decisive action by the court.

In the period 1983 to 1992, 16 year old boys receiving community **19–022** service as a percentage of all males aged 14 and under 17 sentenced for indictable offences rose from one per cent to a stable five per cent, without any erosion of the market share of the supervision order. The comparable figure for females in that age group in 1992 was two per cent. Concern has been expressed that community service orders are more likely to be imposed upon males than females and that young women may thus be discriminated against in gaining access to this non-custodial disposal. Males aged 17 and under 21 sentenced for indictable offences are more than twice as likely to receive a community service order as females (15 per cent compared with seven per cent in 1992). Additionally, females have been twice as likely to be placed on community service having had no previous convictions, as the following Table illustrates:

19–023   Table: Percentage of persons commencing CSOs without previous convictions, 1991

	Age 16	Age 17–under 21
Male	16%	18%
Female	34%	35%

Source: Probation Statistics 1991 (Home Office) (this statistic has not been published subsequently)

The evidence for discrimination and explanations for such differential treatment are by no means clear and more information is needed before the statistics can be properly interpreted. The duty imposed on the Home Secretary by CJA 1991, s. 95 to publish information which will facilitate the avoidance of discrimination in the criminal justice system should at least promote greater clarity and awareness. The earlier *National Standard* (1992, para. 17) encouraged ("within available resources") the exercise of Probation Committee powers to meet certain expenses of those subject to community service orders (see para. 19–034) in paying child minding costs, so that women offenders and single parents should have equal opportunity to undertake this sentence.

19–024   Given its broad appeal as a measure in its own right, considerable attention was focused during the decade prior to CJA 1991 on whether community service could be demarcated and preserved as an "alternative to custody", as initially suggested possible by the Advisory Council, or should also be open to use in a wide range of cases where custody was not a real possibility but the circumstances of the offender made it an attractive non-custodial penalty. Could the imposition of a number of CS hours, particularly in the higher range, be legitimately regarded as the equivalent of a certain length of custodial sentence? In *Lawrence* (1982) 4 Cr. App. R.(S.) 69 Lord Lane C.J. suggested that 190 hours of community service could be regarded as equating with around nine months in custody. This observation led to attempts to construct detailed sliding scales of equivalence (see, for example, *The Magistrates Association*, 1990). *Lawrence* was commonly interpreted to hold that where community service was used as a punishment in its own right rather than as an "alternative to custody", the length of the order should be correspondingly short. This proposition received a degree of support in cases such as *Barley* (1989) 11 Cr. App. R.(S.) 158 in which the Court of Appeal declared that the community service system should not be overloaded with long orders imposed for offences where an immediate custodial sentence would be unjustified or with short orders. However, in *Porter* (1992) 13 Cr. App. R.(S.) 258 the Court of Appeal indicated that *Lawrence* had simply ruled that longer orders should be imposed when CS was being used as an alternative to custody. The converse did not follow and it was possible to impose a long CSO even where custody was not being considered.

This controversy was swept aside by the new framework of **19–025** sentencing in the 1991 Act which presented community service as a restriction on liberty in the community, suitable where the aim is "to deprive the offender of leisure as a punishment and to make some reparation to the community" (*Crime, Justice and Protecting the Public*, para. 4.8).

Sentencers can gain comparatively little help from pre-1991 case law in deciding what length of hours is appropriate for different levels of seriousness of offence. There have been very few appeals against the length of CS orders and the Court of Appeal in *Bushell* (1987) 9 Cr. App. R.(S.) 537 indicated that it would only rarely interfere with the length of an order. Perhaps the most striking example of non-interference is presented in *Cordner* (1992) 13 Cr. App. R.(S.) 570 where an order of 100 hours imposed on a man aged 25 for a theft of 50 pence from a railway ticket machine and attempted theft of a like nature was upheld uncritically.

In so far as any trend can be discerned from past decisions in **19–026** interpreting the "so serious" criterion justifying custody under CJA 1982, s. 1 (4A)(c), it may be helpful to note:

(a) Though burglary of a dwelling house will frequently be considered "so serious", community service has often been considered very appropriate for young offenders whose offence or role in the burglary was not particularly serious or culpable and whose previous record is favourable (*e.g. Mole* (1990) 12 Cr. App. R.(S.) 371).

(b) In criminal damage cases, community service may have strong appeal, *e.g. Ferreira* (1988) 10 Cr. App. R.(S.) 343 where CS was said to be "designed" for a case of spraying graffiti on carriages at a London Underground depot: "They have done this wanton damage and therefore it behoves them to do some service to the public to put it right".

(c) Community service has quite frequently been considered appropriate in cases of violence where mitigation is available such as previous good character or 'out of character' loss of temper, employment or training opportunities, genuine remorse etc. For example, in *McDiarmid* (1980) 2 Cr. App. R.(S.) 130 an offender aged 18 of previous good character threw a beer glass at a man during a public house disturbance, cutting the victim's lip. See also *Grant* (1990) 12 Cr. App. R.(S.) 441.

(d) Community service can be considered "tailor-made" for offences of dishonesty even if in breach of trust and involving a substantial sum, *e.g. Brown* (1981) 3 Cr. App. R.(S.) 294, where a 19 year old with no previous convictions had joined with another in burgling his employer's premises, taking goods worth £2,850.

19-027 The Life Span of a Community Service Order
The administration of community service is specified partly by statute, partly by statutory instrument and partly by the Home Office's National Standard. Prior to 1989, the management of community service within the broad boundaries of the Powers of Criminal Courts Act 1973 was left to the discretion of area probation services and local relevant officers. Concern was expressed whether sentencers could have confidence that community service would be administered with sufficient discipline and consistency and about the variations in interpretation and practice between different areas. The Community Service Rules (S.I. 191/1989, now revoked) aimed to standardise the administration of CSOs and place this on a statutory footing. The Rules were supported by the "National Standards for Community Service" (HOC 18/1989), an innovatory device to ensure greater clarity, consistency of practice and accountability. The 1989 Rules have now been superseded by the Community Service and Combination Order Rules (CSCOR) 1992 (S.I. 2076/1992), which are less comprehensive, many aspects of practice being now incorporated in the *National Standard for Community Service Orders* (Home Office, 1992; revised 1995). The *National Standard* does not have any legal status but forms the basis on which sentencers can expect CS orders to be administered and on which offenders can expect to be treated.

19-028 *Assessment (National Standard,* 1995, paras. 8–12)

Before a placement is arranged or work begins an assessment should be made, considering risk to staff and to the public, the likelihood of re-offending or of serious harm. This should take place within five working days of sentence and should be repeated periodically as part of the normal review process. Regard should be given to any indication given by the sentencing court as to the kind of task which might be suitable for that offender. In the exceptional circumstances that an assessment concludes that work cannot be undertaken without undue risk to the public, "the court should be informed immediately so that it may consider the case for revocation and re-sentencing" (para. 9). This presumably means that the relevant officer shuld make application for revocation as there is no other basis on which the court can have the matter referred to it.

19-029 *Commencement (National Standard,* 1995, paras. 13–15)

The *National Standard* aims to ensure that a prompt start is made, with the first work session taking place as soon as possible after assessment and in any event within 10 working days of the making of the order. Before work commences, the offender should be seen so that their co-operation and compliance with the order can be received, a copy of the order served and written information and instructions provided setting out the required standards of behaviour. Instructions should be accompanied by a statement explaining the consequences of non-compliance, the procedures for revocation and amendment of the order and the complaints procedure. The offender should sign to acknowledge receipt of both the order and the related instructions.

The question may arise whether the offender should be required to commence work while an appeal against conviction or sentence is pending. The opinion of the Home Office in this respect has varied but the current advice (letter to Chief Probation Officers of November 26, 1992) states that offenders should be instructed to work in the normal manner pending the outcome of the appeal, albeit that a successful outcome would render redundant the hours worked in the interim. It is open to question whether anticipation of an appeal would provide reasonable excuse for failure to attend for work if a breach of that requirement is alleged during that period. One comfort to the appellant is that if the conviction or order is overturned, any breach action pending will automatically fall and any penalty imposed for the breach will be voided.

Work Performance, Non-Compliance and Lateness   **19–030**

CSSOR 1992, r.4

"(1) While performing work under an order an offender shall be required to comply with any reasonable directions of the supervisor as to the manner in which the work is to be performed and with any rules reasonably imposed by the supervisor in the place of work having regard to the circumstances of that workplace, the interests of health or safety or the interests and well-being of other persons present.

(2) Where an offender—

(a) fails to comply with any such direction or rule as is mentioned in the preceding paragraph;

(b) in any way fails satisfactorily to perform the work he has been instructed to do;

(c) behaves in a disorderly or disruptive manner or in a manner likely to give offence to members of the public or any person for whose benefit the work is being performed; or

(d) reports for work later than the appointed time

he may (without prejudice to any proceedings for failure to comply **19–031** with the requirements of the order under schedule 2 to the Criminal Justice Act 1991) be required to cease work that day and may, in addition, be required to leave the place of work forthwith; and where he is so required to cease work, the relevant officer may direct that some or all of any period of work for that day shall not be reckoned as time worked under the order."

The *National Standard* (1995, para. 14) specifically prohibits:

(a) attendance while unable to participate properly because of alcohol or non-prescribed drugs;

(b) fighting, violent or aggressive behaviour, or threats of violence;

(c) other conduct or language that might reasonably give serious offence to others;

(d) other wilful or persistent non co-operation or behaviour designed to frustrate the purposes of the offender's or others' orders;

(e) work which fails to demonstrate the required level of effort and commitment.

19–032 *Work Hours and Rate*

The *National Standard* (1995, para. 16) demands a minimum work rate of five hours a week (calculated as an average over the whole of the order) and a ceiling of 21 hours in any one week. Overall, however, work requirements should not conflict with the offender's entitlement to welfare benefits nor should placements prevent the unemployed offender from being readily available to seek or take up employment. The requirement introduced in the 1989 Community Service Rules that a minimum number of hours should be worked on a group placement has not been included in the 1992 Rules and is now obsolete. Where a work session spans lunch time and the offender is required to remain on site, up to half an hour may be counted towards the order, provided that the offender remains under supervision throughout (1995, para. 20).

19–033 *Calculating Time for Travel and Bad Weather*

CSSOR 1992, rr. 3 and 5

"3. The time spent by an offender in travelling in connection with the performance of work under an order shall not be reckoned as time worked under the order except where his relevant officer or supervisor decides that all the time so spent, or such part of it as he so decides, shall be so reckoned.

5. (1) Where bad weather prevents the performance of work, it shall be open to the supervisor to require the offender to remain in the expectation of its being possible to begin or resume work, as appropriate, or he may make arrangements for the offender to perform work at some other place or, where it is not practicable to make such arrangements, he shall dismiss the offender for the remainder of that day.

(2) Any time during which bad weather prevents the performance of work may not be reckoned as time worked under an order except where the offender remains at the place of work either in the charge of the supervisor or because he is required by him so to remain."

The *National Standard* (1995, para. 19) indicates that while travel time **19–034** to and from the placement or assembly point will normally be the offender's own responsibility, travel time necessarily incurred in excess of half an hour should normally be credited as time worked under the order, subject to an overall limit of 10 per cent of the hours prescribed.

A Probation Committee has power to "defray travelling and other expenses in connection with the performance of work by persons in respect of whom community service orders are in force" (PCCA 1973, Sched. 3, para. 10(3)(d)).

Recording and Reports **19–035**

CSCOR, r.6

"(1) The relevant officer or a person nominated by him shall make a report on an offender in respect of any week during which the offender has been instructed to perform work under the order.

(2) A report made on an offender under paragraph (1) above shall include a record of the time worked by him during the week in question, the total time worked under the order and the number of hours which remain to be worked.

(3) A copy of each report on an offender made under paragraph (1) above shall be given to him and, if it is made by another person, to the relevant officer."

Twelve Months Duration

PCCA 1973, s. 15 **19–036**

"(2) Subject to paragraph 15 of Schedule 2 to the Criminal Justice Act 1991, the work required to be performed under a community service order shall be performed during the period of twelve months beginning with the date of the order but, unless revoked, the order shall remain in force until the offender has worked under it for the number of hours specified in it."

The statutory expectation is thus that the work should be completed within a year of the date of the order but the order nevertheless remains in force (and subject to enforcement proceedings) beyond that period until the offender has completed the outstanding hours. Offenders have sometimes erroneously interpreted this provision to imply that they can determine their own pace of work, provided that they fulfil the requirements within 12 months. It is clear, however, that the pace is determined by the relevant officer and that the expectation is that offenders will work steadily from the commencement of the order until completion. Even the longest order should normally be attainable within 12 months if an average minimum of five hours per week is achieved. Problems will arise, however, where illness, injury, work commitments, suspension from CS work or a period in custody intervene.

19–037　　CJA 1991, Sched. 2, para. 15 makes provision for a community service order to be amended on the application of either the relevant officer or the offender by extending the period (see para. 22–013). However, as section 15(2) indicates, an offender can continue to be given work instructions after the expiry of 12 months and it might be queried, in the light of this, why there is any power or necessity to seek an extension. It is nevertheless good practice to seek a time extension because this provides a helpful revised target date by which the obligation to work should be satisfied. Notwithstanding this, proceedings for revocation or breach may, however, be validly initiated after the initial 12 months have elapsed, even though an extension has not been sought, without being out of time.

Apparent Default

The *National Standard* seeks to promote the offender's compliance, by ensuring that instructions are clear and that the placement tasks are suitable, and by giving appropriate encouragement and advice. Any apparent failure to comply "should be dealt with as soon as possible and in any event within two working days" (para. 24).

> "The incident, the offender's explanation (or lack of one) and the relevant officer's opinion of whether any explanation is acceptable and the likely consequences for successful completion of the order must be recorded. If the explanation is not considered acceptable, the incident must formally be recorded as an instance of failure to comply with the order".

19–038　Breach proceedings under CJA 1991, Sched. 2, Pt. II may be appropriate immediately without prior warning if the failure to comply is serious, involving either an attempt to avoid completion or serious misconduct. In other instances the offender should be given a formal warning of the consequences of further failure. The warning should be given in person and confirmed in writing. At most, two warnings within any 12 month period of the order may be given before breach proceedings are instituted (para. 27).

　　　Absence through sickness should be treated as failure to comply unless the relevant officer has reasonable grounds to believe that the sickness is genuine and serious enough to prevent attendance for work and that reasonable efforts have been made by the offender to contact the service to explain the circumstances (para. 28).

19–039　　If breach proceedings are pending, offenders may be allowed to continue working, provided this does not involve undue risk to others, though it should be explained to the offender that it will be for the court to decide whether or not to revoke the order if the breach is established, and to what extent the offender's conduct in the meantime should be taken into account (para. 29).

Successful Outcome

Research has sought to identify characteristics of community service work which enhance the prospects for a successful outcome. McIvor's study of CS schemes in Scotland (1992) found lower levels of unacceptable absences among offenders who considered their experience on community service to have been very worthwhile. Placements which were particularly valued by offenders were characterised by work which:

(a) maximised their contact with the beneficiaries;

(b) enabled offenders to acquire practical or inter-personal skills;

(c) provided offenders with a sense of benefit to recipients.

McIvor thus advocates proper attention to the potential value of com- **19–040** munity service to the offender, as well as the punitive element, by the provision of interesting, enjoyable and worthwhile tasks. She notes that though community service is not an explicitly rehabilitative sentence, offenders who had found CS to be particularly worthwhile were:

(a) slightly less likely to be reconvicted;

(b) reconvicted less often in the three years following sentence;

(c) markedly less likely to be reconvicted of offences involving dishonesty.

In 1993 59 per cent of community service orders imposed on offenders aged 16–17 terminated upon completion of the specified hours, compared with 71 per cent for all age groups. Offenders under 18 showed a higher rate of termination because of failure to comply with requirements (25% compared with 16 per cent for all age groups).

Amendment, Breach and Revocation of Community Service Order

CJA 1991, Sched. 2 provides a common code for the amendment, breach and revocation of community service orders, probation orders and combination orders. Much of the pre-Act case law relating to the regulation of community service orders is now relevant to all three kinds of community order and is therefore addressed in Chapter 22.

COMMUNITY SERVICE AS PENALTY FOR BREACH OF **19–041** A COMMUNITY ORDER

With the introduction of CJA 1991, Sched. 2, Pt. II, a community service order may be imposed as a penalty where failure to comply with a probation order, community service order or combination order is admitted or proved and the court permits the continuance of that order. This is a new provision in respect of breach of community service orders. Statutory provision for such a power previously existed in regard to probation orders under PCCA 1973, s. 6 (now repealed) but was never brought into force.

19–042   The number of hours that may be ordered shall not exceed 60 in aggregate, and where the breached order is a community service order, the aggregate total number of hours under both orders shall not exceed the maximum specified in PCCA 1973, s. 14(1A), *i.e.* 240 hours (para. 6(3)). Where the breached order is a combination order, the aggregate total under both orders shall not exceed 100 hours, the maximum number that can be imposed under a combination order. The Act is not fully clear whether the maximum aggregate allowable refers to the total number of hours ordered or remaining to be served. No minimum length of order is specified and thus the Act allows very short orders, though relevant officers may have doubts about the appropriateness of inducting offenders into work for orders below a certain viable minimum length.

An order imposed as a breach penalty is administered and regulated in the same way as a community service order imposed as a community sentence, under the provisions of PCCA 1973 and CJA 1991. Courts acting for the relevant petty sessions area thus have essentially the same powers of amendment, breach and revocation as if the order was made as a community sentence. This issue is addressed further in Chapter 22.

Chapter 20

Combination orders

The only genuinely innovatory sentence introduced into practice by **20–001**
CJA 1991, the combination order is actually a marriage of the familiar
powers of probation and community service in a single community
order. Under section 11(1) the combination order requires the offender:

(a) to be under the supervision of a probation officer for a period
     specified in the order, being not less than 12 months nor more
     than three years; and

(b) to perform unpaid work for a specified number of hours, being in
     the aggregate not less than 40 nor more than 100.

The probation "element" can be regarded as the senior partner as the
intention of the legislation and the clear view of the Home Office
(*National Standard for Combination Orders*, 1995, para. 10) is that the
community service element will normally be completed first. Though a
single order, the 1991 Act makes little explicit provision for the
enforcement of combination orders, treating the order essentially as two
separate legal entities, thus requiring the courts to borrow as
appropriate from provisions relating to probation and community
service orders. This generates substantial ambiguity in enforcement
proceedings (see para. 22–045).

Power to Make a Combination Order **20–002**
The offender must be aged 16 or over and, as with a community service
order, must be convicted of an offence punishable with imprisonment
(other than an offence for which sentence is fixed by law). As in respect
of a probation order, the court must be of the opinion that the making of
such an order is desirable in the interests of:

(a) securing the rehabilitation of the offender, or

(b) protecting the public from harm from the offender or preventing
     the commission by the offender of further offences.

There is no requirement that such further offences shall be of the same
nature as the offence for which the offender is being sentenced. In
addition, because Part 1 of PCCA 1973 applies to combination orders as
if the probation element were a probation order and the community
service element were a community service order (s. 11(3)) the court

267

must comply with the procedural requirements of the 1973 Act essential in the making of probation and community service orders, *e.g.* in obtaining the consent of the offender.

The court is required to obtain and consider a pre-sentence report before determining the suitability of a combination order for the offender. As with other community orders being imposed as a community sentence, the restriction on liberty imposed under a combination order should be commensurate with the seriousness of the offence or that offence combined with other associated offences, taking into account the suitability of the order for the offender and the likely impact of the order upon the offender in the light of their personal circumstances and characteristics.

A combination order may be imposed upon an offender who resides or intends to reside in Scotland (where the power to combine a probation order with a community service order was already possible) but not if the offender resides or intends to reside in Northern Ireland.

The form of a youth court combination order is specified by the Magistrates' Courts (Forms) Rules 1981, f. 92F (as amended by the Magistrates' Courts (CJA 1991) (Miscellaneous Amendments) Rules 1992. The standard requirements combine those which are specified in community service orders and standard probation orders.

20–003 Additional Requirements
CJA 1991, s. 11(3) specifies that the probation element of a combination order shall be governed by PCCA 1973, Pt. I as if it were a probation order. This means that the court is empowered to insert any additional requirement that may be imposed in a probation order into the supervision element of a combination order, though the court would have to consider to what extent such requirements would be compatible with the performance of the community service element of the order and with full alertness to the overall restriction upon the offender's liberty entailed. The scope to impose additional requirements was clearly anticipated in the White Paper (para. 4.16).

20–004 Combining a Combination Order with other Sentences and Orders
The general rule broadly applies that "courts should avoid mixing sentences which fall into well established and different categories" (*McElhorne* (1983) 5 Cr. App. R.(S.) 53). The scope for combining a combination order with other sentences and orders in respect of either the same or different offences on the same sentencing occasion can be summarised as follows:

Combining a Combination Order with Other Penalties   **20–005**

	Dis- charge	Fine	At- tend- ance Centre	Super- vision Order	Proba- tion Order	CSO	Cur- few Order	Cus- tody
Same Offence	No	Yes	Yes	No	No	No	Yes	No
Different Offences	Yes	Yes	Yes	No	Yes	Yes	Yes	No

CJA 1991, s. 6(3) specifies that a community sentence shall not consist of or include both a probation order and a community service order except as elements of a combination order. By implication a combination order cannot lawfully be combined with either a probation order or a community service order for the same offence. Whether it is good sentencing practice to impose this mix for different offences has not yet been the subject of Court of Appeal guidance. It appears to be legally possible but may be considered undesirable or confusing in practice. To combine a combination order with a supervision order appears clearly wrong, as this juxtaposes two distinct statutory regimes. The court should decide which form of statutory supervision is more appropriate for the offender. A combination order should be combined with an attendance centre order only with considerable hesitation, in view of the triple burden of responsibility which the offender would be required to sustain.

Appropriate Use of a Combination Order   **20–006**
Authoritative guidance is awaited on the sentencing principles applicable to the use of this sentence and its particular weight and merits in sentencing have yet to emerge clearly. The White Paper anticipated that the new order "should be particularly suitable for some persistent property offenders. About 10,000 of those in custody sentenced for burglary, theft, handling, fraud and forgery have three or more previous convictions" (4.16). This bid to provide a particularly demanding non-custodial sentence combining an element of reparation with an opportunity to reduce the likelihood of future offending and thus have particular appeal for sentencers in dealing with those who are on the borderline of custody was echoed in the original *National Standard* (Home Office, 1992, para. 8):

"A combination order is likely to be most appropriate for an **20–007** offender who has:

* committed an offence which is amongst the most serious for which a community sentence can be imposed;

* clearly identified areas of need that have contributed to the offending and which can be dealt with by probation supervision; and

* a realistic prospect of completing such an order, including both the probation and CS elements."

The *National Standard* went on to suggest (para. 9) that amongst those who might not be well suited to a combination order would be:

* those whose lifestyle is particularly chaotic, *e.g.* as a result of drug or alcohol misuse and who might therefore have particular difficulty in keeping to a programme of CS work; or

* offenders with well-ordered lifestyles who have little need of (or alternatively little prospect of responding to) probation supervision.

"Combination orders that include demanding additional requirements within the probation element are particularly onerous and are likely to be difficult to complete, especially for younger offenders."

20–008 A further attempt to demarcate the appropriate constituency of the combination order has been made by the Magistrates Association, the Justices' Clerks Society and the Association of Chief Officers of Probation in a discussion paper (1992) on Community Sentences and Restriction on Liberty:

"Combination orders are appropriate only where a high level of restriction is required. It may be that few cases dealt with in Magistrates' Courts—and even fewer in youth courts—are likely to come within this sentencing band."

However, as Ashworth (1992, 272) has cautioned:

"Whilst the Government's intention is laudable, the outcome in practice will depend heavily on whether the courts do use the order for offenders who might previously have received custody and do not indulge in net-widening by moving up tariff certain offenders who would previously have received either probation or community service alone."

20–009 Many probation areas have hoped to restrict the use of the combination order as far as possible to the Crown Court but in 1993 only 24 per cent of orders were imposed in that court. Seven per cent of orders were imposed by youth courts. Eight per cent of all orders made in 1993 were imposed on persons aged 16–17 (Home Office, 1994a). Combination orders constituted two per cent of all sentences and orders imposed on male offenders aged 14–under 18 for indictable offences (one per cent for all female offenders in that age group.

The Management of a Combination Order 20–010

The probation and community service elements of a combination order are regulated in accordance with the relevant National Standards pertaining to probation and community service as if they were separate orders, but subject also to a supplementary *National Standard for Combination Orders* (1995) which addresses the status of the combination order as a single order of the court. The broad aim is to ensure harmony and co-ordination so that the two elements are administered compatibly with an appropriate overview of the totality of the sentence.

CJA 1991, s. 15(3) does not identify a "responsible officer" for combination orders, recognising the function of the "relevant officer" for community service purposes and the supervising officer for probation supervision purposes. The *National Standard* (1995, para. 6), however, is clear that one officer should be identified as the supervising officer with overall responsibility for the order and should be kept informed of significant developments within the order to ensure that the elements are properly integrated. That officer should regularly review the order as a whole and should take the decision whether to institute breach proceedings. The supervision plan should address the combination order as a whole. The aim should be to maximise the effectiveness of the order as a whole, to reinforce the different elements and to promote compliance with both elements.

Enforcement of a Combination Order

The generic provisions of CJA 1991, Sched. 2 do not designate the combination order as a "relevant order" but instead specify (para. 1(2)):

"... this Schedule shall apply in relation

(a) in so far as they impose such a requirement as is mentioned in paragraph (a) of subsection (1) of section 11 of this Act, as if they were probation orders; and

(b) in so far as they impose such a requirement as is mentioned in paragraph (b) of that subsection, as if they were community service orders."

This leaves open to question whether it is possible for a court to revoke 20–011 one element of the order while leaving the other intact, either in breach proceedings or on hearing a revocation application or subsequent to a custodial sentence imposed for a further offence. The provisions of paragraph 1(2) appear to empower such a split and Ward and Ward (1993) have questioned whether it is possible for a court to revoke the order as a whole upon a single application. The logic of the combination order suggests that the order is best regarded as an indivisible entity. Clear problems would be presented in dealing with the offender afresh for the original offence upon revocation of only one element of the order. On what basis could the court assess what sentence is appropriate for the original offence when a part of the original sentence for that offence remains in force? Pending authoritative determination of this issue, it seems appropriate and in accord with current practice to act on the basis that a combination order should be addressed and revoked as a whole, either upon a single application or by a single decision of the court. This is reinforced by the Magistrates' Court (Forms) Rules 1981, f. 92P, specifying a form for use in "revocation of a probation, community service or combination order". The issue is addressed further in Chapter 22 in regard to breach proceedings.

Chapter 21

Curfew orders

The power to make a curfew order, somewhat akin to "night re- **21–001** striction" as a requirement of a supervision order (para. 17–018) was introduced in Criminal Justice Act 1991, s. 12 but not brought into force in October 1992 with other community sentencing provisions, pending the resolution of technical problems and uncertainties regarding oversight and enforcement. The order is being introduced and tested in three experimental pilot areas (Manchester, Norfolk and Reading) from July 1995, using electronic monitoring operated by commercial contractors

Power to Make a Curfew Order

CJA 1991, s. 12

"(1) Where a person of or over the age of 16 years is convicted of an **21–002** offence (not being an offence for which the sentence is fixed by law), the court by or before which he is convicted may make a curfew order, that is to say, an order requiring him to remain, for periods specified in the order, at a place so specified.

(2) A curfew order may specify different places or different periods for different days, but shall not specify—

    (a)   periods which fall outside the period of six months beginning with the day on which it is made; or

    (b)   periods which amount to less than two hours or more than 12 hours in any one day.

(3) The requirements in a curfew order shall, as far as practicable, be such as to avoid—

    (a)   any conflict with the offender's religious beliefs or with the requirements of any other community order to which he may be subject; and

    (b)   any interference with the times, if any, at which he normally works or attends school or other educational establishment.

(7) The Secretary of State may by order direct— **21–003**

(a) that subsection (2) above shall have effect with the substitution, for any period there specified, of such period as may be specified in the order; or

(b) that subsection (3) above shall have effect with such additional restrictions as may be so specified."

A youth court or the Crown Court may make a curfew order in respect of an offender aged 16 or over who has been convicted of any offence, whether imprisonable or not, other than one carrying a mandatory sentence. A curfew restriction may not extend beyond six months from the date on which the order is made. The "place" need not be the offender's home but will probably be so. The range of restriction which can be imposed is clearly wide, ranging, in theory at least, from as little as two hours up to over 2,000 hours within the six month period. In the anticipation period before the experimental trials, a query has been raised whether a curfew order must contain requirements affecting each day of the total duration of the order. It is difficult to know why subsections (1) and (2) should receive such interpretation and the White Paper (Home Office, 1990) clearly anticipated that the order could specify only certain days, *e.g.* weekends.

21–004 **Procedural Requirements**

Information about Place of Confinement

Though there is no statutory requirement under CJA 1991, s. 7(3) to obtain a pre-sentence report, the court is required to consider whether imposition of restrictions on liberty under a curfew order is commensurate with the seriousness of the offence(s) and whether the order is the most suitable for the offender (CJA 1991, s.6 (2)(a) and (b)). In addition, the court must obtain particular information specified by section 12(6), best secured through a pre-sentence report.

CJA 1991, s. 12

"(6) Before making a curfew order, the court shall obtain and consider information about the place proposed to be specified in the order (including information as to the attitude of persons likely to be affected by the enforced presence there of the offender)."

21–005 This requirement appears to place practical limitations upon the suitability of a curfew order. Apart from questions of the impact of the proposed confinement upon the lives of family members or others who would be affected, an offender who does not enjoy the security of tenure of an owner occupier or a tenant is not necessarily in a position to consent to remaining indoors at the specified "place" where this depends on the goodwill, hospitality or tolerance of the occupier. Though the subsection does not make this explicit, the curfew would seem viable only if the occupier of the premises (if other than the defendant) gives active consent to the proposal (consent which can, of course, be withdrawn at any time, thus requiring a referral back to the supervising court). These questions arise particularly in regard to electronic monitoring (below). Subsection (6) does not specify who will be responsible for making inquiries to provide information for the court but this task is likely to fall to the probation service or social services. It is anticipated that the consent of the defendant will be sought before inquiries are made with third persons and, in the case of a young person who is not living with their parent or person *in loco parentis*, it would seem to follow that the consent of the parent or responsible person should also be secured.

Explanation and Consent

CJA 1991, s. 12

"(5) Before making a curfew order, the court shall explain to the offender in ordinary language—

    (a)   the effect of the order (including any additional requirements **21–006** proposed to be included in the order in accordance with section 13 below);

    (b)   the consequences which may follow under Schedule 2 to this Act if he fails to comply with any of the requirements of the order; and

    (c)   that the court has under that Schedule power to review the order on the application either of the offender or of the supervising officer, and the court shall not make the order unless he expresses his willingness to comply with its requirements."

Responsible Person and Monitoring Arrangements

CJA 1991, s. 12

"(4) A curfew order shall include provision for making a person responsible for monitoring the offender's whereabouts during the curfew periods specified in the order; and a person who is made so responsible shall be of a description specified in an order made by the Secretary of State.

(4A) A court shall not make a curfew order unless the court has been notified by the Secretary of State that arrangements for monitoring the offender's whereabouts are available in the area in which the place proposed to be specified in the order is situated and the notice has not been withdrawn."

21–007 Combining a Curfew Order with Other Sentences or Orders

The scope for combining a curfew order with other disposals is subject to the general rule that "courts should avoid mixing sentences which fall within well-established and different categories" (*McElhorne* (1983) 5 Cr. App. R.(S.) 53, and may be summarised as follows:

21–008   *Combination of Curfew with Other Penalties*

	Dis-charge	Fine	At-tend-ance Centre	Super-vision Order	Proba-tion Order	CSO	Com-bina-tion Order	Cus-tody
Same Offence	No	Yes	Yes	Yes*	Yes	Yes	Yes	No
Different Offences	Yes	Yes	Yes	Yes*	Yes	Yes	Yes	No

* Appears legally permissible but, given the power to make a night restriction requirement in a supervision order, this may be regarded as undesirable or inappropriate in practice.

21–009 Electronic Monitoring

A curfew order may in addition include "requirements for securing the electronic monitoring of the offender's whereabouts during the curfew periods specified in the order" (s. 13(1)). Commonly known as "tagging", this provision for electronic surveillance is not a sentence in its own right but an optional regulatory inclusion in a curfew order and is thus subject to the general requirement that the offender consents to such an order (s. 12(5)). The offender is required to wear a device attached to the ankle or wrist which relays a signal to monitoring equipment located at the place of confinement. Violations are relayed by telephone line to the monitoring centre.

CJA 1991, s. 13

"(2) A court shall not make a curfew order which includes such requirements unless the court—

(a) has been notified by the Secretary of State that electronic monitoring arrangements are available in the area in which the place proposed to be specified in the order is situated; and

(b) is satisfied that the necessary provision can be made under those arrangements."

By section 13(3) the Secretary of State is empowered to "enter into contracts with other persons for the electronic monitoring by them of offenders' whereabouts". Experiments with the use of electronic monitoring of persons remanded on bail during 1990 were far from encouraging, showing that courts were reluctant to use this option, that there were frequent equipment failures and that the violation rate was high (Mair and Nee, 1990). The technology has since been modified and improved and the government intends electronic monitoring to be an integral feature of curfew orders rather than simply an optional extra, allowing offenders to be policed routinely on a continuous basis. The technical demands of such monitoring will limit the number of offenders who are suitable for a curfew order. The offender will need to reside in a property with an existing telephone line or to which a line can be readily connected, thus eliminating defendants who lack a settled address. If the offender is not the property occupier, the permission of the occupier will be necessary for the telephone equipment to be installed or adapted for monitoring purposes. The offender also has to be able to offer a constant electricity supply to power the monitoring equipment.

In the 1995 pilot trials, the installation of equipment and the monitoring of curfew periods will be undertaken by private sector commercial companies under contract with the Home Office. A representative of the contractor will act as "responsible person" for the purposes of section 12(4) and enforcement proceedings (see below).

Sentencing Principles 21–010

Though the Court of Appeal has yet to give guidance on the use of this measure, *Crime, Justice and Protecting the Public* (Home Office, 1990) suggested that curfew orders would be:

> "helpful in reducing some forms of crime, thefts of or from cars, pub brawls and other types of disorder. A curfew order could be used to keep offenders away from particular places such as shopping centres or pubs, or to keep them at home in the evenings or at weekends" (para. 4.20)

The White Paper pointed out that "it is not the intention to keep people at home for most of the day" but to enable them to undertake constructive pursuits whether employment, training, community service or treatment for drug abuse.

Enforcement 21–011

Curfew orders are subject to the common enforcement code contained in CJA 1991, Sched. 2 and jurisdiction is vested in the 'magistrates' court acting for the petty sessions area in which "the place" specified in the order is situated (Sched. 2, para. 1(1)(b)). The "responsible officer" for the purposes of enforcement proceedings is "the person responsible for monitoring (the offender's) whereabouts during the curfew periods specified in the order (CJA 1991, s. 15(3)(c)).

Chapter 22

Enforcement of Community Orders

AMENDMENT OF COMMUNITY ORDERS

22–001 Four community orders (probation, community service, combination and curfew orders) are regulated in common by CJA 1991, Sched. 2, Part IV. Supervision and attendance centre orders are regulated separately by the Children and Young Persons Act, 1969 and the Criminal Justice Act, 1982 respectively.

On Change of Residence
This is the most common reason to seek variation of an order.

Probation, Community Service and Combination Orders (Sched. 2, para. 12)

Where a magistrates' court acting for the petty sessions area specified in the order is satisfied that the offender proposes to change or has changed residence to another petty sessions area, the court may, and on the application of the responsible officer shall (*i.e.* must), amend the order by substituting the other petty sessions area. The offender is not required to be summoned or to consent or to be present when the application is considered (para. 17(2)). The effect is that the order will be regulated for the purposes of amendment, breach or revocation by a court acting for the new petty sessions area.

22–002 If the order is a probation order or a combination order the probation element of which includes additional requirements which can only be complied with if the offender continues to reside in the currently specified petty sessions area, the court shall not amend the designated area without first either cancelling those requirements or substituting other requirements which can be complied with in the proposed area (para. 12(3)). If the order thus has to be amended by substituting fresh requirements that can be complied with in the proposed area then the offender must either be summonsed to attend and give consent or must make the application, under the normal rules for the variation of an order (para. 17(1)).

In the case of a community service order or a combination order, the court shall not transfer the order unless satisfied that arrangements can be made for the offender to perform work in the proposed area (para. 12(4)).

278

Probation Rules 1984, r. 39 places a duty upon a probation officer **22–003** supervising a probation order or community service order (or, by implication, a combination order) to apply for amendment of that order under paragraph 12 unless the probation officer has reason to believe that the offender is unlikely to reside in the area for a reasonable time or, in the case of a probation order, has ascertained from the supervising court that that court and the court acting for the offender's new petty sessions area are satisfied that the special circumstances of the case make it desirable that the offender should remain under his or her supervision (r. 39(3)).

If the offender has moved or intends to move to Scotland or Northern Ireland, the special provisions of CJA 1991, Sched. 3 apply and the order will be amended as follows:

	Scotland	*Northern Ireland*
Probation Order	specify "locality" of proposed or new residence and the appropriate court of summary jurisdiction	specify appropriate petty sessions district
Community Service Order	specify "locality" of proposed or new residence and require officer of appropriate regional or islands council to exercise responsibilities of "relevant officer"	specify appropriate petty sessions district and require officer of Probation Board of Northern Ireland to exercise responsibilities of "relevant officer"

A combination order cannot be transferred to Northern Ireland by **22–004** amendment because this sentence does not exist in that jurisdiction. It will thus be necessary to initiate revocation proceedings so that the original sentence can be considered afresh. If the community service order in respect of an offender aged 16 who is moving to Northern Ireland requires work for an aggregate number of hours exceeding 120 hours, and thus in excess of the maximum number of hours still prevailing in Northern Ireland, the court amending the order to effect transfer of jurisdiction may reduce the number of hours specified in the order (Sched. 3, para. 4(2)).

If applying to amend an order under paragraph 12 it is not necessary to secure or to indicate the consent of the probation service responsible for supervision or the provision of work in the proposed area. The responsibility for application lies with the current supervising or relevant officer. In practice, the supervising or relevant officer will have requested the co-operation of their counterpart in the proposed area to establish that the offender's new residence is likely to last and thus to form the basis of new supervisory or working arrangements. Once this has been established, the transfer should not be delayed because in the meantime the officer in the new area does not have any legal basis for giving binding instructions to the offender, except as agent of the current responsible officer and the court of the existing petty sessions area retains enforcement jurisdiction. The problem posed by the first drawback can be overcome in the short term if the current supervising or relevant officer clearly and directly instructs the offender to co-operate with the supervisory or working instructions given by the officer in the new area operating as the supervising or relevant officer's agent. This would appear to satisfy the standard requirement of the probation order regarding "keeping in touch" in accordance with instructions and the provisions of PCCA 1973, s. 15(1) in respect of a community service order. Any breach proceedings will, however, have to be initiated by the supervising or relevant officer in the court acting for the petty sessions area currently named in the order. The offender under a probation order might argue that the statutory obligation is to be "under the supervision of a probation officer assigned to that area" (PCCA 1973, s. 2(2)) and that supervision cannot be exercised indirectly through an intermediary, but this seems a doubtful defence.

22–005   If the order is amended under paragraph 12, the clerk of the court shall send a copy of the amending order to the clerk to the justices for the new petty sessions area, together with such documents and information relating to the case as are considered likely to be of assistance to the new court in exercising its functions. The clerk for the new area shall give copies of the amending order to the responsible officer and to the person in charge of any institution in which the offender is or was required by the order to reside (para. 18).

If the offender will be residing in Scotland or Northern Ireland the amending order is sent to the "home court", *i.e.* the Sheriff Court having jurisdiction in the offender's new locality in Scotland, or to the court of summary jurisdiction acting for the petty sessions district in which the offender will reside in Northern Ireland.

No order may be made under paragraph 12 while an appeal against the relevant order is pending (para. 16).

22–006 *Curfew Orders*

Where a magistrates' court acting for the petty sessions area in which the place specified in the order is situated is satisfied that the offender proposes to change or has changed residence to another petty sessions area, the court may, and on the application of the responsible offer shall (*i.e.* must), amend the order by substituting a place in that other area for the place so specified (para. 12(2)). If the order contains a requirement which, in the opinion of the court, cannot be complied with in the new area, the amendment shall not be made unless the court either cancels those requirements or substitutes other requirements which can be complied with in the proposed area (para. 12(3)). The most likely problems in practice will arise, particularly in the developmental or experimental phase of electronic monitoring, where the offender has moved to an area where monitoring arrangements are not in place. In such circumstances an amendment is not practicable and the alternative course may be revocation of the order, with scope for re-sentencing.

Supervision Orders   **22–007**

CYPA 1969 does not make specific provision for a supervision order to be amended upon change of address to a new petty sessions area or local authority area but section 15(1) provides a general power to substitute for any of the present provisions of the order a further provision which could have been included if the court was now making the order. Variation can be made on the application either of the supervisor or the supervised person. Application shall be made to a youth court acting for the specified petty sessions area if the supervised person has not attained the age of 18, but otherwise to an adult magistrates' court for that area. The provisions of section 15(1) are detailed at para. 22–016.

Attendance Centre Orders   **22–008**

By CJA 1982, s. 18(6) the offender or the officer in charge of the relevant attendance centre can apply to vary the order by substituting another centre which the court is satisfied is reasonably accessible to the offender, having regard to age, means of available access and any other circumstances. Prior to CJA 1991 this power could only exercised where the offender had changed or was about to change address but section 18(6)(b) was amended by CJA 1991, s. 67(3) to permit variation in any circumstances. Application is made to a magistrates' court (normally a youth court) acting for the petty sessions area in which the centre is situated or, in the case of an order made by a magistrates' court, to that court (s. 18(5)). Where an application is made by the officer in charge, the court may deal with it without summoning the offender (s. 18(7)). A copy of the order for variation shall be given to the offender or sent to the offender's last or usual place of abode. A copy should also be supplied to the officer in charge of the new centre.

Variation, Cancellation or Addition of Requirements   **22–009**

Probation Orders

CJA 1991, Sched. 2, para. 13 empowers a magistrates' court acting for the petty sessions area specified in the order to:

(a)   cancel any requirements in the order;

(b)   insert an additional requirement in the order;

(c)   substitute a new requirement for an existing requirement in the order.

This power applies both to orders made by a youth court and the Crown Court. The Crown Court cannot reserve power of variation to itself. There are three variations which the court cannot make (para. 13(2)(a)):

(a) reducing the length of the probation period;

(b) extending the length of probation period beyond three years from the date of the original order;

(c) inserting a requirement under Sched. 1A, paras. 5 or 6 that the offender shall submit to treatment for mental condition or dependency on drugs or alcohol, *unless* the amending order is made within three months of the date of the original order.

No application may be made while an appeal against the probation order is pending (para. 16).

22–010 Power of variation is exercisable only upon the application of either the probation officer responsible for the order or the offender. The supervising officer is under a duty to make an application as follows:

(a) Probation Rules, r. 39(4) requires the officer to make application where it appears that an application for amendment can properly be made, unless the offender makes application;

(b) where the offender is subject to an additional requirement of treatment either for mental condition or for dependency on drugs or alcohol, and the medical practitioner or the person directing that treatment is of the opinion:

(i) that the treatment of the offender should be continued beyond the period specified in that behalf in the order;

(ii) that the offender needs different treatment, being treatment of a kind to which he could be required to submit in purusuance of a probation order;

(iii) that the offender is not susceptible to treatment; or

(iv) that the offender does not require further treatment;

or, alternatively, is for any reason unwilling to continue to treat or direct the treatment of the offender, then he or she shall make a report in writing to that effect to the supervising officer. That officer must then apply for the variation or cancellation of the requirement (Sched. 2, para. 14).

22–011 If application is made by the supervising officer, the offender must be summonsed to appear before the court and, in the event of non-attendance, may be brought before the court on warrant. In accordance with the general principle that the offender must give valid consent to the making of a probation order, the offender must express willingness to comply with the requirements of the order which the application for variation seeks to impose. If, however, the effect of the proposed amendment is simply to cancel a requirement or to reduce the operational length of any requirement, then the offender does not have to be present or summonsed to attend, nor to give consent. There is not even a formal requirement for the offender to be notified that application is to be made, though this would be good practice.

If the application is made by the offender, Schedule 2 makes no formal provision for the supervising officer to be notified or consulted, but it is most unlikely that the court would grant such an application without giving the Probation Service the opportunity to be heard.

In regard to variation of an order by adding a requirement, it is worth **22–012** noting that the effect will be to increase the restrictions upon the offender's liberty yet Schedule 2 does not require the court to consider the provisions of CJA 1991, s. 6(2). If the original order was deemed to impose restrictions on liberty commensurate with the seriousness of the offence, on what basis might additional restrictions be inserted? The only logical interpretation would seem to be that if the restrictions contained in the original order fell below the ceiling demanded by commensurability, in the light of the offender's personal circumstances and considerations of suitability, but the offender's circumstances have now changed, then the offender could now be considered suitable for additional requirements, provided that these do not exceed that ceiling. This power of amendment is thus unlikely to be used frequently. In any case, the offender has, in effect, power of veto upon any proposed amendment adding requirements and is perhaps unlikely to agree voluntarily to greater restrictions unless such consent is perceived to gain access to resources or opportunities which are not available unless linked to formal requirements.

Community Service Orders   **22–013**

The scope for variation of a community service order is very limited. There is no power to increase or reduce the number of hours specified in the order. The appropriate application in seeking to achieve such an effect would be for revocation of the order. The only application that can be made is for extension of the period of 12 months (specified by PCCA 1973, s. 15(2)) within which the order should be completed (Sched. 2, para. 15). This power rests with a magistrates' court acting for the petty sessions area specified in the order, even if the order was made by the Crown Court which cannot reserve power of variation to itself. No application may be made while an appeal against the order is pending (para. 16).

Application may be made by either the offender or the responsible officer. If application is made by the relevant officer then unless the offender is already before the court (for example in breach procedings where the order is to continue) s/he must be summonsed to appear before the court and, in the event of non-attendance, may be arrested on warrant (para. 17(1)). Paragraph 15 does not specify any maximum time beyond which the order cannot be extended. It is not clear whether a second extension can be sought as paragraph 15 refers only to extending "the period of 12 months". This appears to limit use of the power to a single instance. However, the fact that the time period specified either in the original order or in the amended order upon extension has elapsed does not affect the offender's liability to work. PCCA 1973, s. 15(2) is clear that the order remains in force until the offender has worked for the hours specified (*Tebbutt* (1988) 10 Cr. App. R.(S.) 88).

22-014 Proceedings for breach or revocation may still be validly initiated after the period has elapsed. An extension of time is nevertheless helpful, if not strictly essential, because it provides a clear target date by which the obligation to work should be satisfied. Whether the offender's failure to complete the hours specified in the order within 12 months (or the extended period if an extension is ordered) is in breach of requirements is discussed at para. 22–029. The amendment cannot be made unless the offender expresses willingness to comply with the order under the proposed new time-scale. In this unlikely event the offender is likely to default on the order, as valid instructions to attend for work may still be issued, and thus breach proceedings may be initiated in due course.

22-015 *Combination Orders*

CJA 1991 does not empower variation of a combination order as such. Application may be made to vary either the probation element or the community service element, or both, in accordance with provisions pertaining to probation or community service orders. In considering any application to vary either element, the court will be able to weigh the overall effect upon the combination order as a whole.

Curfew Orders

CJA 1991, Sched. 2, para. 13 empowers a magistrates' court acting for the petty sessions area in which the "place" specified in the order is situated to

(i)   cancel any requirement in the order;

(ii) insert an additional requirement in the order; or

(iii) substitute a new requirement for an existing requirement in the order.

This power applies to orders made by a youth court and the Crown Court. However, the court shall not amend the order by extending the curfew periods beyond the end of six months from the date of the original order (Sched. 2, para. 13(2)(b)). Power of variation is exercisable only upon the application of the offender or the responsible officer. Variations (ii) or (iii) above will require the offender's expression of willingness to comply with the proposed requirement. If application for such a variation is made by the responsible officer, the offender must be summonsed to appear before the court and, in the event of non-attendance, may be brought before the court on warrant. No application may be made while an appeal against the order is pending (para. 16).

22-016 *Supervision Orders*

CYPA 1969, s. 15 empowers the relevant court, upon application either by the supervised person or the supervisor, to vary a supervision order as follows:

(a)   by cancelling any additional requirements (*i.e.* imposed under ss. 12, 12A, 12AA, 12B, 12C or 18(2)(b)); or

(b)   inserting an additional requirement; or

(c)   substituting a new requirement for an existing requirement.

In adding or substituting a requirement, the court can insert "any **22–017** provisions which could have been included in the order if the court then had power to make it and were exercising that power" (s. 15(1)(b)). Thus in determining the powers of the court, the age of the offender at the time of the proposed variation is the crucial consideration. If the supervised person has attained the age of 18 it could be argued that there is no power to insert new requirements, though the counter-argument would be that the offender was aged under 18 at the time of conviction and thus remains eligible to receive a supervision order. Similarly, the present age of the offender will determine whether the offender or the offender's parents should give any required consent (*e.g.* to a requirement under s. 12A(3)). CYPA 1969, s. 16(7) makes specific provision that where the supervised person has attained the age of 14, then a requirement of treatment for mental condition shall not be inserted (or varied in any way other than by removing or reducing the duration of the requirement) under section 15 powers unless the supervised person consents. This is in line with the provision specifying the necessity of a young person's consent in section 12B(2)(b).

The supervisor is under a duty to make application for variation as **22–018** follows:

(a)   Probation Rules 1984, r. 39(3) requires a probation officer supervising a supervision order to make application where it appears that "an application can properly be made".

(b)   Where the supervised person is subject to a requirement of treatment for mental condition under section 12B and the medical practitioner responsible for that treatment is of the opinion:

(i)   that the treatment should be continued beyond the period specified in that behalf in the order; or

(ii)   that the supervised person needs different treatment; or

(iii)   that he is not susceptible to treatment; or

(iv)   that he does not require further treatment,

the practitioner shall report this in writing to the supervisor who must refer it to the relevant court (s. 15(9) and (10)).

The court's powers are subject to the following limitations:

(a)   there is no power to increase the length of the supervision period;

(b)   a new requirement of treatment for mental conditions under section 12B cannot be inserted *unless* the amending order is made within three months of the date of the original order (s. 15(2)(a));

(c) a new requirement of "night restriction" under section 12A(3)(b) cannot specify a day which falls outside the first three months of the order (s. 15(2)(b)).

22–019 The relevant court for a variation application depends upon the age of the supervised person at the time of the proposed variation. If the young person has not reached their eighteenth birthday, application should be made to a youth court; if they have attained the age of 18, application should be made to an adult magistrates' court. If the supervised person attains the age of 18 while an application to a youth court is pending, the court shall have power to deal with the application as if the offender had not attained that age (s. 16(11)).

The normal requirement for a section 15 variation is that the supervised person shall be present before the court (s. 16(1)). Where the supervisor makes application this may be achieved by the supervisor bringing the supervised person before the court (s. 16(1)) but it may also be achieved by summoning the supervised person to attend (s. 16(2)). If satisfied on oath that the summons cannot be served or if the supervised person fails to answer to summons, then a justice may issue a warrant to secure attendance. The court may, however, act in the supervised person's absence to vary an order as follows (s. 16(5):

(a) cancelling an additional requirement;

(b) reducing the duration of the order or of any additional requirement;

(c) changing the supervisor (*e.g.* from a local authority to a probation officer);

(d) altering the name of any specified local authority and/or petty sessions area (*i.e.* to amend the order upon change of address).

22–020 When considering whether to insert a requirement under sections 12, 12A, 12AA, 12B or 12C or to vary or cancel such a requirement, a youth court must be satisfied either (a) that the supervised person is unlikely to receive the care or control he or she needs unless the court makes the order, or (b) is likely to receive such care and control notwithstanding the order being made (s. 16(6)).

The provisions of section 15 and the related supplementary requirements of section 16 are complex and apply a generic approach to variation, breach and discharge of supervision orders. This complex set of powers is detailed further at para. 22–047.

22–021 *Attendance Centre Orders*

CJA 1982, s. 18 gives power to vary the date/time at which the offender is first to attend. There is no power to vary the number of hours of attendance. Application may be made, by either the offender or the officer in charge of the specified centre, to a magistrates' court (normally a youth court) acting for the petty sessions area in which the specified centre is situated, or to the court which made the order. If the application is made by the officer in charge, the offender does not have to be summonsed to attend for the hearing (s. 18(7)) but a copy of the variation order should be served upon the offender (s. 18(8). If the application is made by the offender, there is no statutory requirement that the officer in charge shall be notified or heard by the court but a copy of the variation order should be served upon the officer (s. 18(8)).

BREACH OF COMMUNITY ORDERS   **22–022**

Probation Orders, Community Service Orders, Combination Orders and Curfew Orders

Breach of a requirement of these orders is regulated by a common code set out in CJA 1991, Sched. 2, Pt. II, paras. 2–6.

Jurisdiction

Jurisdiction in breach proceedings lies with a magistrates' court acting for the petty sessions area specified in the order (or, in the case of a curfew order, the petty sessions area in which the place specified in the order is situated), here described as the supervising court. This applies equally to orders made by the Crown Court which does not have power to reserve breach issues to itself but the Crown Court alone can revoke an order made by that Court and if a magistrates' court is of the opinion that revocation is appropriate, the matter must be remitted back to the Crown Court.

Breach proceedings may be initiated while the relevant order is "in force". Proceedings cannot be commenced once the order is completed. If the order ceases to remain in force after an information has been laid, the question arises whether the court retains jurisdiction to hear the allegation and what are the powers of the court if the breach is admitted or proved.

This point was tested prior to the 1991 Act in regard to the completion **22–023** of community service hours. In the leading case of *Tebbutt* (1988) 10 Cr. App. R.(S.) 88, breach proceedings were commenced when the offender had 27 hours work outstanding of an order for 100 hours imposed by the Crown Court. The magistrates chose to remit the matter back to the Crown Court. Whilst waiting to appear at Crown Court, the offender completed the remaining hours. Though revocation in breach proceedings normally signifies that the relevant order lacks future viability, the Crown Court here revoked the order despite its completion and imposed a (suspended) custodial sentence by way of re-sentence. The Court of Appeal dismissed the offender's appeal that the Crown Court had no power to revoke because the order was by then non-existent, stating:

"Once a magistrates' court is seized of a case under PCCA 1973, s. 16 (which then governed breach of community service), the powers of the court to deal with an offender are complete and the performance of hours after that time is a matter only to be considered in mitigation of sentence." (*per* Tudor Evans J.)

The Court of Appeal stated that to conclude otherwise would effectively hand control of the matter to the offender who would be able to wait until breach proceedings had been instituted and could then opt to work and so escape the consequences, including the risks of being dealt with for the original offence. It would also mean that the court's jurisdiction and powers could turn on the speed with which the matter came before the court. The longer it took for the case to be listed, the greater the opportunity for the offender to avoid the consequences. The custodial sentence was also upheld despite completion because the offender had been "extremely unco-operative in carrying out the order, ignoring repeated warnings". Mitigation earned by completion had been reflected in suspension of the prison term.

22-024   The logic of *Tebbutt* applies as validly in the case of probation orders (or supervision orders) which terminate after the commencement of proceedings, not by any effort of the offender but by simple passage of time. The court retains the power to adjudicate upon the breach, to impose a disciplinary penalty to mark the default and to revoke and re-sentence for the original offence, despite the intervening expiry. If the law were otherwise, the offender could avoid the consequences of breach simply by evading the court until the date of expiry.

Where an offender is subject to community service orders imposed on different sentencing occasions and is breached while the first order remains uncompleted, it is not open to the offender to claim that he is in breach only of the first order. This was tested in *Meredith* [1994] Crim. L.R. 142 where the offender had been sentenced to 80 hours community service by a magistrates' court and a further 160 hours by the Crown Court. Dismissing the appellant's claim that, as he had completed only 14 hours, he was not in breach of the second order, the Court of Appeal stated that, if he was right, it would "lead to the remarkable result that he could never be in breach of the second order, because the time would never arrive for him to start performing" that order. "Once two community service orders are made, they are for all practical purposes one order and he was in breach of both."

Meredith does, however, leave unclear important questions of jurisdiction to deal with breach where orders are imposed separately on an offender by courts of different levels. This issue is addressed later in this Chapter (at para. 22–041).

22-025 *Grounds for Breach*

The general grounds for breach action are that the offender "has failed without reasonable excuse to comply with any of the requirements of the relevant order" (Sched. 2, para. 2(1)). The requirement must be one which could lawfully be imposed. The court will need to be satisfied as follows:

(a) the relevant order is in force (or was so at the point where information was laid, see para. 22–022);

(b) the offender is the person subject to that order;

(c) the offender has failed to comply with a valid requirement of that order;

(d) that failure was without reasonable excuse (though the responsibility for raising and establishing such excuse rests with the offender).

Conviction of a further offence while the order is in force, whether committed during the period of that order or not, does not constitute a failure to comply with any requirement of the order (Sched. 2, para. 5(1)).

Probation Orders 22–026

The particular grounds on which a breach may be alleged are:

(i) failure to keep in touch with the responsible supervising officer (either directly or indirectly through a substitute supervisor nominated by the supervising officer) in accordance with instructions (*e.g.* a failure to keep appointments, though the basis may be that the offender has not been at home to receive a visit from the responsible officer as reasonably notified and requested. This would apply in areas where distance between the office and the offender's home and the lack of public transport requires home visiting as normal practice);

(ii) failure to notify the responsible officer of a change of address;

(iii) failure to comply with any additional requirement(s) of the order.

An offender who is required to receive treatment for mental condition or 22–027 for dependency on drugs or alcohol under PCCA 1973, Sched. 1A, para. 5 or 6 shall not be treated as having failed to comply with that requirement on the ground of refusal to undergo any surgical, electrical or other treatment if, in the opinion of the court, that refusal was reasonable, having regard to all the circumstances (Sched. 2, para. 5(2)).

In addition to a claim of "reasonable excuse", an offender may have a valid defence that the additional requirement of which a breach is alleged is too vague or uncertain, or gives undue discretion to the supervising officer, or is outside of the lawful scope of Schedule 1A.

It is not completely clear whether breach action can properly be brought on the grounds of unacceptable behaviour while fulfilling probation requirements, *e.g.* persistent racist abuse or sexual harassment. Such misbehaviour may make it impossible to fulfil the aims of the order and thus provide the basis for an application for revocation but it is less certain that the offender is in breach of a specific requirement of the order. For a breach allegation of this nature to succeeed, it will be necessary to establish that:

(i) the ambit of "instructions" went beyond merely specifying the time and location of appointments;

(ii) instructions were explicitly and unambiguously given by the supervising officer with regard to language and conduct;

(iii) such instructions were "reasonable";

(iv) the behaviour in question was a clear failure to comply.

22–028 For a suggestion that instructions to attend for appointments should make a clear stipulation prohibiting "language or conduct that might reasonably give rise to serious offence in probation staff, other persons under supervision, or members of the public with whom the probationer has contact, when on probation service premises or accompanied by probation personnel", see Cooper and Cooper (1994).

If the probation order contains a requirement of hostel residence, attendance at a probation centre or participation in specified activities, then there is an in-built obligation to comply with instructions, which can properly include the prohibition of oppressive behaviour.

22–029 Community Service Orders
The particular statutory grounds on which a breach may be alleged are:

(i) failure to keep in touch with the relevant officer in accordance with instructions;

(ii) failure to notify the relevant officer of a change of address;

(iii) failure to work at the times instructed by the relevant officer;

(iv) failure to comply with reasonable work directions of the supervisor;

(v) failure to comply with a rule reasonably imposed by the supervisor in the interests of health, safety or the well-being of others present.

It is less clear whether it is a ground for breach that the offender failed to complete the hours specified in the order within 12 months. Non-completion will usually arise either out of a failure to comply with work instructions, which would give sounder grounds for breach action, or because of legitimate unavailability for work because of work commitments or health problems which may constitute grounds for an application to revoke, so the issue may not be of great practical significance. If the offender received insufficient work instructions to complete the order within 12 months, there would obviously be a good defence of reasonable excuse to such a breach allegation. The relevant officer has full discretion to allow the offender to continue working after the expiry of 12 months and is under no obligation to institute breach proceedings (*Tebbutt* (1988) 10 Cr. App. R.(S.) 88).

Dispute may arise from the uncertain ambit of 'reasonable' directions **22–030** and rules issued by the work supervisor in pursuance of CSCOR 1992, r. 4(1). Obvious instances of gross misconduct, disorderly behaviour or the consumption of alcohol at the workplace will clearly constitute breach. In *Caton v. Community Service Office, The Times,* February 27, 1995, the Divisional Court was clear that unacceptable and violent behaviour towards a community service officer could constitute a failure to comply with the requirements of a community service order, even though the required number of hours had been performed. More difficulty may be encountered in regard to less clear cut misbehaviour such as sexist, racist or other oppressive language or harassment which can be the cause of considerable discomfort. This issue is addressed further (at para. 22–027) in the context of probation orders.

If breach proceedings are initiated, the relevant officer has a discretion whether to allow the offender to continue working, "provided that this does not involve undue risk to the public, probation staff or other offenders" (*National Standard,* 1995, para. 29). Suspension from work is likely to follow an incident of alleged gross misconduct or if the offender's continuing failure to attend for work interferes with the efficiency of work arrangements.

Curfew Orders

The particular grounds on which a breach may be alleged are:

(i)   absence from the place where the offender is required to remain during a period specified in the order.

If the curfew order is subject to a requirement of electronic monitoring, a further basis for breach arises:

(ii)   failure to comply with electronic monitoring arrangements (*e.g.* failing to co-operate with the installation of equipment, interference with/damage to equipment, removing the device worn on the body or culpable failure to maintain electricity supply to equipment).

Procedure

Commencing Proceedings   **22–031**

To commence proceedings, an information must be laid before a justice acting for the relevant petty sessions area. If it appears to that justice that the offender has failed to comply with any of the requirements of the order the justice may either:

(a)   issue a summons requiring the offender to appear at the place and time specified in it; or

(b)   if the information is in writing or on oath, issue a warrant for the offender's arrest.

Forms 92I, J and K are prescribed by the Magistrates' Courts (CJA 1991) (Miscellaneous Amendments) Rules 1992 for the form of information, summons and warrant. The information will normally be laid by the responsible officer, either the supervising officer in the case of a probation order, the relevant officer in the case of a community service order or the responsible person in the case of a curfew order (CJA 1991, s. 15(3)). The responsible officer for the purposes of breach of a combination order will depend upon which element it is alleged the offender has breached, though the *National Standard* requires that the decision to take breach action should be taken by the overall supervising officer in consultation with the other supervisors (1995, para. 12). The allegation should normally proceed by summons in the first instance, unless the offender's whereabouts are unknown.

22–032 *Substantiating the Breach*

The offender must always be present in breach proceedings. The offender will be asked to confirm acceptance that the order is (or was) in force. Brief details of the alleged breach are then put to the offender who is asked whether he or she admits or denies the allegation.

22–033   If the offender denies breach of the order, the burden of proof is upon the prosecutor on behalf of the Probation Service (or the responsible person in the case of a curfew order). The standard of proof is that pertaining to criminal proceedings generally, so that the court has to be satisfied beyond reasonable doubt. If the offender claims reasonable excuse for their failure to comply, the onus rests with the offender to establish such excuse on the balance of probabilities (*i.e.* more probable than not). If the offender's defence is that the requirement or instruction was unreasonable, then the prosecution retains the burden of proof that the requirement or instruction was valid. It should be noted that the *National Standards'* requirements and provisions do not have any legal force and do not provide conclusive answers to claims made by offenders in their defence. For example, the relevant *National Standard* (1995, para. 28) requires that an offender subject to a community service order who claims absence through sickness should be asked to provide a medical certificate. If a certificate is not produced and breach proceedings are initiated, the offender is perfectly entitled to supply medical evidence to the court or give an explanation based on health grounds to try to establish a reasonable excuse for non-attendance.

Powers of the Court

If breach of an order is admitted or proved, the powers of the supervising court depend on:

(a) whether the court opts to allow the order to continue or feels that the order should be revoked;

(b) whether the order was made by a youth court or the Crown Court.

22–034 *Powers where the Order Continues*

If the court decides, in the light of any views expressed by the responsible officer about further viability of the order and any indications that the offender is willing to complete the order, that the order should be permitted to continue, the offender may be dealt with in any one of the following disciplinary ways (para. 3(1)), irrespective of which court made the order:

(i)   A *fine* not exceeding level 3 on the standard scale. The fine is deemed to be a sum adjudged to be paid on a conviction for enforcement purposes (para. 6(2)).

(ii) A *community service order* not exceeding 60 hours in the aggregate (para. 6(3)). The Schedule does not specify a minimum number of hours. Courts often have a convention that a breach will attract a standard number of hours, such as five or ten. Where the breached order is a community service order, "the total number of hours under both orders" (*i.e.* the original order and that imposed for the breach) shall not exceed the maximum specified in PCCA 1973, s. 14(1A), *i.e.* 240 hours (para. 6(3)(b)). Where the breached order is a combination order, then the total number of hours under both orders should not exceed the lower maximum of 100 hours permitted as the community service element in a combination order (Sched. 2, para. 1(3)).

The Act does not make entirely clear whether the relevant **22–035** consideration in assessing that maximum should be the number of hours as specified in the orders or the number of hours still to be served. By PCCA 1973, para. 6(4), s. 14(2) and subsequent relevant provisions of that Act shall apply to a community service order made under Schedule 2. The interpretation of section 14(3) when orders are made as sentences on the same or different occasions is clear (see para. 19–003) but the specific wording of paragraph 6(3)(b) appears to limit the aggregate to 240 or 100 hours irrespective of any hours already worked, where the subsequent order is being imposed as a disciplinary penalty following breach. This interpretation would clearly limit the capacity of the court to order additional hours where the offender is already subject to a long order and has not yet worked for any significant number of hours. An order made under Schedule 2, Part II will almost certainly be intended to run consecutively to the original community service order but it will avoid doubt or confusion if the court clarifies that this is the intention.

Power to impose a community service order as a disciplinary **22–036** penalty following breach is unusual in that it involves the use of a disposal which normally amounts to a community sentence in its own right. A community service order may only be imposed as a community order after consideration of a pre-sentence report (CJA 1991, s. 7(3)(b)) but this is not procedurally required under Schedule 2 powers. The court is nevertheless obliged to consider the offender's suitability and to consult either a probation officer or a social worker under PCCA 1973, s. 14(2) (see para. 19–008) which is specifically made applicable by Schedule 2, paragraph

6(4). The effect of section 14(2) is that the offender must also consent to the making of the order.

22-037   Community service orders made under Schedule 2, Part II are regulated and enforced by the Schedule in the same way as an order imposed as a sentence (para. 6(4)(b)). Paragraph 6(5) qualifies the application of the Schedule by specifying that powers conferred by Schedule 2 to deal with the offender for the offence in respect of which the community service order was made (*i.e.* upon revocation in either breach or revocation proceedings) "shall be construed as powers to deal with the offender for the failure to comply with the requirements of the relevant order in respect of which the community service order was made". This clearly means that the offender may be dealt with by a further disciplinary penalty but the position is far less clear as regards the court's powers of revocation. If, for example, an offender subject to a community service order of 120 hours for burglary is made subject to a further 40 hours consecutive community service following a breach of the relevant order, completes the initial 120 hours but breaches the remaining order of 40 hours, the court will have power to impose a fine or a further period of community service, but what are its powers of revocation, if any? A simple revocation without re-sentence would be straightforward but if the court wishes to deal with the offender afresh for the burglary offence, the sub-paragraph appears to give the option to deal with him or her in any manner open to it if the initial breach had just been proved. The offender's extent of compliance would be taken into account in the course of re-sentencing.

(iii) Where the breached order is a probation order, an attendance centre order, subject to the provisions of CJA 1982, s. 17 concerning the permissible aggregate of hours (see para. 16–007). That section will also govern enforcement.

22-038 It is submitted that it is also possible for the court to opt to impose no penalty for the breach. This is not made explicit in Schedule 2 but appears to follow from the phrase: "the court may deal with (the offender) ... in any one of the following ways ..." (para. 3(1)). Some courts, however, have taken the view that a penalty must be imposed, albeit a nominal fine. Note that if the informations allege a number of breach allegations, *e.g.* a failure to perform work on two or more dates, each instance or occasion of breach must be dealt with, albeit that the court may opt to impose no separate penalty for one or more of these.

22-039 *Power of Revocation or Remittal*

If the court is of the opinion that the order should not continue, its alternative power depends upon whether the order was imposed by a youth court or the Crown Court.

Youth Court Order: The court may revoke the order and deal with the offender for the offence in respect of which the order was made, in any manner in which it could deal with the offender if he or she had just been convicted by the court of the offence (para. 3(1)(d)). The option to revoke without dealing with the offender afresh is not available to the court. An offender re-sentenced under paragraph 3(1)(d) may appeal to the Crown Court against sentence (para. 3(5)).

Crown Court Order: A magistrates' court has no power to revoke an **22–040** order made by the Crown Court but may remit the offender back to the Crown Court either on bail or in custody (para. 3(3)). (Note that a probation order made by the Crown Court on appeal is deemed to have been made by the court from which the appeal was brought PCCA 1973, s. 12(2).) The magistrates' court must provide a certificate showing that the offender has failed to comply with the requirements of the order and send "such other particulars of the case as may be desirable". The certificate shall be admissible as evidence of the failure before the Crown Court (para. 3(4)). The Crown Court has to be satisfied that the offender "has failed to comply with any of the requirements of the relevant order" (para. 4(1)). The words "without reasonable excuse" in paragraph 3(1) in regard to the jurisdiction of the supervising court are not contained in paragraph 4(1) and thus the question of any reasonable excuse is an issue to be resolved prior to remitting the matter to the Crown Court. Whether the offender has failed to comply is a matter to be determined by the court and not by a jury (para. 4(3)). If the Crown Court finds that there has been a failure to comply, its discretion is not tied by the magistrates' decision not to impose a disciplinary penalty allowing the order to continue. Its disciplinary powers are identical to those available to a magistrates' court, except that its maximum power of fine (£1,000) is not linked to the standard scale provisions. If the Crown Court decides that the order should terminate, it may revoke the order and deal with the offender in any manner in which it could deal with the offender if he or she had just been convicted by the court of the offence (para. 4(1)(d)).

Meredith [1994] Crim. L.R. 142 (see para. 22–024) demonstrates the **22–041** problems that can arise where an offender in breach is subject both to a youth court order and an order imposed by the Crown Court. The magistrates sought to remit both orders to the Crown Court which then revoked them and re-sentenced the offender to custody. The Court of Appeal upheld this exercise of jurisdiction but the statutory basis for this judgement is questionable. CJA 1991, Schedule 2, paragraph 3 does not empower a magistrates' court to commit an offender to the Crown Court to be dealt with for breach of a magistrates' court order. There was clear power to remit the Crown Court order back to that Court for the breach to be dealt with but Schedule 2, paragraphs 4 and 8 do not empower the Crown Court when opting to revoke its own order and deal with the offender afresh, by custodial sentence or otherwise, to assume jurisdiction over the order of the magistrates' court. None of the requirements of paragraph 8(1)(a),(b) or (c) are thereby satisfied (the

Crown Court is able to assume jurisdiction over the lower court's order only if the Crown Court order is remitted back to the Crown Court in *revocation* proceedings). The Court of Appeal adopted the common-sense approach of claiming that "once two community service orders are made, they are for all practical purposes one order" but if this is the case it is not clear whether the fused order, combining orders made at different court levels, counts as a magistrates' court order or a Crown Court order for purposes of enforcement. In *Meredith* the Crown Court claimed the authority to deal with the offender's total community service liability. What if an offender first receives an order of 100 hours from the Crown Court and subsequently an order of 40 hours from a youth court, and breach proceedings are initiated after completion of 110 hours? The logic of *Meredith* might suggest that the offender could face enforcement proceedings before the Crown Court and yet this would seem singularly unfair. The offender would surely only be in jeopardy before the youth court. A more cumbersome but more statutorily correct approach in *Meredith* would have required the Crown Court to resolve the future of the order made by that court and then for the offender to have appeared before the magistrates to resolve the outstanding order made by that lower court in the light of the Crown Court's decision.

22–042 *Re-Sentencing following Revocation*

The exercise of re-sentencing powers upon revocation is akin to that applying in revocation proceedings under Schedule 2, Part III, outlined later in this chapter and thus not repeated here. Here too the court must take into account the extent to which the offender has complied with the requirements of the relevant order (para. 3(2)(a) and para. 4(2)(a)). There is one crucial difference in the provisions for revocation and re-sentence following breach. The court "may assume, in the case of an offender who has wilfully and persistently failed to comply with those requirements, that s/he has refused to give his/her consent to a community sentence which has been proposed by the court and requires that consent" (para. 3(2)(b)). This relates to CJA 1991, s. 1(3) which empowers a court to pass a custodial sentence if the offender refuses to give consent to a proposed community sentence which requires consent. The offender's non-co-operation with the order allows (but does not oblige) the court to deem that the offender has refused consent and thus entitles the re-sentence to be a custodial sentence, even though the normal threshold requirement of seriousness has not been met.

22–043 *Role of Probation Officer*

Given that the court must first determine whether an offender is in breach of the relevant order and, if so satisfied, proceed to determine the appropriate action to be taken in respect of the breach, the Probation Service is required to fulfil a double role, firstly in prosecuting the complaint and subsequently in assisting the court in determining the appropriate course of action, for example in advising on the suitability of the offender to continue the order. The tension between these roles is obvious, and the valid compatibility of functions was challenged in *Liverpool City Magistrates' Court, ex p. Atkinson* (1987) 9 Cr. App. R.(S.) 216, where the probation officer prosecuting the breach of a community service order had also invited the court to revoke the order, drawing attention to other alleged instances of breach behaviour which had not been the subject of proceedings. The Divisional Court dismissed the argument by way of judicial review that the probation officer should not have contributed to the decision-making following proof of breach. Woolf L.J. stated:

> "... in relation to establishing the matters which it is necessary to **22–044** establish so that the justices can exercise their powers, in practice the probation officer performs a function very similar to a prosecutor. However, once the breach of the requirement has been established, the magistrates will have an option as to what particular course to adopt and, as with any other court who is responsible for deciding how to deal with an offender, it will require the assistance of the probation officer. Speaking for myself, I can see no objection because of the principle which I made reference to at the outset of this judgement (that the prosecutor does not advocate a particular sentence) to the probation officer then providing that assistance.
>
> Of course, the probation officer shall not indicate that a particular fine should be imposed, nor is it his responsibility to decide whether or not the order which has been made should be or may be revoked, or in a case where the Crown Court is involved whether the offender should be committed to the Crown Court. However, what he can properly do in my view, based on his experience of supervising the offender who was the subject of the community service order, is assist the court as to whether or not there is any purpose in his view, as an experienced probation officer, in the community service order being allowed to continue. Sometimes he may take the view that a purpose could be served and he will then give the benefit of that view to the court; in other cases he may not."

Powers upon Breach of a Combination Order   **22–045**

As indicated in Chapter 20, the 1991 Act does not make fully clear the position when a breach of a combination order is established. Given that the order is a single order, breach of one element of the order is a breach of the order as a whole. It seems to follow that the court can opt to revoke the order and re-sentence, taking into account the extent of compliance with both elements of the order. It is doubtful whether the court can instead simply revoke the element of the order which has been breached, leaving the other element standing alone. If that is permissible, it is unclear how the court could re-sentence for the original offence, if part of the original sentence remains in force. The better view appears to be that the whole order must be revoked, allowing the re-sentencing exercise to take account of the offender's suitability for an order embodying that element of the erstwhile combination order which has not been the subject of breach complaint.

22–046 Supervision Orders
Power to deal with breach of a supervision order is provided within the wide-ranging ambit of CYPA 1969, s. 15.

CYPA 1969, s. 15

"(3) If while a supervision order made under section 7(7) of this Act is in force in respect of a person it is proved to the satisfaction of a relevant court, on the application of the supervisor, that the supervised person has failed to comply with any requirement included in the supervision order in pursuance of section 12, 12A, 12AA, 12C or 18(2)(b) of this Act, the court—

(a) whether or not it also makes an order under subsection (1) above, may order him to pay a fine of an amount not exceeding £1,000 or, subject to section 16A(1) of this Act, may make an attendance centre order in respect of him; or

(b) in the case of a person who has attained the age of 18, may (if it also discharges the supervision order) make an order imposing on him any punishment, other than a sentence of detention in a young offender institution, which it could have imposed on him if it—

(i) had then had power to try him for the offence in consequence of which the supervision order was made; and

(ii) had convicted him in the exercise of that power."

22–047 *Jurisdiction and Procedure*

The "relevant court" depends on the age of the supervised person (s. 15(11)). If the supervised person has not attained the age of 18, jurisdiction is exercised by a youth court acting for the specified petty sessions area. If the supervised person has attained that age, jurisdiction rests with a magistrates' court acting for the specified area. If the offender attains the age of 18 while an application is pending to a youth court, that court "shall deal with the application as if he had not attained" that age (s. 16(11)).

Power to deal with breach exists only while the supervision order is in force and only upon the application of the supervisor. The statute does not specify that an information should be laid. No form of application is specified by the Magistrates' Courts (Children and Young Persons) Rules 1992, Sched. 2.

22–048 The court may not make an order under section 15 unless the supervised person is present. Securing that attendance is regulated by the supplementary provisions of section 16. The supervisor "may bring the supervised person before the court" (s. 16(1)) or a justice may issue a summons or warrant to secure attendance (s. 16(2)), subject to the limits on the use of a warrant imposed by MCA 1980, s. 55(3) and (4). Where the supervised person is arrested in pursuance of a warrant and cannot be brought before the court immediately, arrangements may be made for his or her detention in a place of safety for not more than 72 hours from time of arrest (s. 16(3)(a)). If not brought before the court within that period, the supervised person shall be brought before a justice who may direct immediate release or, if the person is aged under 18, a remand to local authority accommodation (s. 16(3A)) to be provided by the authority named in the supervision order (s. 16 (3B)). If the person has attained 18, remand will be to a remand centre or, if no centre is available, a prison (s. 16(3C)). A youth court considering whether to make an order varying or discharging the supervision order under section 15 (1) may remand the supervised person to local authority accommodation pending the outcome of proceedings, providing that a warrant has been issued to bring the supervised person before the court or the court considers that remanding that person will enable information to be obtained which is likely to assist the court in deciding whether and, if so, how to exercise its powers under that subsection. Unlike CJA 1991, Sched. 2, para. 3(1), s. 15(3) does not require that the offender's failure to comply should be "without reasonable excuse". It is not clear whether "failure" implies the lack of reasonable excuse or whether reasonable excuse becomes a relevant consideration only in determining how a breach should be dealt with.

Powers upon Breach   **22–049**

The powers of the court if the failure to comply is admitted or proved depend on the age of the supervised person.

Under 18 years: The court has the discretion to discharge or vary the order under section 15(1) but power of variation is subject to the limits imposed by section 15 (2) in regard to time limits on the insertion of a new requirement of medical treatment or of night restriction and by section 16(7) with regard to consent (see para. 22–017). A youth court is also subject to the over-arching requirement of section 16(6) regarding the supervised person's care and control (see para. 22–020). Whether or not the court exercises this power, it may also impose a disciplinary penalty of either a fine or an attendance centre order. A fine must not exceed level 3 (subject to the lower maximum for under–14s) and is enforced as if the sum was ordered to be paid on conviction for a summary offence (s. 15(7)). Any attendance centre order made in this context is enforceable as if imposed under CJA 1982, s. 17 (CYPA 1969, s. 16A(1)). Upon discharging the order, there is no general power to re-sentence for the original offence but scope to re-sentence arises in the special instance of an order containing a requirement of specified activities under section 12A(3)(a) where the court imposing that requirement specified under section 12D that it was doing so instead of passing a custodial sentence (s. 15(4) and (6), see below).

22–050 *Aged 18 and over:* The court has the same powers as it has in respect of an offender aged under 18 but in addition has the power, if it discharges the order, to impose any punishment for the original offence, other than detention in a YOI, as if it then had power to try him or for the original offence and had convicted them (s. 15(3)(b)). Any fine thus imposed shall not exceed level 5 (s. 15(7)(b)).

22–051 *Breach of Specified Activities Requirements with s. 12D Statement*

In this special instance, where an offender has failed to comply with a requirement imposed under CYPA 1969, s. 12A(3)(a), the court has a power of re-sentence, applicable whether the offender has attained age 18 or not, including power to impose a sentence of YOI detention, provided that the requirement was specifically imposed instead of a custodial sentence under section 12D (s. 15(4) and (6)). The wording of section 15(4) indicates that the failure to comply leading to breach proceedings must be in respect of the specified activities requirement and that it is not sufficient that the supervised person has failed to comply with another requirement of the order.

CYPA 1969, s. 15

"(4) If while a supervision order is in force in respect of a person it is proved to the court under subsection (3) above that the supervised person has failed to comply with any requirement included in the supervision order in pursuance of section 12A(3)(a) of this Act directing the supervised person to participate in specified activities, the court may, if it also discharges the supervision order, make an order imposing on him any sentence which it could have imposed on him if it—

(a) had then had power to try him for the offence in consequence of which the supervision order was made; and

(b) had convicted him in the exercise of that power.

(6) A court may not make an order by virtue of subsection (4) above unless the court which made the supervision order made a statement under section 12D(1) of this Act; and for the purposes of this subsection a certificate under that section shall be evidence of the making of the statement to which it relates."

22–052 If the court has no jurisdiction to try the offender for that offence (*i.e.* where an adult court is dealing with a supervision order was imposed by a youth court for an offence triable only on indictment in the case of an adult), its powers of re-sentence shall not exceed the powers of the court which does have that power (s.15(5)(a)) and, additionally, shall not exceed a term of six months custody and a fine not exceeding £5,000 (level 5) (s. 15(5)(c)).

Credit for Partial Compliance

In all cases where a court deals with breach under section 15(3) or (4), whether discharging and re-sentencing or not, it is required to "take into account the extent to which (the offender) has complied with the requirements of the supervision order" (s. 15(8)).

Appeal 22–053

The supervised person may appeal to the Crown Court against any order made under section 15(3) and (4), except an order which could have been made in the supervised person's absence under section 16(5) (*i.e.* a straight discharge of an order or a cancellation or reduction of a requirement) or a variation to which s/he gave any required consent (s. 16(8)(a)).

Attendance Centre Orders
Breach is regulated by CJA 1982, s. 19 which provides that proceedings may be brought on two grounds:

(a) failure to attend, or

(b) committing a breach of the rules of the centre which cannot be dealt with adequately under those rules.

Procedure

Proceedings are initiated by information to a justice acting for the relevant petty sessions area who may issue a summons requiring the offender to appear before a court acting for that area at the time specified in the summons. If the information is in writing and on oath, the justice may issue a warrant for the offender's arrest to bring them before the court. The relevant PSA is that in which the specified centre is situated or, in the case of a magistrates' court order, the PSA for the court which made the order (s. 19(2)).

Powers upon Breach 22–054

If on the offender's appearance the court is satisfied that he or she has failed without reasonable excuse to attend as required or has broken a rule, the powers of the court depend on whether the order was made by a magistrates' court or the Crown Court.

Magistrates' Court Order

The court may either fine the offender and allow the order to continue, or revoke the order and deal with the offender afresh for the original offence (s. 19(3)(a)). If the first option of a fine is chosen, the breach shall be treated as if a level 3 offence (and thus carrying a maximum fine currently of £1000, or £250 in the case of an offender under 14) and enforcement for non-payment follows accordingly.

22–055 *Crown Court Order*

The court may either fine the offender as above and allow the order to continue or may remit the matter back to the Crown Court, committing the offender in custody or release him on bail to appear at Crown Court, sending a certificate giving particulars of the breach. This certificate shall be admissible at Crown Court as evidence of the breach but the breach must be specifically proved at Crown Court. If the Crown Court is satisfied of the breach, the court may revoke the order and deal with the offender afresh for the original offence (s. 19(5)). Though the Crown Court is not expressly empowered to deal with the breach by fine, thus allowing the order to continue (compare CJA 1991, Sched. 2, para. 4(1)), this option would seem validly open to the court.

Re-Sentencing upon Revocation

The court revoking the order may deal with the offender for the offence in respect of which the order was made "in any manner in which it could have dealt with him for that offence if it had not made the order" (s. 19 (3(a)) and (5)). It would seem that, contrary to the provisions dealing with revocation of probation, community service and combination orders contained in CJA 1991, Sched. 2, the offender should be dealt with on the basis of their age when the attendance centre order was made and subject to the powers and restrictions that applied at that time in that court (see *Wyre Magistrates Court, ex p. Boardman* (1987) 9 Cr. App. R.(S.) 214).

22–056   In re-sentencing for the original offence, the court shall take into account the extent to which the offender has complied with the requirements of the order (s. 19(5A)(a)). This scope to give credit for partial performance was introduced into section 19 by CJA 1991, s. 67(6), mirroring the provisions of CJA 1991, Sched. 2 and CYPA 1969, s. 15.

Another addition to section 19 under CJA 1991, s. 67(6) allows the court to assume, "in the case of an offender who has wilfully and persistently failed to comply" with their attendance centre order, that they have refused to give their consent "to a community sentence which has been proposed by the court and requires that consent" (s. 19(5A)(b)). This is clearly intended to allow the court to deal with the offender by way of a custodial sentence under the provision in CJA 1991, s. 1(3) which creates an exception to the normal criteria permitting a custodial sentence in the case of an offender refusing to give consent to a community sentence requiring such consent. An attendance centre order does not, of course, require consent but section 19(5A)(b) allows the offender to be treated as if consent is required and is being withheld. Though a custodial sentence thus becomes a possible option, it does not follow that this is an inevitable consequence, as the offender may well be suitable for (and willing to consent to) another community order.

Appeal against Re-Sentence   **22–057**

The offender may appeal against the sentence imposed for the original offence under section 19(3)(a). If the sentence was imposed by a magistrates' court, appeal is permitted by section 19(6); if imposed by the Crown Court, by CJA 1982, Sched. 14, para. 23.

Parental Liability to Forfeit Recognisance

CJPOA 1994 introduced an additional power into CJA 1991, s. 58(2) so that a court binding over the parent or guardian of a juvenile aged under 16 at the same time as it passes a community sentence (*i.e.* an attendance centre or supervision order) upon that juvenile can also include in the recognisance a provision that the parent or guardian ensures that the juvenile complies with the requirements of that sentence. Enforcement of such a recognisance upon the juvenile's non-compliance with their community order is addressed in Chapter 14.

TERMINATION OF COMMUNITY ORDERS   22–058

Orders will, of course, terminate upon normal expiry of the period for which the order was made or upon completion of the hours prescribed. Such "natural" termination does not directly concern the court, though successful completions may be reported to the probation liaison committee or to the sentencers who originally dealt with the case if they specially requested to be kept informed of the offender's progress (see para. 11–039). Of concern here are the instances in which the order may terminate other than upon normal completion. Termination following breach of a requirement of a community order is also addressed earlier in this Chapter.

Probation Orders, Community Service Orders, Combination Orders   **22–059**
and Curfew Orders

CJA 1991, Sched. 2, Pt. III provides a generic framework for the revocation of these four community orders.

Powers of Revocation

Broadly speaking, an order may be revoked in four sets of circumstances:

(a) upon application by the offender or the responsible officer to a court acting either for the specified petty sessions area or, in the case of a curfew order, for the petty sessions area in which the specified place is situated (here designated the supervising court, as a convenient shorthand, though this term is not used in the Schedule);

(b) upon application by the offender or the responsible officer to a magistrates' court other than the supervising court, if the offender is convicted of a further offence by that court and receives a custodial sentence;

    (c)   in certain instances where the offender is appearing before the Crown Court;

    (d)   upon breach of the order being proved, where the court is of the view that the order should not continue. Revocation in this context is outlined earlier in this Chapter.

22–060 An order made by the Crown Court can only be revoked by that court so that in circumstances (a), (b) and (d) the magistrates having initial jurisdiction who believe that revocation is appropriate will always need to remit the order back to the Crown Court. A probation order made by the Crown Court on appeal is deemed to have been made by the court from which the appeal was brought (PCCA 1973, s. 12(2)).

    As outlined in Chapter 20, Sched. 2, para. 1(2) specifies that, for the purposes of the Schedule, the probation element of a combination order should be regarded as a probation order and the community service element as a community service order. Uncertainty may thus arise if it is proposed to seek revocation of the whole combination order. Given that the order is a single order it should be open to the court to consider a single application rather than requiring two separate applications upon two separate summonses. The Magistrates' Courts (Forms) Rules 1981 prescribe a form (92P) on the basis that a single application will be appropriate.

22–061 *Upon Application to the Supervising Court*

The court does not have power to revoke the order on its own initiative in any circumstances. Application must be made by either the offender or the responsible officer. The court has jurisdiction to receive an application whether the order was made by a youth court or the Crown Court. If application is made by the responsible officer (as defined by CJA 1991, s. 15(3)), the offender must be summonsed to appear before the court and, in the event of non-appearance, a warrant for arrest may be issued (para. 7(7)). If the offender is already before the court, the summons procedure will be superfluous. Although paragraph 7 specifies that the offender must be summonsed before powers of revocation can be exercised, this can be conveniently achieved by an oral information on the spot. It is not clear whether, in the case of the supervising officer's application for simple revocation of a probation order on grounds of good progress (see para. 22–064), the court can proceed in the offender's absence if the offender consents in writing both to the application and to the matter being heard in his or her absence, though some courts adopt this practice.

22–062 If application is made by the offender, there is no formal requirement that the relevant officer should be either notified or heard but the court is very unlikely to grant the offender's application without consulting the Probation Service. An offender may not make application while an appeal against the relevant order is pending (para. 7(8)) but this does not preclude application pending appeal against conviction or an appeal against another element of the sentence.

The court has to consider whether, "having regard to circumstances which have arisen since the order was made, it would be in the interests of justice:

(a)   that the order should be revoked; or

(b)   that the offender should be dealt with in some other manner for the offence in respect of which the order was made". (para. 7(1))

As the court does not have power to revoke a Crown Court order, the latter consideration would be appropriate in circumstances where the court takes the view that an order made by the Crown Court does not have any likely prospect of being completed satisfactorily and thus should be remitted back to the Crown Court for re-consideration. There is thus a distinction between the court's powers depending upon whether the order was made by a youth court or by the Crown Court.

Youth Court Order: The court can either—   **22–063**

(a)   revoke the order, without imposing any penalty for the original offence (para. 7(2)(a)(i)); or

(b)   revoke the order and re-sentence the offender in such manner as it would if the offender had just been convicted (para. 7(2)(a)(ii)). (Note that for community service orders, the previous power of revocation under PCCA 1973, s. 17(2) permitted the court to deal with the offender in any manner in which the offender could have been dealt with by the court which made the order if the order had not been made).

Crown Court Order: The court should remit the matter back to the Crown Court, either committing the offender to custody or granting bail in the interim, and sending "such particulars of the case as may be desirable" (para. 7(2)(b) and (6)).

Circumstances where Revocation may be Appropriate   **22–064**

(i) *Early Termination of Probation for Good Progress*
The most common instance where revocation is sought arises where an offender subject to a probation order or a combination order has responded satisfactorily and early termination is sought as a mark of good progress. This possibility is explicitly acknowledged in paragraph 7(3) which states that the circumstances in which a probation order may be revoked without re-sentence "shall include the offender's making good progress or responding satisfactorily to supervision". The *National Standard for Probation Orders* (1995, para. 20(a)) indicates that an application for early termination should be considered "where the offender has made good progress in achieving the objectives set out for the order and where there is not considered to be a significant risk of re-offending and/or of serious harm to the public" but not before the half-way point of the order. The 1992 version of the *Standard* stated that

an application "should not normally be sought before half-way through the term of the order" but "should be considered by two-thirds of the term unless there are clear reasons for not doing so".

The court is neither obliged to follow the supervising officer's proposal for early revocation nor, if it does, to revoke without imposing an alternative penalty. However, if the court is not of the view that simple revocation is appropriate then it is more likely to refuse the application.

22-065 If the offender makes the application, this saves the additional procedure of summonsing the offender to court. It does not appear essential that the offender should apply in person. If the offender makes application in writing and the supervising officer supports the application, preferably with a written report outlining progress, then this would seem procedurally sufficient to enable the application to be considered and the order to be revoked, though if the court wishes to hear from the offender in person the application can be adjourned to give them the opportunity of attendance.

The supervising court does not have power of revocation of a Crown Court order even in a straightforward case of good progress and the matter always has to be remitted to Crown Court, a somewhat cumbersome and time-consuming process. At some Crown Court centres, the resident judges have indicated their willingness to receive applications of this nature directly in chambers, thus bypassing an initial application to the supervising court. This is certainly a cost and labour-saving device, albeit of questionable legality.

Though the early termination of the probation order continues the previous tradition of early "discharge" of orders, this device seems less appropriate under the sentencing framework of the 1991 Act where the length of the order as a sentence should be commensurate with the seriousness of the offence. Early termination thus serves as a form of reduction of sentence. There is no provision for a community service order to be revoked prior to completion as a mark of satisfactory effort as a form of incentive or reward. This is because a community service order is not statutorily intended to achieve aims regarding the offender's future conduct and attitude. In regard to combination orders, the *National Standard* indicates that early termination should be considered only after completion of the community service element of the order. In 1993, 10 per cent of probation order terminations where the order was made upon an offender aged 16–20 were on grounds of good progress (Home Office, 1994a).

22-066 (ii) *Conviction of a Further Offence*

A further offence during the course of an order does not constitute a failure to comply with the requirements of that order and so cannot render the offender liable to be dealt with afresh for the original offence, as was the case for probation orders prior to CJA 1991 under PCCA 1973, s. 8 (now repealed). Nevertheless, further offending may provide grounds for the revocation of the order, particularly where the court is imposing a custodial sentence for the further offence. The supervising court cannot act upon its own initiative, however, but only upon an application by the offender or the relevant officer. Clearly a community order cannot be complied with if the offender is not at liberty but if the order is not revoked then it will continue in force and liability will resume upon release. One obvious consideration will be the length of the new custodial sentence, the time remaining for the community order upon the offender's release from custody, the demands of any statutory early release licence or supervision requirements which the offender will face upon release, the efforts made by the offender in response to the order to date, and the advantages or otherwise for the offender of being subject to community order requirements on release. Some guidance in regard to the continuance or otherwise of a probation order can be gained from *Rowsell* (1988) 10 Cr. App. R.(S.) 411. The offender had been placed on probation for three years for driving while disqualified and committed a similar offence a few weeks later. He received a custodial sentence of nine months for the fresh offence but the probation order was allowed to continue. The Court of Appeal commented:

> "In some cases it may be clear that an offender who has broken a **22–067** probation order within a matter of days has shown that he has no intention of taking advantage of the help he has been offered, and it will be right to pass sentence for the original offence. In other cases where ... the probation order has not had time to have effect, it may be correct to leave the order in being. In other cases it may be that so little will remain of the probation period after the offender's discharge from custody that it would be futile to leave the order in being. Each case will be different, and must be decided on its own facts." (*per* Ian Kennedy J.)

See also the more recent case of *Cawley* (1994) 15 Cr. App. R.(S.) 209 (see para. 22–087).

The question of revocation may also arise in the light of other, non-custodial sentences being imposed for the further offence, *i.e.* whether the existing community order is compatible with the new sentence. For example, if the offender received a combination order for the new offence, application for revocation of an existing probation order might be appropriate and desirable to avoid the complexities and duplicating nature of two sets of supervisory requirements. If an order is revoked because the offender is convicted of a further offence and the order is considered incompatible with the new sentence or no longer viable, *e.g.* because the offender has received a custodial sentence, and the offender appeals successfully against conviction of the further offence, the revocation automatically becomes void and the order is thus re-activated (*Woodley, The Times*, November 27, 1991).

22–068 *(iii) Other Changes of Circumstances*

Revocation may also be sought appropriately where the offender's present circumstances suggest that the order is no longer an appropriate or viable sentencing measure. For example, if the offender has become ill or disabled to the extent that it is no longer possible to comply with a community service order for reasons beyond the offender's control. The circumstances may, however, relate to the choice or conduct of the offender so that there has arguably been a breach of the order. There may thus be borderline cases where it is unclear whether it is more appropriate to apply for revocation of the order or to institute breach proceedings.

22–069   A court invited to revoke an order may consider that the offender is in breach of the order. In *Goscombe* (1981) 3 Cr. App. R.(S.) 61 the relevant officer applied to the supervising court for a review of a community service order under PCCA 1973, s.17, now repealed and incorporated within the general provisions of CJA 1991, Sched. 2, as the offender had completed only 22 hours in the first six months of an order for 120 hours. As the order was imposed by the Crown Court, the magistrates remitted the matter back to the Crown Court. The judge found that though the offender had experienced health problems these were not the decisive factor in his failure to work and that he was in breach of the order (under PCCA, s. 16, as then applied). Though the relevant officer had not alleged any culpable failure, the Court of Appeal nevertheless upheld the sentence of imprisonment imposed for the original offence upon revocation, stating:

> "We do not feel there is any important distinction to be drawn between (s. 16 and s. 17) in so far as the powers and the approach of the court having to review the order are concerned."

22–070 While it is true that the court has powers of revocation in both revocation and breach applications, and thus the point may be somewhat academic, *Goscombe* does, however, point to the possibility that if revocation is sought on "non culpable" grounds such as ill-health, the offender may nevertheless be at risk of a custodial sentence if the court considers that non-compliance has arisen, in part at least, through their own fault. Compare *Fielding* [1993] Crim. L.R. 229 (see para. 22–081).

22–071   The issue was further considered in *Jackson* (1984) 6 Cr. App. R.(S.) 202 where an offender aged 19 subject to a community service order had begun to absent herself, initially on medical grounds but subsequently on the basis that she had obtained regular employment on six days each week and was unwilling to undertake community service on her day off. The relevant officer applied for the order to be revoked on the ground that the offender was now unable to comply with the order because of her work commitments. The order was revoked and a custodial sentence was imposed in its place, the Crown Court judge being sceptical about her excuses. On her appeal, the Court of Appeal held that where a revocation is sought relying upon facts which, if proved, would amount to a breach of the order, it is preferable for breach proceedings to be brought and for the facts to be placed on a proper evidential basis rather than leaving the court to decide the matter on the basis of a report from the responsible officer. The *Jackson* decision leaves unclear what the position regarding revocation would be if breach could not be established in such circumstances. Ward and Ward (1993) suggest that there remains no valid basis for revocation. It is submitted, however, that it is still open to the court to consider whether revocation would be in the interests of justice.

It may be instructive to consider the hypothetical case of an offender **22-072** subject to a probation order who is continually moving around the country to such an extent that no basis of regular reporting and supervision can be established. It would probably be difficult to substantiate a breach allegation, if the offender calls at the probation office of the area where he or she is temporarily staying, yet the order appears to lack any meaningful basis upon which to persevere. Revocation may thus be the only way of resolving the impasse.

Revocation by another Magistrates' Court

Schedule 2, paragraph 9 gives a very limited power of revocation to a magistrates' court other than that acting for the specified petty sessions area. The following conditions must be satisfied:

(i)   the offender is convicted of an offence by the court;

(ii) the court imposes a custodial sentence for that offence;

(iii) the offender or the relevant officer applies for the order to be revoked.

If the court considers that it would be in the interests of justice, having **22-073** regard to circumstances which have arisen since the order was made, the court may:

(a) in the case of a youth court order, revoke it (but without have any power to re-sentence) (para. 9(2)(a));

(b) in the case of a Crown Court order, remit the matter to the Crown Court to be considered, sending such particulars "as may be desirable" (para. 9(2)(b) and (3)).

As there is no power to re-sentence for an offence for which an order was imposed by a youth court, in cases where the non-supervising court feels that re-sentencing is appropriate the court should decline to revoke. This then allows application to be made to the supervising court which does have power to re-sentence. However, the non-supervising court does not have any power to remit the matter to the supervising court for consideration. As the offender is probably unlikely to seek revocation, the matter is thus primarily in the discretion of the relevant officer.

22-074 *Revocation by the Crown Court*

Schedule 2, paragraph 8(1) gives power to the Crown Court to revoke an order in force, imposed either by a youth court or the Crown Court, if the offender:

(a) is convicted of another offence by the Crown Court; or

(b) appears before the Crown Court on committal for sentence for a further offence; or

(c) has been remitted to the Crown Court in respect of an order made by the Crown Court, either by the supervising court under paragraph 7(2)(b), or by another magistrates' court under paragraph 9(2)(b).

No application to the Crown Court by the responsible officer of the offender is required, though in circumstance (c) the Court will receive any report prepared by the responsible officer in making application to the lower court. If the Crown Court considers it to be in the interests of justice, having regard to circumstances which have arisen since the order was made, it may under paragraph 8(2):

(a) revoke the order; or

(b) "revoke the order and deal with the offender, for the original offence in respect of which the order was made, in any manner in which it could deal with him if he had just been convicted by or before the court of the offence."

If the offender was remitted under paragraph 9(2)(b), the Crown Court is merely given power to revoke without power to re-sentence (para. 10). The circumstances in which a probation order may be revoked under paragraph 8(2)(a) include the offender's good progress or satisfactory response to supervision (para.8(3)).

22-075 The Crown Court can revoke in any circumstances it deems fit, irrespective of the offender's compliance, and its power is not limited to cases where it imposes a custodial sentence for the new offence. However, the community order must be in force when the offender appears before the Crown Court. If the order has terminated, *i.e.* by lapse of time in the case of a probation order, the Crown Court can neither revoke the order nor re-sentence the offender, even though the further offence occurred during the term of that order. Note also that the mere fact that the offender is subject to a community order is not a valid basis for a youth court to commit the offender to the Crown Court for sentence for the further offence. If the Crown Court imposes a custodial sentence for the new offence, revocation of the community order should not follow automatically but the court should consider whether there is any merit in allowing the order to continue after the offender's release and whether the two sentences are compatible (see *Cawley* (1994) 15 Cr. App. R.(S.) 209 detailed at para. 22–087).

Re-Sentencing following Revocation   **22–076**

When a court which has power to revoke has decided to exercise that power, it must decide whether to revoke simpliciter or to opt to revoke and re-sentence. This will depend on the court's consideration of what is desirable in the interests of justice and the reasons why revocation is required. If the option to re-sentence is chosen, the offender is re-sentenced on the basis that he or she has been freshly convicted by the court. If the offender is convicted of a further offence by the Crown Court and that Court chooses to re-sentence for the original offence, the question arises, in respect of a youth court order, whether the Crown Court may re-sentence using powers available to that Court or is restricted to using powers that are available to the lower court. The wording of paragraph 8(2)(b)—"if he had just been convicted by or before the court"—is ambiguous. In *Mackness* and *Wilson* [1995] Crim. L.R. 341 the Court of Appeal considered that "the court" must mean the Crown Court, thus giving that Court unrestrained powers, but in *Kosser* and *Armstrong* [1995] Crim. L.R. 342 the Court of Appeal led by Lord Tayler CJ reached the opposite conclusion that "the court" means the court that made the order. Though this opinion appears to be *obiter*, it may be appropriate for the Crown Court to limit itself to magistrates' powers. The wording of Sched. 2 paras.3(1)(d), 4(1)(d), 7(2)(a)(ii) and 8(2)(b) that the re-sentencing court should deal with the offender "as if he had just been convicted by the court of the offence" strongly suggests that the age of the offender for the purposes of determining the sentencing powers of the re-sentencing court is the offender's age on the date of re-sentencing. However, in *McDonagh* [1995] Crim. L.R. 512 the Court of Appeal reached a different conclusion in respect of a combination order, imposed by the Crown Court when the offender was aged 17 but revoked following breach when he was 18. The appellant successfully argued that he should not have been re-sentenced to two years YOI as the maximum term for a seventeen year old was then 12 months. The Court of Appeal indicated that the re-sentence should take effect as a 12 month term under CJA 1982, s1B(5) (see para. 24–008) but the basis for this decision is far from clear.

The principles which should be followed in re-sentencing (and which broadly apply also to re-sentencing upon revocation in breach proceedings) can be summarised as follows:

(a) The court must re-sentence in the light of the seriousness of the original offence. However, the fact that the offence was previously considered "serious enough" for a community sentence does not imply that the offence cannot now be considered "so serious" that only a custodial sentence can be justified.
It may be that the offence was earlier considered sufficiently **22–077** serious to pass the custody threshold but there was sufficient mitigation to lead the court to impose a community sentence instead. If a further offence is then committed while the

community sentence is in force and the offender faces re-sentence, "he will have deprived himself of much of the mitigation such as good character, genuine remorse, isolated lapse and similar considerations which led the original court to pass a community rather than a custodial sentence" (*Oliver and Little* [1993] 1 W.L.R. 177, confirming *Webster* (1991) 12 Cr. App. R.(S.) 760). For an instance where the original offence was subsequently considered to merit custody on grounds of public protection, see *Powell* (1992) 13 Cr. App. R.(S.) 202 (see para. 22–080).

(b) In assessing seriousness, the court must apply the sentencing principles of the 1991 Act (as amended). This has particular implications when re-sentencing for offences which were made the subject of community orders prior to implementation of the Act according to pre-CJA 1991 sentencing practice.

22-078 (c) In re-sentencing for the original offence, both a youth court and the Crown Court are required to "take into account the extent to which the offender has complied with the requirements of the relevant order" (Sched. 2, paras. 3(2)(a), 4(2)(a), 7(4) and 8(4)). This principle had been developed in a number of cases prior to the 1991 Act in regard to part-completion of community service orders which indicated that credit should be given if a substantial part of the order had been completed. In *Whittingham* (1986) 8 Cr. App. R.(S.) 116 credit was given where only one-third of the hours had been completed. Credit could enable the re-sentencing court either to allow a non-custodial sentence to be imposed for the original offence or to reduce the length of any custodial sentence imposed. Credit for part-completion of a probation order is a less straightforward matter for the court to assess as compliance is presumably not simply a matter of reporting as instructed but also of engaging actively in the supervisory process. This may prove somewhat difficult to assess. The provisions of paragraphs 7(4) and 8(4) do not indicate if the court taking into account the extent of compliance should simply give credit for satisfactory performance or can draw negative, discrediting conclusions from an unsatisfactory record of performance, even though this has not been the basis of breach proceedings. Practically speaking, the court will be dependent on the extent of information available from the responsible officer.

22-079 Whereas the provisions of paragraphs 3(2)(a), 4(2)(a), 7(4) and 8(4) impose a mandatory requirement upon the court, it is less clear whether CJA 1991, s. 29(1) gives the court re-sentencing for the original offence the discretion to take into account any failure to respond to the now revoked community order in assessing seriousness. While that order is a "previous sentence" within the general ambit of section 29(1), the power to re-sentence "in any manner in which it could deal with him if he had just been convicted by the court of the offence" (paras. 3(1)(d), 4(1)(d), 7(2)(a)(ii) and 8(2)(b)) appears to require the court to disregard the earlier order for this purpose as that order arises from an earlier conviction. The question whether non-compliance with a community service order may be treated as an aggravating factor when a court comes to re-sentence an offender in breach of such an order was raised but left open in *Wiltshire* (1992) 13 Cr. App. R.(S.) 642, in the context of the now repealed PCCA 1973, s. 16 which did not contain any requirement to take extent of compliance into account.

In the more unusual instance that the court is re-sentencing for **22–080** a sexual or violent offence and that offence gives rise to concern about the risk to the public, then the court would be able to take account of the offender's poor response to the order in forming an opinion whether a custodial sentence is necessary to protect the public from serious harm, as use of this information is permitted by CJA 1991, s. 3(3)(b). *Powell* (1992) 13 Cr. App. R.(S.) 202 presents a pre-CJA 1991 example of a young offender originally made subject to a probation order who, upon breach, received a custodial sentence on grounds of protecting the public from serious harm from him. Following conviction for two offences of indecent assault, he was required to reside at a hostel specialising in the treatment of young sexual offenders, as an additional requirement of the probation order. After instances of unacceptable behaviour, for which he was made subject of breach proceedings, he eventually absconded and in subsequent breach proceedings the order was revoked and he was sentenced to custody. His failure to respond was considered to reinforce the nature of the risk he presented.

> "The complete failure of the attempt to help this appellant, a failure which has to be laid at his door, does nothing to detract from the risk of harm to the public: it merely reinforces the concern." (*per* Ian Kennedy J.)

Note that the revocation provisions in Schedule 2, Part III are **22–081** different from those for revocation following breach proceedings under Part II. A court revoking an order following breach is entitled under para. 3(2)(b) and para. 4(2)(b) to assume that wilful and persistent non-compliance amounts to a tacit refusal by the offender to give consent to a community sentence requiring consent, thus permitting the application of CJA 1991, s. 1(3) (see para. 15–017). This assumption cannot be made in Part III proceedings.

(d) If an order is revoked because the offender is now unable to comply with requirements, then although the court in principle has the power to impose a custodial sentence upon re-sentencing in a case where the original offence was sufficiently serious to merit such a penalty, this will not be appropriate where the

offender's inability arises through no fault of his or her own
(*Fielding* [1993] Crim. L.R. 229 where an offender was unable to
continue his community service order because of a back injury
which prevented him working; see also *Davey* (1994) 15 Cr. App.
R.(S.) 852). It is unclear what would be the approach if, say, the
offender's inability to work resulted from a deliberate decision on
his part, *e.g.* to take a job working seven days a week. If the Court
considers that past non-compliance has in part arisen through the
offender's own fault, it seems that the court may nevertheless
impose a custodial sentence (*Goscombe* (1981) 3 Cr. App. R.(S.)
61) (see para. 22–069).

22–082   (e)   Appropriate allowance should be made for any period spent by
the offender in custody (or secure accommodation) before the
now revoked community sentence was passed (*McIntyre* (1985) 7
Cr. App. R.(S.) 196; *MacKenzie* (1988) 10 Cr. App. R.(S.) 299;
Wiltshire (1992) 13 Cr. App. R.(S.) 642).

22–083   (f)   Revocation of a community order does not prevent the re-
sentencing of the offender to a further community order, even an
order of a similar nature to that now revoked. In *Havant Justices,
ex p. Jacobs* [1957] 1 W.L.R. 365, a further probation order
imposed in place of a previous probation order (following breach
proceedings) was upheld as a sound order, despite having the
effect of extending the total period of probation supervision
beyond three years. The offender's suitability for the proposed
order will need to be considered afresh. If the offender receives a
custodial sentence for the further offence, a further community
order for the original offence is unlikely to be appropriate or
compatible.

(g)   The sentence imposed in re-sentencing shall not place the
offender at extended risk of custody for a lengthy period after the
original offence was committed. This principle was expounded in
Robinson (1986) 8 Cr. App. R.(S.) 327 where a suspended term of
imprisonment   was   considered   inappropriate   following
revocation of a community service order. Clearly this situation
will not arise in regard to a young offender and it may be
considered that no other sentence or order of the court in dealing
with a young offender presents "risk of custody" in the same way
as a suspended sentence. If the offender fails to comply with a
further community order and is consequently at risk of a
custodial sentence upon revocation of that order, the question of
staleness of the offence and lapse of time will then be a relevant
consideration in mitigation.

22–084   (h)   If the offender is sentenced to custody for any further offence
which is considered "so serious", the court will be able to impose
a concurrent custodial sentence for the original offence even if
that offence does not warrant custody in its own right. It will

usually be inappropriate for consecutive sentences to be passed for offences which do not themselves satisfy the requirements relating to custody or for sentences to be made longer than strictly justified by reference to those offences which do qualify (*Oliver* and *Little* [1993] 1 W.L.R. 177). If the community order is revoked following the imposition of a custodial sentence for a further offence, the fact that the new offence is of a completely different nature to the offence for which the community sentence was imposed does not prevent the court imposing a custodial sentence in re-sentencing for the original offence (*Fleming* (1989) 11 Cr. App. R.(S.) 137 where the original offences involved theft and handling while the new offence was possession of drugs).

(i) If revocation and re-sentence follow conviction for a further **22-085** offence, the original offence and the further offence can be regarded as "associated" offences within the definition of CJA 1991, s. 31(2) and the court is thus at liberty to weigh their seriousness in aggregate. If, however, the decision to revoke the order is taken only after sentence has been passed for the new offence and in the light of that decision, then clearly the original offence will not be "associated" with the subsequent offence, though the court in considering the seriousness of the subsequent offence may take into account both the conviction of the original offence and any subsequent failure to respond to the community sentence imposed for that offence (CJA 1991, s. 29(1)). It is not clear whether the further offence can properly influence the assessment of seriousness of the original offence. It is possible, borrowing the terminology of the now replaced CJA 1991, s. 29(2), that the circumstances of the further offence may disclose aggravating features of the original offence that were otherwise not apparent.

(j) The sentence for the original offence and the further offence, **22-086** when viewed together as a total sentence, should be proportionate to the overall seriousness of the offending (CJA 1991, s. 28(2)(b)). Thus if a custodial sentence is imposed for the further offence and a consecutive custodial sentence is imposed for the original offence, the court should adjust the sentence downwards if the impact of the combined sentences would be too severe for the overall seriousness of the offender's behaviour (*Anderson* (1982) 4 Cr. App. R. (S.) 252).

(k) The fact that the further offence is of a completely different nature to the offence for which the community order was made does not in itself restrict the re-sentencing court from imposing a custodial sentence in re-sentencing for the offence for which the order was made (see *Fleming* (1989) 11 Cr. App. R.(S.) 137).

(l) If the further offence was committed before the community order **22-087** was made, the court should not normally re-sentence the

offender for the original offence upon revocation. This principle
was established in *Cawley* (1994) 15 Cr. App. R.(S.) 209 where the
young offender had received a probation order at magistrates'
court after committing a burglary. The Crown Court in
sentencing him to a young offender institution for the burglary
also revoked the probation order and imposed a consecutive
custodial sentence. The Court of Appeal held that it could seldom
if ever be in the interests of justice to resentence an offender for
offences for which he was placed on probation after the
commission of the crime for which he was subsequently
sentenced even if it is appropriate to revoke the probation order.
Here revocation was also inappropriate and was quashed as it
seemed helpful and appropriate that the probation order should
still be in place on his release (after sentence of nine months
detention). Presumably the principle would apply if the
community order is a community service order, though the
continuance of such an order may not be considered to be so
potentially "helpful and appropriate". The Court of Appeal
appears to have overlooked that the offender would be subject to
statutory supervision on release under CJA 1991, s. 65 though it
may have felt that this form of supervision could be less intensive
than the oversight offered by a probation order.

22-088   (m) If a compensation order was made at the same time as a
community sentence and the community sentence is later
revoked and the offender is re-sentenced for the original offence,
the compensation order is not affected (*Jama* (1992) 13 Cr. App.
R.(S.) 63). The compensation order may, however, be varied by
the magistrates' court responsible for its enforcement.

Probation Orders: Substitution of Conditional Discharge

22-089 Under pre-1991 law, a court having power to discharge a probation order
had the alternative power under PCCA 1973, s. 11 to substitute a
conditional discharge in respect of the original offence, on the
application of the probationer or the supervising officer. It is uncertain
whether this power has survived implementation of CJA 1991. Section
11 was not repealed by CJA 1991, Sched. 13. On the contrary, section 11
is specifically amended by Schedule 11, paragraph 10 to update it in the
light of the repeal of PCCA 1973, s. 8. This strongly implies that the
drafters of the Act believed that the provision would have continuing
life. On the other hand, the wording of section 11(1) empowers a court
"having power to discharge a probation order". Discharge powers were
specified in PCCA 1973, s. 5(1) and Sched. 1, para. 1, now repealed (CJA
1991, Sched. 13). Discharge of a probation order has been replaced by the
generic powers of revocation contained in CJA 1991 Sched. 2, Pt. III. It is
therefore questionable whether any court now has power of discharge,
thus rendering s. 11 obsolete. Under revocation powers, a court may
revoke the order and deal with the offender in some other manner

(Sched. 2, para. 7(2)). Thus a conditional discharge could be imposed. This does not achieve exactly the same result as a substitution under section 11 because a conditional discharge substituted under that power is deemed to have retrospective effect as if it had been ordered on the date of the making of the probation order and continued for the duration of the probation period as originally specified.

The other differences between the section 11 procedure and the **22-090** Schedule 2 procedure are:

(a) Under section 11, if the applicant is the supervising officer the probationer's attendance at court is not required, provided that the officer "produces to the court a statement that (the probationer) understands the effect of an order under section 11 and consents to the application being made" (s. 11(3)). Under Schedule 2, the offender has to be summonsed to attend.

(b) Under section 11, the court has the power either to discharge the order outright or to substitute a conditional discharge. Under Schedule 2, the court has complete discretion in how it will re-sentence or deal with the matter afresh upon revocation.

(c) Under section 11, the application is made to the supervising court, even if the probation order was made by the Crown Court, unless the Crown Court had specifically reserved power of discharging the order to itself. Under Schedule 2, revocation of a Crown Court order can only be granted by the Crown Court.

A section 11 application thus has certain advantages of simplicity **22-091** which may make it an attractive option. It has been a popular recourse for supervising officers who have felt that a probation order can serve no further useful purpose but that it is too early in the life of the order to seek an outright discharge. However, the power of substitution of a discharge would seem to be much more appropriate in the context of the pre-1991 Act status of the probation order, when it was much more akin to the conditional discharge, being "instead of sentence" and rendering the offender liable for sentence for the original offence if convicted of a further offence committed during the operative period. Section 11 then served in effect to remove the active supervisory element of the order. Now that the probation order is a community sentence in its own right, the logic of section 11 is far less obvious.

Pending authoritative interpretation of this ambiguous issue, a court may feel that it has jurisdiction to consider a section 11 application on the same basis as it could receive an application for revocation. Application may be made by either the probationer or the supervising officer and the court must conclude that the probation order "is no longer appropriate in the case of the probationer" (s. 11(1)). If the conditional discharge is substituted, it will be subject to the normal provisions relating to conditional discharge. If the offender is subsequently convicted of an offence committed between the date of the probation order and the substitution, she or he will be liable to be sentenced for the offence for which the probation order was originally imposed. Whether the offender will be entitled to any credit for the extent of their compliance and the restriction on their liberty during the period of their probation order is nowhere addressed. Questions like this highlight the lack of fit between this provision and the 1991 Act philosophy. No application can be made under section 11 while an appeal against the making of the probation order is pending (CJA 1982, s. 66(3)).

22–092 Supervision Orders
The early termination of a supervision order retains the concept of "discharge" under CYPA 1969 rather than that of revocation. Discharge upon breach of a supervision order is outlined earlier in this Chapter. There is no dedicated statutory provision for the discharge of a supervision order following conviction of a further offence, even if a custodial sentence or an incompatible community sentence such as a probation order has been imposed for that offence and even upon conviction by the Crown Court. In these circumstances it would be open to the supervisor (or the supervised person) to apply for discharge to the relevant court under CYPA 1969, s. 15(1), either "on the spot", if further sentence is imposed by that court, or subsequently.

Children and Young Persons Act 1969, s. 15

22–093   "(1) If while a supervision order is in force in respect of a supervised person, it appears to a relevant court, on the application of the supervisor or the supervised person, that it is appropriate to make an order under this subsection, the court may make an order discharging the supervision order ..."

The relevant court, in the case of a person who has not attained the age of 18, is a youth court acting for the specified petty sessions area; if the supervised person has attained the age of 18, the relevant court is an adult magistrates' court acting for that area (s. 15(11)). Even if the supervision order was made by the Crown Court, the relevant court has power of discharge. The Crown Court cannot reserve power of discharge to itself.

If the application is made by the supervisor, the supervisor may bring the supervised person before the court to hear the application or may seek a summons or warrant to secure the attendance of the supervised person before the court, but the court may order the discharge of supervision in the absence of the supervised person (s. 16(5)). A youth court shall not exercise power of discharge unless satisfied that the supervised person is likely to receive the care and control he or she needs, notwithstanding the discharge (s. 16(6)(a)). The supervised person may appeal to the Crown Court against dismissal of an application under section 15 to discharge a supervision order (s. 16(8)(b)). If the application is dismissed, no further application for discharge shall be made during a period of three months from the date of dismissal, without the consent of the relevant court (s. 16(9)). On discharging a supervision order, the court must send a copy to the supervised person and, if the supervisee is a child, to the parent or guardian of that child.

Early Termination for Good Progress **22-094**

The *National Standard* (1995, para. 25) specifies:

> "Early termination of a supervision order should be considered where the offender has made good progress in achieving the objectives set out for the order and where there is not considered to be a significant risk of re-offending and/or of serious harm to the public. Early termination should not be considered before at least half the order has been successfully completed without breach or re-offending."

The 1992 version of the *Standard* proposed that an application for early termination should normally be considered by two-thirds of the term of the order "unless there are clear reasons for not doing so".

Attendance Centre Orders **22-095**

Early termination of an attendance centre order retains the language of "discharge" under CJA 1982, s. 18 except in the context of breach of the order, outlined earlier in this Chapter, where revocation can follow (s. 19). Discharge may be sought either where the offender moves to an area where a centre suitable for their age group or gender is not available, or if their employment demands make their attendance impossible, or if their state of health has deteriorated, making them unsuitable for the demands of the order. Discharge is not appropriate simply on the ground of "good progress". There is no dedicated statutory provision for the discharge or revocation of an attendance centre order following conviction of a further offence, even if a custodial sentence has been imposed for that offence and even upon conviction by the Crown Court. In these circumstances it would be open to the officer in charge or the offender to apply for discharge to the relevant court under the general provisions of section 18, as will now be outlined.

An attendance centre order may be discharged on an application by **22-096** the offender or the officer in charge of the relevant centre (s. 18(1)). The application is made to either:

(a) a magistrates' court (normally a youth court) acting for the petty sessions area in which the centre is situated, or

(b) the court which made the order (s. 18(3)).

Where an application is made by the officer in charge, the court may deal with it without summoning the offender (s. 18(7)). Magistrates' courts normally have the power to discharge a Crown Court order, an advantage which does not generally apply to community sentences. Where, however, the order was made by the Crown Court and that court reserved to itself the power to discharge the order, application must be made to that court (s. 18(4)).

By CJA 1991, s. 67, the power to discharge an attendance centre order includes power to deal with the offender for the offence in respect of which the order was made in any way in which the offender could have been dealt with by the court which made the order, if the order had not been made (s. 18(4A)). There is no explicit provision for bringing the offender before the court in such instances but the offender would clearly need to be summoned to attend if re-sentencing is anticipated.

22–097 Section 18, unlike section 19, does not provide any power to commit the offender to the Crown Court for re-sentence on discharge of an order made by the Crown Court, even if the order was made for an offence triable only on indictment. This appears to prevent a magistrates' court from dealing with the offender under section 18(4A) for such an offence.

Chapter 23

Custodial Sentences: General

The broad position since the implementation of the Criminal Justice **23–001** Act 1991 and the changes introduced by the Criminal Justice and Public Order Act 1994 is as follows:

(a) A youth court may impose two types of custodial sentence:

(i) a sentence of detention in a young offender institution (YOI) upon male and female young persons aged 15 to 17 for a term between two months and six months (for a single offence) or 12 months in aggregate (for two or more indictable offences);

(ii) a secure training order upon male and female children and young persons aged 12 to 14 for a term between six months and two years, a half of which is spent in detention, for one or more imprisonable offences, provided certain special criteria are satisfied.

(b) The Crown Court may impose four types of custodial sentence: **23–002**

(i) a sentence of YOI detention on the same category of juveniles as a youth court but up to a maximum of 24 months for one or more offences;

(ii) a sentence of detention under section 53(2) and (3) of the Children and Young Persons Act 1933 upon either juveniles aged 10 to 17 convicted on indictment of manslaughter or other grave crimes (primarily offences punishable with imprisonment for 14 years or more) or young persons convicted on indictment of certain specified road traffic offences causing death;

(iii) a secure training order on the same basis as a youth court;

(iv) a sentence of detention during Her Majesty's pleasure as a mandatory sentence upon a juvenile convicted of murder.

With the exception of detention during Her Majesty's pleasure, which is a punishment fixed by law (CJA 1991, s. 1(1)), the imposition of a custodial sentence, including a secure training order, on a child or young person is subject to the same statutory restrictions as apply to the sentencing of adults.

23–003 # RESTRICTIONS ON IMPOSING CUSTODIAL SENTENCES: THE TWO CRITERIA

Criminal Justice Act 1991, s. 1

"(2) Subject to subsection (3) below, the court shall not pass a custodial sentence on the offender unless it is of the opinion—

(a) that the offence, or the combination of the offence and one or more offences associated with it, was so serious that only such a sentence can be justified for the offence; or

(b) where the offence is a violent or sexual offence, that only such a sentence would be adequate to protect the public from serious harm from him."

Subsection (3) creates an exception to the application of the criteria by permitting a court to pass a custodial sentence on an offender who refuses consent to a community sentence requiring that consent (see para. 15–017). Once the sentencer has formed the opinion that the defendant falls within section 1(2)(a), and is not of the view that a longer than commensurate sentence is required, it is unnecessary to consider whether the criterion of section 1(2)(b) is satisfied (*Actie* (1993) 14 Cr. App. R.(S.) 598).

23–004 **The Seriousness Criterion**
As has been outlined in Chapter 9, the central emphasis of the Criminal Justice Act 1991 is upon sentencing according to the seriousness of the offence and this is the predominant criterion justifying custody. It is quite similar to the now superseded criterion justifying custody for a young offender under CJA 1982, s. 1(4A)(c): "the offence ... was so serious that a non-custodial sentence for it cannot be justified". The interpretation of that criterion by the Court of Appeal has been extensively scrutinised in order to gain help in understanding what will make an offence "so serious" under the 1991 Act. The only attempt to give general guidance as to what would bring an offence within CJA 1982, s. 1 (4A)(c) was made by Lawton L.J. in *Bradbourn* (1985) 7 Cr. App. R.(S.) 180:

"... the kind of offence which when committed by a young person would make right thinking members of the public knowing all the facts feel that justice had not been done by the passing of any sentence other than a custodial one."

23–005 Though open to criticism for being unduly sweeping, simplistic and ill-defined, the Lawton test has been approved by Lord Taylor C.J. in *Cox*

[1993] 1 W.L.R. 188: "... we think that Lawton L.J.'s formulation is appropriate to any consideration of the expression 'so serious that only such a sentence can be justified for the offence' and we adopt it". Lord Taylor did not seek to explore whether the new phrasing of the "so serious" criterion sets a different, arguably stricter test. For an illustration of the Lord Chief Justice's use of the feelings of a notional member of the public, see *Husbands* (1993) 14 Cr. App. R.(S.) 709, a case of burglary discussed below (para. 23–013).

In forming its opinion on whether the offence is "so serious", the court must consider or take the following into account:

(i) all such information about the circumstances of the offence (including any aggravating or mitigating factors) as is available to it (CJA 1991, s. 3(3)(a));

(ii) a pre-sentence report (s. 3(1)) though since implementation of the Criminal Justice and Public Order Act 1994 a court dealing with a juvenile for an offence triable only on indictment is not obliged to do so if of the opinion that a report is unnecessary; if the offence is triable either way or only summarily, (s. 3(1) and (2)), the court can dispense with a report if a report prepared for a previous sentencing occasion is available to it (s. 3(2A) see para. 11–005).

Is the prevalence of an offence a pertinent factor in the assessment of **23–006** seriousness? Lord Taylor C.J. has lent support to this proposition in early cases interpreting CJA 1991. In *Cox* [1993] 1 W.L.R. 188, he said "the prevalence of offences of a particular class and public concern about them are relevant to the seriousness of an instant offence, as we made clear in *Cunningham* [1993] 1 W.L.R. 183". In *Cunningham*, however, he approved of prevalence as a legitimate factor in determining the length of the custodial sentence to be passed, under section 2(2)(a) (see para. 23–004), once a decision in principle had been taken that the offence was "so serious". *Cox* concerned an 18 year old who had ridden a trials motorcycle recklessly without lights at night, in wet weather with poor visibility and had mounted the pavement in an attempt to avoid the police. *Cunningham* involved robbery of a small shop at knife-point. Both kinds of offence cause obvious concern, but it is unclear on what basis a court can conclude that a particular crime is increasing or is causing particular alarm. As Faulkner and Gibson (1993) have remarked:

"What will clearly not suffice is for the sentencer to rely solely on their recollections of previous cases heard in court or reports in local newspapers, or on public statements by the police, by interest groups or by local or national politicians. The court will need to be satisfied about prevalence and this implies that evidence of some sort will be needed to be considered and tested before the court has any sound basis for aggravating seriousness. Arguably the cases in which prevalence can be reliably established will be few in number, perhaps arising from local outbreaks of offences such as racial harassment, or the stealing and racing of motor vehicles."

23–007 For a recent example of prevalence being cited as a factor in the assessment of seriousness, without any apparent supporting evidence, see *Percy* (1993) 14 Cr. App. R.(S.) 10, a case of "ram raiding". See also *Pimm* (1993) 14 Cr. App. R.(S.) 730 (para. 23–025) and *Bennett* (1995) 16 Cr. App.R.(S.) 438 (para. 24–055) which are indicative of the Court of Appeal's wish to take a firm stand against the reckless use of vehicles by adolescents.

If the court considers that an offence is "so serious" and the offender thus qualifies for custody, this is not conclusive in determining sentence, as Lord Taylor C.J. pointed out in *Cox* and *Oliver* [1993] 1 W.L.R. 177 and 188:

"The court is still required to consider whether such a sentence is appropriate, having regard to the mitigating factors available and relevant to the offender, as opposed to such factors as are relevant to the offence." (*Cox*)

"There may well be cases where, notwithstanding that the offence itself passes the custody threshold, there is sufficient mitigation to lead the court to impose a community sentence." (*Oliver*)

23–008 The scope for mitigation on which the court is able to draw to allow the imposition of a non-custodial sentence is very wide. It may, for instance, relate to the personal circumstances of the offender, as illustrated in the case of an adult by *Jones* (1992) 13 Cr. App. R.(S.) 275 (intense financial worry), or may arise from the particular appeal of a community sentence. Thus in *Cox*, the pre-sentence report proposed a period of probation supervision that would allow the offender the opportunity to examine his offending in more detail and enable him to recognise the danger in which he placed both himself and the public when he engaged in that type of offence (reckless driving). The past preparedness of courts to take "a calculated risk in the hope that the public will in the longer term be better protected" in respect of adult offenders is illustrated by *Bradley* (1983) 5 Cr. App. R.(S.) 363 (four years imprisonment for burglary varied to a 'last chance' probation order) and *Heather* (1979) 1 Cr. App. R.(S.) 139 ("well-deserved" five years imprisonment for robbery of a chemist's shop for drugs at knife-point varied to a probation order to try to prevent the offender from becoming completely addicted to drugs) though such decisions now have to be viewed circumspectly and are clearly out of line with the tenor of sentencing since the 1991 Act.

23–009 If the offender receives a community sentence in circumstances where their offence satisfies the "so serious" criterion and subsequently re-offends while the community sentence is in force, the offender "would have deprived himself of much of the mitigation such as good character, genuine remorse, isolated lapse and similar considerations which had led the original court to pass a community rather than a custodial sentence" (*per* Taylor C.J. in *Oliver*).

Pending a comprehensive new body of case law on the interpretation of the "so serious" criterion of CJA 1991, it is still helpful to look at the Court of Appeal's view of seriousness within CJA 1982, s. 1(4)(c), as amended by CJA 1988, s. 123. These pre-1991 Act cases nevertheless have to be viewed with caution as they concentrate on appeals from Crown Court sentences, largely concerning young offenders aged over 17, and may reflect either the 1988 Act's wording of the criterion which required sentencers to have regard to only one offence in assessing seriousness or the decision in *Roberts* (1987) 9 Cr. App. R.(S.) 152 that the 1982 version of the criterion should be applied to each offence individually rather than to the aggregated gravity of all the offences for sentence.

Burglary of Dwellings

Mussell and Others (1991) 12 Cr. App. R.(S.) 607 confirmed that **23–010** although always a serious offence, a dwelling-house burglary is not always "so serious" and automatically requiring a custodial sentence. Each offence has to be judged individually. Among features likely to be considered are: the extent to which the particular burglary was planned or pre-meditated, the numbers involved in it, whether it was committed by day or night, and whether any person was or may have been at home or may have witnessed any part of the burglary.

Coulston (1990) 12 Cr. App. R.(S.) 286 and *Mole* (1990) 12 Cr. App. R.(S.) 371 illustrate circumstances where the role played by the offender contributed to the Court of Appeal's conclusion that the offence was not "so serious". In *Coulston* the appellant aged 16 had committed two burglaries of dwellings whilst the owners were away, in the company of an 18 year old co-offender. He was said to have been infatuated with his accomplice, had not caused the mess inflicted and had played a passive role in the offences. In *Mole* the appellant aged 17 was concerned with two others in a daytime burglary. His role was the familiar one of knocking on the door of the house to establish whether anyone was in. On receiving no reply, he kept watch whilst his accomplices broke in, ransacked the property and stole items worth £3,000. They were **23–011** apprehended quickly and nearly all the stolen property was recovered. The Court of Appeal said that it did not wish to detract from the seriousness of domestic burglary, which involved an invasion of privacy and caused distress and anxiety even when householders were not at home at the time of the offence, but the offender was not the prime mover and, given that this was a daytime burglary whilst the householder was out, it was a "classic case" for a community service order.

Suker (1990) 12 Cr. App. R.(S.) 290 illustrates a night-time burglary of occupied premises where the particular facts made the case insufficiently serious for a custodial sentence. The appellant, aged 19, was seen attempting to climb through the bathroom window of a house in the early hours of the morning. The occupant was alerted, pulled the offender into the house and detained him until the police arrived. The offender was somewhat inebriated and claimed that he had been hoping to find enough money to pay for a taxi to take him home and did not intend to take any other property.

23–012   *Bates* (1985) 7 Cr. App. R.(S.) 105, *Roberts* (1987) 9 Cr. App. R.(S.) 152 and *Littler and Dooley* (1990) 12 Cr. App. R.(S.) 143 appear to provide instances of quite typical domestic burglaries which the Court of Appeal did not consider to be individually "so serious". In *Bates* the appellant aged under 21 had entered the house of an acquaintance with other youths to steal a video recorder. They were caught in the act. The Court of Appeal said that the appropriate sentence was a community service order. In *Roberts* the appellant aged 18 had broken into a number of premises, including dwellings, over around two months, but selected only unoccupied houses during the day. In *Littler and Dooley*, two offenders aged 18 had broken into a house whilst the owner was away by smashing a pane of glass in a rear door. They stole electrical items and jewellery worth £1,660 in total.

Past examples of instances where dwelling-house burglary has been considered "so serious", on unsurprising grounds, include:

> *Dolby* (1989) 11 Cr. App. R.(S.) 335: the offender aged 20 broke into the house at night and entered the bedroom of the sleeping occupant, a woman living alone.
>
> *Marsden* (1990) 12 Cr. App. R.(S.) 274: the offender aged 18 broke into the home of his former foster parents whilst they were away on holiday. He ransacked the house, stole property worth £3,000 and displayed his feelings of resentment against the owners for allegedly letting him down by smearing excrement in a lavatory and urinating in their bedroom.
>
> *Stokoe* (1991) 12 Cr. App. R.(S.) 726: the offender aged 20 called at the home of an 83 year old woman, ostensibly to check repairs previously undertaken. Whilst his accomplice kept her talking, he stole £1,000 in cash and a valuable bracelet.

23–013   The first case of domestic burglary held not to be "so serious" under CJA 1991, *Bennett* (1995) Cr. App. R.(S.) 438, C.A., involved a break-in at night, the offender aged 20 knowing that the occupier was away on holiday. He attempted to escape empty-handed when disturbed by a neighbour and was arrested immediately. He pleaded guilty. The Court of Appeal considered that the "so serious" criterion was not satisfied by these facts and it was wrong to impose a custodial sentence.

Husbands (1993) 14 Cr. App. R.(S.) 709 suggests that repeated house burglary is highly likely to satisfy the "so serious" criterion. The offender (now aged 17) had burgled a house stealing items worth £1900. Around six months later he was interrupted in the course of another domestic burglary. Endorsing the "right-thinking member of the public" test, Lord Taylor C.J. stated:

> "Putting ourselves in the position of a member of the public considering this criminal conduct, we could well understand that had there only been the offence which was committed in June 1991

it might have been possible to say that it was not 'so serious' ... But if that member of the public were to hear that six months later the offender had done the same thing again in another private dwelling house, we consider that the only conclusion to which that member of the public would come would be that a custodial sentence was required."

Though of previous good character, the offender had been in **23–014** employment and had been motivated by the idea of extra money and also by boredom and the influence of his new association with criminally-minded friends. His expression of shame, his dissociation from his new associates and the proposal of a combination order did not persuade the Court of Appeal to set aside sentence of 12 months YOI.

Non-Domestic Burglary

Eddy and Monks (1991) 11 Cr. App. R.(S.) 370 presents the best-known illustration of "so serious" burglary of commercial premises. The two co-offenders, one aged under 21 (20), committed a series of systematic break-ins. A high-powered car would be taken and concealed, the premises would be entered and then immediately left to test if there was an alarm system and, if the police did not respond, the burglary would proceed, involving theft of property worth, in two instances, around £10,000. The Court of Appeal concluded that each of these two burglaries taken in isolation was so serious that a non-custodial sentence could not be justified.

In *Hassan and Khan* (1989) 11 Cr. App. R.(S.) 148, the appellants aged **23–015** under 21 had burgled a number of schools, in some cases more than once, stealing property such as video recorders and computers, worth £3,000 in total. The Court of Appeal considered that none of the offences viewed individually were "so serious" and that the proper sentence would have been a community service order.

Since the implementation of CJA 1991, the Court of Appeal has made clear that "young men who indulge (in ram raiding) must know that heavy sentences will follow", given the reliance on organised teams, surprise, brute force, affront and danger caused to the public and the prevalence of this kind of crime (*Percy* (1993) 14 Cr. App. R.(S.) 10). For a more mundane instance of non-dwelling burglary considered "so serious", see *Dorries and Dorries* (1993) 14 Cr. App. R(S) 605, where custody was upheld for a 20 year old man with no previous convictions who had co-burgled a lock-up shop at night using a crowbar and a radio scanner, stealing goods worth £600, driving off when the police intervened. Compare *Tetteh* [1993] Crim. L.R. 629 where a community sentence was considered appropriate for a 35 year old man who had "opportunistically" burgled a social club, forcing open the spirits store but was intercepted before anything was taken.

23–016 *Robbery*

In the reported cases this offence has almost always been judged "so serious", irrespective of the particular facts. Among cases which have indicated that a custodial sentence was necessary:

> *Willis and Willis* (1984) 6 Cr. App. R.(S.) 68. The offenders, one aged 16 and the other slightly older, had demanded money from a shopkeeper using an imitation firearm, an air rifle, and obtaining £40. This assessment is in line with guideline judgements such as *Attorney-General's Reference Nos. 3 and 4 of 1990* [1991] Crim. L.R. 304, indicating that vulnerable small businesses such as small shops, off-licences and take-away outlets, serving the community, should be protected by the courts.
>
> *Curtis* [1987] Crim. L.R. 66. The appellant aged 16, with two older co-offenders, robbed a man working in a multi-storey car park, stealing his wage packet containing £65. He admitted kicking the victim as he lay on the ground and accepting £25 of the proceeds.
>
> *Pretty* [1992] Crim. L.R. 68. The appellant aged 16 and another youth approached two boys of their own age and demanded money, threatening to beat them up if they did not co-operate. Sums of £3.50 and 50 pence were obtained.

23–017
> *Golding* (1992) 13 Cr. App. R.(S.) 142. The appellant aged 18, in company with other youths, approached the victim aged 16 and threatened to beat him up unless he handed over his new bicycle, a Christmas present worth £200. The bicycle was handed over and ridden off by the appellant who later sold it.
>
> *Hiscock* (1994) 15 Cr. App. R.(S.) 287. The appellant aged 17 twice demanded items from schoolboys aged 15, on the first occasion obtaining a wallet under threat of violence and on the second a bus pass by intimidation. Sentence of nine months YOI for this "most unpleasant incident" was held to be "neither manifestly excessive nor wrong in principle".

23–018 Though cases like *Pretty* would appear to suggest that no robbery, however petty, can be regarded as insufficiently serious for a custodial sentence, there are occasional instances where a non-custodial sentence has been considered appropriate:

> *Balogum* (1983) (unreported). The appellant aged 17 robbed a youth of the same age with learning difficulties as they walked home after receiving their wages. He hit the victim in the face and stole £5. Though the offender was considered a bully, his sentence of three months YOI was replaced by a probation order.
>
> *Keane* (1990) 12 Cr. App. R.(S.) 132. The appellant aged 18 accosted a 17 year old youth on a bus and took his personal stereo whilst his co-offender held the victim's arms.

Theft and Deception in Breach of Trust **23–019**

The following cases illustrate instances of breach of trust which were not considered to be "so serious".

> *Bradbourn* (1985) 7 Cr. App. R.(S.) 180. The appellant, aged 20, was a shop assistant. Following unexplained shop losses, a security check was commenced and she was observed to ring up less on the till than she had received in payment for goods and to keep the difference of £2.
>
> *Scott* (1990) 12 Cr. App. R.(S.) 23. A supermarket check-out assistant aged 20, a single mother living alone with a two month old baby, allowed customers to take goods out through her check-out desk either without paying or for nominal payment. She pleaded guilty to one offence of attempted theft and nine offences of theft. The full extent of the loss was impossible to assess accurately but the offender estimated that the goods totalled around £4,000. She had gained little for herself apart from temporary popularity, receiving only two jumpers and a baking set from the goods stolen. The Court of Appeal said that, even viewing the offences as a whole rather than individually, the case did not fulfil the "so serious" criterion.
>
> *Wilson* (1990) 12 Cr. App. R.(S.) 284. A post office worker aged 18 **23–020** had opened various postal packets and stolen the contents: two telephones, two track suits, a jumper and a medallion. He pleaded guilty to one count of opening a postal packet and two of theft.
>
> *Morris* [1991] Crim. L.R. 563. A cashier aged 20 stole various sums of money between £40 and £80 from receipts from customers over two to three months, to spend on gambling. The total loss was in excess of £1,000. He pleaded guilty to six counts with 41 similar offences being taken into consideration.
>
> *Choudhary* (1992) 13 Cr. App. R.(S.) 290. The appellant aged 19, employed as a part-time petrol station cashier, used a dishonestly obtained credit card to steal from his employer, taking amounts of £20 to £30, totalling over £3,000. He pleaded guilty to one offence of handling and three of theft, with 136 thefts being taken into consideration. The Court of Appeal said that no single offence, taken alone, was "so serious" and substituted a conditional discharge for two months YOI.

Compare two pre-CJA 1991 cases which were considered to satisfy the **23–021** "so serious" test:

> *Stanley* (1986) 8 Cr. App. R.(S.) 404. The appellant aged 16 used his position as a jewellery shop assistant to steal jewellery worth about £5,000 over a period of about six months. He pleaded guilty to six counts of theft and asked for 24 similar offences to be taken into consideration.
>
> *Carthy* (1991) 12 Cr. App. R.(S.) 622. The appellant aged 19, a

solicitor's clerk who was responsible for taking the firm's receipts to the bank and to draw cash, presented cheques stolen from the firm on four occasions, forging a partner's signature, to obtain sums ranging from £270 to £820. The total obtained was about £2,745. He pleaded guilty to four offences of obtaining property by deception. He claimed that he was being threatened to repay a debt of nearly £1,000 and had originally taken the money to settle his liability, using the surplus for himself and his family.

23–022 Two cases decided since implementation of CJA 1991 (but prior to the amendments introduced by CJA 1993) illustrate circumstances falling either side of the "so serious" threshold:

In *Small* (1993) 14 Cr. App. R.(S.) 405 a pizza shop manager aged 19 had failed to pay in sums received as takings, totalling £1,800. The Court of Appeal considered that he was not sufficiently mature to cope with the heavy volume of work, the long and unsocial hours and the excessive level of responsibility placed on him at too early a stage in his career. Three months YOI was replaced by a community service order.

In *Hill* (1993) 14 Cr. App. R.(S.) 556, a warehouse assistant aged 18 had systematically stolen goods worth £1,500 from his employer over a period of weeks, taking the goods back to other branches to obtain a refund, using forged till receipts and pretending to be a dissatisfied customer. Custodial sentence was upheld.

Theft in Other Circumstances

23–023 *Munday* (1985) 7 Cr. App. R.(S.) 216 presents an early example of the application of the "so serious" criterion to run-of-the-mill theft from shops. The appellant aged 17 and a female co-offender took clothing with a total value of about £168 from shops in the course of a single afternoon. Sentence of six months custody was quashed and a fine was substituted.

Scorey (1988) 9 Cr. App. R.(S.) 536 illustrates a more substantial episode of theft which was considered "so serious". The appellant aged 19 had joined with others on three occasions in stealing radio cassette players from new cars parked at a depot whilst awaiting delivery. Thirty two sets worth £6,400 were taken on the first occasion, 28 sets worth £5,600 on the second, 55 sets worth £11,000 on the third. Given that the raids were very skilfully carried out and planned well in advance, the Court of Appeal considered that each raid in isolation was "so serious" and sentence of nine months custody was upheld.

Car Crime

Two cases illustrate episodes of taking without consent which were considered to fall on either side of the "so serious" threshold. In *Emery* [1985] R.T.R. 415 the appellant aged 20, together with a co-offender, had taken a motor cycle without consent and when pursued by the police tried to evade arrest by driving through two sets of red lights, exceeded the speed limit and drove on the wrong side of the road, causing on-coming vehicles to brake suddenly. The machine eventually mounted the pavement and the riders fell off. The Court of Appeal said that even though the taking was premeditated and the reckless driving was both bad and extended, nevertheless the appropriate sentence, taking account of the appellant's good character, was a community service order.

Compare *Jeary* (1987) 9 Cr. App. R.(S.) 491 where the appellant aged **23–024** 18, together with other youths, had taken two cars for a "bit of fun", using keys in their possession, had driven round a city area at high speed, colliding with each other on several occasions. After finally colliding head on, damaging one car beyond repair, the youths had driven off in the remaining car, eventually crashing it into a tree. The Court of Appeal considered sentence of four months custody fully justified, having particular regard to the deliberate destruction of the vehicles.

Two further cases throw light on the evaluation of reckless or dangerous driving without the element of taking. In *Osborne* (1990) 12 Cr. App. R.(S.) 55, the appellant aged 20 had drunk about four pints of lager and, whilst returning home, had driven at high speed on to a housing estate. He lost control and the car mounted the pavement hitting two lamp posts. He was chased by the police at speeds of 60 to 70 mph before stopping and attempting to hide. His breath alcohol level was twice the legal limit. The Court of Appeal upheld the sentencer's view that the offence was "so serious". In *Winterton* [1993] Crim. L.R. 322, the appellant aged 19, driving his father's high-powered car, had crossed double white lines to overtake but had swerved back to avoid a collision with an on-coming car. He lost control and hit another vehicle killing the driver. The offence of causing death by reckless driving was considered "so serious" but elements of mitigation (his youth and previous good character, his inexperience as a driver, his remorse and the interval of 15 months between incident and trial) allowed reduction of sentence.

> "This was a case in which, if the public at large knew all the facts, **23–025** they would say that when a life had been lost through the deliberate flouting of road markings at excessive speed, only a custodial sentence was appropriate."

Strong indication of the Court of Appeal's concern about youthful recklessness behind the wheel causing death was provided in *Pimm* (1993) 14 Cr. App. R.(S.) 730. The offender was convicted of manslaughter, having tried to flee in his vehicle when seen by the victim in the course of attempting to take a car. The victim had tried to block his escape and was run down. The Court of Appeal felt that sentence of nine years YOI (and 10 years disqualification) was fully justified for a bad case involving excess alcohol and gross disregard for human life and limb.

"The prevalence of this kind of offence is among those of the appellant's age group. It is that group which needs to be deterred."

23–026 This lead was followed in *Evans* (1994) 15 Cr. App. R.(S.) 137, a case of aggravated vehicle taking causing death. Sentence of two years YOI was upheld where a "hard-working, honest and usually conscientious" 19 year old had taken a car with its keys left in it after he had been drinking (blood alcohol level of 42 mg per 100 ml of blood). He lost control and hit a tree, killing his passenger. Similarly, in *Ore and Tandy* (1994) 15 Cr. App. R.(S.) 620, where the 19 and 20 year old offender had taken a car, engaged in a race with another car, lost control, mounted the pavement and killed a boy pedestrian, sentences of four years YOI were upheld. The Court of Appeal commented that this kind of offending had reached "epidemic proportions" and required specific and more drastic penalties. "If the sentences ... served to deter one young person from a similar escapade, and protected one other person from death or maiming, they would have served their purpose."

23–027 *Ore and Tandy* and *Sealey* (1994) 15 Cr. App. R.(S.) 189 (also a case of aggravated vehicle taking) serve to indicate that a passenger can expect to be treated just as culpably as the driver. The Court of Appeal held that the appellant's presence in the car amounted to encouragement.

"He must have known that the vehicle would be driven dangerously to escape police attention if necessary ... The Act is designed to deter young people, whether drivers or passengers, going off in stolen cars which are driven dangerously."

In *Robinson and Scurry* (1994) 15 Cr. App. R.(S.) 452, however, the Court of Appeal felt able to make some distinction between driver and passenger in an "appalling" case of aggravated vehicle taking (see para. 24–006), stating that differentiation is appropriate "unless the passenger can be shown to have given some positive encouragement to the driver". This approach suggests that mere presence is insufficient to amount to equal culpability.

Offensive Weapon

23–028 *Camp* (1989) 11 Cr. App. R.(S.) 196 provides a rare instance of an appeal case considering this offence simpliciter. The appellant aged 20 was stopped by police late at night in a town centre and a carving knife was found in the sleeve of his jacket. He explained that he had earlier been "done over by 15 blokes" and that he carried it for self-defence purposes because he still considered he was at risk. The Court of Appeal not surprisingly considered that the facts did not justify custody and sentence of four months YOI was quashed.

Criminal Damage

Ferreira and Belic (1988) 10 Cr. App. R.(S.) 343 provides an example of criminal damage to public property causing expense and inconvenience which was nevertheless not considered to satisfy the "so serious" test.

The appellants aged under 21 were found in the early morning at a train depot where carriages had been damaged with paint sprays. One appellant admitted being present when the carriages were sprayed and the other was in possession of spray cans which he admitted intending to use to spray graffiti. The Court of Appeal said that this was the kind of case for which community service was designed.

The criminal damage in *Hunter* [1991] Crim. L.R. 146 was in the context of a larger violent incident (see para. 23–037). The appellant aged 20 had resented the break up of his relationship with a young woman and reacted, *inter alia*, by breaking the windscreen of a van belonging to her employers and causing damage worth £1,384 to furniture and fittings in her parents' home. The Court of Appeal considered that the windscreen damage was not "so serious" but that the second count did satisfy the criterion.

Bomb Hoax   23–029

Wilburn [1992] Crim. L.R. 129 illustrates the seriousness with which this kind of irresponsible alarm can be viewed. The appellant aged 21 placed an imitation bomb made of flour and putty in a department store toilet and telephoned the store with a warning that two bombs would explode within ten minutes. The store was evacuated, causing substantial loss of trading, bomb disposal teams were called, streets were cordoned off and emergency services attended. The offender said he had been pressured by friends to carry out the hoax. A custodial sentence was upheld. In *McClennon* (1994) 15 Cr. App. R.(S.) 17 (where an adult woman with two young children had planted a bomb-like article in a shopping precinct lavatory) the Court of Appeal stated that the serious nature of the offence was a more important factor in sentencing than the background and position of the offender.

Arson   23–030

This offence is often of sufficient seriousness to merit consideration of CYPA 1933, s.53(2) powers of detention and is discussed further at para. 24–054. *Corsi* (1990) Crim. L.R. 435 offers a further example of an episode considered "so serious" in the range of detention in a young offender institution. The appellant aged 17 had been drinking to celebrate the completion of school examinations. He and another youth then entered a bus parked at a bus depot. He ripped open a seat and his co-offender set light to it. The fire spread and destroyed four buses at a replacement cost of £50,000, together with damage to the depot costing £17,000. The Court of Appeal said that the seriousness of the offence outweighed all other considerations in mitigation and upheld sentence of nine months YOI.

Street Violence   23–031

Most of the reported cases illustrating the application of CJA 1982, s. 1(4A)(c) to assault or public order offences concern incidents of street fights and disturbances, often outside clubs, pubs or take-aways, usually between rival groups of young people. Among cases which were considered to be "so serious":

> *Jeoffrey and Others* (1985) 7 Cr. App. R.(S.) 135. Following an incident at a dance, which doubtless fired their tempers, the offender aged under 21 and others attacked a youth who was unknown to them as he walked in the street with his girlfriend, causing various injuries of a not especially serious nature. The victim was discharged from hospital within an hour and was believed to have made a complete recovery. Though the offenders were either in work or on training courses and were suitable for community service, the Court of Appeal upheld sentence of three months detention for assault occasioning actual bodily harm.
>
> *Poyner* (1989) 11 Cr. App. R.(S.) 173. A group of men, including the appellant aged 20, attacked another man as he walked in the early hours of the morning. He was knocked down, kicked about the head and forced to hand over his watch and some money. Poyner denied involvement in the robbery but admitted punching the victim and pleaded guilty to affray. Despite a proposal in the social enquiry report that a probation order would help to stabilise his life, six months detention was upheld.

23–032
> *Hebron and Spencer* (1989) 11 Cr. App. R.(S.) 226. During a New Year's Eve disturbance in a city centre, fighting broke out among a large crowd and bottles were thrown. Spencer's contribution was to shake his fist and shout "Kill the Bill" but this was part and parcel of an alarming and potentially dangerous situation and sentence of detention for violent disorder was upheld, though reduced from 18 months to 12 months.
>
> *McQueen* (1989) 11 Cr. App. R.(S.) 305. A group of eight youths, including the appellant aged 19, attacked another youth for no apparent reason, causing cuts and bruises to his head amounting to actual bodily harm.
>
> *Wilson* (1989) 11 Cr. App. R.(S.) 344. In a fight outside a nightclub where they had been drinking, the appellant aged 20 knocked the victim over and continued to punch him as he lay on the ground, causing a fractured cheekbone, two black eyes, a cut lip and internal haemorrhage to one eye, though without permanent damage. Though "so serious", sentence was reduced to allow his immediate release, having served six weeks in custody.

23–033
> *Furnell* (1990) 12 Cr. App. R.(S.) 306. The appellant aged 20 was one of several young people who were creating a disturbance in a street and cutting flowers from adjoining gardens with a pair of shears. A householder who believed that his car had been damaged tried to remonstrate with them and engaged in a scuffle with one of the group. As the householder walked away from that encounter he was struck on the head from behind by the appellant using the pair of shears. The blow knocked him to the ground and caused a 1½ cm laceration, concussion, nausea and blurred vision. Though the use

of a weapon and the attack from behind as the victim was walking away justified a custodial sentence, six months detention for actual bodily harm was reduced to three months.

Beddoes (1990) 12 Cr. App. R.(S.) 363. A group of 15 young men including the appellant aged 20 attacked a group of soldiers outside a pub using snooker cues and throwing glasses. Two people required hospital treatment afterwards. Sentence for violent disorder was reduced from nine months to six months detention.

Johal (1991) 12 Cr. App. R.(S.) 695. The offender aged 19 and his   **23–034** brother had been subjected to racist abuse by a group of youths in a fish and chip shop. They later encountered two of the group and attacked one with baseball bats from behind, striking blows to the head and body. The second victim was hit on the head when he tried to help the first youth. Two years detention for wounding with intent was upheld, despite mitigating factors including the offender's positive good character, the element of provocation and the improbability of his offending again in the future.

Cripps (1991) 12 Cr. App. R.(S.) 689. The offender aged under 21 was one of a group of young men who set upon another such group in the street because the ex-girlfriend of one of the attackers had left a nightclub with some of the victims. Injuries included two broken noses. The appellant was convicted of violent disorder after a trial lasting four and a half days. Though his involvement was recognised to be limited, having become involved after the fight had already started, the Court of Appeal deferred to the trial judge's conclusion that the offence was "so serious" but reduced sentence from 18 months to six months detention.

Bray (1992) 13 Cr. App. R.(S.) 5. As the victim was walking in the   **23–035** street with his girlfriend, a car stopped and the offender aged 20 got out carrying a metal bar, threatened him and lunged at him with the bar. The victim avoided injury until the co-offender joined in using a sawn-off snooker cue. The victim was struck with the bar and the cue causing a head wound requiring four stitches. The Court of Appeal described this as a disgraceful and unprovoked incident of racial violence and upheld sentence of 18 months detention for unlawful wounding.

The following are examples of cases where a custodial sentence was not upheld:

Pearson (1989) 11 Cr. App. R.(S.) 391. Having been asked to leave a pub, the appellant aged under 21 and a friend joined with other youths in the car park and attacked two others as they arrived. A number of people were injured in the ensuing fight. The appellant admitted being involved in the fight but denied starting it. In a later incident, whilst on bail for the previous matter, the appellant was with a group outside an off-licence who were taken to task by the proprietor for urinating at the side of the shop. In the ensuing fight the appellant claimed that he had merely shouted and encouraged the trouble without hitting anyone, but admitted struggling with a man who was trying to restrain his friend. Four months detention for each offence of threatening behaviour was quashed and a community service order was substituted.

23–036   *Smith and Gilhooley* (1990) 12 Cr. App. R.(S.) 172. Two young women aged 19 who had been drinking encountered two other young women in the street late at night and a fight ensued. After the fight broke up, the appellant chased one of the victims, kicking and punching her, causing fractures to her nose and floor of the left orbit, multiple bruises and abrasions. The Court of Appeal concluded that the "so serious" criterion was not satisfied and substituted community service and compensation orders.

23–037 *Other Violence*

McDermot (1984) 6 Cr. App. R.(S.) 377 offers an example of a case where the Court of Appeal found sufficient personal mitigation to substitute a community service order in place of detention, despite the unlawful wounding of a fish bar proprietor by an 18 year old offender who struck the victim over the head with a piece of wood. There may have been an element of provocation in that the offender claimed that the attack was in revenge for an incident some weeks earlier when he had been stabbed in the back by the proprietor. The offender was serving an apprenticeship which was still open to him.

Personal mitigation seems to have proved highly persuasive in *Grant* (1990) 12 Cr. App. R.(S.) 441. Following the break up of his relationship with a girlfriend, the appellant aged 20 encountered her in a nightclub in the company of another man. After upsetting the young woman, he punched her companion in the face and pushed him, causing him to fall down a flight of stairs. The victim suffered a wound requiring seven stitches and two broken teeth. As this behaviour was "out of character" and he stood to lose his employment and his home if sentenced to custody, the Court of Appeal concluded that the case was "tailor made" for community service and quashed sentence of three months detention for unlawful wounding.

Compare *Hunter* [1991] Crim. L.R. 146, where three assaults occasioning actual bodily harm were considered to involve "horrifying personal violence" and thus to be sufficiently serious for custodial sentences, despite the fact that the offender had been reconciled with his first victim and had resumed living with her since the incident. The appellant aged 20 attacked a young woman with whom he had been living and who had terminated the relationship. The assault took place in her parents' home. He dragged her by the hair and punched her repeatedly. He then attacked her father who had tried to intervene, kicking him as he lay on the floor after falling over. He finally attacked another man who intervened, kicking him unconscious as he lay on the floor.

23–038   *Rhoades* (1989) 11 Cr. App. R.(S.) 538 demonstrates that assault on a police officer, even if leading only to conviction for common assault, can be considered sufficiently serious to justify custody. The appellant aged 20 who had spent the evening drinking was stopped by uniformed police officers whilst driving and requested to take a breath test. Following his refusal and arrest, he struggled and resisted being taken to the police car. One officer was kicked and another received a fist blow but it was accepted that the offender had not caused deliberate injury.

In the light of *Rhoades*, it is not surprising that an assault on a police officer occasioning actual bodily harm was considered "so serious" and a custodial sentence justified in *Leather* (1993) 14 Cr. App. R.(S.) 736. A young woman aged 17 of previous good character had seized a police officer by the testicles as he was seeking to arrest her boyfriend, intending to prevent that arrest. The assault was noted to be sustained with considerable force and intensity.

Two other cases of assault occasioning actual bodily harm **23-039** adjudicated since the introduction of CJA 1991 suggest that, for adult offenders at least, the Court of Appeal is likely to consider that the "so serious" threshold is reached in most cases of ABH. In *Audit* (1994) 15 Cr. App. R.(S.) 36, the offender attacked a man he had been drinking with after they had left the public house, punching him in the face and again as he lay on the ground, causing a cut eyebrow requiring stitches and bruises to the face and jaw. A custodial sentence was appropriate for "an unprovoked, gratuitous drunken attack on an innocent man in a public place." In *Graham* [1993] Crim. L.R. 628, the victim had invited the offender aged 21 to "come outside" with her in the course of an argument in a restaurant. The offender struck the victim twice on the nose and face in what she claimed was "pre-emptive self-defence". While custody was considered right in principle, a short, sharp sentence was considered adequate.

In a cluster of cases reviewing sentencing for wounding or causing **23-040** grievous bodily harm with intent, on the Reference of the Attorney-General, the Court of Appeal has given a strong indication that, in the case of adults at least, conviction for a section 18 offence will almost always deserve a custodial sentence. Thus in *Attorney-General's Reference No. 27 of 1993 (Piff)* [1994] Crim. L.R. 465, where the offender aged 21 had butted a football match opponent on the side of the face during the course of the game, causing a shattered cheekbone and eye socket among other injuries, six months imprisonment was substituted for a probation order with an additional requirement to attend a "violent offenders' programme". Condemning violence on the field of play and acknowledging the public perception that "there are too many offences of this kind", Lord Taylor C.J. stated:

> "The idea that conduct involving an intention to do really serious bodily harm is to be dealt with by putting a person on probation should not be allowed to become current".

Unlawful Sexual Intercourse and other Sexual Crime

23-041 *Tonks* (1990) 12 Cr. App. R.(S.) 282 shows the weighing of aggravating
and mitigating factors, leading to the conclusion that the offence was
"so serious". The offender aged 19 started going out with a 12 year old
girl when he was aged 18 and after a month they had sexual intercourse
on five occasions, resulting in her pregnancy. Mitigation included the
offender's emotional immaturity, the genuine affection between them,
his frankness when interviewed by police and his remorse. However,
the Court of Appeal considered his continued association with the girl
after he had been warned to stop by her step-father and his father and his
gross irresponsibility in causing her to become pregnant made a
custodial sentence inevitable.

In *Attorney-General's Reference No. 13 of 1993 (Gambrill)* [1993]
Crim. L.R. 892, the offender, then aged 18, had attempted sexual
intercourse with a nine year old girl for whom he had babysat. The
defence claimed in mitigation that the offence was an isolated, brief and
temporary loss of control from which he had voluntarily desisted when
he had been unable to achieve penetration, at a time when he was
immature and sexually inexperienced. The offence came to light two
and a half years later. The Court of Appeal agreed that a probation order
was an unduly lenient sentence and that it had a duty to impose a
custodial sentence in a case of unlawful sexual intercourse or attempted
USI against a very young girl.

23-042   Compare *Fuller* (1992) 13 Cr. App. R.(S.) 680 where a babysitter aged
16 at the time of the offences admitted a single brief occasion of buggery
of a boy aged 10, stopping when the boy complained of pain, and eight
occasions of indecent assault (placing his penis between the boy's
buttocks in simulation of intercourse to ejaculation). Though the Court
gave general guidance that those who babysit for other people's children
have a particular responsibility and in virtually all cases any breach or
abuse of trust will result in "severe punishment", it was not persuaded
that a custodial sentence was required in this instance. The offender had
made a full admission of what should be regarded as sexual
experimentation by an adolescent boy who was immature, naive and a
slow developer, without deep-rooted problems. The difference in age
between perpetrator and victim had to be diminished because of the
former's immaturity. A probation order was imposed to further the
assistance on offer outlined in the probation and psychiatric reports.

23-043   *Kendall* (1994) 15 Cr. App. R.(S.) 187 and *Oriss* (1994) 15 Cr. App.
R.(S.) 185 provide examples of indecent assault that did not require a
"punitive sentence". In *Kendall* the offender aged 15 had intercourse
with a 14 year old girl who, though not an enthusiastic participant, was
found to have given consent. The Court of Appeal overturned a
custodial sentence, in recognition of their similarity in age and his
immaturity, and imposed a conditional discharge, recognising that he
had already spent a month in custody. In *Oriss*, a young adult aged 18 to
19 at the time of the offences had twice touched a boy aged 12 between

his knee and thigh, on one occasion after masturbating in the boy's presence. As there was no genital contact nor use or threat of violence and the assaults were over clothing and not prolonged, the Court of Appeal felt able to replace a sentence of nine months YOI with a probation order, commenting that it would have been sensible to have adjourned sentence for a psychiatric assessment to see if treatment could assist the offender.

Simon John K. (1994) 15 Cr. App. R.(S.) 271 illustrates indecency under the Indecency with Children Act 1960 s. 1(1). Sentence of three months YOI imposed on an 18 year old youth for rubbing his erect penis against his brother aged 4½ was overturned, being "both unimaginative and wholly wrong" and out of all proportion to the harm caused. The incident lasted ten minutes and caused no physical injury. The offender was said to show a significant degree of emotional insecurity and sexual immaturity. He had obtained a good job and a college place and was due to commence training for managerial responsibility. A conditional discharge was imposed in recognition of time spent in custody. A pre-sentence report had proposed a probation order with a requirement of attendance at a group for sexual offenders.

Length of Sentence   **23–044**

If an offence, either on its own or in combination with one or more associated offences, is considered to satisfy the "so serious" criterion and mitigation does not permit any sentence other than custody, the length of such sentence is determined according to CJA 1991 s. 2:

CJA 1991, s. 2

"(2) The custodial sentence shall be—
  (a) for such term (not exceeding the permitted maximum) as in the opinion of the court is commensurate with the seriousness of the offence, or the combination of the offence and other offences associated with it; or

  (b) where the offence is a violent or sexual offence, for such longer term (not exceeding the maximum) as in the opinion of the court is necessary to protect the public from serious harm from the offender."

On the face of it, it appears possible for a violent or sexual offence to   **23–045** qualify for a custodial sentence not under CJA 1991, s. 1(2)(b) but under section 1(2)(a) and yet receive a longer than commensurate sentence in pursuit of section 2(2)(b). In practice (and in principle), any offence which is deemed to require such longer sentence should qualify for a custodial sentence under section 1(2)(b). In reaching an opinion as to the proper length of sentence under section 2(2)(a), the court must once more take into account all such information about the circumstances of the offence, including any aggravating or mitigating features (s. 3(3)(a)), and must also obtain and consider a pre-sentence report before forming such opinion (subject, of course, to the familiar exception for an offence triable only on indictment and the safety net clause that no custodial sentence passed without the benefit of a PSR will thereby by invalidated).

In *Cunningham* [1993] 1 W.L.R. 183, the Court of Appeal posed the question: does the provison (of s. 2(2)(a)) permit the sentencing judge to take the need for deterrence into account? Lord Taylor C.J. answered in the affirmative, reiterating that the purposes of a custodial sentence "must primarily be to punish and deter ... 'commensurate with the seriousness of the offence' must mean commensurate with the punishment and deterrence which the seriousness of the offence requires." This contrasts somewhat with the cautious note of realism sounded in the 1990 White Paper (2.8) that though deterrence has much immediate appeal, "it is unrealistic to construct sentencing arrangements on the basis that most offenders will weigh up the possiblities in advance and base their conduct on rational calculation". This seems particularly true of young offenders.

23–046 Given the apparently mandatory requirement of section 2(2)(a) that the custodial sentence *shall* be commensurate with the seriousness of the offence, proportionality appears on the face of it to be not merely a starting point but the finishing point in determining sentence. However, this must be qualified by the scope to mitigate sentence under CJA 1991, s. 28(1), taking account of any such matters which the court considers relevant.

Protection of the Public Criterion
The second and alternative ground justifying a custodial sentence is where the court is of the opinion:

> "where the offence is a violent or sexual offence, that only such a sentence would be adequate to protect the public from serious harm from him." (CJA 1991, s. 1(2)(b))

It is thus the successor to the now superseded criterion justifying custody for a young offender under CJA 1991, s. 1(4A)(b), that "only a custodial sentence would be adequate to protect the public from serious harm from him". Whereas the earlier version of the criterion was non-specific in regard to the nature of the offence, the offence must now be either a violent or sexual offence within the definitions provided by CJA 1991, s. 31(1). Use of this justification for a custodial sentence is likely to be highly exceptional in youth courts and cases raising public protection concern are much more likely to be committed to Crown Court for trial.

23–047 *Violent Offence*

This is defined as "an offence which leads, or is intended or likely to lead, to a person's death or to physical injury to a person, and includes an offence which is required to be charged as arson (whether or not it would otherwise fall within this definition)". This definition does not include psychological harm nor does it require that the injury caused or risked need be of a serious nature. The expansive drafting would appear to include such offences as dangerous driving, supplying dangerous drugs and more serious public order offences.

The ambiguity of the definition was highlighted in two decisions by **23–048** differently constituted courts of the Court of Appeal considering whether robbery at knifepoint, where the victim suffers no physical injury, is a "violent" offence. In *Murray* [1994] Crim. L.R. 383, the Court ruled not, finding it impossible to say what the offender would have done if the victim had resisted. In *Cochrane* [1994] Crim. L.R. 382, the Court ruled that it was a violent offence; it is not necessary to show that injury was a necessary or probable consequence and the act could have led to physical injury if a struggle ensued. It seems difficult to distinguish the two cases on their facts and the view in *Cochrane* may seem the more persuasive. Difficulty also arises where an imitation or unloaded firearm is used (*Touriq Khan* (1995) 16 Cr. App.R.(S.) 180 and *Palin* [1995] Crim. L.R. 435). As Thomas notes in his commentary on the latter case:

> "An offence which is likely to cause fear or shock is not a violent offence unless it does unintentionally result in physical injury (if the victim injures himself in trying to escape , or if the intended victim injures the offender in an attempt to apprehend him, for example). In a case when no physical injury has occurred, it seems essential to establish that the offence was intended or likely to lead to physical injury, if necessary by a Newton hearing, before the court exercises the powers given by section 2(2)(b)."

Sexual Offence   **23–049**
This is defined more narrowly by reference to specific statutes and means an offence contrary to any of the following (as revised by CJPOA 1994, Sched. 9, para. 44(1)):

(a)   Sexual Offences Act 1956, except under ss. 30, 31, 33–36;

(b)   Mental Health Act 1959, s. 128;

(c)   Indecency with Children Act 1960;

(d)   Theft Act 1968, s. 9 (burglary with intent to commit rape);

(e)   Criminal Law Act 1977, s. 54;

(f)   Protection of Children Act 1978;

(g)   Criminal Law Act 1977, s. 1 (conspiracy to commit any of the offences in (a)–(b);

(h)   Criminal Attempts Act 1981 (attempting to commit any of those offences);

(i)   Inciting another to commit any of those offences.

The amended definition resolves the problems highlighted in *Robinson* [1993] 1 W.L.R. 168 in dealing with an attempted rape offence. Indecent exposure is not an offence within any of the specified statutes and so does not constitute a sexual offence for the purposes of CJA 1991, Pt. I.

Protection from "Serious Harm"

This is defined by section 31(3) as "protecting members of the public from death or serious personal injury, whether physical or psychological, occasioned by further such offences committed by" the offender.

23-050   In the process of forming an opinion whether the public protection criterion is satisfied, the court must:

(i)   obtain and consider a pre-sentence report before forming any such opinion (s.3(1)), though if the offence is triable only on indictment the court is not obliged to do so if of the opinion that a report is unnecessary (s.3(2));

(ii)   take into account all such information about the circumstances of the offence (including any aggravating or mitigating factors) as is available to it (s.3(3)(a)).

In addition, the court is at liberty to take into account any information about the offender which is before it (s.3(3)(b)). There is thus no restriction on the use of information before the court. This was demonstrated in *Attorney General's Reference No. 4 of 1993 (Bingham)* [1993] Crim.L.R. 795 where the court took wide account of the offender's efforts to contact, pressurise and make sexual advances to a number of boys. Mitigating factors under CJA 1991, s. 28(1) will have less significance in circumstances where the protection of the public becomes the over-riding factor.

23-051   Clearly, the fact that an offence is "violent" or "sexual" does not preclude a non-custodial sentence. On the other hand, because the criterion is primarily based on the future risk posed by the offender, a custodial sentence may be justified even if the instant offence is insufficiently serious to merit a custodial sentence under the "so serious" criterion. What is less clear is whether *any* violent or sexual offence within the statutory definition could be regarded as sufficient to come within the public protection criterion, irrespective of level of seriousness. The nature and seriousness of the instant offence will clearly be a significant factor in the evaluation of risk but it is not necessary to show that the offender has caused serious harm either through the present offence or in the past. This is illustrated by *Bowler* (1994) 15 Cr. App. R.(S.) 78 where the defendant (aged 27) faced sentence for indecent assault on a girl aged six. He had a record of indecent assault, not of a prolonged nature or involving any attempt at penetration. His sexual pre-occupation was fetishistic, the touching of women's knickers. The Court of Appeal considered that such indecent assault may well lead to a serious psychological harm and some victims could be more than usually vulnerable. The offender thus presented a sufficient danger of serious harm and sentence of six years imprisonment was upheld, despite the relatively minor nature of the assault.

Powell (1992) 13 Cr. App. R.(S.) 202 (see para. 22–080) illustrates **23–052** circumstances of indecent assault where the offender aged under 21 was initially given the opportunity of a non-custodial sentence, a probation order with a requirement of residence at a probation hostel specialising in sexual offenders, but was subsequently sentenced to two years detention, following breach proceedings because of his failure to comply with that order. The Court of Appeal upheld the sentence, being satisfied that this was justified under the public protection criterion under the 1982 Act. The two incidents of indecent assault concerned, first, a mid-morning attack on a girl aged 13 as she was walking home. He put his arms around her waist from behind, pushed her to the ground and shouted "let me have it". He was intercepted and detained by a passing driver. He then admitted an earlier assault on a two and a half year old child whilst baby-sitting. He had one previous conviction, for indecently assaulting a woman aged 19. It is not clear whether the criterion would have been satisfied at the time of his conviction or whether the court was only able to reach that conclusion in the light of the evidence of his unsuitability for or his unwillingness to comply with the hostel regime and accept therapeutic help.

In practice, cases which satisfy the public protection criterion of section 1(2)(b) will also satisfy the "so serious" criterion of section 1(2)(a). The practical impact of the public protection provision focuses upon section 2(2)(b) and the justification for imposing a longer than commensurate term of custody.

Length of Sentence

Use of section 2(2)(b), cited at para. 23–044, to impose a longer than **23–053** commensurate term where this is considered necessary to protect the public from serious harm from the offender should be used with considerable caution, albeit that the exercise of this power, where the conditions set out are satisfied, is mandatory and not merely discretionary (*Bowler* (1994) 15 Cr. App. R.(S.) 78). As Thomas has argued (1993), the power to sentence under section 2(2)(b):

> "... is an extremely blunt instrument as the offender given such a longer sentence is not entitled to any special consideration under Part 2 of the Act (early release), and must serve at least half of the sentence before becoming eligible for release, even though he ceases to be dangerous during the sentence. It seems that the most sensible approach to the use of the new power would be to confine it to cases where there is the clearest possible basis for inferring that the offender is dangerous, and in such cases allowing a sentence which is substantially longer than would be proportionate to the seriousness of the offence on the analogy of life imprisonment. It would be regrettable if the power were to be used rather casually, on

the basis of slender evidence for inferring dangerousness, to justify sentences which are only marginally more severe than could be justified as commensurate sentences under section 2(2)(a). Such an approach would provide no significant degree of protection for the public in those cases where it is needed, and serve to confuse the difference in approach required by the two limbs of section 2(2)."

23-054 There have been no reported cases to date on the application of section 2(2)(b) to juveniles and it is to be anticipated that this power will be exercised in respect of young people only extremely rarely, in the Crown Court. Drawing upon the reported adult cases, it is possible to summarise the experience to date as follows, drawing particularly upon the guidance by Lord Taylor C.J. in *Crow* and *Pennington* (1995) 16 Cr. App. R. (S.) 409.

a. The court should take account of the circumstances of the current offence(s), the nature and circumstances of previous offences, medical and other evidence about the offender in determining whether there is a substantial risk of the offender committing violent/sexual offences in the future which may cause serious harm. A serious risk of some harm is insufficient basis for a longer than commensurate sentence (*Creasy* [1994] Crim. L.R. 308 which presents puzzling comparison with *Bowler* (see para. 23–051) in that following a boy aged 13 home from school and attempting to masturbate him through his trousers was considered merely "unpleasant and distressing").

b. If the offence is an isolated instance or there is no reason to fear a substantial risk of further violence or sexual offending, a longer than commensurate sentence will not be appropriate (see, for example, *Walsh* (1995) 16 Cr. App. R. (S.) 204). However, the absence of previous convictions for violence or sexual crime does not rule out a longer sentence provided that there is clear evidence of dangerousness and if other circumstances of the case show a substantial risk (*Nicholas* [1994] Crim. L.R. 76 and *Thomas* (1995) 16 Cr. pp. R. (S.) 616).

23-055 c. It is not essential for the threat to be to the public at large and may be presented to a very small number of specific people, as in *Hashi* (1995) 16 Cr. App. R. (S.) 121 where the offender's continuing obsession with his former partner created a serious risk to any man who associated with her. It may be, however, that a limited range of risk can be adequately covered by safeguards such as child protection procedures (*S.* (1995) 16 Cr. App. R. (S.) 303) or an injunction (*Nicholas* [1994] Crim. L.R. 76).

d. It is not necessary to obtain a psychiatric report for the purposes of s.2(2)(b), if the court is satisfied of the need for public protection in the light of all the circumstances of the case (*Hashi* (1995) 16 Cr. App. R.(S.) 121) but it will be common practice to seek such an assessment, if the danger appears to stem from a medical or personality problem, in order to find out whether a psychiatric disposal is more appropriate (*Fawcett* (1995) Cr. App. R. (S.) 55). There is, of course, a statutory requirement to obtain a psychiatric report if the offender is or appears to be mentally disordered, under CJA 1991 s.4.

e. Even where the maximum sentence is a determinate one, it will **23–056** usually be inappropriate to impose that maximum as some allowance should be made even in the worst cases, for a plea of guilty.

f. Account must be taken of the offender's age; with younger offenders, protection of the public must be balanced against the possible added risk that may be presented on release from a crushingly long sentence.

g. In dealing with co-offenders, they should be assessed separately so that it may be legitimate to impose a longer than commensurate sentence on one but a commensurate sentence upon the other. In *Bestwick and Huddlestone* (1995) 16 Cr. App. R. (S.) 168 a case of two young men involved in arson offences, the younger was assessed as a normal personality who enjoyed the excitement of fires but had no urge to light fires to experience that excitement. His co-offender was a seriously disturbed personality obsessed with lighting fires and likely to continue to set fire to property to gain excitement.

h. When the court is contemplating the imposition of a longer than commensurate sentence under section 2(2)(b), the proper practice is for the court to give an express indication to the defence advocate that such a sentence is being considered so that appropriate submissions can be made (*Baverstock* [1993] 1 W.L.R. 202).

Giving Reasons for Custody   **23–057**

CJA 1991, s. 1

"(4) Where a court passes a custodial sentence, it shall be its duty—
  (a) in a case not falling within subsection (3) above, to state in open court that it is of the opinion that either or both of paragraphs (a) and (b) of subsection (2) above apply and why it is of that opinion; and

  (b) in any case, to explain to the offender in open court and in ordinary language why it is passing a custodial sentence on him.
(5) A magistrates' court shall cause a reason stated by it under subsection (4) above to be specified in the warrant of commitment and to be entered in the register."

CJA 1991, s. 2

"(3) Where the court passes a custodial sentence for a term longer than is commensurate with the seriousness of the offence, or the combination of the offence and other offences associated with it, the court shall—

(a) state in open court that it is of the opinion that subsection (2)(b) above applies and why it is of that opinion; and

(b) explain to the offender in open court and in ordinary language why the sentence is for such a term."

23–058 The working reality of section 1(4) was clarified by the Court of Appeal in *Baverstock* [1993] 1 W.L.R. 202. Lord Taylor CJ indicated that (a) and (b) should not normally be a two-stage process:

"... the judge should be able at one and the same time to explain in ordinary language the reasons for his conclusions and tell the offender why he is passing a custodial sentence. When complying with this second requirement, however, the judge will be addressing the offender directly and if, in complying with subsection 4(a), he has not used ordinary language, it will be necessary for him to go on to do so in order to comply with subsection (4)(b) ... the precise words used by a judge are not critical. The statutory provisions are not to be treated as verbal tightropes for judges to walk. Given that the judge's approach accords with the effect of the statutory provisions, this court will not be sympathetic to appeals based on fine linguistic analysis of the sentencing remarks."

Though a magistrates' court is required to record on the warrant of commitment and in the court register its reason for passing a custodial sentence (s. 1(4)), it is not required to record its reasons for determining the length of the sentence.

23–059 **Effect of Time Spent on Remand on Length of Sentence**
Under the provision of CJA 1967, s. 67 that the length of any custodial sentence imposed on an offender shall be treated as reduced by any relevant period spent in police detention or prison custody, section 67(1A)(c) specifies that the following also counts for that purpose:

"any period during which, in connection with the offence for which the sentence was passed, he was remanded or committed to local authority accommodation by virtue of an order under CYPA 1969, s. 23 or MCA 1980, s. 37 and in accommodation provided for the purpose of restricting liberty."

23–060 Thus time so spent is treated as having been served for the purpose of determining whether the offender has served a half or other portion of his or her sentence for the purposes of early release provisions, as detailed below in regard to YOI and CYPA, s. 53 detention. In *Collins*

[1994] Crim. L.R. 872, the Court of Appeal indicated that "accommodation provided for the purpose of restricting liberty" is not limited to "secure accommodation" and that time spent in a "structured and supervised" unit thus counted towards sentence of section 53 detention.

Chapter 24

Specific Custodial Sentences

24–001 DETENTION IN A YOUNG OFFENDER INSTITUTION

Detention in a young offender institution (YOI) is the primary custodial sentence for young persons and the only custodial sentence available to a youth court. This sentence was introduced by the Criminal Justice Act 1988 amending the Criminal Justice Act 1982, replacing the previous orders of detention centre and youth custody by amalgamating them into a single sentence. The justification for two forms of custodial regime had become increasingly untenable. Whereas juvenile courts had not had power to sentence to borstal training, borstal's successor, the determinate sentence of youth custody, had been available to magistrates from its inception in CJA 1982. In the period following implementation of the 1982 Act there was evidence of a shift in magisterial sentencing away from shorter detention centre sentences towards longer youth custody sentences. Meanwhile, the regimes provided in the two kinds of establishment ceased to be so distinctively different. The borstal training tradition, or what was left of it, was replaced by a more routine custodial ethos in youth custody centres whilst the attempt in the early 1980s to restore the element of "short, sharp shock" into detention centres by a rigorous regime of drill, parades, physical education and inspections proved to be futile (Home Office, 1984).

24–002 There were no discernible differences in terms of re-conviction rates between those centres in which the experimental approach was introduced and other centres. Furthermore, the "tough" regimes were not perceived as significantly tougher by their trainees. Rather than reporting the desired deterrent effect, they appeared to find many aspects of the tough approach easier, more enjoyable and less stressful. As spare capacity in detention centres increased, so it became pragmatically convenient to transfer young offenders subject to youth custody to detention centre accommodation. The differentiation became increasingly artificial.

Power to Order YOI Detention

Criminal Justice Act 1982, s. 1A

"(1) Subject to ... CYPA 1933 s. 53, where—

(a) an offender under 21 but not less than 15 years of age is convicted of an offence which is punishable with imprisonment in the case of a person aged 21 or over; and

(b) the court is of the opinion that either or both of paragraphs (a) **24–003** and (b) of subsection (2) of section 1 of the Criminal Justice Act 1991 apply or the case falls within subsection (3) of that section,

the sentence that the court is to pass is a sentence of detention in a young offender institution."

Whereas the power to order YOI detention was previously subject to special criteria applicable only to young offenders by which a defendant could be judged to qualify for a custodial sentence, the sentence is now determined on exactly the same statutory basis as imprisonment, and subject to the restrictions on imposing custodial sentences set out in CJA 1991, Pt I. Note that there is no power to impose a sentence of YOI detention on an offender under the age of 18 for contempt of court (CJA 1991, s.63(5) amending CJA 1982, s.9; see *Byas* [1995] Crim. L.R. 439). As a probation order may not be imposed for contempt (*Palmer* (1992) 13 Cr. App. R.(S.) 595, which appears also to exclude a community service order or supervision order), the only available sanction would appear to be a fine.

Maximum Term

Criminal Justice Act 1982, s. 1A

"(2) Subject to section 1B(2) below, the maximum term of detention in a young offender institution that a court may impose for an offence is the same as the maximum term of imprisonment that it may impose for that offence."

Criminal Justice Act 1982, s. 1B

"(2) In the case of an offender aged 15, 16 or 17 the maximum term of **24–004** detention in a young offender institution that a court may impose is whichever is the lesser of—

(a) the maximum term of imprisonment the court may impose for the offence; and

(b)   24 months.

(4) A court shall not pass on an offender aged 15, 16 or 17 a sentence of detention in a young offender institution whose effect would be that the offender would be sentenced to a total term which exceeds 24 months."

The maximum term for youths was increased from 12 months to 24 months by the Criminal Justice and Public Order Act 1994, s. 17, thus extending the powers of the Crown Court. Youth courts remain subject to the limitation upon the use of custody contained in MCA 1980, ss. 31 and 32 which specify a maximum of six months in respect of any one offence. The maximum aggregate term which magistrates can impose is six months, unless two of the terms are imposed for offences triable either way, in which case the maximum aggregate term is 12 months. This change may promote a greater use of committals for sentence from the youth courts (MCA 1980, s. 37(1), see para. 12–003). The new maximum does not apply to offences committed before the commencement date for this provision, February 3, 1995 (CJPOA 1994 Commencement Order No.5).

24–005   Where an offender is convicted of more than one offence for which a sentence of YOI may be passed or is convicted of such an offence whilst already serving a previously imposed YOI term, the court may pass consecutive sentences in the same way as applies to sentences of imprisonment (s. 1A(5) but subject to s. 1B(4)). "Total term" in section 1B(4) is defined in section 1B(6) (see para. 24–008).

The question has arisen in a number of cases whether it is legitimate to sentence a young offender who pleads guilty to the maximum available term of YOI, bearing in mind the familiar principle that those who plead guilty can expect credit for having done so. As a general rule maximum sentences in such instances are not appropriate, in order to preserve the discount principle (see *Stewart* (1983) 5 Cr. App. R.(S.) 320 and, for more recent examples, *George* (1993) 14 Cr. App. R.(S.) 12 where sentence for a "quite disgraceful" offence of criminal damage worth £33,000 to a church committed by a 16 year old was reduced from 12 to 10 months and *Murphy* (1994) 15 Cr. App. R.(S.) 176). The exceptions where the maximum term can properly be imposed are:

24–006   (a)   where the offender is eligible for a sentence of detention under CYPA 1933, s. 53(2) and credit is given by passing a YOI sentence instead (*Reynolds* (1985) 7 Cr. App. R.(S.) 335);

       (b)   where the offence is a specimen charge;

       (c)   in the most exceptional circumstances, where the nature of the offence requires the maximum term in the public interest, though case law is not clear cut. In *Reay* [1992] Crim. L.R. 457, a 15 year old had pleaded guilty to offences of taking without consent and reckless driving. Sentence of 12 months YOI was upheld because of the seriousness and local prevalence of the offence and the danger to life and limb involved. See also

Winspear (1987) 9 Cr. App. R.(S.) 243 where a 16 year old had committed two offences of domestic burglary on the same house on the day he was released from a custodial sentence imposed for that kind of crime. Stephen Brown L.J. commented that "there are cases which merit the maximum term", irrespective of plea. Compare *Robinson and Scurry* (1994) 15 Cr. App. R.(S.) 452, where the Court of Appeal concluded that an 24–007 episode of aggravated vehicle taking, in which two 20 year olds had taken a car and used it to commit a burglary, later driving it at speeds of up to 110 mph, through a road block, eventually colliding with another vehicle at 102 mph, causing severe cuts and other injuries to the occupants, did not fall into the "exceptional" category, despite the "appalling and dangerous driving". Maximum sentence of YOI was thus reduced to reflect their guilty plea at the earliest opportunity, thus saving expense and sparing witnesses the ordeal of reliving their experience.

More recently, *Sharkey and Daniels* (1995) 16 Cr. App. R.(S.) 257 further illustrates that the "discount" principle will apply even in cases (such as episodes of extremely reckless high speed vehicle taking) where the pressure to dilute its application is very strong. The Court of Appeal there indicated two circumstances in which the maximum sentence may properly be imposed: where the maximum term for the offence is demonstrably too low, having been fixed some while previously, and where the offender is a danger to the public and the need to protect the public outweighs the usual discount policy. In *McDonogh* [1995] Crim. L.R. 512 (outlined at para. 22–076), the Court of Appeal declined the appellant's argument that he should have received less than the maximum term of YOI available to a 17 year old on being resentenced for burglary, as he had pleaded guilty prior to initial sentence of a combination order, now revoked. The Court stated that the restriction of the maximum sentence did not mean that the court should start with the proposition that the maximum term was the proper sentence and then make an appropriate reduction where there had been a guilty plea. Unfortunately, the judgement does not make clear whether the basis for the decision was that the offender had received benefit of discount by avoiding sentence of s.53(2) detention. As the Crown Court had initially felt able to impose a community sentence, this would not seem a plausible explanation for the Court of Appeal's decision. In *Hastings*, [1995] Crim. L.R. 661 1995 the court of appeal upheld a maximum term for dangerous driving because the offender aged 22 has no realistic prospect of contesting the matter and this was one of the worst instances of this offence, without any mitigating factors.

CJPOA 1994, s. 48 now places the principle upon a statutory footing, requiring the sentencing court to take into account the stage in the proceedings at which the offender indicated an intention to plead guilty and the circumstances in which this indication is given (see para 9–018).

24–008 *Sentence in Excess of Maximum Term*

Criminal Justice Act 1982, s. 1B

"(5) Where the total term of detention in a young offender institution to which an offender aged 15, 16 or 17 is sentenced exceeds 24 months, so much of the term as exceeds 24 months shall be treated as remitted.

(6) In this section 'total term' means—

    (a) in the case of an offender sentenced (whether or not on the same occasion) to two or more terms of detention in a young offender institution which are consecutive or wholly or partly concurrent, the aggregate of those terms;

    (b) in the case of any other offender, the term of the sentence of detention in a young offender institution in question."

The exercise of remission was illustrated in *Anderson* [1992] Crim. L.R. 171 where a 16 year old was sentenced to three years YOI, no reference being made by CYPA, s. 53(2). As the sentence was not referred back to the sentencer for review and variation under Supreme Court Act 1981, s. 47, the Court of Appeal held that sentence should take effect as one of 12 months YOI, the maximum term permissible. See also *Venison* (1994) 15 Cr. App. R.(S.) 624 where a sentence of "two years' detention" passed without reference to section 53(2) was varied to 12 months detention in YOI (the maximum term of YOI then available). Although the sentencer may have had section 53(2) in mind, the Court of Appeal stated that it was incumbent on sentencers to make plain the precise statutory provisions under which they were passing sentence. The ambiguity could only be resolved in favour of the defendant. See also para. 24–042

24–009 *Minimum Term*

Juveniles are subject to a greater minimum term than young adults, two months instead of 21 days. The Criminal Justice Bill which preceded the 1991 Act had originally proposed two months as the standard minimum for 15 to 20 year olds, to emphasise that custody should be reserved for more serious offences and to encourage sentencers to impose community penalties instead of very short detention periods. A backbench amendment reducing the minimum for 18 to 20 year olds was subsequently accepted by the Government, to provide flexibility by allowing magistrates to sentence young adults to shorter periods of detention for offences which would not attract a custodial sentence for juveniles. CJA 1991 amended CJA 1982 by abolishing differences between males and females in regard to the minimum age at which sentence of YOI could be imposed and the minimum length of sentence.

Criminal Justice Act 1982, s. 1A   **24-010**

"(3) Subject to subsection (4) below, a court shall not pass a sentence for an offender's detention in a young offender institution for less than the minimum period applicable to the offender under subsection (4A) below.

(4) A court may pass a sentence of detention in a young offender institution for less than the minimum period applicable for an offence under section 65(6) of the Criminal Justice Act 1991.

(4A) For the purposes of subsections (3) and (4) above, the minimum period of detention applicable to an offender is—

(a) in the case of an offender under 21 but not less than 18 years of age, the period of 21 days; and

(b) in the case of an offender under 18 years of age, the period of two months."

CJA 1991, s. 65(6) specifies penalties for failure to comply with supervision requirements on release from YOI (see para. 24-029).

Determination of Age

The offender's age shall be deemed to be that which it appears to the **24-011** court to be after considering any available evidence (CJA 1982, s. 1(6)). Where the court has imposed sentence on the basis of the defendant's apparent age, the sentence is not invalidated if it is subsequently discovered that the assumption was incorrect (*Brown* (1989) 11 Cr. App. R.(S.) 263). *Brown* concerned a defendant who appeared to be 21 but was in fact only 20. He was clearly liable to a custodial sentence of some kind. If the age uncertainty turns on whether the defendant is 14 or 15 and there is thus a more significant issue of sentencing power at stake, it is questionable whether the approach in *Brown* should apply. In the event of dispute about the offender's age, the best course will probably be to adjourn until the matter can be resolved (*Steed* (1990) 12 Cr. App. R.(S.) 230).

YOI Accommodation   24-012

An offender sentenced to YOI shall be detained in such an institution unless the Secretary of State has directed their detention in a prison or remand centre, but if the offender is under 18 at the time of that direction, this shall be "only for a temporary purpose" (CJA 1982, s. 1C).

YOI Regime: "High Impact Programmes"

As part of the Prison Service's Corporate Plan 1995–98, a pilot project providing "a longer and more active day and a more demanding regime" will be introduced in at least one YOI, Thorn Cross. This will be modelled on "boot camps", a penal initiative in the United States since 1983 to impose quasi-military discipline or "shock incarceration" on young offenders, involving drill, inspections, hard physical work and exercise, education, rope skills and life skills, in spartan conditions for around 16 hours a day. Not surprisingly, this has been quickly identified as an attempt to re-introduce the discredited concept of the "short, sharp shock" and has attracted criticism from the Penal Affairs Consortium (1995) and the Prison Reform Trust (Nathan, 1995) and scepticism from the Prison Service officials who reported on a visit to various camps in the United States (Brooks *et al.*, 1994), in the light of research evaluations of the American experience to date.

Recent Trends in YOI Sentencing
The reduction in numbers of young persons sentenced to immediate custody, reflecting not only the demographic shrinkage of this age group within the general population but also the greater use of non-custodial options, is illustrated in the following Table, though the most recent figures suggest that a re-expansion of the use of custody may now be in train (figures available for males only).

Age	15	16	17
1988	1,014	1,908	4,110
1990	395	879	2,227
1992	433	819	1,908
1993	504	957	1,806

Early indications of changes in sentencing practice as a result of the implementation of the 1991 Act suggested a slightly reduced use of immediate custody. The Home Office provided the following estimate of the percentage change between the first three quarters and the final quarter of 1992 in the use of custody for indictable offences.

Age Group	Quarters 1–3	Quarter 4
14–17	8.4	5.8
17	11.5	9.3

24–013 A NACRO survey (1993) of sentencing in the youth courts in the first six months following implementation of the Act showed that YOI sentences were imposed upon three per cent of 15 year olds, 6.6 per cent of 16 year olds and five per cent of 17 year olds in the sample. Figures are awaited to illuminate the impact of the amendments to the Act introduced in August 1993, though the population of sentenced male offenders aged under 21 began to rise from that date, expanding from 2,600 60 2,800 by the end of 1993. The population of sentenced male offenders aged under 18, as of 30 June, stood at 1,571 in 1988, falling to 726 in 1992, but rising to 753 in 1993 (Home Office 1994b).

The recent use of immediate custody as a percentage of all persons of the relevant age group sentenced for indictable offences further illustrates the trend.

Aged 14 and under 18

	Males			Females			Persons		
	Magist.	Crown	All Courts	Magist.	Crown	All Courts	Magist	Crown	All Courts
1983	10.9	61.6	15.3	6.7	22.5	1.6	9.8	59.6	13.9
1988	8.9	48.4	13.7	1.4	20.1	2.6	8.2	46.8	12.6
1992	6.5	39.2	10.4	0.9	14.8	1.7	5.8	37.8	9.4
1993	9.3	35.8	11.1	1.9	18.5	2.6	8.5	34.7	10.2

Source: Criminal Statistics 1993

Average length of sentence (in months) for male persons over the last six years for which figures are available, showing a slight increase for 15-year-olds and a recent reduction for 17-year-olds, were as follows:

Age	15	16	17
1988	3.3	4.4	8.7
1989	4.2	4.8	9.7
1990	4.2	4.8	9.9
1991	4.0	4.7	9.7
1992	4.1	4.7	10.0
1993	4.2	4.6	5.2

Source: Criminal Statistics 1993

The percentage distribution of sentence lengths for male persons in **24–015** 1993 (including also s.53(2) deletion) were as follows:

Age	less than 3 months	3–4 months	4–6 months	6–12 months	12 months - 2 years	2–4 years	4 + years
15	19	26	30	23	2	*	*
16	16	24	30	26	5	*	*
17	16	19	26	32	7	*	*

Early Release
Sentences of YOI detention are treated on almost exactly the same **24–016** footing as sentences of imprisonment for the purposes of CJA 1991, Part II (s. 43(1)). Thus the detainee serving less than four years has the status of "short-term prisoner" subject to release after serving one-half of sentence (CJA 1991, s. 33(5)). There are, however, two important differences distinguishing the young offender from the adult prisoner. The first affects those serving sentence of YOI of exactly 12 months. Whereas the adult offender serving sentence of 12 months or more is

subject to "automatic conditional release" (ACR) on licence after serving half of their sentence, short-term young offenders serving sentence of 12 months or less are released unconditionally at that point, *if under the age of 18* (s. 43(4)(a)). This difference is made less significant by the fact that all young offenders, unlike adult prisoners serving less than 12 months imprisonment, are subject to statutory supervision on their release from young offender institution, even if they are not subject to licence under automatic conditional release arrangements (CJA 1991, s. 65; see para. 24–028).

24–017   Section 43(4) does not state the relevant date at which the offender's age is determined but implies that the moment for deciding whether the offender is under 18 is the halfway point of their sentence.

Release on Licence

Detainees serving a sentence of 12 months YOI who are 18 at the halfway point of sentence will be released on licence at that point under ACR arrangements.

Length of Licence

Licence remains in force until the date on which the detainee would (but for their release) have served three-quarters of their sentence (CJA 1991, s. 37(1)). This is subject to a statutory minimum period of one-quarter of the total sentence term, even if this takes the licence period beyond the three-quarters point. This minimum is designed to ensure a sufficiently useful and viable period of oversight. It has most significance when time on remand contributes to the calculation of early release (see para. 23–059). However, the licence cannot run beyond the full term 100 per cent point of sentence, even if this falls within the minimum period.

24–018   In the case of young offenders covered by CJA 1991, s. 65, however, section 65(4) provides that if licence expires in less than three months (*i.e.* because the full term of sentence is reached), the offender will remain subject to a requirement of statutory supervision under section 65(1), beginning on the date of expiry and ending three months from the date of release.

The Licence period in respect of a sexual offender (as defined by CJA 1991, s. 31(1)) may be extended to run until the completion of the full term of sentence, if so ordered by the sentencing court (CJA 1991, s. 44; see para. 24–061).

Licence Conditions

The primary licence requirement is that the offender "must place (him or herself) under the supervision of whichever probation officer or social worker is nominated for this purpose from time to time", the objectives of such supervision being the protection of the public, the prevention of re-offending and the achievement of successful re-integration in the community. The specific standard conditions of supervision are as follows:

"While under supervision you must: **24–019**

(i)   keep in touch with your supervising officer in accordance with any reasonable instructions that you may from time to time be given;

(ii) if required, receive visits from your supervising officer at your home at reasonable hours and for reasonable periods;

(iii) live where reasonably approved by your supervising officer and notify him or her in advance of any proposed change of address;

(iv) undertake only such employment as your supervising officer reasonably approves and notify him or her in advance of any proposed change in employment or occupation;

(v)   not travel outside the United Kingdom without obtaining the prior permission of your supervising officer;

(vi) not take any action which would jeopardise the objectives of your supervision, namely to protect the public, prevent you from re-offending and secure your successful reintegration into the community." (HOC 104/1992 Annex A)

As release on licence is automatic, the Home Office envisages that most   **24–020** short-term detainees will be released on a "standard licence". However there is provision for the governor of the establishment from which the detainee is released to approve special additional conditions in exceptional cases, when recommended to do so by the supervising officer in the interests of devising an effective programme of supervision. Any such extra conditions must be chosen from a list of approved conditions, detailed at para. 24–078.

As Circular Instruction 27/1992, para. 25 points out:

"there is no mechanism to delay release if a prisoner declines to co-operate with supervision ... the prisoner may have refused to give a release address. If the home area is known, the prisoner should be instructed to report to the duty officer at a probation office in the home area. If the home area is not known, it may be necessary to instruct the prisoner to report to the duty officer at a probation office in the petty sessional area where the prisoner was tried for the current offence. If agreed with the Probation Service, and as a last resort, part or all of the discharge grant may be sent to the reporting office as an incentive to turn up".

If the prisoner is willing to co-operate but is genuinely homeless, the   **24–021** Probation Service will be responsible for trying to find accommodation but it is recognised that this cannot be guaranteed, thus making licence requirements very difficult to enforce if the offender is moving around frequently between temporary bases.

Release Direct from Court

An offender may be entitled to be released on licence direct from court if they have spent a sufficient period of time on remand in custody or following a reduction of their sentence on appeal. (Note that the former "five day rule" which operated to ensure that remission could not reduce the actual term to be served to less than five days was abolished upon introduction of early release under CJA 1991.) Such offenders are still liable to compulsory supervison and should be issued with licence and notice of supervision at the court. Court duty probation officers will identify the supervising officer and determine reporting instructions. Detailed guidance is provided by Circular Instruction 39/1992.

24–022 *The Process of Supervision*

In the revised *National Standard for Supervision Before and After Release from Custody* (1995) the Home Office stipulates the following procedures to be exercised by probation officers and local authority social services departments:

First interview after release: the supervising officer should see the offender where practicable on the same day as release and in any event on the next working day after release (para. 28).

Home Visit: a home visit should take place within five working days of the first interview so that the offender's address can be confirmed and arrangements made for a second interview (para. 31).

24–023 *Second Interview:* within ten working days of release (para. 32).

Communication with Police: the police should be given release, licence and address information as soon as possible and in any case within 15 working days of release (para. 33).

Supervision Plan: a plan setting out the purpose, desired outcomes, timetable of key targets and the nature/frequency of contact should be finalised by the conclusion of the second interview (para. 32) and should be reviewed at least quarterly (para. 39).

Subsequent Contact: after the second interview, meetings should occur weekly for the remainder of the first four weeks after release. Thereafter, there should be at least fortnightly contact for the second and third months following release; subsequently, contact should be not less than monthly (para. 40).

24–024 *Failure to Comply:* any apparent failure to comply with requirements should be followed up promptly and within two working days at most. Where an offender fails to attend an appointment or to comply with any other licence condition, the supervising officer should institute breach action immediately or issue a formal warning of the likely consequences of further failure to comply. A warning should be given in writing to the offender and, in the case of a young person under 18, to his or her parents or other responsible adult. The supervising officer should confirm that the offender (and the parents or other responsible adult where relevant) has clearly understood the warning and should note their response on the record. At most, two warnings within any 12 month period of the licence may be given before breach proceedings are instituted (paras. 48–51).

Breach of Licence

Criminal Justice Act 1991, s. 38

"(1) A short-term prisoner—
    (a)   who is released on licence under this Part; and   **24–025**

    (b)   who fails to comply with such conditions as may for the time being be specified in the licence,
shall be liable on summary conviction to a fine not exceeding level 3 on the standard scale.

(2) The magistrates' court by which a person is convicted of an offence under subsection (1) above may, whether or not it passes any other sentence on him—
    (a)   suspend the licence for a period not exceeding six months; and

    (b)   order him to be recalled to prison for the period during which the licence is so suspended.
(3) On the suspension of the licence of any person under this section, he shall be liable to be detained in pursuance of his sentence and, if at large, shall be deemed to be unlawfully at large."

Failure to comply with an ACR licence requirement is thus a summary **24–026** offence punishable on conviction by a fine not exceeding level three. The convicting magistrates' court also has the power, whether or not it imposes a fine (or another measure available for a non-imprisonable summary offence such as discharge), to suspend the licence for a period not exceeding six months and order the licensee to be recalled to custody for the suspension period. If recalled, the detainee, if not already released at the end of the specified suspension period, is entitled to be released unconditionally at the three-quarters point of sentence. Unlike the provisions of the 1991 Act regarding breach of community orders (Sched. 2, para. 3(2)) and the offence of failure to comply with post-custody supervision (s. 65(6)), s. 38(1) does not refer to failure "without reasonable excuse" and thus appears to expect stricter liability. This would appear to be an unintended omission and it seems open to the court to construe the subsection accordingly. The *National Standard* (1995, para. 48) certainly anticipates that the supervising officer should not enforce the licence by prosecution where the offender's explanation for an apparent default is acceptable.

24–027   This provision does not specify the manner in which the person on licence should be brought before the court and thus is subject to the general provisions of MCA 1980, s. 1 governing issue of summons, *etc.* A warrant in the first instance could not ordinarily be issued as the offence is not punishable with imprisonment (only suspension of licence) unless the person's address is not sufficiently established for a summons to be served on him or her (s. 1(4)), *e.g.* if their breach of licence arises from an un-notified change of address. However, these restrictions do not apply to persons who have not attained the age of 18, though courts may apply the restrictions as persuasive guidelines in the case of youths.

If the person does not attend in answer to summons, MCA 1980, s. 13(3) places similar restrictions on the issue of a warrant, *i.e.* a warrant may only be issued if the offence is imprisonable or the court proposes to impose a disqualification. This would mean that the court would ordinarily be unable to use a warrant to bring the licensee before the court, despite the power to return him or her to custody and would have no option but to proceed in the licencee's absence. If licence is then suspended, the short-term prisoner is unlawfully at large and liable to arrest and return to prison custody. Here too, the restrictions do not apply to persons under 18 but may be followed as appropriate guidelines. To proceed in the young person's absence would be extremely unusual. If a warrant is to be issued, the court may initially prefer a letter to be sent to the juvenile's parents warning them of the court's powers in the hope of prompting attendance. Suspension of licence in the licensee's absence can be an important consideration if their whereabouts are unknown for otherwise their avoidance of court appearance until after the expiry of their licence will leave the court simply with power to impose a fine.

24–028 *Release on Post-Custody Supervision*

The long-standing tradition of compulsory benevolence in imposing statutory supervision upon young persons leaving custody continues under Part III of the 1991 Act, separate from the early release provisions of Part II and applicable to sentences which in the case of an adult would lead to automatic unconditional release. This oversight is intended to ensure help in resettlement for those who may be particularly vulnerable and inexperienced, perhaps facing independent life for the first time and with a particularly high risk of reconviction. Nevertheless, many trainees completing their YOI terms can resent this form of additional obligatory oversight and it can sometimes appear that the sanctions exist to ensure contact yet the contact is sought simply to avoid the risk of sanction. It is a challenge to those charged with supervisory responsibility to make the link a more rewarding opportunity rather than a merely formal exercise.

Criminal Justice Act 1991, s. 65

"(1) Where a person under the age of 22 years ('the offender') is released from a term of detention in a YOI ... he shall be under the supervision of a probation officer or a social worker of a local authority social services department."

The period of supervision for those serving YOI sentences is three **24–029** months commencing on date of release (s. 65(3)). The previous provision under CJA 1982, s. 15 for a sliding scale of supervisory period depending on the length of sentence is superseded.

Supervision Requirements

The offender shall comply with such requirements as may be specified by the Secretary of State (s. 65(5)). The requirements of supervision are currently the same as the standard conditions of ACR licence (see para 24–019).

Failure to Comply with Requirements

Criminal Justice Act 1991, s. 65

"(6) A person who without reasonable excuse fails to comply with a requirement imposed under subsection (5) above shall be liable on summary conviction—

(a) to a fine not exceeding level 3 on the standard scale; or

(b) to an appropriate custodial sentence for a period not exceeding 30 days, but not liable to be dealt with in any other way."

The appropriate sentence for an offender aged under 21 at the time of **24–030** sentence is detention in a young offender institution (s. 65(7)(b)). If sentenced to custody under s. 65(6), the offender is not liable to an additional period of supervision on release but their original liability to supervision remains in force and, if still current, continues after their release (s. 65(8)).

Early Release on Compassionate Grounds

The Home Secretary may release a YOI detainee at any time if satisfied that "exceptional circumstances exist which justify the release on compassionate grounds" (CJA 1991, s. 36(1)). For the Home Office's interpretation of what constitutes compassionate grounds, see para. 24–082. If the detainee would otherwise have been released under "automatic conditional release" arrangements (*i.e.* as a "short-term prisoner", if serving sentence of 12 months and aged 18 at the halfway point of sentence) then their release will be on licence and subject to supervision, expiring at the three-quarters point of sentence.

If the detainee would have been otherwise subject to unconditional **24–031** release (other than being liable to supervision under CJA 1991, s. 65) their release will be on licence expiring at the half-way point of sentence. If licence in either case expires in less than three months from date of release, then the detainee will be subject to supervision under section 65 until the expiry of three months from their date of release.

Time on Remand in Custody before Sentence

The provisions for early release specify proportions of sentence which have to be served or expire before a detainee is either released on licence or is entitled to unconditional release or is no longer subject to licence. The critical points of sentence are one-half, two-thirds and three-quarters. Any time on remand in custody or in local authority secure accommodation which counts under CJA 1967, s. 67 towards the reduction of the sentence to be served also counts in the calculation of the relevant proportions (s. 41(1) and (2)).

24–032   However, time on remand does not have the effect of reducing any licence period below the minimum specified by section 41(3) which, in the case of short-term detainees, is one-quarter of sentence. Thus an offender sentenced to 12 months YOI, having spent eight months on remand, who is aged 18 at the halfway point of their sentence, will be entitled to immediate release on licence but the licence will not terminate after one month when the three-quarters point of sentence is reached, but after three months (*i.e.* after one-quarter of sentence). However, licence requirements expire at the full term point of sentence, even if the minimum period has not been satisfied.

Disciplinary Offences in Custody

CJA 1991 replaced the previous system of granting or forfeiting "remission" with a new procedure permitting "additional days" to be awarded for misbehaviour in custody. Additional days extend the time to be served before entitlement to release either on ACR licence or young offender supervision. The period of any licence or supervision to be served remains unchanged but is completed correspondingly later. "Additional days" may be remitted in certain circumstances, *e.g.* for subsequent good behaviour.

Conviction during Currency of Original Sentence

24–033 On release from young offender institution, an offender is subject to the provisions of CJA 1991, s. 40 in respect of any conviction for a new imprisonable offence committed prior to the expiry of the full term of their YOI sentence (CJA 1991, s. 43(1)).

Criminal Justice Act 1991, s. 40

"(1) This section applies to a short-term or long-term prisoner who is released under this Part if—
    (a) before the date on which he would (but for his release) have

served his sentence in full, he commits an offence punishable with imprisonment; and

(b) whether before or after that date, he is convicted of that offence ('the new offence').

(2) Subject to subsection (3) below, the court by or before which a person to whom this section applies is convicted of the new offence may, whether or not it passes any other sentence on him, order him to be returned to prison for the whole or any part of the period which—

(a) begins with the date of the order; and

(b) is equal in length to the period between the date on which the new offence was committed and the date mentioned in subsection (1) above.

(3) A magistrates' court—   **24–034**

(a) shall not have power to order a person to whom this section applies to be returned to prison for a period of more than six months; but

(b) may commit him in custody or on bail to the Crown Court for sentence and the Crown Court to which he has been so committed may make such an order with regard to him as is mentioned in subsection (2) above.

(4) The period for which a person to whom this section applies is ordered under subsection (2) above to be returned to prison—

(a) shall be taken to be a sentence of imprisonment for the purposes of this Part;

(b) shall, as the court may direct, either be served before and be followed by, or be served concurrently with, the sentence imposed for the new offence; and

(c) in either case shall be disregarded in determining the appropriate length of that sentence."

This section embodies a new concept of being "at risk", designed to restore greater meaning to the sentence passed by the court so that it carries meaning and consequences through to the end of the full term, even after the expiry of any licence or post-release supervision period.

The critical date is the date of the new offence, not of conviction for **24–035** that offence. This means that the later the fresh offending occurs in the passage of time towards full term, the less the offender's liability to serve their unserved period of sentence.

The new offence must be imprisonable, so that a failure by a "short-term detainee" to comply with a condition of licence under automatic conditional release arrangements does not trigger section 40 consequences as the breach is not an imprisonable offence under section 38, even though the offender may be returned to custody following suspension of their licence. However, failure to comply with a section 65 supervision requirement is punishable with detention or imprisonment (section 65(6)) and thus appears to attract section 40 consequences, though this may seem an unnecessary or unintended degree of double jeopardy.

24–036   The court dealing with the new offence should first decide the apropriate sentence for that offence without regard to the fact that it may also be considering a return to custody under section 40. If the court imposes a custodial sentence, it then has to decide whether to exercise its power under section 40 and, if so, whether this should be served concurrently or not. If the court decides that the new offence is insufficiently serious to justify a custodial sentence but is serious enough to justify a community sentence, and then wishes to exercise power under section 40 to return the offender to custody, the court will face the difficulty that the offender will be unable to embark on their community order until their release after serving their outstanding custodial liability. It is unclear, for instance, whether a section 40 order would be considered incompatible with a probation order imposed for the new offence (see para. 18–014), though in practice this will probably depend on the length of delay before the new probation order can be supervised.

24–037 DETENTION FOR GRAVE CRIMES

Children and Young Persons Act 1933, s. 53

"(1) A person convicted of an offence who appears to the court to have been under the age of eighteen years at the time the offence was committed shall not, if he is convicted of murder, be sentenced to imprisonment for life ... but in lieu thereof the court shall (notwithstanding anything in this or any other Act) sentence him to be detained during Her Majesty's pleasure, and if so sentenced he shall be liable to be detained in such place and under such conditions as the Secretary of State may direct.

(2) Subsection (3) below applies—

  (a) where a person of at least 10 but not more than 17 years is convicted on indictment of—

    (i) any offence punishable in the case of an adult with imprisonment for 14 years or more, not being an offence the sentence for which is fixed by law, or

    (ii) an offence under section 14 of the Sexual Offences Act 1956 (indecent assault on a woman);

  (b) where a young person is convicted of—

    (i) an offence under section 1 of the Road Traffic Act 1988 (causing death by dangerous driving), or

    (ii) an offence under section 3A of the Road Traffic Act 1988 (causing death by careless driving while under influence of drink or drugs).

(3) Where this subsection applies, then, if the court is of opinion **24–038**
that none of the other methods in which the case may legally be
dealt with is suitable, the court may sentence the offender to be
detained for such period, not exceeding the maximum term of
imprisonment with which the offence is punishable in the case of
an adult, as may be specified in the sentence; and where such a
sentence has been passed the child or young person shall, during
that period, be liable to be detained in such place and on such
conditions as the Secretary of State shall direct.

(4) A person detained pursuant to the directions of the Secretary of
State under this section shall, while so detained, be deemed to be in
legal custody."

Life Detention under section 53(1)   24–039
A mandatory sentence of life detention during Her Majesty's pleasure is
prescribed for murder by young offenders aged under 18 at the time of
the offence. The sentencer has no power to make a minimum
recommendation under the Murder (Abolition of Death Penalty) Act
1965, s.1(2).
   Though young persons sentenced to detention during Her Majesty's
pleasure for murder under section 53(1) are to be treated as persons
serving life imprisonment (CJA 1991, s. 43(2)), they are not affected by
early release procedures initiated by the 1991 Act. The Secretary of State
may refer their case to the Parole Board at any stage, but in practice they
are dealt with under the same procedures as apply to all mandatory
lifers. The Secretary of State thus determines the minimum period (the
'tariff') to be served by them to satisfy the requirements of retribution
and deterrence, after consultation with the trial judge and the Lord
Chief Justice. The offender is informed of the substance of this judicial
advice and has the opportunity to make written representations as to
why this recommended period should not be increased. Reasons will be
given to the offender for any departure from the judicial view. Of 217
young offenders detained under section 53(1) in February 1995, two have
been given a tariff of five years or less; 33, six to nine years; 139, ten to 14
years; and 43, 15 to 20 years. Their first review by the Parole Board will
normally take place three years before the end of their tariff period.
Since April 1993, offenders have been able to have access to the reports
before the Parole Board and to receive reasons for the Board's decisions
and recommendations. The question whether persons detained under
section 53(1) should be treated on a basis more akin to discretionary
lifers and thus subject to judicial review procedures (as provided by the
discretionary lifer panel system, see para. 24–074) is currently the
subject of applications before the European Commission of Human
Rights (*Hussain and Prem Singh v. United Kingdom*).
   If release on licence is recommended by the Parole Board, the
Secretary of State has the discretion to accept or reject that advice. In
exercising the discretion to release the offender, the Secretary of State

shall consult the Lord Chief Justice and the trial judge, if available. If released on licence, section 53(1) detainees remain on licence in accordance with CJA 1991, s. 37(3), *i.e.* until death, unless licence is revoked upon recall to custody under section 39(1) or (2) (see para. 24–080). While on licence, the offender shall comply with conditions including supervision by a probation officer (or local authority social worker if released under the age of 22). Licence requirements are as outlined at paras. 24–019 and 24–078.

24-040 Detention under section 53(2) and (3)
The maximum length of a sentence of detention in a young offender institution which can be passed on an offender aged under 18 before the Crown Court, is 24 months. However, in the case of a juvenile convicted of a very serious crime, a longer sentence of detention may be imposed under section 53(3) powers. Seventeen year olds now qualify for this sentence by virtue of their new status as "young persons" (CJA 1991 Sched. 8, para. 1(3)). Offences for which this sentence is available are restricted to those punishable with imprisonment for 14 years or more, the only exception (for all juveniles) being indecent assault on a woman, which qualifies even though it carries a maximum sentence of 10 years. In the case of juveniles aged 14 or over, two further offences qualify despite carrying a maximum sentence of 10 years: causing death by dangerous driving and causing death by careless driving while under the influence of drink or drugs.

Since the reduction of the maximum sentence for non-dwelling-house burglary to 10 years (CJA 1991, s. 26), this offence is not eligible for section 53(3) detention. Among the more common offences which qualify for section 53(3) powers are:

(i)   wounding with intent to cause grievous bodily harm or assault occasioning grievous bodily harm with intent: OPA 1861, s. 18 (max. term: life imprisonment);

(ii)   rape: SOA 1956, s. 1 (max. term: life imprisonment);

(iii)   unlawful sexual intercourse with a girl aged under 13 years: SOA 1956, s. 5 (max. term: life imprisonment);

(iv)   arson: CDA 1971, s. 1 (max. term: life imprisonment);

(v)   robbery: TA 1968, s. 8 (max. term: life imprisonment);

(vi)   aggravated burglary: TA 1968, s. 10 (max. term: life imprisonment);

(vii) burglary of a dwelling: TA 1968, s. 9 (max. term: 14 years).

24-041 The length of detention shall not exceed the statutory maximum term of imprisonment available in respect of an adult but, if the offence carries a maximum of life imprisonment, detention for life may be ordered (*Abbott* [1964] 1 Q.B. 489 CCA).

CJA 1991, s. 31(1) includes section 53 detention within the definition of a custodial sentence and so power of detention under section 53(3) is subject to all the restrictions and related requirements contained in CJA 1991, Part I upon imposing custodial sentences. Previously, section 53 was not subject to the restrictions on the use of custody for young offenders contained in CJA 1982, s. 1, now superseded.

Detention under section 53(3) can only be imposed on conviction on **24–042** indictment in the Crown Court and is thus not available either to a youth court or to the Crown Court when a juvenile has been committed for sentence after a finding of guilt by a youth court. A youth court retains discretion whether to commit a juvenile to the Crown Court for trial under this provision but if an eligible offence appears to merit a greater penalty than is available under CJA 1982 powers of detention in a young offender institution, the magistrates should take this course (*Learmonth* (1988) 10 Cr. App. R.(S.) 229).

If the Crown Court intends to pass sentence under section 53(3), this must be exercised with great care and made plain and explicit, without ambiguity; simple reference to "detention" is insufficient (see *Venison* (1994) 15 Cr. App. R. (S.) 624 applying CJA 1982, s. 1B(5) to resolve ambiguity in favour of the defendant and also *Egdell* [1994] Crim. L.R. 137). If, however, the sentencer indicates that detention under section 53(3) is in mind when adjourning to allow a report to be prepared, but does not explicitly refer to section 53 when subsequently passing sentence, the sentence should nevertheless be regarded as clear and unambiguous (*Marriott and Shepherd* (1995) 16 Cr.App.R.(S.) 428).

Power of detention under s.53(3) was extended to children by CJPOA 1994. Home Office Circular 70/1994, amplifying CJPOA 1994 Commencement Order No. 2, has clarified that the extension does not apply to offences committed before date of implementation of the provision, January 9, 1995.

Sentencing Principles   **24–043**

In regard to young offenders aged 15 or over the Court of Appeal has made it clear that the maximum term applicable to detention in a young offender institution (or youth custody, prior to CJA 1988) reflects specific legislative policy that young people should not be detained for longer than that period except in exceptionally serious cases (*Oakes* (1983) 5 Cr. App. R.(S.) 389).

Thus section 53(3) power should not be used routinely to enlarge the **24–044** options available to the court. In *Oakes* (a case of burglary) the Court of Appeal appeared to be of the view that the use of section 53(2) (as then applied) should be confined to offences of serious violence, noting that when first introduced it was available only for attempted murder, manslaughter and wounding with intent (it was subsequently extended to other grave crimes by CJA 1961). Previously, in *Mulkerrins* [1981] Crim L.R. 512, the Court of Appeal had referred to section 53(2) detention as a "sentence of last resort", to be used very sparingly.

In *Fairhurst* [1986] 1 W.L.R. 1374, the Court of Appeal resolved much uncertainty in a guideline judgement by Lord Lane C.J. Referring to the balance to be struck between, on the one hand, the desirability of keeping youths out of long terms of custody and, on the other hand, the necessity to meet serious offences with sufficiently substantial sentences, Lord Lane outlined the following principles (updated here to refer to YOI instead of youth custody and to the current age range but not taking account of the subsequently increased maximum term of YOI):

1. It is not necessary, in order to invoke the provisions of section 53(2), that the crime committed should be one of exceptional gravity, such as attempted murder, manslaughter, wounding with intent, armed robbery or the like.

24–045   2. On the other hand it is not good sentencing practice to pass a sentence of detention under section 53(2) simply because a 12 months YOI sentence seems to be on the low side for the particular offence committed.

3. Where the offence plainly calls for a greater sentence than one of 12 months YOI and is sufficiently serious to call for a sentence of two years YOI or more had the offender been aged 18 or over, then it will be proper to sentence to a similar term of section 53(2) detention. If the offence would merit a sentence of less than two years but more than 12 months YOI for an offender aged 18 or over, then the sentence should normally be one of YOI and not of section 53(2) detention. It cannot be said that the difference between a sentence of, say, 21 months and one of 12 months YOI is so great that the 12 months could be regarded as an inappropriate term.

24–046   4. Where more than one offence is involved for which section 53(2) detention is available, but the offences vary in seriousness, provided that at least one offence is sufficiently serious to merit section 53(2) detention, detention sentences of under two years duration, whether concurrent or consecutive, may properly be imposed in respect of the other offences: see *Gaskin* (1985) 7 Cr. App. R.(S.) 28.

5. Where an offender is aged under 15 and thus ineligible for YOI, a section 53(2) detention sentence of less than two years may well be appropriate. (This is pursued in more detail later in this section.)

6. Where there are two offences committed by a 15 or 16 year old and one of them, A, carries a maximum sentence of 14 years, and the other, B, carries a lower maximum, then generally speaking it is not proper to pass a sentence of section 53(2) detention in respect of offence A, which would not otherwise merit it, in order to compensate for the fact that 12 months' YOI is grossly inadequate for offence B. Where, however, it can truly be said that the defendant's behaviour giving rise to offence B is part and

parcel of the event giving rise to offence A, such a sentence may properly be passed.

7. Where an offender faces sentence for two or more offences, one of **24-047** which is eligible for section 53(2) detention and the other is not, it is better to pass no separate penalty for the latter rather than a concurrent sentence of youth custody. This principle has been confirmed in *Collins* [1994] Crim. L.R. 872 where it was pointed out that a concurrent YOI term would inhibit the offender's allocation to a local authority or other establishment outside the Prison Service.

By proposing the "two year test" as the threshold criterion for the use of section 53(2) the Court of Appeal has thus initiated a 12 months buffer zone to keep the power of long-term detention separate from the conventional young offender institution sentence. Now that the maximum term of YOI for this age group is two years, it seems likely that a higher threshold will be set for the use of section 53(3) powers. If the same buffer zone is used then a normal minimum term of three years detention can be anticipated.

The *Fairhurst* judgement did not refer to the principle of restraint first **24-048** proposed in *Storey* (1984) 6 Cr. App. R.(S.) 104 that the section 53(2) sentence should not be of such length:

> "that it would seem to the young men involved, particularly if they are not outstanding intellectually, that the far end of it is out of sight ... The sentencer should take care to select a duration on which the offender can fix his eye with a view to emerging in the foreseeable future."

Not only should a section 53(3) term not be longer than would be appropriate as a sentence of imprisonment for an adult (*Burrowes* (1985) 7 Cr. App. R.(S.) 106), the *Storey* principle requires sentences to be scaled down from the length of sentence appropriate for an older offender to a level which reflects the extreme youth of the defendant and their relative grasp of the passage of time. David Thomas (in his commentary on *Marshall* [1989] Crim L.R. 520) suggested that any sentence over three years would require particular justification (though in the light of speculation about the normal minimum term now applicable, this would seem to require upward revision). On the other hand, the Court of Appeal in *McFarlane and Burke* (1988) 10 Cr. App. R.(S.) 10, approving terms of five years and four years upon 15 year olds for robberies of young women walking alone in the evening, using a degree of violence coupled with sexual threats, stated that the *Storey* principle did not mean that the courts should automatically pass a shorter sentence where the circumstances of the case merit a substantial period of detention.

Because children and young persons aged under 15 are not eligible for **24-049** sentence of detention in a young offender institution, different principles apply to the use of 1933 powers of detention and the *Fairhurst* guidelines are not so applicable. A shorter term of section 53(3) detention may be appropriate for a qualifying offence. Thus in *McHugh* (1994) 15 Cr. App. R.(S.) 192 sentence of 10 months detention was upheld for a boy aged 14 with no previous convictions who pleaded guilty to two offences of burglary of occupied dwellings at night, one involving a relatively sophisticated means of entry, ransacking, vandalism and soiling and, in the second instance, the deliberate targeting of an elderly woman's home to facilitate escape if she woke and confronted the intruders. Though the boy was "under the malign influence of a more sophisticated criminal" and reports made a determined bid for a supervision order, the Court of Appeal noted the strong element of public interest in the case and held that

> "the message must go out loud and clear ... to all of a like age and of a like mind, that offences of this extremely serious and degrading character will be met by severe and unpleasant punishment".

24-050 See also *Clews* (1987) 9 Cr. App. R.(S.) 194 and *Probert* (1994) 15 Cr. App. R.(S.) 891 where a sentence of 12 months detention was imposed.

The relationship of section 53(3) detention upon younger juveniles to the new powers to impose a secure training order (for which the defendant in *McHugh* would have been ineligible as he had no previous convictions) awaits clarification.

Cases illustrative of the use of section 53(2) detention include:

Manslaughter: *Coffey* (1994) 15 Cr. App. R.(S.) 754 where a 15 year old boy had sustained an attack upon another youth in the street without provocation, ultimately striking him on the head with some force with a road direction sign. The pre-sentence report described him as "very quiet, polite, extremely likeable with a ready smile, genuine in attitude and impossible to fault". A subsequent report from the Special Unit where he had been held since sentence indicated his very good behaviour, being "a pleasure to teach" and getting on well with staff. Sentence of five years detention was considered excessive and reduced to four years.

In *Sherwood and Button* (1995) 16 Cr. App. R.(S.) 513 sentence of seven years detention was upheld for "almost as bad a case of motor manslaughter as could be envisaged". In the course of a 80 m.p.h. chase in a built up area, the 17 year old driver of a car taken without consent struck a pedestrian, killing her instantly. The offender drove on for some time without slowing, even though her body remained wedged in the shattered windscreen until eventually flung off. In *Attorney-General's Reference No.28 of 1994* (1995) 16 Cr. App. R.(S.) 589, sentence of nine months YOI detention was replaced by three years section 53(2) detention for an "eggshell skull" homicide. In the course of a violation confrontation with two boys, the 17 year old offender had inadvertently also struck the mother of one of them, causing her death through a heart rhythm abnormality. Though he had not hit the deceased deliberately and did not anticipate the very serious outcome, he had acted in the course of a persistent episode of aggressive conduct and had previous convictions for violence.

Rape: *Hippolyte* [1987] Crim L.R. 63 where sentence of five years **24–051** was upheld on a 15 year old who together with an older co-offender broke into the flat of the victim and raped her, following which the accomplice pushed objects into her vagina. Compare *McIntosh* (1994) 15 Cr. App. R.(S.) 163 where the offender when aged 16 had broken into the home of a very old woman while she was asleep in bed and had threatened to kill her before raping her and forcing his penis into her mouth. He was arrested 18 months later at age 18. Sentence of nine years YOI was reduced to seven years. See also *Powell* (1994) 15 Cr. App. R.(S.) 611, outlined at para. 9–028, and *Suleman* (1994) 15 Cr. App. R.(S.) 569 where sentence of seven years and eleven months was upheld. The offence would have deserved 12 years if committed by an adult and there had been an adequate reduction for youth.

In *Stone* (1995) 16 Cr. App. R.(S.) 406, sentence of four years detention was reduced to two years six months for a 15 year old who had persistently raped and indecently assaulted a girl aged six who was in the care of the same foster-parents as himself, having been received into care following parental sexual abuse.

Buggery: *Baxter* (1994) 15 Cr. App. R.(S.) 609 where sentence of two years was upheld on a 15 year old for three counts of buggery of a boy aged nine living in the same household as the offender. Though no violence or bribery had been used, the Court of Appeal declined the defence invitation to impose a supervision order.

Wounding with Intent: *Adams* (1994) 15 Cr. App. R.(S.) 466 where **24–052** sentence of three years was upheld on a 15 year old girl who, out of jealousy over the affections of a boy, sought out the other girl and challenged her to a fight, in the course of which she stabbed the victim a number of times causing multiple wounds to various parts of her body. When questioned, the offender expressed satisfaction rather than remorse and stated she had wanted to kill the victim. She was said to suffer "poor impulse control" arising from her repeated experience of loss of significant males in her life. In *Anderson* (1994) 15 Cr. App. R.(S.) 553, sentence of 10 years was reduced to eight years for a boy aged 16 who had left a recreation ground after the victim had intervened to prevent him abusing an Asian youth, returning with two firearms including a sawn-off shotgun, firing at the victim at close range and causing multiple puncture wounds to his ankles. Though this was a vicious and planned attack on someone acting as a good citizen, the original sentence was considered excessive in the light of the offender's age.

For recent cases involving long terms of YOI detention on 17 year old offenders, prior to the extension of section 53 to that age group, see *Bierton* (1995) 16 Cr. App. R.(S.) 309 where sentence of ten years was upheld for an episode of driving a stolen car at high speed for nearly two miles, trying to dislodge the owner who was clinging to the bonnet, having sought to prevent the vehicle taking, and was eventually flung off in a collision with a tree causing him grievous injuries. The Court of Appeal was very sceptical of defence claims for the offender's remorse. In *Cosgrove* (1995) 16 Cr. App. R.(S.) 76 the offender pursued an earlier quarrel with his victim by stealing a knife and attacking him, striking out at his stomach but hitting him in the arm. Though he had little self-control and tended to retaliate violently to real or imagined insults, ten years detention was longer than absolutely necessary, given his age and plea, and the Court substituted seven years.

24–053   **Robbery:** *Marshall* [1989] Crim L.R. 520, where sentence of six years on a 16 year old for robberies of school children aged 15 or 16, who were threatened with a knife or a bottle, was reduced to four years. More recently, in *Conlon* (1994) 15 Cr. App. R.(S.) 110, sentence of three years was upheld for a 14 year old boy for three robberies of off-licences using an imitation firearm. The Court of Appeal noted reports that he was progressing well during his sentence and commented that this was a "reflection of the value of this type of sentence". See also *Marti* (1992) 13 Cr. App. R.(S.) 1.

In *Taylor and Andrews* (1995) 16 Cr. App. R.(S.) 570, the 17 year old offender had attacked a 70 year old man in his home in the belief that he kept a large sum of money there. Though a considerable degree of gratuitous violence was used, causing a legacy of continuing fear, he had acted under the influence of his 21 year old co-offender and showed evidence of very real remorse, thus allowing a "modest reduction" of sentence from seven to six years.

24–054   **Burglary:** *Wilson* [1987] Crim L.R. 64, where sentence of four years was upheld on a youth who broke into the home of a woman aged 86 in the late evening, woke her, dragged her into her backyard and left her there unconscious. In the earlier case of *Butler* (1984) 6 Cr. App. R.(S.) 236, sentence of two years detention imposed on a 16 year old convicted of numerous dwelling-house burglaries, in some of which substantial damage had been caused, was upheld on appeal. But Lord Lane in *Fairhurst* commented that the decision in *Butler* may have gone too far in the opposite direction to the restrictive interpretation in *Oakes* (see para. 24–043). In *McHugh* (1994) 15 Cr. App. R.(S.) 192, sentence of 10 months detention was upheld for a 14 year old boy of previous good character who had burgled and ransacked an occupied residence at night, despite strong proposals for a supervision order. The Court of Appeal stated:

> "The message must go out loud and clear ... to all of a like age and like mind that offences of this extremely serious and degrading character will be met by severe and unpleasant punishment."

In *Probert* (1994) 15 Cr. App. R.(S.) 891, sentence of 12 months detention was imposed on a boy aged 14 who had broken into an unoccupied house with an accomplice aged 16, smashing fixtures, spraying paint and causing flooding, the damage amounting to £12,000. Both youths received the same term as there was no basis for distinguishing one as the ringleader and they were regarded as equally culpable.

Arson: *Storey* (1984) 6 Cr. App. R.(S.) 104 where sentence of five years on youths aged 16 who had set fire to a school, after splashing petrol around, causing damage worth £370,000, was reduced to three years. It should not be assumed, however, that arson will always attract a section 53(2) sentence. In *Dewberry and Stone* (1985) 7 Cr. App. R.(S.) 202, 12 months youth custody imposed on the less culpable youth was set aside and a community service order was substituted; three years detention on the more culpable youth was replaced by 12 months youth custody on the basis that a sentence of 18 months would have been the appropriate length if permitted.

In *Parkes* (1995) 16 Cr. App. R.(S.) 74, sentence of five years YOI imposed on a 17 year old girl (before s.53 was extended to that age group) for arson being reckless whether life was endangered was reduced to three years, albeit that this was a planned attack in setting fire to the door of a house with petrol, showing total disregard for the safety of the occupants, a mother and her two young children.

Kidnapping: *Henry* (1994) 15 Cr. App. R.(S.) 539 where sentence of 30 months was reduced to 18 months for the abduction of a 15 year old boy who owed money to one of the perpetrator group. He had been forced into the boot of a car, driven for a short distance and left tied to a tree from which he was able to free himself, being detained for some 20 minutes in total. The Court of Appeal gave credit for the fact that no weapon was used, little violence applied, no injuries suffered, no ransom demanded and no threat offered to public safety.

Car Crime: In *Bennett* (1995) 16 Cr. App. R.(S.) 438, the offender **24–055** aged 15 had taken a van and driven it at high speed round a housing estate, in a bravado display, egged on by an audience, taunting the police in pursuit and driving deliberately at police vehicles. Upholding sentence of five years detention for criminal damage being reckless whether life was endangered, the Court of Appeal indicated that a clear message was necessary, that punishment for this kind of behaviour must be severe and liberty will be lost for a substantial period, "however young the driver and however good his previous character".

> "It is unacceptable to the public ... for neighbourhoods to be terrified and people awakened in the middle of the night by the roar of engines, the squeal of tyres and the flash of lights, for life and limb recklessly to be put at risk, for property to be endangered and for the police to be mocked when they seek to

intervene, all because selfish youths think it amusing to display over a significant period of time what they foolishly believe to be their driving skills. It is not the role of police officers or police cars ... to serve as Aunt Sallies for unbridled hooliganism." (*per* Rose L.J.)

Deterrence

24–056

A number of cases have emphasised the important element of deterrence in s. 53(2) sentencing, *e.g. Storey* (1984) 6 Cr. App. R.(S.) 104:

> "offences by schoolboys using incendiary devices on schools are not out of the ordinary. The courts should make plain that arson is a serious offence, capable of having grave consequences, and will be dealt with very severely."

Deterrence as a basis for sentencing is less clear under the proportionality principles which underlie CJA 1991 but, following the comments of Lord Taylor C.J. in *Cunningham* [1993] 1 W.L.R. 183, there appears to remain scope for sentencers to take into account the need for deterrence (see para. 23–045).

In *Marriott and Shepherd* (1995) 16 Cr. App. R.(S.) 428, the Court of Appeal emphasised the importance of deterrence, tempered by considerations of age, when dealing with robbery targeted upon and attacking vulnerable old people. The 16 and 17 year old offenders had watched and followed the 88 year old victim, snatching her bag and causing her to fall to the ground, sustaining a fractured skull.

> "It is not inappropriate to impose a deterrent sentence; there may be a very real need to deter others and indeed young others from offending in a like manner. But when one is passing ... a deterrent sentence, it is necessary to keep a balance between that aspect of the matter, the youth of the offender and the effect of a long sentence upon the perception of the offender, it being trite to observe that young offenders see time stretching ahead of them in a different way to that in which adults see it." (*per* Ebsworth L.J.)

Noting that the robbery had involved serious but not grave violence, though with foreseeably grave consequences, the court of Appeal reduced sentence of seven years to five years.

24–057 *Dangerousness and Public Protection*

Prior to provision in CJA 1991, s. 1(2)(b) and 2(2)(b) for custodial sentences on the criterion of public protection, it was acknowledged that section 53(2) powers could appropriately be used to pass a very long preventive sentence on young offenders considered to present a considerable risk to the public (see commentary by Thomas on *Woodbridge* [1978] Crim. L.R. 376).

The case normally cited to illustrate this use is *Storey* (1973) 57 Cr. App. R. 840 where a youth of 16 received a term of 20 years detention for attempted murder. The Court of Appeal regarded it as a very exceptional case where a shorter period might prove insufficient for the protection of the public but questioned whether any case would ever arise in which a longer determinate term would be appropriate. The court in *Storey* felt able to predict a time by which the offender would cease to be dangerous, though the basis of that assessment is not clear from the report of the case.

Use of the alternative option of detention for life is illustrated in *Bell* [1990] Crim. L.R. 206. The offender aged 16 was convicted of assault with intent to rob and indecent assault, having approached the victim whilst she was pushing her two year old child in a pram, pointing a Stanley knife at her stomach and demanding her money. He then demanded to handle her indecently, threatening to slash the victim or her child in the throat. She had submitted and had been forced to take his penis in her mouth. The offender had previous convictions for indecent assault. Dismissing his appeal against sentence of life detention under section 53(2) for the assault with intent to rob (at that stage indecent assault was not a qualifying offence, despite being the more serious offence), the Court of Appeal held that whilst there are some cases where it is better for the sentencer to specify the number of years which the offender should serve, this was a case where no court could predict how long it would be before the appellant would be safe to be released.

Detention for life will be justified, as in the case of discretionary life **24-058** imprisonment, in most exceptional circumstances where three conditions are satisfied, as propounded by several pre-1991 leading cases (*e.g. Hodgson* (1968) 52 Cr. App. R. 113, *Wilkinson* (1983) 5 Cr. App. R.(S.) 105, *de Haviland* (1983) 5 Cr. App. R.(S.) 109, *O'Dwyer* (1986) 86 Cr. App. R. 313):

1. The offence is grave enough in itself to merit a very long sentence on the basis of proportionality, even if not in the very first rank of seriousness.

2. The nature of the offence and the offender's history show that the offender has a continuing mental instability and, if at liberty, is likely to re-offend and present a grave danger to the public. The threat may be to a particular person (*Allen* (1987) 9 Cr. App. R.(S.) 169), though is more likely to be to the public in general or to a particular section of the community. Psychiatric and psychological reports and evidence should be presented to the court (*Pither* (1979) 1 Cr. App. R.(S.) 209).

3. The offender will remain unstable and a potential danger for a **24-059** long and/or uncertain period. As Widgery C.J. stated in *Bryson* (1973) 58 Cr. App. R. 464, in upholding sentence of detention for life on a 14 year old for arson causing £20,000 worth of damage and considerable risk to life: "None of the experts give any sort of indication that a particular period of years can in this case be chosen to ensure that the public can be properly protected."

A court will be hesitant to conclude that these criteria are met in the case of young offenders except in the most rare instances of sexual or other violence of a most disturbing, pathological nature. It would clearly be wrong for the court to opt for an indeterminate sentence as a "more merciful" alternative to a long determinate term, in order to allow continual review and release as soon as it is safe to do so (*Hall* (1986) 8 Cr. App. R.(S.) 458 where the 17 year old offender, affected by glue-sniffing, had set fire to a house where he was staying, leaving the other occupants, a woman and her two young children, asleep. The Court of Appeal noted that while the offender was immature, with a disturbed childhood in local authority care and lengthy criminal record, this did not amount to "mental abnormality"). See also *Turton* (1986) 8 Cr. App. R.(S.) 174. For a recent example of custody for life imposed for rape upon a 20 year old who was diagnosed as suffering an untreatable psychopathic disorder and a propensity to commit sexual attacks, see *Attorney-General's Reference No. 6 of 1993 (Musgrove)* (1994) 15 Cr. App. R.(S.) 375.

24-060   Under the provisions of CJA 1991, ss. 1(2)(b) and 2(2)(b) allowing the imposition of a custodial sentence where only such a sentence would be adequate to protect the public from serious harm (see para. 23–046 *et seq.*), the use of section 53(3) power to impose a long determinate period of detention or detention for life because of the risk posed by the offender is restricted by the requirement that the offence must be a "violent" or "sexual" offence, as defined by CJA 1991, s.31(1) (see para. 23–047). This restriction is unlikely to impede the scope of the court as the kind of case for which lengthy or indeterminate detention will be under consideration will almost certainly fall within one or both of these categories.

In the most highly exceptional of circumstances there remains the scope, in theory at least, to pass sentence of detention for life for an offence carrying life imprisonment on grounds not of public protection but of seriousness. As this would presumably be justified only in the case of the most heinous instance of that kind of crime where no mitigation can be identified, it seems in practice impossible to envisage use of such a sentence upon a defendant aged under 18.

Sexual Offences: Extension of Licence

24-061 CJA 1991, s. 44 empowers the sentencing court to specify that an offender convicted of a sexual offence (as defined by CJA, s. 31(1)) shall be subject to licence upon early release until the completion of the full term of the sentence instead of the normal three-quarters point of sentence. This power is available even if only part of the sentence is imposed for a sexual offence. In taking this step the court should have regard to the criteria to be taken into account in considering parole, *i.e.* the protection of the public from serious harm and the desirability of preventing further offending by the offender and securing their rehabilitation.

Discretionary Life Detention Sentences

CJA 1991, s. 34 empowers a judge, when passing a non-mandatory sentence of life imprisonment, including life detention under section 53(3), for a violent or sexual offence, to specify such part ("the relevant part") as should be served before the offender can require their case to be referred to the Parole Board. When this power is exercised, the prisoner or detainee has the status of "discretionary life prisoner" and their sentence falls into two parts:

(a) the relevant part consisting of the period of detention imposed for punishment and deterrence, taking into account the seriousness of the offence; and

(b) the remaining part of sentence, the continuation of which is governed by considerations of risk to the public.

In determining "the relevant part" under section 34(2), the judge has to **24-062** consider not only the seriousness of the offence but also the fact that a detainee serving a determinate long-term sentence would be entitled to release after serving two-thirds of their term and could be released after serving one-half only (see para. 24-073). This consideration appears to suggest that the judge shall first decide the appropriate determinate term on the basis of seriousness, ignoring the risk factors which require an indeterminate term, and then reduce that by between a third and a half to produce the "relevant part".

The Lord Chief Justice gave further guidance on the exercise of s.34 powers in a *Practice Direction: Crime: Life Sentences* [1993] 1 W.L.R. 223:

(a) The judge is not obliged to make use of section 34 provisions when passing a discretionary life sentence but should do so, "save in the very exceptional case where the judge considers that the offence is so serious that detention for life is justified by the seriousness of the offence alone, irrespective of the risk to the public". In such a case the judge should state that in open court when passing sentence.

(b) In cases where the judge proposes to specify the relevant part **24-063** under section 34 the judge should permit counsel for the defendant to address the court as to the appropriate length of the relevant part. Where the judge does not propose to specify the relevant part, defence counsel should be permitted to address the court as to the appropriateness of the course of action.

(c) In specifying the relevant part the judge should indicate the reasons for reaching a decision as to the length of that part.

(d) Whether or not ordering that section 34 should apply, the judge should not make a written report to the Lord Chief Justice, contrary to practice in recent years.

The importance of specifying a period for the purposes of section 34 was emphasised in *Lomas* [1995] Crim. L.R. 576.

Time on Remand

Prior to CJA 1991, an anomalous feature of the section 53(2) sentence was that time spent remanded in custody did not count towards sentence. CJA 1991, Sched. 11, para. 2(3) amends CJA 1967, s. 67(5) by providing that time spent on remand in custody or in local authority secure accommodation shall count towards determinate sentences under section 53(2), as it has towards other custody sentences. See also para. 23–059 *et seq* in regard to remand time and early release provisions.

Placement

24–064 Section 53(2) tries to combine two objectives: secure containment and public protection appropriate to the nature of the offence; treatment and rehabilitation appropriate to the comparative youth of the offender. Placement inevitably reflects this duality. The 1933 Act stipulates that section 53 detainees may be detained "in such a place and under such conditions as the Secretary of State may permit", and this could obviously be at a Prison Department establishment. CYPA 1969, s. 30 specifically mentions the power of the Secretary of State to allocate section 53 detainees to "community homes" (LACHs), residential child care establishments run by local authorities, some of which provide secure accommodation. Since 1971, there has been a third option as a result of practice rather than legislation. Youth Treatment Centres (YTCs), controlled directly by the Department of Health, have been developed to provide secure residential treatment facilities for highly disturbed adolescents, including a small number of section 53 offenders. There is currently only one such specialist centre, St. Charles in Essex, Glenthorne in Birmingham being closed in July 1995. Allocation policy within the Home Office is currently set out in Circular Instruction 31/1987 which states that:

24–065   "The decision where to place a s. 53(2) offender must balance the best interests of the offender against the wider responsibilities of the Secretary of State. Of paramount importance among these are the protection of the public and the maintenance of confidence in the operation of the criminal justice system, including confidence on the part of courts in what happens to offenders."

C.I. 31/87 emphasises the need for flexibility and careful consideration of individual cases. The foremost consideration proves to be age: those aged under 16½ on conviction are likely to be referred to Department of Health for placement in either an LACH or YTC. Immaturity or vulnerability in older detainees, or lack of prior criminal experience are also taken to indicate that allocation to a community home would be more appropriate.

24–066 A number of abscondings by section 53 offenders from LACHs during

1987, together with concern about the higher cost of helping young offenders in local authority establishments, caused the Home Office Research and Planning Unit to study the advantages of LACHs compared with the provision for section 53 offenders in young offender institutions. Broadly, the study (Ditchfield and Catan, 1992) found that the regimes provided were very different. For example, LACHs "provided significantly more and better quality education and training, a greater variety of physical exercise and recreational activity, a higher level of throughcare, and more help and advice with detainees' problems". The general quality of life was demonstrably better in community homes than in YOIs. The study also found that "offenders released from community homes were statistically less likely to have been reconvicted after two years than offenders released from YOIs", the proportions being 40 per cent and 53 per cent respectively. For a further examination of the experiences of section 53 offenders see Boswell (1991) who also identifies the comparative lack of counselling, training and education in custodial regimes and recommends closer liaison between the authorities to ease the transition from child care facilities to the prison system.

Following a management review in 1993 of both YTCs by the Social Services Inspectorate (SSI) of the Department of Health, which found serious problems at both centres, the Home Office made the decision to stop placing new section 53 cases in either centre until the concerns raised by the SSI have been fully addressed. Difficulties identified included confusion over aims, staff demoralisation, disjointed management and, in the case of one centre, "an arbitrary, reactive and at times apparently punitive approach which exacerbated tensions and made the exercise of control more problematic" (cited in Howard League, 1995). As a consequence of the Home Office's decision, some young people serving section 53 sentences have not been placed in appropriate long-term units but have had extended stays in short-term secure units or have been located in the YOI system.

Recent Use of section 53
Concern has been expressed about increased use of section 53 since 1970 when only 11 sentences were passed, five being under section 53(1). The subsequent increase has been most evident in the use of section 53(2), from six instances in 1975 to 156 in 1986. The biggest increase was in the use of section 53(2) for robbery and burglary, reflecting the increased numbers of juveniles being tried and sentenced at Crown Court for these offences.

This upward trend in the use of section 53(2) sentencing against a **24–067** downward trend in the overall number of juvenile custodial sentences suggested that the sentence had been transferred "from a last ditch social defence to a tariff sentence" (Harris and Timms, 1988), contrary to the original intention of the 1933 Act. The figures since 1986 when the *Fairhurst* judgement clarified the use of section 53(2), showing a recent decrease in use, and the rise following the availability of this sentence for 17 year olds, are as follows:

	1987	1988	1989	1990	1991	1992	1993
s.53(1)	19	22	15	10	12	11	24
s.53(2) (total)	154	177	115	125	102	93	315
Violence	29	21	23	12	25	21	60
Sexual	11	16	16	23	13	14	20
Burglary	24	32	16	15	12	7	52
Robbery	68	84	44	52	45	41	137
Theft/ Handling	–	–	1	–	–	–	1
Arson	17	20	14	21	7	7	24
Drug	1	2	–	–	–	2	4
Other	4	2	1	2	–	1	17

Source: Home Office, *Criminal Statistics England and Wales*
Note: The Home Office believes that some under-recording may have occurred in 1989 and 1990.

24–068   The annual *Criminal Statistics* do not indicate the gender and ethnic origins of juveniles detained under section 53(2) but unpublished Home Office figures for 1986 made available to a NACRO Working Group (NACRO 1988) on the use of section 53 showed that of 129 juveniles detained in Prison Department establishments under section 53(2), six were female and 123 male. Receptions under section 53(2) sentence by ethnic origin showed that 80 per cent were white, 16 per cent were black or Asian and four per cent were categorised as "other". NACRO commented that "young black people are over-represented in the group attracting section 53(2) sentences, as compared to those receiving detention centre and youth custody sentences".

24–069   Now that 14 year olds can no longer be sentenced to YOI and 17 year olds have the benefit of the YOI ceiling applicable to juveniles, it is possible that section 53(3) sentences will be passed more frequently upon these age groups. Some indication of trends is provided by figures for the first six months following implementation of the 1991 Act (NACRO, 1993). A total of 72 young people received section 53(2) sentences, nine being aged 14 and 35 being aged 17/18. Thus only 37 young offenders aged under 17 received such a sentence which would suggest a projected 12 month figure of 74, a clear drop from the 1992 figure of 93. Black young people continued to be over-represented, 10 out of the 70 for whom ethnic origin was known being from non-white minorities. Robbery remained the most prevalent main offence, accounting for 43 per cent of cases, with burglary accounting for nearly 24 per cent of cases.

Early Release

Prior to CJA 1991 juveniles sentenced under section 53 neither came within the normal parole scheme arrangements nor were they entitled to remission of sentence. The Home Secretary could refer section 53(2) detainees to the Parole Board and release them on licence at any point in their sentence but was not required to do so. Most served well over two-thirds of the sentence in custody. This unfair anomaly was rectified by CJA 1991, s. 43(1) which specifies that determinate sentences under section 53(2) shall be treated as determinate sentences of imprisonment for the purposes of Part II of the Act. Young offenders serving indeterminate sentences under section 53 are treated as though they are life-sentence prisoners for the purposes of early release procedures (s. 43(2)).

Transitional Arrangements 24–071

The transitional arrangements in CJA 1991, Sched. 12, para. 11 specify that Part II of the Act shall apply to those who are serving a determinate section 53(2) sentence, or are on licence following such a sentence, at the date of the Act's commencement (October 1, 1992) as if the offender were or had been a life prisoner rather than a long-term or short-term prisoner, with the following two exceptions:

1. If recommended to release the offender on licence, the Home Secretary may do so without the usual requirement pertaining to non-discretionary life prisoners under CJA 1991, s. 35(2) of consultation with the Lord Chief Justice, together with the trial judge if available.

2. Licence shall remain in force until the date on which the offender would (but for their release) have served the whole of their sentence.

The transitional arrangements for those serving an indeterminate section 53 sentence at the time of the commencement of the Act are that they will be treated in the same way as "discretionary life prisoners" under CJA 1991, s. 34 where the Home Secretary has issued a certificate to that effect, specifying the part of sentence which the court would normally specify under section 34(2) to reflect the seriousness of the offence. Of 21 young offenders detained for life under section 53(2) in February 1995, seven had been given a "tariff" term of five years or less; eight, six to nine years; and six, ten to 14 years.

"Short-Term" Detainees

As in the case of adult prisoners, "short-term" status applies to 24–072 detainees serving sentence for a term less than four years (CJA 1991, s. 33(5)). These detainees are entitled to be released on licence as soon as they have served one-half of their sentence (s. 33(1)(b)). This is normally referred to as "automatic conditional release" (ACR). Their licence remains in force until the date on which the detainee would (but for their release) have served three-quarters of their sentence (CJA 1991, s. 37(1)), though subject to a statutory minimum period of one-quarter of the total sentence term, even if this takes the licence period beyond the three-quarters point (s. 41(3)). This is designed to ensure a minimum desirable period of oversight. The licence period in respect of a sexual offender may be extended to run until the completion of the full term of sentence, if so ordered by the sentencing judge (CJA 1991 s. 44; see para. 24–061).

24-073 *Licence Conditions*

A person subject to ACR licence shall comply with the conditions specified in the licence. The standard licence for short-term prisoners including section 53(2) detainees currently specifies six requirements of supervision, as detailed at para. 24–019. The process of supervision has been described earlier in this Chapter (para. 24–022).

The nominated supervising officer is normally a probation officer (s. 37(4)) but, in relation to a detainee released on licence under the age of 22, may be a social worker of a local authority social services department (s. 43(5)). Additional licence conditions may be included at the discretion of the prison governor, on the recommendation of the supervising officer or with that officer's agreement. Such extra requirements must be from a list of approved conditions (see para. 24–078).

Breach of Licence

Failure to comply with an ACR licence requirement is a summary offence punishable by fine and also by suspension of licence, as detailed at para. 24–025.

"Long-Term" Detainees

"Long-term" status applies to detainees serving sentence for a term of four years or more (CJA 1991, s. 33(5)). Long-term detainees are entitled to "automatic conditional release" on licence only after serving two-thirds of their sentence. They are, however, eligible for "discretionary conditional release" on parole after serving a half of their sentence, if this is recommended by the Parole Board. In the case of detainees serving sentence of less than seven years, the Parole Board's recommendation for release is decisive. If the Parole Board recommends the release of a detainee serving sentence of seven years or longer, the Home Secretary retains discretion not to release if this is considered to be contrary to the public interest. However, the Home Secretary cannot release a detainee when the Parole Board have not recommended release.

24-074 *Discretionary Life Detainees*

In cases where the sentencing judge specified a "relevant part" of sentence under CJA 1991, s. 34 (see para. 24–061) (or the Home Secretary has specified the tariff term under transitional arrangements) the discretionary life detainee is eligible for release on licence after serving the specified part (s. 34(3)). Release is upon the direction of the Parole Board after referral by the Home Secretary and an oral hearing before a "discretionary lifer panel" in accordance with the Parole Board Rules 1992. The Board must be satisfied that detention is no longer necessary for the protection of the public (s. 34(4)(b)). The detainee may require the Home Secretary to refer the case to the Parole Board at any time after completion of the relevant part, though if the detainee is also serving a determinate term of detention or imprisonment, then a half of that sentence must also have been served. If a detainee is referred to the Board but release is not directed, the detainee has the right to be referred again after a period of two years from the date of the disposal of the previous reference (s. 34(5)).

Criteria for Selection for Parole   **24–075**

In exercising powers to give the Parole Board directions as to the matters to be taken into account in considering individuals for parole, the Home Secretary shall in particular have regard to (s. 32(6)):

(a) the need to protect the public from serious harm from offenders; and

(b) the desirability of preventing the commission by them of further offences and of securing their rehabilitation.

The Home Secretary has announced the following guidelines to be applied from October 1, 1992 in considering all determinate sentence offenders, whether commencing sentence before, on or after that date.

(i) The decision whether or not to recommend parole should focus primarily on the risk to the public of a further offence being committed at a time when the offender would otherwise be in prison. This should be balanced against the benefit, both to the public and the offender, of early release back into the community under a degree of supervision which might help rehabilitation and so lessen the risk of re-offending in the future.

(ii) Each case should be considered on its individual merits, without discrimination on any grounds.

(iii) Before recommending parole, the Parole Board should be satisfied **24–076** that:

(a) the longer period of supervision that parole would provide is likely to reduce the risk of further imprisonable offences being committed. In assessing the risk to the community, a small risk of violent offending is to be treated as more serious than a larger risk of non-violent offending;

(b) the offender has shown by his attitude and behaviour in custody that he is willing to address his offending and has made positive efforts and progress in doing so;

(c) the resettlement plan will help secure the offender's rehabilitation.

(iv) Before deciding whether or not to recommend parole, the Parole Board must take into account the supervising officer's recommendation as to suitability for release, including co-operation with a programme of supervision and adherence to the conditions of the licence.

24–077 *Licence Conditions*

Long-term and life detainees who are released on licence are subject to such conditions as may be specified in the licence, including requirements as to supervision by a probation officer. The standard requirements are as specified for short-term detainees but together with any additional conditions which may be included after consultation with the Parole Board, usually on the recommendation of the officer who will supervise the licensee. In the case of a discretionary life detainee, the conditions of the licence shall be as recommended by the Parole Board (s. 37(5)). The supervising officer is normally a probation officer (s. 37(4)) but, in relation to a detainee released on licence under the age of 22, may be a social worker of a local authority social services department (s. 43(5)). The process of supervision has been described earlier in this Chapter (see para. 24–022).

24–078 Extra conditions should be limited to appropriate choices from the following list of approved conditions:

1. Attending upon a duly qualified psychiatrist/psychologist/ medical practitioner for such care, supervision or treatments as that practitioner recommends.

2. Not to engage in any work or other organised activity involving a person under a specified age.

3. To reside at a specified address and not to leave without prior approval of supervising officer; thereafter to reside as directed by supervising officer.

4. Not to reside in the same household as any child under a specified age.

5. Not to seek to approach or communicate with wife/former wife/child(ren)/grandchildren/other named persons without prior approval of supervising officer and named social services department.

6. Comply with any requirements reasonably imposed by supervising officer for purpose of ensuring that licensee address alcohol/drug/sexual/gambling/ solvent abuse/debt/offending behaviour problems at specified course or centre (where appropriate).

24–079 Conditions in a licence may be inserted, varied or cancelled during the course of the licence period. This is usually upon the application of the supervising officer to the Parole Unit of the Home Office. The Parole Board must be consulted and, in the case of discretionary life detainees, any change should not be made except in accordance with the recommendations of the Board (s. 37(5)). Because the original licence is issued by the Governor of the establishment from which the offender is released, any changes have to be notified to the Governor so that a fresh licence can be issued.

Length of Licence

Long-term detainees remain subject to licence until the date on which, but for their release, they would have served three-quarters of their sentence (s. 37(1)), subject to a statutory minimum period of one-twelfth of the total sentence term (s. 41(3)). The licence period in respect of a sexual offender may be extended to run until the completion of the full term of sentence, if so ordered by the sentencing judge (CJA 1991, s. 44; see para. 24–061). Life detainees remain subject to licence until death (s. 37(3)).

Revocation and Recall   **24–080**

Whereas short-term detainees are liable to prosecution for failure to comply with their licence conditions, long-term detainees and life detainees are instead subject to revocation of licence and recall to custody, either on the recommendation of the Parole Board (s. 39(1)) or by order of the Home Secretary where expediency in the public interest requires urgent intervention (s. 39(2)). In either instance revocation will usually follow a written report and recommendation from a probation officer of Chief Officer grade of the Probation Service supervising the licensee. Apart from the licensee's response to licence conditions, the factors to be taken into account include: the likelihood of further serious offending; risk to the public safety; behaviour by the licensee which is likely to bring the licence system into disrepute.

Rights and Procedure Following Recall

Upon recall to prison, the detainee shall be informed of the reasons for their recall and of their right to make representations in writing with respect to that recall (s. 39(3)). The Home Secretary shall refer to the Parole Board any detainee who either was recalled without the Board's recommendation under section 39(2) or has made representations under section 39(3). Where the Board then recommends (in the case of a long-term detainee) or directs (in the case of a discretionary life detainee) their immediate release on licence, this will be put into effect (s. 39(5)).

If not released on the recommendation or direction of the Parole **24–081** Board, a long-term detainee who has been recalled by the Board under section 39(1) shall be released unconditionally at the three-quarters point of sentence, *i.e.* the point at which the licence would have expired (s. 33(3)(b)). CJA 1991 is silent as to the fate of the long-term detainee recalled directly by the Home Secretary under section 39(2), though it would seem anomalous that these detainees should (by implication) remain in custody until completion of the full term of their sentence. This appears to be a statutory oversight rather than an intended consequence.

Release on Compassionate Grounds

A detainee (subject to s. 53 or YOI detention) may be released at any time during their sentence if the Home Secretary is satisfied that "exceptional circumstances exist which justify ... release on compassionate grounds" (s. 36(1)), though, in the case of a long-term or life detainee, the Home Secretary shall consult the Parole Board unless circumstances make consultation impracticable (s. 36(2)). CI 36/1992 identifies two main categories justifying compassionate release, but only in "the most exceptional circumstances":

24–082 (a) medical conditions, including terminal illness, severe incapacitation and circumstances where continued detention would endanger the prisoner's life;

(b) tragic family circumstances which could not have been foreseen at the time of sentencing.

On release, detainees are subject to licence and consequent liability to prosecution or recall, depending on their status, until the usual expiry point of licence, the three-quarters point of sentence.

Time on Remand in Custody Before Sentence

The provisions for early release specify proportions of sentence which have to expire or be served before the detainee is either released on licence or is entitled to unconditional release or is no longer subject to licence. The critical points of sentence are one-half, two-thirds and three-quarters. Any time on remand in custody prior to sentence which counts under CJA 1967, s. 67 towards the reduction of the sentence to be served also counts in the calculation of these proportions (s. 41(1) and (2)).

24–083 *Disciplinary Offences in Custody*

CJA 1991 abolished the previous system of granting remission and thus detainees no longer receive "loss of remission" as a penalty for misbehaviour in custody. Instead CJA 1991, s. 42 provides for "additional days" to be awarded which extend the time to be served before entitlement to automatic conditional release on licence or discretionary early release on parole licence. The actual period of licence remains unchanged but commencement and completion are correspondingly delayed. The Prison Rules allow "additional days" to be remitted in certain circumstances, *e.g.* for subsequent good behaviour.

Conviction During Currency of Original Sentence

Short-term (*i.e.* serving sentence of less than four years) and long-term section 53(2) detainees sentenced after the commencement of CJA 1991 (October 1, 1992) are subject to the provisions of CJA 1991, s. 40 in respect of any conviction for a new imprisonable offence committed prior to the expiry of the full term of their section 53(2) sentence (see para. 24–033 *et seq.*). This liability does not apply to life sentence detainees who remain subject to recall to custody indefinitely.

SECURE TRAINING ORDERS **24–084**

Introduced by the Criminal Justice and Public Order Act (CJPOA) 1994, to address government concern for a small number of children alleged to be responsible for a disproportionately large number of offences and to give courts power to "send really nasty little juveniles away to somewhere where they will be looked after better and where they will be educated" (Kenneth Clarke as Home Secretary, 1993), this new order is available for 12, 13 and 14 year old offenders, both male and female, and may be imposed by the Crown Court or a youth court. An offender in respect of whom a secure training order is made "shall be subject to a period of detention in a secure training centre followed by a period of supervision" (CJPOA, s. 1(2)) and the sentence thus has a dual effect.

Power to Make a Secure Training Order

Criminal Justice and Public Order Act 1994, s. 1

"(1) Subject to CJA 1982, s. 8(1) and CYPA 1933, s. 53(1) (sentences **24–085** of custody for life and long term detention), where—

 (a) a person of not less than 12 but under 15 years of age is convicted of an imprisonable offence; and

 (b) the court is satisfied of the matters specified in subsection (5) below,

the court may make a secure training order.

(5) The court shall not make a secure training order unless it is satisfied—

 (a) that the offender was not less than 12 years of age when the offence for which he is to be dealt with by the court was committed;

 (b) that the offender has been convicted of three or more imprisonable offences; and

 (c) that the offender, either on this or a previous occasion—
  (i) has been found by a court to be in breach of a supervision order under the Children and Young Persons Act 1969, or

        (ii)   has been convicted of an imprisonable offence committed whilst he was subject to such a supervision order.

24–086   (7) Where a court makes a secure training order, it shall be its duty to state in open court that it is of the opinion that the conditions specified in subsection (5) above are satisfied."

Though the criteria to be satisfied are designed to ensure that a secure training order is imposed only where the juvenile has persistently re-offended and has failed to respond to supervision, these requirements could be satisfied on the basis of a relatively limited pattern of offending. However, a secure training order counts as a "custodial sentence" for the purposes of CJA 1991, ss. 1–4 (CJPOA, s. 1(6)) and thus the criteria for justifying custody under CJA 1991, s. 1(2)(a) and (b) apply. The exception permitting a custodial sentence under CJA 1991, s. 1(3) where the offender refuses consent to a proposed community sentence will also be applicable. The age of a person shall be deemed to be that which it appears to the court to be after considering any available evidence (CJPOA 1994, s. 1(9)).

24–087 Length of Order

Criminal Justice and Public Order Act 1994, s. 1

"(3) The period of detention and supervision shall be such as the court determines and specifies in the order, being not less than six months nor more than two years.

(4) The period of detention which the offender is liable to serve under a secure training order shall be one half of the total period specified by the court in making the order."

The period of detention is spent in a new form of custodial institution, a secure training centre, defined as a place "in which offenders not less than 12 but under 17 years of age ... may be detained and given training and education and prepared for their release" (Prison Act 1952, s. 43(1)(d)). Purpose-built establishments, likely to be funded by the private sector, are unlikely to be available before 1996. Five secure training centres are planned for England and Wales, each holding a maximum of 40 offenders. Where such accommodation "is not immediately available", the court may commit the offender to such place as the Secretary of State may direct or arrange (such as local authority secure accommodation), for a period not exceeding 28 days, extendable upon application (CJPOA 1994, s. 2(2)).

24–088 Supervision following Detention
The offender shall be under the supervision of a probation officer or local authority social worker for the area in which the offender resides, (or such other fit and proper person as the Secretary of State may designate) (CJPOA 1994, s. 3(2)). The choice of supervisor will be made by the Home Office in the light of a recommendation by the operator of the

centre concerned, based on an assessment of the offender's needs. The decision will be made as early as possible following sentence. The Secretary of State will specify the requirements to be complied with (s. 3(6)(b)), backed by enforcement sanctions. It will be possible to include additional supervision notice requirements, including conditions of compliance with specified activities or refraining from participating in specified activities. Supervision will be undertaken in accordance with a *National Standard for the Provision of Pre and Post Release Supervision*, based on the *National Standard for Supervision Before and After Release from Custody* (1995), specifying the minimum levels of contact during and following the custodial phase. The draft of this standard reflects the ministerial view that offenders should be closely supervised. A minimum of three appointments per week is specified for the first month following release, with two per week in the second month and one per week thereafter. It will be necessary to involve parents at all stages and to keep teachers (or employers) up to date with progress (and vice versa).

Enforcement Proceedings 24-089

Criminal Justice and Public Order Act 1994, s. 4

"(1) Where a secure training order has been made as respects an offender and it appears on information to a justice of the peace acting for a relevant petty sessions area that the offender has failed to comply with requirements under section 3(6)(b) the justice may issue a summons requiring the offender to appear at the place and time specified in the summons before a youth court acting for the area or, if the information is in writing and on oath, may issue a warrant for the offender's arrest requiring him to be brought before such a court.

(2) For the purposes of this section a petty sessions area is a relevant petty sessions area in relation to a secure training order—

  (a) if the secure training centre is situated in it;

  (b) if the order was made by a youth court acting for it; or

  (c) if the offender resides in it for the time being.

(3) If it is proved to the satisfaction of the youth court before which an offender appears or is brought under this section that he has failed to comply with requirements under section 3(6)(b) that court may—

  (a) order the offender to be detained in a secure training centre for such period, not exceeding the shorter of three months or the remainder of the period of the secure training order, as the court may specify, or

  (b) impose on the offender a fine not exceeding level 3 on the standard scale."

24-090 The provisions of section 4 have a hybrid appearance, specifying that a prosecution will be initiated in the manner prescribed by CJA 1991, Sched. 2 for breach of a community order while providing that a breach is punishable in a manner akin to a failure to comply with short-term prisoner licence under CJA 1991, s. 38. Section 4(1) does not require the order still to be "in force" when the information is laid but the court's power to order the offender's return to a secure training centre under section 4(3)(a) is only available while the order remains in force. As with CJA 1991, s. 38, "failure to comply" is not qualified by the words "without reasonable excuse".

If the offender is returned to a secure training centre (for a period not exceeding three months), supervision requirements will resume on further release if the order has not expired in the meantime, but the offender's liability to supervision is not extended by the period of time spent back in custody, nor does the further custodial period incur a fresh liability to supervision.

24-091 Why a New Sentence?
The Government's arguments for the secure training order have been highly controversial and have encountered considerable and influential opposition, particularly in the House of Lords during the passage of the enabling legislation. The following considerations have dominated the debate.

The Extent of the Problem

The Government has claimed that secure training centres are needed to accommodate up to 200 very persistent young offenders who are said to account for a considerable proportion of juvenile crime and are "a menace to the community". The evidential basis for this demand does not appear to be well grounded. Firstly, there is no clear basis on which to identify the persistent offender. Competing definitions of persistence are arbitrary and inconsistent; no two definitions lead to the identification of the same discrete group of problematic children. Further, persistent offending does not equate with seriousness of offending.

24-092   The Policy Studies Institute (Hagell and Newburn, 1994) examined the pattern of youth crime in two London boroughs and a Midlands county using three definitions of persistence:

(a)   frequency of offending in one year;

(b)   frequency of offending during a period of three months;

(c)   the statutory criteria for secure training orders.

Only three children satisfied all three definitions. Seventeen of the 25 children identified using test (c) were not identified by either of the other two definitions. On examining the records of the children who satisfied at least one definition, the researchers found that they accounted for between a seventh and a twelfth of all known juvenile offending in the two police areas. There was no evidence to support the belief that a small number of young offenders account for an extremely large proportion of known offending.

"Very few frequent offenders were identified and fewer still whose frequent offending continued over an extended period of time. Few juveniles appeared to offend very frequently for more than short periods".

In a study conducted by the Dartington Research Unit in Cardiff in 1992 **24–093** (The Children's Society, 1993) 20 of the more persistent offenders aged 10–17 were responsible for 878 offences, representing 32 per cent of detected crime involving juveniles but only 1.5 per cent of the total reported crime in the city. Only six of these 20 young people were aged 12–15 years and their contribution to the overall crime rate was only 0.5 per cent.

The Adequacy of Existing Powers of Sentence

The Government claims that the children in question cannot be dealt with adequately within existing sentencing powers, which include supervision orders with either requirement of intermediate treatment or a residence requirement (which requires the local authority to place the young person in local authority accommodation for a specified period of up to six months), as well as detention under CYPA 1933, s. 53 for the most serious crimes.

To test this claim, the Save the Children charity (1994) surveyed **24–094** children aged 12 to under 15 in nine local authority areas in the North of England, who were subject to a supervision order (imposed in criminal proceedings) on September 1, 1993. Of the 95 children identified, 76 were subject to standard orders without additional requirements. Of the 19 subject to an additional requirement, only one was subject to a residence requirement removing him from home. The report concludes that there is no evidence of a "log jam" of cases requiring greater sentencing powers. Fourteen (15 per cent) of the supervised children were accommodated by the local authority because of their welfare needs rather than as a result of prosecution, suggesting that their needs would be better met through appropriate use of the provisions of the Children Act 1989 rather than new criminal justice measures.

The Need for Specialised Centres   **24–095**

The Government is committed to the provision of five new centres, each serving large geographical areas and accommodating some 40 young people, at a capital cost of £75 million. The Save the Children research mentioned above also surveyed children aged 15 from the same nine areas either serving sentence of YOI detention (25 or 42 per cent) or supervision orders with intermediate treatment requirements (34 or 58 per cent). If the same proportion were to hold true for children under the age of 15, it is estimated that only seven younger children from that region might be considered in need of custody at any one time, only one of whom was a female child. Save the Children suggests that this likely demand could be readily accommodated through a modest expansion of local authority secure accommodation, at far less cost. A separate system will mean that many of the young people concerned will be held a long way from their home areas, inhibiting the maintenance of close links with their families and social workers and thus undermining their prospects for re-settlement on release.

24-096 *The Evidence of Past Experience*

Research into the effectiveness of previous experiments in institutional care or custody for young offenders, such as approved schools, community homes with education and secure units, has indicated that these increased rather than reduced the likelihood of re-offending. Thus Cawson and Martell (1979), following up a sample of 40 children on discharge from four secure units, found that 78 per cent re-offended in the year following discharge and 40 per cent of them committed six or more offences during that 12 month period. Those leaving approved schools had a reconviction rate 49 per cent higher than would otherwise have been expected from their characteristics and records (Home Office, 1975). Similar discouraging results have been reported by Millham et al (1978) and Thorpe et al (1979). Plans for the proposed new centres are said to be based on the Lisnevin training school in Northern Ireland and more recent research (New Approaches to Juvenile Crime, 1994) suggests that the reconviction rate of young people leaving that establishment has been over 85 per cent.

Past experience also suggests that bullying and intimidation among trainees is likely to be a considerable, negative cultural feature of such institutions and that there is also a real risk of misuse of staff power. The Government has been keen to emphasise the positive elements of the planned regimes but the draft rules for the new centres have been described as "a recipe for child abuse and concealed horrors" (Crook, 1994) because of the discretion afforded to staff in regard to strip searches, the use of force, restrictions upon contact with families, the use of removal from association as a punishment by being placed in a locked room and prevention of communication with any outside person. The Howard League intends to challenge the legality of the proposed rules, alleging contravention of the Children Act 1989 and other welfare legislation.

Chapter 25

Ancillary Issues

ANCILLARY SENTENCING POWERS

Forfeiture and Deprivation

Courts have the general power to order the forfeiture of property connected with the commission of an offence under PCCA 1973, s. 43, together with other statutory powers of forfeiture provided in respect of specific offences.

PCCA 1973, s. 43

"(1) Subject to the following provisions of this section, where a person is convicted of an offence and—

  (a) the court by or before which he is convicted is satisfied tht any property which has been lawfully seized from him or which was in his possession or under his control at the time when he was apprehended for the offence or when a summons in respect of it was issued—

   (i) has been used for the purpose of committing, or facilitating the commission of any offence; or

   (ii) was intended by him to be used for that purpose; or

  (b) the offence, or an offence which the court has taken into **25–002** consideration in determining his sentence, consists of unlawful possession of property which—

   (i) has been lawfully seized from him; or

   (ii) was in his possession or under his control at the time when he was apprehended for the offence of which he has been convicted or when a summons in respect of that offence was issued,

the court may make an order under this section in respect of that property, and may do so whether or not it also deals with the offender in respect of the offence in any other way and without regard to any restrictions on forfeiture in an enactment contained in an Act passed before the Criminal Justice Act 1988.

(1A) In considering whether to make such an order in respect of any property a court shall have regard—

(a) to the value of the property; and

(b) to the likely financial and other effects on the offender of the making of the order (taken together with any other order that the court contemplates making)."

25–003 Forfeiture orders should be used only where the facts are 'simple and uncomplicated' and are thus not appropriate where the property in question is subject to joint ownership (*Troth* (1980) 71 Cr. App. R. 1). However, the order should not be made without "full and proper investigation" of the prosecution's application (*Pemberton* (1982) 4 Cr. App. R.(S.) 328), though in most cases affecting juveniles the circumstances are likely to be straightforward and obvious.

The power should not be used to forfeit property used in the commission of an offence by some person other than the offender and section 43(1)(a)(i) should be read as "... any offence by him", not "by anyone" (*Slater* [1986] 1 W.L.R. 1340, *Neville* (1987) 9 Cr. App. R.(S.) 222).

25–004 Though a forfeiture order may be seen primarily as a preventive measure, it almost inevitably has a punitive impact and the court should thus have regard both to the effect any order would have on the offender and to the totality of sentence. Thus if forfeiture would "overdo the punishment" (*Budds* (1982) 4 Cr. App. R.(S.) 268) or would have a disproportionately severe impact upon the offender (*Tavernor* [1976] R.T.R. 242), an order would be inappropriate. A forfeiture order may, however, be combined with an order of discharge (*i.e.* in a case where it is "inexpedient to inflict punishment") (PCCA 1973, s. 12(4)) though the fact that the offender is considered to merit an absolute discharge may cause the court to feel that forfeiture is not appropriate (*Hunt* [1978] Crim L.R. 697, where the defendant received an absolute discharge for handling stolen goods placed in the boot of his car by friends; an order depriving him of his car was set aside on appeal). Forfeiture can be combined with a compensation order and PCCA 1973, s. 43A specifically provides for the sale of property connected with an offence to finance compensation for the victim where the means of the offender would otherwise be inadequate to meet a compensation order. The most likely and straightforward use of section 43 powers against juveniles will be to ensure the confiscation of keys or implements used in the course of taking or stealing from motor vehicles or in burglary.

25–005 *Effect of Forfeiture*

Forfeiture deprives the owner of any property rights but does not affect the rights of any other person. The property is taken into the possession of the police and is thus subject to the Police (Property) Act 1897. No application to the court can be made by a claimant after six months from the date of the forfeiture order.

A claimant seeking to recover the property must satisfy the court either that he or she did not consent to the offender having possession of the property or, in the case of property seized under PCCA, s. 43(1)(a), that he or she did not know and had no reason to suspect that the property was likely to be used for the purpose of crime. The police may dispose of the property and the proceeds of any sale are applied to public funds.

Other Statutory Powers   **25–006**

Statutes giving power of forfeiture and disposal or destruction which are most likely to be applied to juveniles are as follows:

Prevention of Crime Act 1953: Section 1(2) permits an order for the forfeiture or disposal of any weapon concerned in the offence of possessing an offensive weapon in any public place without lawful authority or excuse.

A similar provision applies under the *Crossbows Act 1987* in respect of the summary offence of possession of a crossbow without adult supervision by a person under 17. No power of forfeiture is attached to the offence under CJA 1988, s. 139 of having an article with a blade or point (other than a folding pocket knife) in a public place, but use may be made following conviction of the general power under PCCA 1973, s. 43.

Firearms Act 1968: A number of offences under the Act prohibiting the **25–007** possession of firearms or ammunition by young persons are subject to forfeiture/disposal orders under Schedule 6, Part II, paras. 7 and 8:

(i)   s.22(3)—person under 15 having a shotgun without adult supervision;

(ii) s.22(4)—person under 14 having an air weapon or ammunition without lawful authority;

(iii) s.22(5)—person under 17 having an air weapon without a securely fastened cover in a public place;

(iv) s.23(1)—person under 14 making improper use of an air weapon when under supervision.

In addition, section 52 of the Act gives broad authority to the court to make such order as to forfeiture or disposal of any firearm or ammunition as it deems appropriate in the following circumstances:

(i)   where an offender is sentenced to a young offender institution;

(ii) where an offender is bound over to keep the peace and the recognisance carries a condition not to possess, use or carry a firearm;

(iii) where the offender is placed on probation with an additional requirement of the order not to possess, use or carry a firearm.

This section is widely worded and does not require either that the offence should relate to the firearm or that the offender was in possession of the firearm at any particular time.

Misuse of Drugs Act 1971: Where a person is convicted of an offence under this statute or a drug trafficking offence under the Drug Trafficking Offences Act 1986, the court may order "anything shown to the satisfaction of the court to relate to the offence to be forfeited and either destroyed or dealt with in such other manner as the court may order" (s. 27(1)). Property relating to the offence may include money (*Beard* [1974] 1 W.L.R. 1549) provided that the relationship is established but this power should be distinguished from the Crown Court's power of confiscation of the profits of dealing under the Drug Trafficking Offences Act 1986, s. 1.

25–008 Exclusion Orders

Of the two powers of the court to order the offender's exclusion from specified places, licensed premises and football grounds, the latter is more likely to be used upon juveniles.

Football Grounds

Under the Public Order Act 1986, s. 30, a person convicted of an offence satisfying the specified criteria may be prohibited from entering football grounds for the purpose of attending prescribed matches (*i.e.* involving a Football League team) for a minimum of three months (no maximum is specified). The criteria to be satisfied are as follows:

(a) The offence was either—

    (i) committed during the period from two hours before to one hour after a prescribed match while the offender was at or entering/leaving a ground; or

    (ii) involved the use or threat of violence to another person or property or of threatening behaviour or racial hatred under the 1986 Act, committed on a journey to or from a prescribed match; or

25–009   (iii) was committed under the Sporting Events (Control of Alcohol etc) Act 1985 s. 1(3), (4) or s. 1A(3) or (4).

and

(b) The Court is satisfied that the making of such an order in relation to the offender would help to prevent violence or disorder at or in connection with prescribed football matches.

The order can only be made in addition to any sentence or order for the offence of which the offender is convicted. On the application of the prosecution, the court may also order that a photograph of the defendant shall be taken and may require the offender to attend a specified police station within seven days for that purpose.

Entering grounds in breach of an order is a summary offence punishable by a fine not exceeding level 3 and/or one month detention.

A person subject to such an exclusion order may apply to the court which imposed it to terminate it, provided that at least one year has elapsed since the making of the order. Where the application is refused, a fresh application cannot be made for a further six months.

Licensed Premises   **25–010**

Under the Licensed Premises (Exclusion of Certain Persons) Act 1980, s. 1, if a person is convicted of an offence committed on licensed premises and the court is satisfied that the offender resorted to violence or offered or threatened to resort to violence, the court may make an exclusion order prohibiting the offender from entering those premises or any other specified licensed premises for a period of not less than three months and not more than two years. Home Office Circular 51/1993 was issued to draw sentencers' attention to the availability of this power. Such an order can be made only in addition to any penalty or order imposed for the offence, including an absolute or conditional discharge. Entering licensed premises in breach of such an order is a summary offence punishable with a level 3 fine (£1,000) or one month's detention or both. At the time of such conviction, the court shall consider whether the order should continue, be terminated or varied by deleting the name of any specified premises. The order is not otherwise affected by a conviction for non-compliance.

It is unclear how wide the ambit of the order can be. In *Grady* [1990] Crim. L.R. 608, the court sought to exclude the offender from entering "licensed premises in Norfolk" for 12 months. The order was quashed on appeal because the offender was a woman of mature years of previous good character and the Court of Appeal stated that exclusion orders were designed for those who could be said to be making a nuisance of themselves in public houses. The Court did not comment on the scope of the order appealed against.

Restitution Order   **25–011**

A restitution order is intended either to restore goods stolen or unlawfully removed to the person entitled to them or, if the goods are not recovered, to restore to that person the cash or goods equivalent out of money found in the offender's possession on apprehension or goods representing the proceeds of the misappropriated property.

Theft Act 1968, s. 28

"(1) Where goods have been stolen, and either a person is convicted of any offence with reference to the theft (whether or not the stealing is the gist of his offence) or a person is convicted of any other offence but such an offence as aforesaid is taken into consideration in determining his sentence, the court by or before which the offender is convicted may on the conviction (whether or not the passing of sentence is in other respects deferred) exercise any of the following powers—

(a)   the court may order anyone having possession or control of the goods to restore them to any person entitled to recover them from him; or

(b) on the application of a person entitled to recover from the person convicted any other goods directly or indirectly representing the first-mentioned goods (as being the proceeds of any disposal or realisation of the whole or part of them or of goods so representing them), the court may order those other goods to be delivered or transferred to the applicant; or

(c) the court may order that a sum not exceeding the value of the first mentioned goods shall be paid, out of any money of the person convicted which was taken out of his possession on his apprehension, to any person who, if those goods were in the possession of the person convicted, would be entitled to recover them from him."

25–012 Restitution shall only be ordered where the question of title to goods is straightforward and the evidence is clear. A criminal court is not the appropriate forum to determine complex issues of ownership (*Calcutt* (1985) 7 Cr. App. R.(S.) 385). Under section 28(1)(c), it is not necessary to show that money found in the offender's possession is the proceeds of the offence, merely that it belongs to the offender (*Lewis* [1975] Crim. L.R. 353). *Lewis* also established that a restitution order can be made for a greater sum than the offender realised from the offence, provided that it is not a sum greater than the loss occasioned by the offence. An order may be made under both section 28(1)(b) and (c), provided that the entitled person does not thereby recover more than the value of the original goods.

25–013 Disqualification and Endorsement

Juveniles are subject to the same provisions of disqualification and endorsement as adult offenders, even though they may be too young to hold a licence to drive a motor vehicle. These provisions are not detailed here but attention is drawn to considerations relating to the youth of the offender which may influence a court having discretion in regard to disqualification or the length of any period of disqualification.

The Persistent Offender

It may be considered counter-productive to impose a long period of disqualification on an offender who has shown a tendency to drive without a licence, exposing them to greater likelihood of ignoring the licence requirements. In *Thomas* [1983] 1 W.L.R. 1490, Lord Lane C.J. said:

"... with persons like the present appellant, who seem incapable of leaving motor vehicles alone, to impose a period of disqualification which will extend for a substantial period after their release from custody may well, and in many cases certainly will, invite the offender to commit further offences in relation to motor vehicles. In other words a long period of disqualification may well be counter-productive and so contrary to the public interest."

This reasoning also appears valid in cases where a custodial sentence is **25–014** not imposed at the time of disqualification. The court may feel it proper not to make the prospect of lawful driving seem so remote and unattainable as to be not worth waiting for. On the other hand, the risks arising from the defendant's bad driving may indicate that a long ban is necessary to protect the public.

Protection of the Public

In considering its duty to protect the public from danger, the court may feel that a lengthy period of disqualification is justified to enable the young offender to develop in maturity (*Gibbons* (1987) 9 Cr. App. R.(S.) 21).

Inhibiting the Offender's Prospects

The court may consider that it is important not to inhibit unduly the young offender's employment prospects if there is a real possibility that their ability to drive will enhance their chances in the job market (see *Aspden* [1975] R.T.R. 456).

Recommendations for Deportation 25–015
By the Immigration Act 1971, s. 6(3) a court may, on sentencing an offender who is aged 17 or over, who is not a British citizen and who is convicted of an offence punishable for an adult with imprisonment, make a recommendation that the offender be deported. The final decision whether to deport is for the Home Secretary. The offender must be given a minimum of seven days notice in writing that a recommendation is being considered and the defence should have the opportunity to address the court on the matter. The order should be considered on the criterion whether the offender's continuing presence in the United Kingdom would be detrimental to the community, in the light of the seriousness of the offence, the offender's record and the likely impact of deportation upon third parties such as the offender's family.

It may seem unlikely that a juvenile will be considered to present sufficient likelihood of community detriment. Though no precise statistics are available, the use of this power upon 17 year olds is extremely rare, the majority of offenders who are subject to recommendation being drug couriers. In *Ariquat* (1981) 3 Cr. App. R.(S.) 83 no evidence of community detriment was found in regard to a young offender, a 19 year old who was convicted of indecent assault, having had sexual intercourse with a girl of 15, believing her to be aged 16. The court is entitled to consider whether the offender would suffer special hardship if deported, *e.g. Walters Current Sentencing Practice*, K1–5H01, quashing a recommendation to send a 17 year old back to a country which he hardly knew and which his parents had since left.

25–016 APPEALS

Appeals from a Youth Court

A decision of a youth court, like that of any Magistrates' Court, may be challenged in three ways:

(a) by an appeal by the defence to the Crown Court against conviction (if the juvenile did not plead guilty) and/or sentence, under MCA 1980, s. 108;

(b) by appeal by an aggrieved person or party to the Divisional Court on a point of law by way of case stated, under MCA 1980, s. 111, complaining that a decision was wrong in law or in excess of jurisdiction;

(c) by application to the High Court for judicial review of the magistrates' decision.

Because the juvenile is in essentially the same position as an adult defendant, the provisions for appeal are not detailed at length here but the following summary points may be helpful for those unfamiliar with the procedures.

25–017 Appeal to the Crown Court

* In an appeal against sentence, "sentence" means "any order made on conviction" (s. 108(3)), including a conditional discharge, disqualification from driving, a recommendation for deportation, a compensation order or a hospital order. The only exceptions are an order for costs, an order for the destruction of an animal or "an order in pursuance of any enactment under which the court has no discretion as to the making of the order or its terms" (s. 108(3)).

* Appeal to the Crown Court is commenced by the appellant's notice of appeal which must be lodged in writing with the justices' clerk and the prosecutor within 21 days, stating whether the appeal is against conviction or sentence or both. The 21 day time limit runs from the date of the court's order, even though conviction occurred earlier and the appeal is against conviction only. The Crown Court has discretion to extend the 21 day limit and to give leave to appeal out of time on receipt of an application in writing specifying the grounds of the application (Crown Court Rules 1982, r. 7(5) and (6)).

25–018 * The appeal at the Crown Court takes the form of a re-hearing.

* The powers of the Crown Court in considering an appeal against sentence are to make such order or sentence as the magistrates could have imposed, even if this means increasing the sentence imposed by the magistrates (Supreme Court Act 1981, s. 48). On hearing an appeal against conviction, the Crown Court may confirm, reverse or vary any part of the decision appealed against or may remit the matter back to the lower court.

"Case Stated" Procedure   25–019

* Appeal by way of case stated must be made within 21 days of the justices' decision by applying in writing to the clerk of the court concerned asking the magistrates to state a case, identifying the question of law or jurisdiction on which the High Court's opinion is sought.
If it is contended that there was no evidence on which the magistrates could reasonably have come to a particular finding of fact, the questions of fact in dispute should be stated.

* Within 21 days of receipt of the application, the clerk should prepare an initial draft of the case and supply this to the parties who then have a further 21 days in which to make representations on the draft. The magistrates then have a further 21 days in which to prepare the final version of the case stated.

* Following receipt of the final version, the applicant has ten days within which to lodge the case with the Divisional Court and within a further four days must serve notice of entry of the appeal on the respondent.

* Upon application to the magistrates for a case to be stated, the applicant loses any right of appeal to the Crown Court (MCA 1980, s. 111(4)).

Bail pending Appeal against a Custodial Sentence   25–020
Where a person has given notice of appeal to the Crown Court against the decision of a youth court or has applied to a youth court to state a case for the opinion of the High Court, then if the appellant is in custody, the youth court has power under MCA 1980, s. 113(1) to grant bail. This power is entirely at the court's discretion and there is no presumption in favour of bail under the Bail Act 1976, s. 4. When a Crown Court judge grants a certificate that a case is fit for appeal, he or she may also bail the defendant pending determination of the appeal (Supreme Court Act 1981, s. 81(1)(f)). Finally, the Court of Appeal may grant an appellant bail pending determination of the appeal (Criminal Appeal Act 1968, s. 19(1)(a)).
Whether bail is appropriate in instances where the offender will otherwise be commencing a custodial sentence is a delicate question. On the one hand, it would seem unjust if the defendant is obliged to serve time in custody which is later overturned; on the other hand, the court may feel that its authority to pass sentence is undermined by releasing the defendant, whose hopes are likely to be raised by the grant of bail, only to be dashed if the appeal is unsuccessful.
In *Watton* (1979) 68 Cr. App. R. 293, the Court of Appeal gave some **25–021** guidance on its approach to granting bail pending appeal, stating that "the true question is, are there exceptional circumstances which would drive the court to the conclusion that justice can only be done by the granting of bail". The defendant in *Watton* claimed that his

circumstances were "very special"—his wife's health was poor, his daughter suffered mental instability, he needed time to put his business affairs in order as he had not anticipated a prison sentence—but the Court of Appeal concluded that his case was not exceptional. A pertinent consideration may be whether there are very strong factors relating to mitigation which may not have been accorded full enough weight. The time that will elapse before appeal, coupled with the length of the custodial sentence, may also be relevant but the alternative and perhaps preferable course may be for the court to take steps to see whether the appeal can be expedited, to resolve matters as quickly as possible (see *Practice Direction (Crown Court: Bail Pending Appeal)* [1983] 1 W.L.R. 1292). This preference was expressed in *Imdad Shah* (1980) 144 J.P. 618 and 637 where a 16 year old had received three months detention at Crown Court. Having served a month of that sentence, he was given leave to appeal by a single judge of the Court of Appeal who also released him on bail. The Court of Appeal disapproved noting that, if the appeal failed, the offender would have to return to custody for a brief period to complete his sentence and this would be unsatisfactory and disruptive for the institutional regime.

25–022   "When these short sentence cases come up on applications for leave to appeal, bail in the ordinary way should not be granted because these ... cases can always at short notice be put in the list ... Judges who are minded to grant leave, rather than grant bail, should take steps to see that the case is expedited."

If bail is granted but the appeal ultimately fails, the fact that there has been a long delay between release on bail and the determination of the appeal, and that the sentence would have by then been served if bail had not been sought or granted, cannot be grounds for any substantial reduction in sentence. If an appellant applies for bail, he or she should realise that if the appeal is unsuccessful then the sentence will have to be served (*Callan, The Times*, July 1, 1993 in which sentence of five months for possession of a firearm was reduced to four months in recognition of the substantial period spent on bail pending appeal).

25–023 Appeal by Parents

As a court sentencing a juvenile may also make orders in respect of their parent or guardian, it should be noted that the parent has a right of appeal as follows:

(a) against an order under CYPA 1933, s. 55 to pay a financial penalty, either to the Crown Court against a magistrates' court order (s. 55(3)) or to the Court of Appeal against an order made by the Crown Court (s. 55(4));

(b) against an order under MCA 1980, s. 81(1)(b) directing the parent to pay a defaulting juvenile's unpaid sum, to the Crown Court (s. 81(6));

(c) against an order under CJA 1991, s. 58 binding over the parent to exercise proper care and control of the juvenile, either to the Crown Court against a magistrates' court order (s. 58(6)) or to the Court of Appeal against an order made by the Crown Court (s. 58(7)).

"Appeal Strategy"   25–024

Following the introduction of criteria restricting the making of custodial sentences on young offenders under CJA 1982 as amended by CJA 1988, there was a sharp rise in the number of appeals against custodial sentences, encouraged by juvenile justice workers in some social services departments and organisations such as the Association of Juvenile Justice and the National Association for the Care and Resettlement of Offenders (NACRO). This strategy of encouraging appeals is credited with real success in obliging sentencers to recognise the importance of the criteria and apply them more rigorously. Stanley (1992), a NACRO officer, has reported the experience of an appeals strategy in Kent. Between May 1984 and October 1987, 234 custodial sentences were passed by juvenile courts in that county, of which 41 (18 per cent) were appealed. Thirty six (86 per cent) of the appeals resulted in a lower sentence, either a reduced custodial period or a non-custodial sentence.

> "As magistrates' decisions were increasingly challenged and a second opinion sought ... magistrates in Kent took notice and looked more carefully into why they were making custodial sentences. They appeared to be considering (the statutory criteria) more seriously, stating fuller reasons in court and only making custodial sentences after first having considered all alternatives."

Stanley has since argued (1993) that an appeals strategy can be extended under the framework of the 1991 Act to promote tighter and more disciplined regard not only for the criteria for custody but the new criteria of seriousness for community sentences.

REHABILITATION AND SPENT CONVICTIONS   25–025

The Rehabilitation of Offenders Act 1974 provides that most convictions can become "spent" so that the convicted person is entitled to be regarded for a range of purposes as if never convicted of the offence concerned. The convicted person becomes "rehabilitated" after the "rehabilitation period" specified for the sentence or order imposed following that conviction has elapsed, provided that the offender has not been convicted of an indictable offence during that period. The primary benefits are that the ex-offender does not need to disclose a spent conviction when applying for a job, joining an organisation or taking out insurance. For certain specified occupations and purposes, for example involving work in the health service, criminal justice system or with children, a conviction can never be regarded as spent. In recognition of the fact that young offenders predominantly "grow out of crime", that their offending is a transient feature of adolescence and that changes of outlook, personality and behaviour can occur more quickly during their teen and young adult years, the Act provides that the rehabilitation period for some sentences should be shorter for young offenders than for adults.

25–026 Excluded Sentences

Sentences applicable to young offenders which are excluded from the scope of the 1974 Act by s. 5(1) and in respect of which a young offender can never become rehabilitated are as follows:

(a) detention during Her Majesty's pleasure;

(b) custody for life;

(c) detention under CYPA 1933, s. 53 for a term exceeding 30 months;

(d) detention in a young offender institution for a term exceeding 30 months.

25–027 Rehabilitation Periods

The rehabilitation periods from the date of conviction for qualifying sentences where the offender was under 18 at the date of conviction specified by section 5(2) unless otherwise indicated are:

(a) detention under CYPA 1933, s. 53 for more than 6 months but not more than 30 months	5 years
(b) detention in a young offender institution for more than 6 months but not more than 30 months	5 years
(c) detention in a young offender institution for 6 months or less	3½ years
(d) secure training order	1 year after the order ceases (s. 5(6)(d)).
(e) combination order	2½ years
(f) community service order	2½ years
(g) curfew order	2½ years

(h) probation order	(i) 1rs (for persons placed on tion after the date of impntation of CJPOA 199. 9 para. 11(1) amg s. 5(4)). (ii) r or until the order cea/hichever is the lonpr persons placed on pron before that date).
(i) supervision order	1 yuntil the order ceases, whier is the longer (s. 5(5
(j) attendance centre order	1 yter the order ceases (s. 5(6
(k) fine or compensation order	2½
(l) conditional discharge	1 or until the order exp whichever is the lon. 5(4)).
(m) absolute discharge	6 ms (s. 5(3)).
(n) bind over to keep the peace or to be of good behaviour	1 or until the order exp whichever is the lon. 5(4)).
(o) hospital order	5 y or 2 years after the ordpires, whichever is the lon. 5(7)).
(p) an order imposing disqualification, disability, prohibition or other penalty	the the order ceases to havrder ceases to have eff(5(8)).

25–028

25–029

Where more than one sentence is imposedespect of a conviction (whether or not in the same proceedings) elevant rehabilitation period for that conviction shall be the lr or longest of those applicable (s. 6(2)).

The rehabilitation period runs from the daconviction even where sentence was initially deferred. Where an der receives more than one sentence or order for a single offence, ertinent rehabilitation period is that relating to the longest applical 6(2)).

Further Conviction   **25–030**

Section 6(4) specifies that the offender can me rehabilitated if not reconvicted of an indictable offence duringrelevant rehabilitation period. If the offe is reconvicted of any offence other than a summary offence, ehabilitation period for the previous offence is extended to run une expiry of the rehabilitation period pertaining to the later offence e offender receives an excluded sentence for the later offence, the e conviction is also excluded permanently from the possibility of reitation. The subsequent conviction rule applies even if the later off was committed prior to conviction or sentence for the previous off

25–031 Spent Convictions Criminal Proceedings
Convictions cannecome spent for the purposes of criminal proceedings and if ænder is convicted of a further offence, the court must be provided w statement of the defendant's previous record, whether spent or However a *Practice Direction (Crime: Spent Convictions)* [1975.L.R. 1065 requires that those which are spent should, wherever piable, be marked as such and that no one should refer in open court spent conviction without the authority of the judge. Such authonould be only be given where the interests of justice so require. ᵌ arrangements apply to magistrates' courts in furtherance of HOC 975.

BIBLIOGRAPHY

Advisory Council on the Penal System (1970) *Non-Custodial and Semi-Custodial Penalties* (London: H.M.S.O.)

Allen, F. (1964) *The Borderland of Criminal Justice: Essays in Law and Criminology* (Chicago: University of Chicago Press)

Allen, R. (1990) "Juvenile offenders left out of the Act" (1990) 70 *Childright* 11–12

Allen, R. (1991) "Out of Jail: the reduction in the use of penal custody for male juveniles 1981–1988" (1991) 30 *Howard Journal* 30–52

Anderson, R. (1978) *Representation in the Juvenile Court* (London: Routledge)

Archbold (1994/5) (London: Sweet & Maxwell)

Ashworth, A. (1983) *Sentencing and Penal Policy* (London: Weidenfeld and Nicolson)

Ashworth, A. (1992) *Sentencing and Criminal Justice* (London: Weidenfeld and Nicolson)

Ashworth, A., Cavadino, P., Gibson, B., Harding, J. and Rutherford, A. (1992) *Materials on the Criminal Justice Act 1991* (Winchester: Waterside Press)

Ashworth, A. (1994) "Abolishing the Presumption of Incapacity: C v DPP" (1994) 6 *Journal of Child Law* 174–176.

Association of Chief Officers of Probation (1992) *Seriousness and Proportionality in the Youth Court under the Criminal Justice Act 1991* (London: A.C.O.P.)

Association of Chief Officers of Probation/NACRO, *A Crisis in Custody* (1995)

Bailey, V. (1987) *Delinquency and Citizenship* (Oxford: Clarendon Press)

Ball, C. (1981) "The Use and Significance of School Reports in Juvenile Court Criminal Proceedings: a Research Note" (1981) 11 *British Journal of Social Work* 479–483

Ball, C. (1983a) "Secret Justice: The Use Made of School Reports in the Juvenile Court" (1983) 13 *British Journal of Social Work* 197–205

Ball, C. (1983a) "A Research Based Comment on Juvenile Panel Sizes and Court Sittings—Narrow Parochial Pride" (1983) 147 *Justice of the Peace* 148–150

Ball, C. (1995) "Youth Justice and the Youth Court: the End of a Separate System"

Ball, C. (1992) "Young Offenders and the Youth Court" [1992] *Criminal Law Review* 277–287.

Ball, C. (1994) "Cautioning: a radical shift in policy?" [1994] *New Law Journal* 295–296

Ball, C. (1995) Research report, University of East Anglia, due for publication.

Bevan, V., and Lidstone, K. (1991) *The Investigation of Crime: A Guide to Police Powers* (London: Butterworths)

Birch, D. (1992) "Children's Evidence" (1992) *Criminal Law Review* 262–276

Bochel, D. (1976) *Probation and After-Care: Its Development in England and Wales* (Edinburgh: Scottish Academic Press)

Boswell, G. (1991) *Waiting for Change* (London: The Prince's Trust)

Bottoms, A.E. (1977) "Reflections on the Renaissance of Dangerousness" (1977) 16 *Howard Journal* 70–96

Bottoms, A.E. and Preston, R.H. (1980) *The Coming Penal Crisis* (Edinburgh: Scottish Academic Press)

Bottoms, A.E. (1974) "On the Decriminalisation of the English Juvenile Court" in Hood, R.(Ed) *Crime, Criminology and Public Policy* (London: Heinemann) 319–346

Bottoms, A. (1989) "The Place of the Probation Service in the Criminal Justice System" in (1989) *The Madingley Papers II* (London: Central Council of Probation Committees)

Bowden, J. and Stevens. (1986) "A corporate strategy in Northamptonshire" (1986) 150 *Justice of the Peace* 345–7

Brookes, M., et al. (1994) *Boot Camps: Report to the Home Office of a visit to the United States,* unpublished.

Brown, D. (1989) *Detention at the Police Station under the Police and Criminal Evidence Act,* Home Office Research Study 104, (London: H.M.S.O.)

Brown, D., Ellis, T., and Larcombe, K. (1992) *Changing the Code: Police detention under the revised the PACE codes of practice,* Home Office Research Study No. 129 (London: H.M.S.O.)

Brown, S. (1991) *Magistrates at Work* (Milton Keynes, Open University Press)

Burney, E. (1979) *JP: Magistrate, Court and Community* (London: Hutchinson)

Burney, E. (1985) *Sentencing Young People* (Aldershot: Gower)

Butler-Sloss, E. (1988) *Report of the Inquiry into Child Abuse in Cleveland 1987* Cm.412 (London: H.M.S.O.)

Cape, E. (1993) *Defending Suspects at Police Stations* (London: Legal Action Group)

Carpenter, M. (1851) *Reformatory Schools for the Children of the Persihing and Dangerous Classes and for Juvenile Offenders* (London: C. Gilpin)

Cawson, P. and Martell, M. (1979) *Children Referred to Closed Units* (DHSS Research Report No. 5) (London: H.M.S.O.)

Cawson, P. (1981) *Young Offenders in Care* (DHSS: London)

Cavadino, M. (1994) "Persistent Young Offenders" [1994] 6 *Journal of Child Law* 2–6.

Cavadino, P. (1995) *Good Practice After the Criminal Justice and Public Order Act* (London: New Approaches to Juvenile Crime)

Children's Society (1988) *Penal Custody for Juveniles: the line of least resistance* (London: the Children's Society)

Children's Society (1993) *A False Sense of Security: the Case Against Locking Up More Children* (London: The Children's Society)

Cicourel, A, *The Social Organisation of Juvenile Justice* (New York: John Wiley)

Cooper, P. and Cooper, J. (1994) "Enforcing Instructions Against Oppression" (1994) 41 *Probation Journal* 14.

Cornish, D., and Clarke, R. (1976) *Residential Treatment and its Effects on Delinquency*, Home Office Research Study No. 32, (London: H.M.S.O.).

Criminal Justice Consultative Council (1994) "Activity in the Criminal Justice System", Unpublished working paper CJCC(94)13

Crook, F. (1994) "A Recipe for Child Abuse", *The Guardian*, July 20, 1994

Crown Prosecution Service (1994) *The Code for Crown Prosecutors* (London: CPS)

Department for Education (1992) *School Reports to the Courts* (London: DFE)

Department of Health (1990) *Children Act 1989 Guidance and Regulations*, Vol. 1 (London: H.M.S.O.)

Ditchfield, J.A. (1976) *Police Cautioning in England and Wales*, Home Office Research Study No. 37 (London: H.M.S.O.)

Ditchfield, J. and Caton, L. (1992) *Juveniles Sentenced for Seriousness Offences: a comparison of regimes in Young Offender Institutions and Local Authority Community Homes* (Research and Planning Unit Paper 66) (London: Home Office)

Dixon, D. (1990) "Juvenile Suspects and the Police and Criminal Evidence Act" in *Children and the Law: Essays in Honour of Professor H. K. Bevan*, Ed. David Freestone (Hull: Hull University Press)

Draycott, A. and Baker, S. (1994) *Stone's Justices Manual*, Vol. 1 (London: Butterworths)

Duquette, D. (1992) "Child Protection Legal process: Comparing the United States and Great Britain" (1992) 5 *University of Pittsburgh Law Review* 239–294

Elkin, W. (1938) *English Juvenile Courts* (London: Kegan Paul)

Evans, R. (1991) "Police Cautioning and the Young Adult Offender" [1991] *Criminal Law Review* 598–609

Evans, R. (1993a) "Comparing Young Adult and Juvenile Cautioning in the Metropolitan Police District" [1993] *Criminal Law Review* 572–578

Evans, R. (1993b) *The Conduct of Police Interviews with Juveniles*, Research Study No. 8, Royal Commission on Criminal Justice (London: H.M.S.O.)

Evans, R. (1994) "Cautioning: Counting the Cost of Retrenchment" [1994] *Criminal Law Review* 566–575

Evans, R. and Ferguson, T. (1991) "Comparing Different Juvenile Cautioning Systems in One Police Force Area". Report to the Home Office research and Planning Unit.

Farrington, D. and West, D. (1990) "The Cambridge Study in Delinquent Development: A long-term follow-up of 411 London males" in Kerner, H. and Kaiser, G. (eds.) (1990) *Criminality: Personality, Behaviour, Life History* (Heidelberg, Germany: Springer-Verdag)

Farrington, D. (1992) "Juvenile Delinquency" in C.J. Coleman (ed.) *The School Years* (2nd ed.) (London: Routledge)

Farrington, D. and West, D. (1993) "Criminal, Penal and Life Histories of Chronic Offenders: Risk and protective factors and early identification" (1993) 3 *Criminal Behaviour and Mental Health* 492

Faulkner, D. (1992) "Magistrates in the Young Court" (1992) 48 *The Magistrate* 133

Faulkner, D. and Gibson, B. (1993) "Seriousness—Right or Wrong?" (1993) 157 *Justice of the Peace* 195

Fenwick, H. (1995) "Curtailing the Right to Silence, Access to Legal Advice and Section 78" [1995] *Criminal Law Review* 132–136

Gibson, B., Cavadino, C., Rutherford, A., Ashworth, A. and Harding, J. (1994) *The Youth Court One Year Onwards* (Winchester: Waterside Press)

Gibson, B. (1995) "Young People, Bad News, Enduring Principles" *Youth and Policy* 48, 64–70.

Giller, H. and Tutt, N. (1987) "Police Cautioning of Juveniles: the Continuing Practice of Diversity" [1987] *Criminal Law Review* 367–374

Hagell, D. and Newburn, T. (1994) *Persistent Young Offenders* (London: Policy Studies Institute)

Hampshire Probation Service and Hampshire Social Services Department (1992) *Criminal Justice Act 1991: Targeting Matrix Youth Courts Supplement* (Winchester: Hampshire Probation Service)

Harris, B. (1978) Editorial note (1978) 142 *Justice of the Peace* 619

Harris, R. and Webb, D. (1987) *Welfare, Power and Juvenile Justice* (London: Tavistock Publications)

Harwin, J. (1981) "The Battle for the Delinquent" in *Yearbook of Social Policy in Britain 1980–81*, ed. Jones, C. and Stevenson, J. (London: Routledge and Kegan Paul) 191–222

Hilgendorf, L. (1981) *Social Workers and Solicitors in Child Care Cases* (London: H.M.S.O.)

Home Office (1927) *Report of the Committee on the Treatment of Young Offenders* Cmnd. 2831 (London: H.M.S.O.)

Home Office (1936) *Report of the Departmental Committee on the*

Social Services in Courts of Summary Jurisdiction Cmnd. 5122 (London: H.M.S.O.)

Home Office (1937) *Report of the Departmental Committee on Corporal Punishment* Cmnd. 5684 (London: H.M.S.O.)

Home Office (1960) *Report of the Committee on Children and Young Persons* Cmnd. 1191 (London: H.M.S.O.)

Home Office (1965) *The Child, the Family and the Young Offender* Cmnd. 2742 (London: H.M.S.O.)

Home Office (1968) *Children in Trouble* Cmnd. 3601 (London: H.M.S.O.)

Home Office (1975) *The Sentence of the Court* (London: H.M.S.O.)

Home Office (1980) *Young Offender* Cmnd. 8045 (London: H.M.S.O.)

Home Office (1984) *Tougher Regimes in Detention Centres: an Evaluation* Home Office Young Offender Psychology Unit (London: H.M.S.O.)

Home Office (1989) *Report of the Advisory Group on Video Evidence (Pigot Report)* (London: Home Office)

Home Office (1990a) *Crime, Justice and Protecting the Public* Cmnd. 965 (London: H.M.S.O.)

Home Office (1990b) *Report of the Working Group on Pre-Trial Issues* (London: Home Office)

Home Office (1992) *National Standards for the Supervision of Offenders in the Community* (original version) (London: Home Office)

Home Office (1993a) *Report of the Royal Commission on Criminal Justice* Cmnd. 2263 (London: H.M.S.O.)

Home Office (1993b) *Cautions, Court Proceedings and Sentencing*, Statistical Bulletin 24/93 (London: Government Statistical Service)

Home Office (1994) *Race and the Criminal Justice System 1994* (London: Home Office)

Home Office (1994a) *Probation Statistics for England and Wales, 1993* (London: H.M.S.O.)

Home Office (1994b) *The Prison Population in 1993 and Long Term Projections to 2001*, Statistical Bulletin 16/94 (London: Government Statistical Service)

Home Office (1995a) *National Standards for the Supervision of Offenders in the Community* (revised version) (London: Home Office)

Hood, R. (1972) *Sentencing the Motoring Offender* (London: Heinemann)

House of Commons (1973) *Eleventh Report from the Expenditure Committee H.C. 534–i* (London: H.M.S.O.)

House of Commons (1993) *Sixth Report from the Home Affairs Committee 1992–3 HOC 441–I* (London: H.M.S.O.)

Howard League (1995) *Banged Up, Beaten Up, Cutting Up* (London: Howard League)

Inspectorate of Probation (1993) *The Criminal Justice Act 1991 Inspection* (London: Home Office)

411

Justices Clerks' Society (1994) "Response to the Law Commission's Report on Binding Over" in (1994) 50 *The Magistrate* iii

Kay, N., and Quao, S. (1987) "To be or not to be an 'appropriate adult'" (1987) *Community Care* July, 22
Kidscape (1994) *Bullying Pays! A Survey of Young Offenders* (London: Kidscape)
Krisberg, B. and Austin, J.F. (1993) *Reinventing Juvenile Justice* (London: Sage)

Law Commission (1994) *Binding Over* (Law Comm. No. 222) Cm. 2439 (London H.M.S.O.)
Laycock, G., and Tarling, R. (1985) "Police Force Cautioning: Policy and Practice" (1985) 24 *Howard Journal* 81–92
Lemert, E.M. (1970) *Social Action and Legal Change: Revolution within the Juvenile Court* (Chicago: Aldine)
Longford, Lord (1964) *Crime—a Challenge to us all*, Report of a Labour Party Study Group (London: Labour Party)

McIvor, G. (1992) *Sentenced to Service: The Operation and Impact of Community Service by Offenders* (Aldershot: Avebury)
Mackay, Lord (1994) Speech to the Annual General Meeting of the Magistrates' Association (1994) 50 *The Magistrate* 194–196
Magistrates' Association (1993a) *Sentencing Guidelines* (London: Magistrates' Association)
Magistrates' Association (1993b) "The Avoidance of Delays in the Magistrates' Court" (1993) 49 *The Magistrate* 69–71
Magistrates' Association, A.C.O.P. and the Justices' Clerks' Society (1993) "Community Sentences and Restriction on Liberty" (1993) 49 *The Magistrate* 89
Mair, G. (1991) *Part-Time Punishment?* (London: H.M.S.O.)
Mair, G. and May, C. (1995) *Practitioners' Views of the Criminal Justice Act: a survey of criminal justice agencies* (Research and Planning Unit Paper 91) (London: Home Office)
Mair, G. and Nee, C. (1990) *Electronic Monitoring: The Trials and Their Results* (Home Office Research Study No. 120) (London: H.M.S.O.)
Martin, F., Fox, and Murray, K. (1981) *Children out of Court* (Edinburgh: Scottish Academic Press)
Millham, S., Bullock, R. and Hosie, K. (1978) *Locking up Children:* (London: Saxon House)
Morris, A. and Giller, H. (1977) "The juvenile court: a Client's perspective" [1977] *Criminal Law Review* 198–205
Morris, A. and Giller, H. (1980) *Justice for Children* (London: Macmillan)
Morris, A. and Giller, H. (1987) *Understanding Juvenile Justice* (London: Croom Helm)
Morris, M. and McIsaac, M. (1978) *Juvenile Justice?* (London: Heinemann)

412

Mott, J. (1983) "Police decisions for Dealing with Juvenile Offenders" (1983) 23 *British Journal of Criminology* 249–262

NACRO (1984) *The First Twelve Months: results of a local authority survey on the sentencing of juveniles since the Criminal Justice Act 1982* (London: NACRO)
NACRO (1987) *Diverting Juveniles from Custody: Findings from the Fourth Census of Projects Funded under the DHSS IT Initiative* (London: NACRO)
NACRO (1988) *Grave Crimes—Grave Doubts* (London: NACRO)
NACRO (1989) *Diverting Juvenile Offenders from Prosecution* (Juvenile Crime Committee Policy Paper 2) (London: NACRO)
NACRO (1990) *Reducing Custody for Juveniles: the DHSS Intermediate Treatment Initiative* (London: NACRO)
NACRO (1991) *Reducing the Use of Custody for Young Offenders*, NACRO Young Offenders Committee Policy Paper, December 1991 (London: NACRO)
NACRO (1992) *Training Material: Criminal Justice Act 1991* (London: NACRO)
NACRO (1993) *Monitoring the Criminal Justice Act in the New Youth Court* (London: NACRO)
NAPO (National Association of Probation Officers) (1992) *Limiting the Damage* (London: NAPO)
Nathan, S. (1995) *Boot Camps: Return of the Short Sharp Shock*
New Approaches to Juvenile Crime (1994) *Creating More Criminals: The case against a new "secure training order" for juvenile offenders* (London: NACRO)

Packman, J. (1981) *The Child's Generation* (Oxford: Blackwell)
Parker, H. Casburn, M. and Turnbull, D. (1981) *Receiving Juvenile Justice* (London: Basil Blackwell)
Parker, H., Sumner, M. and Jarvis, G. (1989) *Unmasking the Magistrates* (Milton Keynes: Open University Press)
Pearson, G. (1983) *Hooligan: a History of Respectable Fears* (London: MacMillan Press)
Penal Affairs Consortium (1992) *The Case against Sentencing 15 year olds to Prison Service Custody* (London: Penal Affairs Consortium)
Penal Affairs Consortium (1995) *'Boot Camps' for Young Offenders*
Pitts, J. (1988) *The Politics of Juvenile Crime* (London: Sage)
Platt, A. (1968) *The Child Savers: the Invention of Delinquency* (Chicago: Chicago University Press)
Pratt, J. (1986) "Diversion from the Juvenile Court" 1986) 26 *British Journal of Criminology* 220.
Priestley, P., Fears, D. and Fuller, R. (1977) *Justice for Juveniles* (London: Routledge and Kegan Paul)

Ralphs, E. and Norman, G. (1992) *The Magistrate as Chairman* (London: Butterworths in association with The Magistrates' Association)

Ravenscroft, L. (1987) "Selection and Appointment of Magistrates and Panel Members for Children's Hearings" (1987) 151 *Justice of the Peace* 475–6

Richardson, N. (1988) *Justice by Geography II* (Lancaster: Social Information Systems)

Royal Commission on Criminal Procedure (1981) *Report*, Cmnd. 8092 (London: H.M.S.O.)

Rutherford, A. (1992) *Growing Out of Crime: The New Era* (Winchester: Waterside Press)

Sanders A., Bridges, B., Mulvaney, A. and Crozier, G. (1989) *Advice and Assistance at Police Stations and the 24 Hour Duty Solicitor Scheme* (London: Lord Chancellor's Department)

Save the Children (1994) *Children Aged 12–14 and the Criminal Justice System* (Interim Report) (London: Save the Children Fund)

Sheehy, N. and Chapman, A. (1989) "Assessing the Veracity of Children's Testimony" (1989) 8 *Medical Law* 311

Shelley, N. (1993) "Probation Orders After the Criminal Justice Act" (1993) 157 *Justice of the Peace* 570

Smith, D. and Gray, J. (1985) *Police and People in London: The PSI Report* (Aldershot: Gower)

Smith, E. (1989) "How to Deal with Children's Evidence" in *Children's Evidence in Legal Proceedings, an International Perspective*

Spencer J. & Flin R. 'The Evidence of Children' (1990)

Social Services Inspectorate (1994) *Responding to Youth Crime: Findings from Inspections in Youth Justice Services in Five Local Authority Social Services Departments* (London: H.M.S.O.)

Stanley, C. (1992) "Criteria for Custody: the role of appeals" [1993] *Criminal Law Review* 568

Stanley, C. (1993) "Appeals Strategy Needed" (1993) 40 *Probation Journal* 174

Steer, D. (1970) *Police Cautions: a study in the exercise of police discretion* (Oxford: Blackwell for the Penal Research Unit)

Stewart, G. and Stewart, J. (1993) *The Social Circumstances of Younger Offenders under Supervision* (London: ACPO)

Stone, N. (1994a) "Losing 'Help and Balance': Dispensing with Pre-Sentence Reports" (1994) 50 *The Magistrate* 75

Stone, N. (1994b) "Cautioning Youth in a Cool Climate" (1994) 158 *Justice of the Peace* 549–551

Stone, N. (1994c) "Sentencing the Near Adult" (1994) 158 *Justice of the Peace* 580 and 595

Stone, N. (1995a) *The Companion Guide to Mentally Disordered Offenders* (Ilkley: Omer Wells)

Stone, N. (1995b) "An Early Facelift for Pre-Sentence Reports" (1995) 159 *Justice of the Peace* 140–143

Tarling, R. and Wetherett, M. (1980) *Sentencing Practice in Magistrates' Courts*, Home Office Research Study No. 56 (London: H.M.S.O.)

Thomas, D. (1993) Commentary on *R. v. Robinson* [1993] *Criminal Law Review* 145

Thorpe, D. (1978) 'Intermediate Treatment' in Tutt, N. (Ed.) *Alternative Strategies for Coping with Crime* (Oxford: Blackwell)

Thorpe, D., Paley, J. and Green, C. "The Making of a Delinquent" (1978) *Community Care*, 26.4.1979, 18–20

Thorpe, D., Green, C. and Smith, D. (1979) *Punishment and Welfare* (Lancaster: University of Lancaster)

Thorpe, D. Smith, D. Green, C.J. and Paley, J. H. (1980) *Out of Care: The Community Support of Young Offenders* (London: George Allen and Unwin)

Tregiglas-Davey, M. (1993) "Judicial Review of Police Cautions" (1993) 157 *Justice of the Peace* 515–517

Tutt, N. and Giller, H. (1983) "Police Cautioning of Juveniles: the Practice of Diversity" [1983] *Criminal Law Review* 587–595

Uglow, S., Dart, A., Bottomley, A., and Hale, C. (1991) "Cautioning Juveniles: Multi Agency Impotence" [1991] *Criminal Law Review* 632–641

van Bueren, G. (1992) "Child-Oriented Justice: An International Challenge for Europe" (1992) 6 *International Journal of Law and the Family* 381

Walker, N. (1985) *Sentencing: Theory, Law and Practice* (London: Butterworths)

Wasik, M. (1985) "The Grant of an Absolute Discharge" (1985) 5 *Oxford J.L.S.* 211

Wasik, M. and von Hirsch, A. (1988) "Non-Custodial Penalties and the Principles of Desert" [1988] *Criminal Law Review* 555

Wasik, M. and von Hirsch, A. (1994) "Section 29 Revised: Previous Convictions in Sentencing" [1994] *Criminal Law Review* 409

Watson, J. (1942) *The Child and the Magistrate* (London: Shaw)

West, D.J. (1973) *Who Becomes Delinquent?* (London: Heinemann)

West, D.J. (1982) *Delinquency: Its roots, careers and prospects* (London: Heinemann)

Zander, M. (1995) *Police and Criminal Evidence Act 1984* (3rd Edition) (London: Sweet and Maxwell)

Zander, M. (1975) "What Happens to Young Offenders in Care", *New Society* July, 24 pp. 185–7.

INDEX

All references are to paragraph numbers